BEFORE THE FLOOD

BEFORE THE FLOOD

THE ITAIPU DAM

AND THE VISIBILITY

OF RURAL BRAZIL

JACOB BLANC

DUKE UNIVERSITY PRESS

Durham and London

2019

Cover designed by Courtney Leigh Baker
Typeset in Minion Pro by Westchester Publishing Services

Library of Congress Cataloging-in-Publication Data
Names: Blanc, Jacob, author.
Title: Before the flood : the Itaipu Dam and the visibility of
rural Brazil / Jacob Blanc.
Description: Durham : Duke University Press, 2019. | Includes
bibliographical references and index.
Identifiers: LCCN 2019006363 (print)
LCCN 2019016266 (ebook)
ISBN 9781478005322 (ebook)
ISBN 9781478004295 (hardcover : alk. paper)
ISBN 9781478004899 (pbk. : alk. paper)
Subjects: LCSH: Itaipu (Power plant) | Itaipu (Power plant)—
Political aspects. | Dams—Brazil. | Land reform—Brazil.
Classification: LCC TK1442.I85 (ebook) | LCC TK1442.I85
B536 2019 (print) | DDC 333.91/415098162—dc23
LC record available at https://lccn.loc.gov/2019006363

Cover art: Itaipu Dam. Alexandre Marchetti /
Itaipu Binacional

This book received a publication subsidy from Duke
University Press's First Book Fund, a fund established by
Press authors who donate their book royalties to help
support innovative work by junior scholars.

FOR IZZY

CONTENTS

ABBREVIATIONS ix

NOTE ON TERMINOLOGY AND ORTHOGRAPHY xi

ACKNOWLEDGMENTS xiii

INTRODUCTION
History as Seen from the Countryside 1

CHAPTER 1
Borders, Geopolitics, and
the Forgotten Roots of Itaipu 20

CHAPTER 2
The Project of the Century and
the Battle for Public Opinion 53

CHAPTER 3
The Double Reality of Abertura: Rural Experiences
of Dictatorship and Democracy 82

CHAPTER 4
Sem Tekoha não há Tekó: Avá-Guarani Lands
and the Construction of Indigeneity 125

CHAPTER 5
The Last Political Prisoner: Borderland Elites
and the Twilight of Military Rule 154

CHAPTER 6
"Men without a Country": Agrarian Resettlement
and the Strategies of Frontier Colonization 170

CHAPTER 7

Land for Those Who Work It: MASTRO and
a New Era of Agrarian Reform in Brazil 197

CONCLUSION

After the Flood 228

NOTES 235

BIBLIOGRAPHY 277

INDEX 291

ABA	Associação Brasileira de Antropologia (Brazilian Anthropological Association)
ABC	Labor strikes in the São Paulo cities of Santo André, São Bernardo do Campo, and São Caetano do Sul
AESI	Assessoria Especial de Segurança e Informação (Special Committee of Security and Information)
ARENA	Aliança Renovadora Nacional (Alliance for National Renovation)
CEB	*Comunidades eclesiais de base* (ecclesial base communities)
CIBPU	Comissão Interestadual da Bacia Paraná-Uruguai (Interstate Commission of the Paraná-Uruguay Basin)
CIMI	Conselho Indigenista Missionário (Indigenous Missionary Council)
CNV	Comissão Nacional da Verdade (National Truth Commission)
CPT	Comissão Pastoral da Terra (Pastoral Land Commission)
CSN	Conselho de Segurança Nacional (National Security Council)
DSN	Doutrina de Segurança Nacional (Doctrine of National Security)
FETAEP	Federação dos Trabalhadores na Agricultura do Estado Paraná (Paraná Federation of Agricultural Workers)
FUNAI	Fundação Nacional do Índio (National Foundation of Indigenous Affairs)

INCRA	Instituto Nacional de Colonização e Reforma Agrária (National Institute for Colonization and Agrarian Reform)
ITC	Instituto de Terras e Cartografia (Institute of Land and Cartography)
LSN	Lei da Segurança Nacional (National Security Act)
MASTER	Movimento dos Agricultores Sem Terra (Movement of Landless Farmers)
MASTRO	Movimento dos Agricultores Sem Terra de Oeste do Paraná (Landless Farmers Movement of Western Paraná)
MDB	Movimento Democrático Brasileiro (Brazilian Democratic Movement)
MJT	Movimento Justiça e Terra (Justice and Land Movement)
MST	Movimento dos Trabalhadores Sem Terra (Landless Workers Movement)
PIN	Plano de Integração Nacional (National Integration Plan)
PMDB	Partido do Movimento Democrático Brasileiro (Brazilian Democratic Movement Party)
PT	Partido dos Trabalhadores (Workers' Party)
PTB	Partido Trabalhista do Brasil (Brazilian Workers' Party)
SNI	Serviço Nacional de Informações (National Information Service)

NOTE ON TERMINOLOGY AND ORTHOGRAPHY

Like the historical actors in this book, I use the word *Itaipu* to refer both to the dam itself and to the enterprise that built and administered it, the Itaipu Binational Corporation.

Throughout the book, *farmers, families,* and *communities* are used interchangeably to describe the populations that mobilized against Itaipu. This matches the phrasing used by participants at the time. The most common terms for individuals were *colono* (settler) or *agricultor* (farmer), and "family" was the unit most commonly used to describe the number of people whose lands would be flooded.

The category of "landless" (*sem terra*) covers a wide range of rural Brazilians who did not own the legal deed to the lands they worked. Among others, this includes squatters (*posseiros*), tenant farmers (*arrendatários*), sharecroppers (*parceiros*), day laborers (*empregados*), and itinerant workers (*boias-frias*).

The term *farmer* was applied to both landowning and landless farmers. When I discuss the Justice and Land Movement as a whole, *farmer* refers to all participants, landed and landless alike. When it is necessary to distinguish between the two, I most often use the labels of *landed farmers* and *landless peasants,* although the former are sometimes referred to just as *farmers,* and the latter are also described as *peasants, peasant farmers, landless farmers,* or *landless workers.*

Because the present narrative focuses almost exclusively on the Brazilian portion of Itaipu's history, I have chosen to use the Portuguese spelling for all place-names and proper nouns in the triple frontier area between Brazil, Paraguay, and Argentina.

Although Guaraní (with an accented *í*) is the spelling for the ethnolinguistic group common to southern Brazil and Paraguay, the specific community involved at Itaipu is the Avá-Guarani, spelled with an unaccented *i*.

All translations are my own.

ACKNOWLEDGMENTS

From Wisconsin, to Brazil, and now to Scotland, I've racked up so many intellectual and personal debts over the course of this project that an acknowledgment section seems as tall a task as the book itself. To everyone who made this project not only possible but better, I offer the stories in this book, and the meanings they hold in Brazil and beyond, as a preliminary thank-you.

As with all students who have had the privilege of studying Latin American history at the University of Wisconsin–Madison, I begin by thanking my three mentors: Steve Stern, Florencia Mallon, and Francisco Scarano. I can only hope this book honors what they taught me and so many others: that intellectual passion and a sense of humility are cornerstones of engaged and important scholarship. Steve's work ethic and commitment to building community will always inspire me, and for the instances—three times by my count—when I had to be put "in the doghouse" for being careless or sloppy in my work, his tough-love approach helped keep me focused and grounded. From Florencia I will always carry the importance of not just writing well but writing meaningfully—and of actually slowing down enough to enjoy the process. Franco was instrumental in pushing my gaze to the Latin American countryside, and his constant good nature showed that one can be both a luminary scholar and an endlessly smiley person.

Also at Wisconsin, Jim Sweet strengthened my historiographic knowledge of Brazil and stressed the need to always follow your own compass. Bill Cronon and Gregg Mitman welcomed me into the world of environmental history and helped teach me what it means to tell stories that matter. From sociology, Gay Seidman gave me new perspectives on development and social movements—and she will always hold a special place as my family's intellectual yenta. Alberto Vargas made the Latin American, Caribbean, and Iberian Studies program a warm second home on campus, and Severino Albuquerque provided an equally vibrant space through the Brazil Initiative. What first drew me to Madison, and what sustained me throughout, was its community of grad students, and I extend my full appreciation to Dave Bresnahan, Phil Janzen, John Boonstra, Dave Murdock, Debbie Sharnak, Elena McGrath, Bridgette Werner, Valeria Navarro-Rosenblatt, Marcelo Casals, Adela Cedillo, Vikram Tamboli, Alberto Ortiz, and Tamara Feinstein. Beyond Madison, I benefited—and continue to benefit—from the help and friendship of a long line of *Brazilianistas*: John French, Barbara Weinstein, Jim Green, Cliff Welch, Victoria Langland, Marc Hertzman, Rebecca Atencio, Chris Dunn, Christine Folch, Jerry Dávila, Frederico Freitas, and Andrew Britt. Although I'm still a newcomer to the University of Edinburgh, I thank my colleagues for their warm welcome, and I look forward to the intellectual exchanges ahead.

Institutional and financial support came from many sources. My fieldwork was funded primarily by fellowships from the Fulbright-Hays program and the Social Science Research Council. Other funding came from the University of Wisconsin–Madison History Department, the American Historical Association, and the Center for Culture, History, and the Environment. The Latin American, Caribbean, and Iberian Studies program made possible a summer award from the Tinker-Nave Foundation and also Foreign Language and Area Studies fellowships to study Portuguese and Guaraní. The University of Edinburgh provided a faculty grant to pay for the indexing of this book and the illustration of its maps, and more important, a reduced course load for my first year that allowed me to put the final touches on this manuscript.

I am extremely grateful to Duke University Press, above all to my editor Gisela Fosado, whose professionalism and *buena onda* shepherded this book through the editing and publication process. Thanks as well to Lydia Rose Rappoport-Hankins and Jenny Tan, the editorial associates at Duke, and to the two peer reviewers who gave such insightful and detailed comments. Portions of chapter 1 appeared in my article "Itaipu's Forgotten History: The 1965 Brazil-Paraguay Border Crisis and the New Geopolitics of the Southern Cone" (*Journal of Latin American Studies* 50, no. 2 [2018]). Portions of chapter 5 appeared in my article "The Last Political Prisoner: Juvêncio Mazzarollo and the Twilight of Military Rule in Brazil" (*Luso-Brazilian Review* 53, no. 1 [2016]). And portions of chapter 6 appeared in my article "Enclaves of Inequality: Brasiguaios and the Transformation of the Brazil-Paraguay Borderlands" (*Journal of Peasant Studies* 42, no. 1 [2015]). I am indebted to all three journals for their help with each publication. Finally, I benefited from feedback and conversations at innumerable conference panels and academic forums. Above all, I'd like to thank the organizers of three invited talks I gave in 2017: John French at Duke University's Global Brazil Lab, Emile Chabal at Edinburgh's Centre for the Study of Modern and Contemporary History, and Christine Mathias at the Institute for Historical Research in London. In each case, the talks proved immensely helpful for fine-tuning arguments and meeting new colleagues.

All the institutional support in the world could have yielded terrible research if not for the support and friendships I found in the field. In Brazil, my biggest thanks go to those who welcomed me into their families and confirmed why I want to devote my professional life to the country's study: Anísio Homem and Mônica Giovannetti, Jorge Venturini, Barbara Corrales, and Rafa D'Alo and Maria Braga. In terms of research, I would have been lost without Pastor Werner Fuchs and Aluízio Palmar, whose contacts throughout the Paraná countryside made possible nearly all of my interviews. A special thanks to Vilma Macedo and Anna Rebeca Mazzarollo for sharing the files of the late Juvêncio Mazzarollo; I wish I had started my research a few years earlier so that I could have met him. Across Brazil, professors at various universities pointed me in the right direction and always reminded me to stop and chat over a *cafezinho* before I ran off to the archives: Maria Lucia Brant de Carvalho, Guiomar Germani, Rinaldo Varussa, Carla Silva, Márcio Both, Francisco Doratioto, Sel Guanaes, Paulo Porto Borges, Alfio Brandenburg, and Leonilde Servolo de Medeiros. It frightens me to imagine this book without my research at the Documentation Center of the Itaipu Binational Corporation, so a sincere thank you to Wanderlei Gregório and Suzanna Alves Martins. Similar thanks go to Solange Rocha at the Public Archive in Curitiba. At less official archives, Mariléia Tonietto provided access to the files of the Paraná Federation of Rural Workers, as did Claudio Rodriguez at the Syndicate of Rural Workers in São Miguel do Iguaçu. In Paraguay, Gustavo Codas was my earliest and most consistent source of support and networking. I also had the privilege of working with the pioneering human rights activist Martin Almada, who helped orient me to the "Archive of Terror" and its harrowingly exhaustive holdings. At the Archive of the Paraguayan Foreign Ministry, Alfredo Blacttler patiently processed all of my document requests. Bartomeu Melià, Daniel Campos, Ignacio Telesca, Ricardo Canese, and Herib Campos all graciously shared their time and their expertise on the history of the Paraguayan countryside.

A profound thank-you to my parents, Alan Benjamin and Lita Blanc, for exposing me from a very young age to the cultures and histories of Latin America, and for showing me how to navigate life with empathy and a critical eye. Any redeeming qualities of mine that may exist in the pages of this book draw directly from the two of them. And I cannot imagine having written this book without the help of my brother, Eric Blanc, who read nearly every draft of every sentence, keeping my arguments sharp and my prose humble. Here's to a lifetime of friendship and nerdiness. And last, but never finally, I thank my brilliant wife, Isabel Pike. Izzy, you entered my life in the second half of this book's progression, but it's as if your happiness and love sustained it from the very beginning. Your discerning intellect and attention to detail made this book better, and your mere presence makes everything else worthwhile.

MAP 1 The Paraná borderlands. Courtesy of Gabriel Moss.

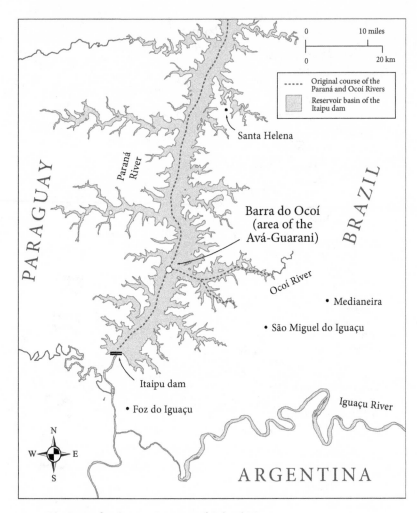

MAP 2 The Itaipu flood zone. Courtesy of Gabriel Moss.

History as Seen from the Countryside

The area was at the mercy of the waters, presenting a vast scene of ruin and desolation. Wandering along the almost 200 kilometers from Foz do Iguaçu to Guaíra, bordering the Paraná River, was a painful experience. It gave the impression of circulating among the rubble caused by a catastrophe.

—JUVÊNCIO MAZZAROLLO, *A TAIPA DA INJUSTIÇA*

On October 13, 1982, the diversion locks of the Itaipu Binational hydroelectric dam closed for the first and final time. To power the turbines of what would become the largest dam in the world, nearly thirty billion cubic meters of water spread out behind Itaipu. When the flooding stopped two weeks later, the dam's reservoir stood as the biggest artificial lake in existence. Previously, this water would have flowed downstream as part of the Paraná River, the natural dividing line that formed the border between southwestern Brazil and eastern Paraguay. But driven by the geopolitical tensions of the Cold War, the neighboring dictatorships of Brazil and Paraguay had collaborated on a project of unparalleled scale that blocked the river and formed a reservoir covering 1,350 square kilometers, equivalent to roughly half the state of Rhode Island.[1] Shocked by the catastrophic scale of the flooding, observers watched the rising waters slowly engulf what had been some of South America's most fertile agricultural landscapes.

The Itaipu flood was the most important step in completing what Brazil's military government heralded as "the Project of the Century." Shortly after seizing power in a 1964 coup, the dictatorship began pursuing a massive energy complex in the Paraná borderlands; only a decade earlier, Brazil was still generating most of its domestically produced energy from firewood, charcoal, and sugarcane by-products.[2] As the new regime oversaw the murder, torture, and imprisonment of thousands of its own citizens, it also pushed for a hydroelectric dam intended to galvanize a new era of modernization. The dictatorship envisioned this project as the touchstone of Brazil's rise as a global power.

From an engineering standpoint, the Paraná River offered unmatched hydroelectric potential, a strategic location on one of Latin America's largest river systems, and proximity to the industrial zones of São Paulo that enabled the efficient transmission of energy. And, more important, given the authoritarian context of the time, the area surrounding Itaipu was rural and sparsely populated, and its inhabitants had never posed a political threat to the current regime. Government leaders, however, did not anticipate that communities living in Itaipu's flood zone would rise up in response.

Beginning in the 1970s, farmers, peasants, and indigenous groups in western Paraná staged a series of land encampments and protests that occupied national headlines and drew solidarity from many of Brazil's most influential opposition groups. Magnified by the international spotlight cast on the Itaipu dam and propelled by the growth of pro-democracy forces throughout the country, the struggle of these rural borderland communities was elevated into a referendum on the dictatorship itself.

By the time of the 1982 flood, a resurgent wave of opposition had loosened the military's grip on power. Over the previous decade, trade unionists, human rights activists, students, urban shantytown dwellers, progressive clergy, politicians, and grassroots networks across Brazil had mobilized to demand the return of democracy. Seeking to stem the tide of popular protest, the military government initiated a series of political reforms intended to maintain control of the return to civilian rule. The official contours of this transition coalesced around the 1979 policy of *abertura*, the Portuguese word for "opening." The abertura included an amnesty law that allowed exiles to return home, the formation of new political parties, and direct elections in 1982 for all positions except the presidency—elections that took place only a few weeks after the Itaipu flood.[3] The rhetoric and policies of abertura implied that a return to civilian rule was increasingly likely, but daily life under military rule suggested a different reality. Despite the official progress of democratization, repression continued to take many forms, including false imprisonment; abusive labor, economic, and urbanization policies; and, as we shall see, the mass displacement caused by the Itaipu megaproject.

As Brazil's military navigated what would become its final years in power, Itaipu symbolized both the legacy of dictatorship and the incomplete promise of a democratic future. In the face of a potential regime change—the dictatorship handed over power in March 1985—the Itaipu dam stood as a monument to military rule that would remain in place long after the return of civilian rule. As such, Itaipu provided a physical link between dictatorship and democracy. And in the context of abertura, Itaipu also provided an arena where the very notions of dictatorship and democracy were contested by popular movements and military leaders.

For nearly a decade, rural communities mobilized against Itaipu and against the Brazilian state, primarily under the banner of the Justice and Land Movement (MJT, Movimento Justiça e Terra). By calling attention to the mistreatment of local farmers, the MJT undermined the dictatorship's triumphalist narrative of development and progress. Over the course of its two defining events—protest camps in front of Itaipu's offices and construction site in 1980 and 1981—the group withstood a prolonged standoff with military authorities and won a series of concessions, both material and symbolic. After nearly twenty years of dictatorship, Brazil's democratic opening was believed to be forthcoming, but the exact path of the transition remained unclear. With the specter of the flood looming, groups in the Paraná borderlands confronted an appendage of the dictatorship and showcased a particular form of politics and rural resistance.

But the immediate backdrop of dictatorship told only part of the story. Long before the 1964 coup, rural violence and rural inequality had existed regardless of whether Brazil was under military or civilian rule. Western Paraná was no exception. For communities displaced by Itaipu, both the dam and the official period of dictatorship marked less an isolated rupture than an escalation of abusive policies and incidents in the countryside. The flood uprooted over forty thousand people, most of whom were either title-holding farmers, landless peasants, or the Avá-Guarani Indians.[4] For these three key groups, the fight at Itaipu functioned as a protest against dictatorship *and* a larger challenge to the marginalized status of rural Brazil.

From the perspective of the dominated rural classes, democracy represented more than simply the absence of dictatorship, more than a return to the pre-1964 status quo. Rather, these groups interpreted the abertura as an opening in which to create a new social order. These alternative visions for democracy included political rights like those being fought over in the urban theaters of abertura, but they were premised above all on the question of agrarian rights in the countryside. By shifting the focus to experiences like those at Itaipu, the dichotomy implied by the terms *dictatorship* and *democracy* begins to dissolve. As a military-era conflict linked to a long history of repression and contestation in the countryside, the history of Itaipu challenges the official periodization of modern Brazil.

Although these three groups lived in the same marginalized rural part of the country, and although they confronted the same immediate obstacle of displacement, they did not form a unified front. The mobilizations against Itaipu exposed a deeply rooted series of internal conflicts. Along with race, class, and ethnic divisions, hierarchies also emerged from diverging perceptions of land. Despite the importance of the waters that formed the dam's reservoir basin and powered its turbines, in many ways the history of Itaipu is a history not of water but of land. As such, this book knowingly focuses less on the technological details and the ecological consequences of building the world's largest hydroelectric project.[5] Instead, it is guided by the following questions: what did the flooded lands mean to different rural groups, how did those meanings shape these groups' experience both before and after the flood, and why has the fight for land lingered as a constant feature of Brazilian society? These questions are relevant to any number of examples. But as a case study that brings together three different populations in the countryside, Itaipu offers a particularly powerful lens for viewing the history of Brazil from a rural perspective.

During Brazil's uncertain path out of dictatorship, these competing relationships to land determined which groups could be seen as valid stakeholders in the nation's democratic future. In the Paraná borderlands, only the title-holding farmers—almost all of European origin—became visible in national debates over political rights and citizenship. These farmers sought more money for their flooded properties, took the leading role in organizing the MJT protest camps, and successfully forced the government to increase expropriation prices. To be sure, these small-scale farmers continued to occupy a marginalized sector of society even after the flood, but their ability to purchase new lands elsewhere helped them navigate the challenges of displacement.

Landless and indigenous communities, in contrast, had neither the legal nor the social resources of their landed neighbors. Despite participating actively in the MJT, the landless received almost nothing in the final agreement negotiated by the movement's leadership. And aside from a few scattered gestures of solidarity, the neighboring farmers ignored the Avá-Guarani. After being overlooked in the initial fight at Itaipu, these displaced groups formed new movements that mobilized, respectively, for agrarian reform and for indigenous rights. Whereas the MJT disbanded its campaign before Itaipu's flood—once it had secured most of its financial goals—the landless and indigenous demands for structural change in the countryside endured long afterward.

This book follows a dual narrative. On the one hand, the case of Itaipu highlights the continuity of land struggles before, during, and after military rule. The mobilizations at Itaipu belonged to a larger history of collective action in the Brazilian countryside, as the fight for access to land and agrarian reform persisted across time and forms of government. In this sense, the history at Itaipu cannot be reduced to a history of dictatorship. Yet, on the other hand, the size of the dam and its centrality to the military regime also triggered a series of profound changes that were, in fact, conditioned by dictatorship. What changed was not necessarily the nature of the underlying issues but rather the scale: the process of confronting the centerpiece of the military's development program cultivated new levels of political consciousness and connected rural livelihoods to national solidarity networks. To this day, displaced farmers describe their movement as a "big political classroom" and a "laboratory of consciousness" where they learned to fight against authoritarian rule. And despite having their demands overruled within the MJT, many landless peasants still credit the campaign at Itaipu with providing the early catalyst for their subsequent campaigns. This mobilizing effect proved particularly important as the landless communities went on to establish a group in western Paraná that played a pivotal—and almost entirely overlooked—role in the 1984 creation of the Landless Workers Movement (MST, Movimento dos Trabalhadores Sem Terra), which has since become one of the largest social movements in the Western Hemisphere.[6] Similarly, the Avá-Guarani underwent their own process of politicization, using the highly visible target of Itaipu to amplify the long-standing indigenous struggle for territorial and ethnic sovereignty.

In the context of abertura, each of the displaced groups sought to position itself as a legitimate social force by basing its campaign on the dictatorship's own laws. The landed farmers relied on the 1967 Constitution to advocate for increased financial compensation, and the landless peasants appealed to the 1964 Land Statute to demand agrarian reform. The Avá-Guarani, for their part, cited the 1973 Indian Statute to protect both their territorial rights as Indians and their political rights as citizens—what Tracy Devine Guzmán calls the challenge of how to be Native and national at the same time.[7] By relying on military laws as a source of political currency, rural Brazilians showed that despite their exclusion from the normative progress of abertura, democracy nonetheless existed as a tangible concept to be invoked by any group wishing to advance their hopes for a more equal society.

As we shall see throughout this book, these movements did not always achieve their goals, nor did they all reach a sense of mainstream legitimacy. But for the displaced communities, the process of taking a stand against a violent dictatorship changed the perception—if not always the realities—of what could be accomplished in the countryside.

This evolution of political consciousness constituted an unintended consequence of the Itaipu megaproject. Although designed as an instrument to affirm state power, in practice the project actually *accelerated* collective action against the dictatorship. The dam did achieve most of its geopolitical and financial goals, but this came at the cost of exposing the contradictions between ideologies of state-directed development and democratic citizenship.[8] The peripheral nature of western Paraná meant that before Itaipu's construction, local farmers had had little contact with the military government; in interviews, many farmers recalled that the dam represented their first direct encounter with the military regime, often using the terms *Itaipu* and *government* interchangeably. When the MJT emerged to confront Itaipu, its members initially aimed not to challenge military rule but to defend their lands. The movement, however, soon became increasingly politicized, in large part owing to the work of progressive clergy and opposition leaders at the local and regional level, but also because news of the abertura traveled by word of mouth and through newspapers and radio programs. By providing the impetus for grassroots mobilizations in the emerging context of democratization, the Itaipu dam created opposition to military rule in the very spaces the dictatorship saw as politically benign and thus ideal for its geopolitical ambitions.

It must be noted that the size of Itaipu and its importance to the dictatorship made outright opposition to the dam dangerous and futile. The MJT never objected to the construction of the dam per se but rather to how government authorities treated the displaced communities.[9] The claimed injustice was not that the project would flood smallholders' homes but that Itaipu's below-market compensation package violated the farmers' legal rights. The 1967 Constitution stipulated that expropriations done in the name of the public interest be paid at "a fair price," and the MJT demanded that farmers receive the actual value of the flooded properties—leaving aside, for the most part, the nonfinancial goals of landless and indigenous families. The MJT fought for Itaipu to increase its compensation by an average of roughly US$5,000 per family, a relatively small sum for a project with a budget that soared to nearly US$20 billion. In public, Itaipu's leadership claimed it could not increase land prices because the added costs would slow construction on the dam. These public statements were often couched in Itaipu's stated commitment to treating the displaced communities in a "fair, Christian, and just" manner. Yet internal documents and the context of democratization reveal a different story: the dictatorship knowingly misled the farmers and refused to meet their demands in an attempt to control the narrative surrounding Itaipu. During the abertura the conflict at Itaipu functioned as a battle for public opinion over who held the legitimacy to determine Brazil's future.

From October 1982 onward, the dam and its immense flood zone became a permanent vestige of dictatorship. Even the most inclusive political victories of the abertura appear temporary compared to the long-term impact of Itaipu; direct elections and democratic freedoms might return, but the flooded homes never would. Yet Itaipu also represented a different legacy, one of struggle and rural resistance. And whereas the flood's physical impact was most immediately felt in the surrounding area, the political lessons forged at Itaipu reverberated far beyond the Paraná borderlands.

By exploring the full range of experiences that converged at the Itaipu dam, this book offers a new approach to the social and political histories of modern Brazil. Itaipu was an arena of social conflict as much as it was an energy source and a geopolitical monument. It projected rural livelihoods into national debates over land, development, and political legitimacy. And in what became the twilight of Brazil's dictatorship, the clashes at Itaipu showcased how a relatively small number of Brazilians in a supposedly isolated borderland could articulate a rural-based vision of democracy at a national level.[10]

This book has two primary goals. The first is to show how the dictatorship was experienced in the countryside. Rather than focusing on large urban centers, this book inverts the conceptual and geographic lens often used to study Brazil's era of authoritarian rule. Even as some scholars of the abertura have moved away from the canonical studies of political parties, labor unions, and elite social networks, the overwhelming majority still concentrate on the urban centers of São Paulo, Rio de Janeiro, and Brasília.[11] While these cities served as major theaters of democratization, the implication is that events in urban zones reverberated outward at a similar—or slightly delayed—timescale across Brazil. In contrast with much of this literature, I show how rural Brazil served as a pivotal site for both the exercise of dictatorship and the practice of resistance. The history of mobilization at Itaipu offers original insights into how struggles for land interacted with broader themes of dissent and democracy.

The book's second goal is to look *inside* the grassroots movements to reveal the shifting meanings of land and legitimacy. Farmers of European descent, racially diverse landless peasants, and the Avá-Guarani not only confronted Itaipu and the military regime but also, through internal disputes over strategies and demands, defended their own conception of land and its role in their particular goals for a future society. Existing scholarship on the Brazilian countryside, while robust, tends to focus on one particular group: either farmers, peasants, or Indians, almost never in connection to one another.[12] The case of Itaipu, in contrast, brings together a uniquely wide spectrum of rural livelihoods, through which I explore the complexities of politics, identity, and struggle in the countryside. The differences among the displaced communities help explain why certain farmers attained mainstream legitimacy while others, despite mobilizing against the same immediate threat, remained invisible in Brazil's reemerging culture of democracy.

These two interventions situate the fight at Itaipu both within and beyond the transition from authoritarian rule. The political climate of the time helped transform the MJT's struggle for higher expropriation payments into an explicit critique of the military regime. Yet the underlying questions of rural citizenship and agrarian rights did not fit neatly into the dominant framework of the abertura. The main protests in Brazilian cities focused on reversing the repressive policies of military rule, but even before the dictatorship, rural communities had rarely benefited from the political freedoms that democratization would ostensibly return. At Itaipu, displaced communities instead mobilized around an issue that long predated the 1964 coup: land. The farmers connected their struggle to the national fight for democracy, but at its core, theirs was a fight unmoored from the immediate context of dictatorship. The underlying problem at Itaipu—access to land and its impact on political legitimacy—emerged long before and persisted well after the official return of democracy in 1985.

This book ties together some of the most important narratives in the making of modern Brazil: development, authoritarian rule, and social protest. At the same time, the history of Itaipu also makes visible the enduring realities of life in the countryside. Far too often, rural livelihoods have remained overlooked and isolated from the national polity. In spite of this exclusion, rural communities have formed complementary, if not entirely independent, attachments to ideas of nationhood and progress. The point here is not to overstate the political impact of rural Brazilians like those at Itaipu, nor to assert that the countryside holds more or less historical value than urban areas. Instead, the case of Itaipu demands that we take rural experiences seriously and on their own terms.

Rural Visibility and the Meanings of Land

In order to connect the question of land to larger issues of politics and development, the book's conceptual framework revolves around the idea of visibility: how do certain rural communities become seen as legitimate social actors, why are others rendered invisible, and what space does the countryside occupy in national imaginaries? Given that the Itaipu dam was so important largely for the image that the government hoped it would project to the world, the idea of visibility tethers the immediate struggle of displaced farmers to the more endemic issue of inequality and representation in the Brazilian countryside. In the shadow of the military's geopolitical shrine, the farmers, peasants, and Indians defended their particular relationships to land as a means to take a political stand against the military while also attempting to position themselves as a visible social force in a postdictatorship landscape.

The question of visibility is especially important for the scale and timing of the movements at Itaipu. Although the dam displaced over forty thousand Brazilians, only a few thousand people actively participated in the MJT protest camps. And of the roughly seventy-five members of the Avá-Guarani—a small community to begin with—only a handful of male leaders publicly advocated against Itaipu. Compare these numbers, for example, to the millions of industrial workers who joined the paradigmatic labor strikes from 1978 to 1980 in the so-called ABC region of São Paulo, or even the hundreds of thousands of rural workers who mobilized in the sugar fields of Pernambuco in northeastern Brazil at roughly the same time. If not for the enormity of the Itaipu dam, it is unlikely that relatively small groups from rural communities could have achieved national prominence. As the farmers' struggle became more visible, the dictatorship monitored it closely through a myriad of surveillance and intelligence systems. Opposition networks also helped amplify the visibility of the borderland communities; for example, Leonel Brizola, arguably the most outspoken political critic of the regime, personally visited the MJT's encampment at Itaipu, as did Luiz Inácio "Lula" da Silva, the leader of the ABC strikes, with the subsequent landless protests. The movements in western Paraná could not have emerged earlier than they did, as openly confronting such an important branch of the dictatorship was possible only because national opposition movements had already opened the initial fissures of dissent and democratization.

For understanding how the struggle at Itaipu was broadcast nationally, the idea of visibility also matters in a literal sense. Despite the ethnic and regional diversity of the communities that mobilized against Itaipu, the leadership of the

MJT was composed almost entirely of white male small farmers. As a result, and conditioned by the fragile social context of abertura, media outlets and even sympathetic opposition politicians often depicted the MJT as a homogeneous group. This sanitized version portrayed an image of humble southern farmers protecting their right to a simple and dignified life of agriculture—a vision that harkened back to the folklore of *bandeirantes* (frontier settlers) who first "tamed" the wild backlands of Brazil's south and southeast in the seventeenth century. The news showed protesters as ethnically European, predominantly male, and nonthreatening—the latter point a reflection of religious leaders' insistence on peaceful tactics. This ignored how the movement as a whole, and not only its leaders, involved people from a wide spectrum of regional, ethnic, and class backgrounds; men and women; and those who sought to push more confrontational tactics to win long-lasting change. As the abertura amplified debates over citizenship and rights, only certain rural livelihoods attracted mainstream attention.

In his analysis of megadams and environmental activism, literary scholar Rob Nixon reinterprets the idea of the modern nation-state not only as the production of imagined communities—as Benedict Anderson famously argued—but as the exclusion of communities that have been actively *unimagined*.[13] This condition of invisibility emerges from both the physical violence of forced displacement and also the "indirect bureaucratic and media violence" underpinning the policies and discourse of hydroelectric projects, whether in Brazil, Kenya, India, China, or the United States. In Nixon's view, heavily indebted to his reading of Arundhati Roy, the treatment of these unimagined communities results in a status of "spatial amnesia" where, "under the banner of national development, [rural people] are physically unsettled and imaginatively removed, evacuated from place and time and thus uncoupled from the idea of both a national future and a national memory."[14] The history of Itaipu offers an important corollary to Nixon's argument: along with the exclusion of select populations, nations also develop through the active unimagining of *places*. The 1982 flood rendered invisible a stretch of Brazil's highly contentious frontier with Paraguay, and the displacement of rural groups—those whom Nixon sees as the actively unimagined—was predicated above all on the loss of land and the destruction of place. Without the inundation of nearly a thousand square kilometers of national territory, the dam would not exist and Itaipu could never deliver its much-heralded progress to the Brazilian nation.

The concept of visibility links the ideas of *imagining* and *seeing*, particularly as theorized by James C. Scott, for whom state-initiated development schemes are inherently misguided attempts to make society more "legible." The Itaipu dam stands as a clear example of Scott's view that such projects emanate from a "high-modernist ideology [that] is best conceived as a strong, one might even say muscle-bound, version of the self-confidence about scientific and technical progress."[15] Yet the case of Itaipu shows how visibility functions as a two-way framework. More than just chronicling the military's logic at Itaipu—Scott's perspective of "seeing like a state"— this book illuminates how grassroots actors can attempt *to be seen*. In their standoff with the crown jewel of the military state's development program, rural Brazilians in western Paraná asserted their right to be seen and to be respected, not only by the dictatorship but by the full range of nonstate actors involved at Itaipu and in the broader fight for democracy. The crystallization of long-simmering struggles in the context of abertura gave shape to ideas that had previously existed only as imagined possibilities. This process was not always linear or evenly distributed, but marginalized groups during this time endeavored to make themselves visible and to reverse their status as unimagined communities.

To add an explicitly rural dimension to the theme of visibility, I also develop a second concept: the dialectic of land and legitimacy. This idea draws out the impact that different perceptions of land have on the beliefs and actions of various rural communities. While remaining indebted to Thomas D. Rogers's argument that landscapes simultaneously exist as both an environment with physical characteristics and "an idea . . . associated with particular meanings," my proposed framework goes a step further to reveal the broader ramifications of that duality.[16] The dialectic of land and legitimacy allows us to see how relationships to land emboldened people's political and social aspirations while at the same time determining whether or not those aspirations were seen as legitimate. The term *legitimacy*, as used both in my own analysis and by different actors quoted in this book, reflects how one's worldviews are considered valid or acceptable in the eyes of mainstream society. This book shows instances when people and groups assume legitimacy for themselves, and also when legitimacy is granted—or denied—by external forces. As such, legitimacy can be claimed, and it can also be conferred.

The dialectic of land and legitimacy argues that in the Brazilian countryside one's sense of legitimacy was fundamentally linked to a particular relationship to land. In the case of Itaipu, the title-holding small farmers in the MJT considered land to be their *individual property*. The landless workers who went on to build a new movement saw land as the basis of their *collective rights*. And the

Avá-Guarani conceived of land as a *way of life*. Beyond simply describing the different meanings imbued in the flooded lands, this dialectic explains how perceptions of land determined the strategies taken by each group to defend their particular livelihoods. In turn, these forms of social mobilization elicited different responses from the military regime and local elites, with the degree of repression corresponding to the threat that each group posed to the existing social order.

For the title-holding farmers, the idea of landownership as legitimacy came from the personal histories of the families who had migrated from the southern states of Santa Catarina and Rio Grande do Sul in the 1940s and 1950s, helping make the region one of Brazil's most fertile agricultural zones. These farmers held the most influence in the MJT, they successfully forced Itaipu to increase its compensation, and, notwithstanding the traumas of displacement, they suffered little repression from the military regime after the Itaipu flood. In many ways, this sequence of events most closely aligns with the official understanding of democratization: after elevating their rural struggle into national debates, and after becoming seen as a valid social force, the landed white farmers celebrated their victory against military rule, and in a certain sense they moved on.

The MJT's almost singular focus on winning better prices neglected the region's landless inhabitants. By July 1981, only a few months after the MJT demobilized its final protest camp, landless farmers had formed an independent struggle seeking to abolish the existing system of land tenure: the Landless Farmers Movement of Western Paraná (MASTRO, Movimento dos Agricultores Sem Terra do Oeste do Paraná). Whereas the MJT used a strategy of protesting in front of their intended target, MASTRO led a series of direct occupations, with hundreds of families seizing control of abandoned or underused lands. Seeking the redistribution of land and national agrarian reform, these communities based their legitimacy around an understanding of land as a collective right for all Brazilians. In response, and determined to protect their properties and the status quo, the military government and wealthy elites reacted violently. During occupations organized by MASTRO in 1983 and 1984, two farmers were killed, and dozens more were beaten, imprisoned, and physically expelled from their homes. These events in western Paraná mirrored a growing trend as hundreds of landless peasants died at similar occupations throughout the country—all this at a time when Brazil was said to be in the final stages of its controlled transition to democracy.

For landless Brazilians, the dialectic of land and legitimacy functioned as both a catalyst of protest and a source of repression. Because the abertura's mainstream political focus did little to disrupt the structural inequalities long embedded in the Brazilian countryside, landless groups mobilized in more radical ways that went beyond the official contours of Brazil's transition. For doing so, they confronted waves of repression that would continue even after the 1985 return of civilian rule.

For the Avá-Guaraní, land embodied a fundamentally different set of meanings than it did for their neighboring farmers. Without romanticizing an indigenous community's connection with the surrounding natural world, the idea of land as a way of life underscores the Avá-Guaraní's historical and cultural constructions of land. The Guaraní word for "land" (*tekoha*) derives from the root *tekó*, meaning a sociopolitical space that expresses "a way of being, system, a culture, a [set of] law and traditions."[17] In defense of this livelihood, the Avá-Guaraní had to contend not only with the Itaipu flood but with the added threat of government policies designed to assimilate indigenous groups into mainstream society. Only legally defined "Indians" had access to federally protected indigenous territory, and the label of "non-Indian" rendered a person invisible in the eyes of the law and removed all rights to land. As part of Itaipu's expropriation process, the government subjected the Avá-Guaraní to "indicators of Indianness" that, among other categories, evaluated an individual's skin pigment, language, clothing, and name. Authorities used this survey to claim that only a small handful of actual Indians lived in Itaipu's flood zone. In response, the Avá-Guaraní mobilized to have all members of their community acknowledged—in both a literal and an ontological sense. The community used solidarity networks to attract media attention, lobby politicians, and gain allies in civil society. Thanks in large measure to the public pressure generated by the Avá-Guaraní, the government soon abandoned the criteria of Indianness as its nationwide policy.

In spite of this victory, however, the community's overall situation changed very little. In June 1982—four months before the Itaipu flood—the military regime relocated the Avá-Guaraní to an indigenous reservation, and in the decades since, the community has shuffled between two additional government reserves that barely maintain poverty levels of subsistence. Being seen by mainstream society became a tool for protecting indigenous lands, yet under dictatorship and democracy alike, the Avá-Guaraní could not fully shed their status of invisibility.

The Pitfalls of Periodization

The official time frame of Brazil's dictatorship is 1964 to 1985. This includes the initial coup in 1964, the peak of state-sanctioned repression from 1968 through 1974, the start of abertura in 1979, the Diretas Já (Direct Elections Now) campaign in the early 1980s that led the significant—though ultimately unsuccessful—fight for direct presidential elections, and, finally, the transfer to civilian rule in March 1985.

Rather than starting with the coup, I have chosen to begin my history of Itaipu in the late 1950s, nearly a decade earlier, and to end it in 1984, a year before the return of democratic rule. Once we take seriously the premise that 1964 and 1985 did not hold the same weight for all Brazilians and for all spaces within the national territory, we can instead choose markers that more accurately reflect the experience of a given community. A different spatial framework, in this case a rural borderland, requires a different temporality. Consequently, this periodization diverges from the paradigmatic urban events that traditionally serve as the bookends of Brazil's dictatorship.

At Itaipu, this alternative chronology draws out the deeper roots of both the dam and the people living in its shadow. In the late 1950s, the dictatorship of Paraguay's Alfredo Stroessner—in power since 1954—and a series of democratic Brazilian governments began a tense pursuit of a hydroelectric dam on their shared border; this conflict over control of the Paraná River revived a bitter rivalry between the nations that stretched back to the nineteenth century. To understand the binational character of the Itaipu dam, it is essential to trace the early negotiations and geopolitical posturing between Brazil and Paraguay. That these initial forays took place roughly a decade before Brazil's military seized power shows that the allure of megadevelopment transcended political systems: civilian presidents in Brazil, including the leftist João Goulart, who was overthrown in the 1964 coup, were prepared to collaborate with the violent Stroessner regime because it enabled access to the energy potential of the Paraná River. Development projects, much like authoritarian regimes, do not emerge in a vacuum, and we must place both in their appropriate contexts.

From a social perspective, an earlier starting point calls attention to the events that stood as key referents for the groups displaced by Itaipu. The year 1957 witnessed the Squatters Rebellion, an uprising of landless farmers in western Paraná that epitomized the region's history of agrarian radicalization. Many of the communities that later mobilized against Itaipu legitimized their actions around the memory of previous conflicts like the 1957 rebellion. Similar to how the abuses of dictatorship belonged to a longer history of repression in the countryside, so too did resistance under military rule draw from rural struggles before 1964.

The book's main narrative ends in 1984 when Itaipu began producing energy, when the journalist Juvêncio Mazzarollo was released from jail, and when the MST held its founding convention in the Paraná city of Cascavel, around a hundred kilometers from Itaipu. The first two events—the dam becoming operational and the freedom of a journalist imprisoned for criticizing Itaipu—indicated that the abertura might soon reach a successful conclusion. The former offered tangible proof that the structures of dictatorship, in this case a massive source of energy, could transition seamlessly into a new civilian society. The latter, for its part, suggested the return of political rights after two decades of authoritarian rule. But the shared financial ambitions of military and civilian leaders, and the end of overt repression such as the false imprisonment of a journalist, masked the realities that still persisted. Although the abertura provided an opening that made long-held hopes for radical agrarian change seem actionable, the platform of democratization fell far short of addressing rural needs. As protests nationwide made the official return of democracy a growing possibility, the 1984 creation of the MST showed that rural Brazilians did not trust the abertura to improve their livelihoods. By de-emphasizing 1985, even if just by one year, we see how social mobilizations were not defined by the context of dictatorship but were instead amplified by it.

This book's temporal sweep also situates Itaipu within the history of agrarian reform movements in twentieth-century Brazil. Although organized rural labor struggles occurred in all periods of Brazil's history, it was not until the 1940s that movements formed explicitly around the question of agrarian reform.[18] In the late 1950s, two new groups in particular took up the fight for land redistribution: the Peasant Leagues in the northeast and the Movement of Landless Farmers (MASTER, Movimento dos Agricultores Sem Terra) in the south. The struggle for agrarian reform continued to escalate into the 1960s, pushed forward by the Brazilian Communist Party, rural labor unions, and the policies of president João Goulart. After the 1964 coup—precipitated in no small measure by the growing struggle for structural change in the countryside—rural activism was suppressed under the doctrine of Cold War counterinsurgency. In the second decade of military rule, however, the regime supported a resurgence of organized rural labor, seeing it as an effective way of controlling the labor market while investing in the mechanization of agriculture, which led, in turn, to increased rural-to-urban migration and a shift toward seasonal, rather than permanent, employment. The unions made agrarian reform their principal cause, but federal law prevented them from representing workers who were not engaged in agriculture on a full-time basis. Inspired by this cause but unable to join the unions, an increasing number of underemployed and landless rural groups in western Paraná and across the country helped revitalize the long-standing struggle for land—and the strategy of direct-action land occupations—as Brazil's potential democratic future began to unfold.

The Itaipu dam helps reimagine military rule as an experience that cannot be reduced to static time frames or thematic boundaries. To unearth the full significance of what took place at Itaipu, we must extend our view to before the flood, to before the start of dictatorship. Only by tracing the continuities of predictatorship life through the realities of a posttransition democracy can we fully understand the histories in between. By exposing the deeply rooted dynamics of land, legitimacy, and rural struggle, the case of Itaipu challenges the standard chronology of modern Brazil.

Sources

This book draws on research from over thirty archives and databases in Brazil, Paraguay, and the United States. These included large, well-organized government archives, dusty closets in union halls, the holdings of university libraries and church parishes, and declassified digital collections. I also received access to the personal files of nearly a dozen individuals who played various roles in Itaipu's history. Additionally, I conducted forty-five interviews with former leaders and members of the rural struggles (including farmers, landless peasants, and indigenous communities), retired military personnel, politicians on both ends of the spectrum, diplomats, government officials, political activists, and labor leaders.

Most significantly, I gained extended access to the internal holdings of the Itaipu Binational Corporation—something no scholar has previously done. I spent almost two months with the files of Itaipu's executive directory, its legal office, its public relations branch, its internal security, and its communication with politicians, government ministries, media outlets, private businesses, and community organizations. Itaipu's security system was so meticulously embedded in the dictatorship's own surveillance apparatus that the dam's resulting documentation center contains confidential reports on seemingly every political event or social activity in the surrounding region. This archive includes folders devoted to political speeches, press releases, newspaper articles, and communication among Itaipu's leadership, the military police, and the federal government. The timing of my research was another crucial element. Because I conducted fieldwork in the immediate aftermath of Brazil's National Truth Commission (whose report was released in December 2014), I benefited from the emerging trend toward public access to documents from the military regime. In particular, the Memórias Reveladas project through the National Archive offered a vast trove of primary material, and this book is the first to incorporate the declassified documents relating to Itaipu and the farmers' movement. This emphasis on government transparency also allowed greater access than might have otherwise been possible at the archive of Itamaraty, the equivalent of Brazil's State Department. The Itamaraty documents provide detailed information on a previously unstudied secret military project called Operation Sagarana that shows the logistical framework for Brazil's incursion into the contested border zone with Paraguay.

Structure of the Book

To emphasize my alternative approach to periodization, the seven chapters are divided into two sections. The first three chapters proceed chronologically until the Itaipu flood in October 1982. The subsequent four chapters then offer a more syncopated chronology of what took place concurrently with the more visible events before the 1982 flood and before the official return to democracy in 1985. These chapters trace, respectively, the history of the Avá-Guarani indigenous group, the saga of a journalist imprisoned for his coverage of local elites and the Itaipu dam, the trajectories of displaced migrants across foreign and internal frontiers, and the escalating struggles of landless peasants. The aim here is that both the content of the book and the process of reading it will help readers rethink the history of modern Brazil and its assumed temporalities.

Chapter 1 explores the geopolitical standoff between Brazil and Paraguay that occurred as the military governments in both countries jockeyed to control the border region and the waters of the Paraná River. Along with exploring the historical roots of the Itaipu dam, this chapter argues that the border conflict was a catalyst for Brazil's rise as the Southern Cone's most powerful nation. Chapter 2 chronicles a subsequent escalation between a pair of more localized forces: Itaipu and the surrounding communities. Looking at the parallel progress of the dam's construction and the rise of local resistance between the 1973 Treaty of Itaipu and the beginning of 1980, this chapter reveals the importance of public opinion in an era of political uncertainty. While the Brazilian government praised the dam as a beacon of national strength, local populations offered a counternarrative that denounced the military's expropriation policies as a violation of their rights.

Chapter 3 focuses on the MJT land encampments in 1980 and 1981. In the context of abertura, the confluence of opposition figures helped catapult the lives of farmers into national debates over development and political legitimacy. Yet because not everyone threatened by Itaipu benefited from the success of the protest camps, we can trace the simultaneous development of political consciousness and exclusion, what I term the double reality of abertura. The chapter ends with a highly visible example of this divergence: the Itaipu flood of October 1982. Although the displaced farmers had invoked the rhetoric of abertura to advance their fight for land and justice, the Itaipu flood showed that the official contours of democratization could not remove the realities of authoritarian rule most intimate to many of the rural inhabitants of western Paraná.

Chapter 4 marks the start of the second half of the book, where each chapter follows a narrative that predated, overlapped with, and ultimately outlasted the MJT movement and the Itaipu flood. This chapter traces the history of the Avá-Guarani indigenous community that also lost its lands to Itaipu. The indigenous struggle overlapped at key moments with the adjacent farmers' movement but was predicated on a much longer history of repression and cultural exploitation. Overlooked by both mainstream society and the neighboring farmers, the community led a parallel campaign against Itaipu based on a particular understanding of land and its corresponding legal rights. Chapter 5 then follows the story of Juvêncio Mazzarollo, the journalist who became known as "the last political prisoner" when his criticism of Itaipu landed him in jail from 1982 to 1984. For the local elites who felt removed from Brazil's democratization process, Mazzarollo's imprisonment was an attempt to preserve their dwindling power. For national authorities, the coverage of the farmers drew attention away from the triumphalist narrative of Itaipu. And for opposition groups across Brazil and globally, Mazzarollo transcended his role as a dissident journalist to become a rallying point for democracy.

Chapter 6 demonstrates that along with meeting the energy and geopolitical ambitions of Brazil, the Itaipu dam also occupied an important sphere in the dictatorship's policies of agricultural colonization and territorial expansion. This approach materialized in two overlapping ways: the emergence of a mass migration of Brazilians into Paraguay (known as *Brasiguaios*) and the resettlement of the displaced Itaipu farmers in the faraway corners of Brazil, above all to the northeast and the Amazon. From this perspective we see Itaipu as an engine of rural population shifts, with the dam serving as a central arc in the reorientation of the Brazilian countryside. The seventh and final chapter details the history of the region's landless farmers and the formation of MASTRO (Movimento dos Trabalhadores Sem Terra de Oeste do Paraná). This chapter shows how the contours of visibility can change: in the early stages of abertura, the landless farmers at Itaipu remained almost entirely overlooked, yet through the creation of independent agrarian movements, Brazilians who fought with groups like MASTRO and later the MST (Landless Workers Movement) succeeded in elevating the profile of rural Brazil. Despite the increased claims to legitimacy, violence against landless communities—a reality that long predated military rule—endured long after the official return to democracy. Finally, a conclusion reflects on the meanings of chronology, asking what changes when we rethink notions of "before" and "after," for the Itaipu flood and also for the official period of dictatorship.

CHAPTER 1

Borders, Geopolitics, and
the Forgotten Roots of Itaipu

In 1972 the Uruguayan writer Eduardo Galeano traveled through the Paraná frontier zone between Paraguay and Brazil. As he prepared to cross the Paraná River and make his way toward Brazil, he saw a message carved into a rock: "Paraguayans have lost their water—but water is not everything." Galeano gazed out on the majestic Guaíra waterfalls, a series of cascades with the highest volume of water on the planet—over twice the flow of Niagara Falls. Amid the deafening buzz of the Guaíra Falls, Galeano reflected on what, if anything, could possibly be more important than the roaring waters in front of him: "Well then, the riverbank?"[1]

Galeano's observation highlights a paradox of how the Itaipu dam came into being. The waters of the Paraná River that eventually powered Itaipu's turbines were initially far less significant than the lands that surrounded them. Disputes over this border date back to the War of the Triple Alliance (1864–1870), a victory for Brazil and its allies that killed well over half of Paraguay's male population.[2] By the middle of the twentieth century, an emerging desire to develop the region pushed Brazil and Paraguay into a fifteen-year standoff for control of the river's hydroelectric potential. This conflict centered on territorial sovereignty in the Guaíra region: what were the limits of the international border, how did it divide the waters of the Paraná River and its famous waterfalls, and who had the right to redraw its boundaries?[3] These issues had existed since the nineteenth century, but only in the late 1950s did questions of topography and geographic demarcation result in a prolonged geopolitical crisis. As Galeano noted, the riverbank very much mattered, and with their sights set on building the largest dam in the world, the governments of both nations jockeyed for control of the border.

This chapter traces the geopolitical relationship between Brazil and Paraguay from the late 1950s through the 1973 Treaty of Itaipu. Among a litany of engineering and bureaucratic details, the binational agreement included stipulations that allowed Brazil to appropriate the overwhelming majority of the dam's future production. The treaty also determined that 1,300 square kilometers of land on both sides of the Paraná River would be flooded to create the dam's reservoir basin. This area included the entire controversial frontier region in Guaíra. After a century of geopolitical problems, Brazil and Paraguay found a way to make their border conflict literally disappear. As Brazil's Foreign Ministry described in a confidential report, the dam "should flood the entire disputed zone, and as such, would finally resolve this problem."[4]

For nearly fifty years, Itaipu's supporters have championed a narrative that the dam helped overcome the historical enmity between Brazil and Paraguay to trigger unprecedented development in each country—a claim that in many ways holds true. But this triumphalist retelling often overlooks how Itaipu also solidified the uneven power relations on display throughout the preceding border crisis.

Although scholars agree that Brazil emerged in this period as the region's major power, they have yet to fully acknowledge the central role of the Guaíra conflict in Brazil's ascent. Given this oversight, we must ask how a border dispute served to fundamentally change the geopolitical landscape of the Southern Cone. Along with exploring the historical roots of the Itaipu dam, this chapter argues that the Guaíra border conflict helped catalyze Brazil's rise to power. With the backing of the United States, Brazil's military regime refused to recognize Paraguay's claim to the frontier zone. Although the Paraguayan government did benefit from entering Brazil's sphere of influence through its participation in a binational dam project, it did so only on the terms dictated by Brazil, one of its greatest historical rivals.

The dictatorship of General Alfredo Stroessner had ruled Paraguay since 1954, and by the mid-1960s the government began to move the country away from its traditional alliance with Argentina (its neighbor to the west) in favor of Brazil (its neighbor to the east). Brazil, meanwhile, saw the overthrow of its democratically elected president João Goulart in April 1964. Determined to transform the country into a global power, Brazil's new military regime maneuvered to surpass its Latin American neighbors in regional and hemispheric dominance. The Argentine government, whose borders lay downstream on the same Paraná River, worried that a Brazil-Paraguay dam upstream would limit its own energy and commercial interests. This chapter will chronicle how Brazil's successful control of the waters and shorelines of the Paraná borderlands helped it become the region's most powerful country.[5]

Brazil's successful use of frontier statecraft in the 1960s had its roots in earlier efforts to bring new territories and resources under national control. At the turn of the twentieth century, for example, Brazil staged similar geopolitical, cartographic, and diplomatic standoffs along its Amazonian frontiers with Peru and Bolivia. Under the direction of José Paranhos, better known as the Baron of Rio Branco, Brazil incorporated an area roughly the size of France.[6] This gave the young Brazilian Republic—established only two decades earlier—a taste of imperial ambitions and set the precedent for subsequent border disputes. And whereas the frontier conflicts in the Amazon had largely been about access to rubber, one of the world's most valuable commodities at the time, the border standoff with Paraguay in the 1960s concerned a different natural resource: the hydroelectric potential of the Paraná River.

The context of the Cold War also shaped the Guaíra border crisis. Especially after the Cuban Revolution of 1959, Latin America served as an important battleground for the global Cold War, and the United States initiated a number of programs intended to stem the tide of communism in the Western Hemisphere. These included public initiatives like the Alliance for Progress that incentivized moderate reforms, and also covert plans to support leaders who would defend US interests.[7] The dictatorships of Brazil and Paraguay saw themselves as important Cold War allies of the United States: each government framed its political legitimacy around a rigid brand of anticommunism, and both sent troops to support the US invasion of the Dominican Republic in 1965—an action that Argentina never took. Although the US government had a positive relationship with Paraguay, Brazil remained its most important partner in Latin America. As such, Brazil's growth was vital to the United States' geopolitical vision. At both an ideological and a material level, the Cold War discourse resonated strongly with Latin American dictatorships. In Brazil the military's Doctrine of National Security (DSN, Doutrina de Segurança Nacional) focused heavily on industrial development, and Paraguay's General Stroessner sought to build a modern nation that could earn the approval of the United States and its global allies.

To fulfill these goals, both military regimes looked to the disputed borderlands and the untapped power of the Paraná River. In an exercise of geopolitical posturing, the Brazilian regime foresaw that despite its overwhelming political and economic strength, it would have to allow its smaller neighbor to participate in a binational project. Yet the Brazilian government concealed its willingness to collaborate and instead strong-armed Paraguay. This set the groundwork for a controversial 1973 treaty requiring Paraguay to sell its unused energy from Itaipu exclusively to Brazil at a below-market price that was fixed for fifty years.[8] In the decade before this treaty, however, the Stroessner regime aimed to consolidate its political legitimacy and become a stronger ally of the United States—even if this meant a rapprochement with Brazil. Paraguayan efforts to deflect internal opposition toward an outside force only partially succeeded; popular dissent formed not only against the Brazilian "invasion" of the border but also against Stroessner's complicity in "selling out" the Guaíra waterfalls. Even with this domestic tension, the government's nationalist rhetoric allowed Stroessner to claim the construction of a Paraná dam as a victory for the Paraguayan people.

The desire to make the Itaipu dam a reality embroiled Brazil and Paraguay in a geopolitical standoff that vacillated between conflict and collaboration. Although punctuated by celebrations of binational agreements in 1966 and 1973, the fifteen-year standoff was defined by the mobilization of troops on opposite sides of the border, the arrest of government leaders, popular unrest in the streets, and a nonstop stream of diplomatic posturing. Despite the claims of international unity that Itaipu's proponents have trumpeted for over half a century, the dam emerged from a partnership built not on trust or mutual respect but on conflict. This chapter will use previously unexamined archival sources and interviews with surviving participants to reveal the depths of Itaipu's prehistory.

Revisiting the forgotten roots of Itaipu casts new light on the legacy of the dam itself. More than just a colossal feat of engineering genius, the dam must be understood as the apex of a geopolitical conflict through which Latin American governments jockeyed for regional and global power. Despite Itaipu's importance—both during its early years and in the decades since—its bellicose beginnings remain largely unknown. This oversight should not be surprising as Itaipu was and continues to be held up as a model of Latin American cooperation. This makes it all the more necessary to explore the tense and at times violent history that paved the way for the so-called Project of the Century.

One Border, Two Interpretations

To properly contextualize the actions and rhetoric that both governments would deploy in the lead-up to the Itaipu dam, one must first understand why Brazil and Paraguay had diverging perceptions of their shared border. This difference of interpretation originated in the 1872 Treaty of Loizaga-Cotegipe

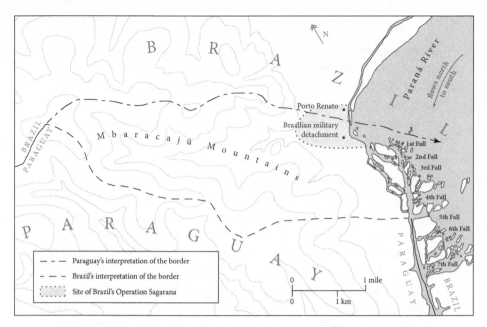

MAP 3 The contested Brazil-Paraguay border and the Guaíra waterfalls. Courtesy of Frederico Freitas.

that followed the War of the Triple Alliance. Signed by the government of Paraguay and the empire of Brazil—and against the desires of both Argentina and Uruguay—the treaty designated the Guaíra waterfalls as the dividing line between the nations. Paraguay referred to the cascades collectively as the Salto de Guairá, an understanding that all seven of the falls belonged to one singular body of water. Brazilians called these the Sete Quedas (seven falls), implying that each existed independently from the others. This distinction is critical because the treaty of 1872 stipulated that the border between Brazil and Paraguay stretched from the Mbaracajú Mountain range toward "the waterway or canal of the Paraná River . . . to the Great Fall of the Seven Falls."[9] Paraguay thus interpreted the treaty to mean that the border extended to the northern end of the waterfalls and encompassed all of them, while Brazil considered the frontier to bisect them at the fifth cascade—the tallest of the seven falls.

In the context of Cold War ambitions to harness the energy of the Paraná River, Paraguay's understanding that the *waterfall* (singular) belonged to both countries protected its claim to participate in any development project that included any portion of the falls. For Brazil, however, the belief that the border bisected the *waterfalls* (plural) justified building a hydroelectric dam on its section of the river that would completely circumvent Paraguayan waters. In the hundred years after the War of the Triple Alliance, Paraguay had consistently emphasized that the 1872 treaty had left twenty kilometers of uncontested land west of the Guaíra waterfalls. Brazil, in contrast, acknowledged no such ambiguity and refused to recognize Paraguay's claims.[10] From 1872 through the early 1960s, dozens of binational meetings discussed unresolved border issues, many of which made reference to the twenty kilometers of undemarcated Mbaracajú Mountains west of the Paraná River.[11]

A parallel controversy imbricated Argentina, a country with an equally important claim to the Paraná. Although the river originates in Brazilian territory, its downstream flow forms the border between Paraguay and Argentina before finally flowing into the basin of the River Plate and the Atlantic Ocean. Throughout the twentieth century, Argentina encouraged river-use regulations based on the principle of prior consultation (*consulta prévia*) in order to protect itself against any damages from upstream development—specifically targeting Brazil. In the first half of the century, when Argentina's regional superiority was more evident, Brazilian governments respected Argentine proposals for river regulation.[12] As Brazil's influence grew, however, it rejected Argentina's attachment to prior consultation and claimed that it had no obligation to share water with any downstream nation.[13] Argentina's major backlash against what would become the Itaipu dam did not take place until the 1970s—when it denounced Brazil in front of the United Nations—but the origins of this river rivalry took shape in the preceding decades. Propelled by these competing visions for the Paraná River, the Guaíra border conflict helped Brazil supplant Argentina as the region's major power.

A deeper legacy of the War of the Triple Alliance also motivated the perceptions of these boundaries. Popular lore, especially in Paraguay, depicts Brazil as the aggressor of the war that nearly wiped out Paraguay's population. Yet the conflict also resulted from the policies of the Argentine Republic and the interests of foreign capital, most notably British merchants.[14] F. J. McLynn has argued that Brazil "fought a bloody war and expended enormous amounts of manpower and treasure for aims which in no sense worked toward its real national interest."[15] Seen from this perspective, the war not only produced a feeling of perpetual victimhood in Paraguay but also greatly frustrated Brazil's leaders, who felt unduly blamed for a costly and violent war. While Paraguayans saw the 1872 treaty as the codification of their country's defeat, Brazilians viewed the treaty as one of the few tangible benefits from their wartime efforts and the stigma of being a victorious invader. As a result, the 1872 treaty became a site of conflict to which all parties attached meaning for the next hundred years.

Given the contentious history of these borderlands, the War of the Triple Alliance stands as an ominous and steady presence in the geopolitical antecedents of the Itaipu dam. In the renewed border standoff, Paraguayan nationalists consistently invoked the specter of the nineteenth-century war, yet Brazilian officials rejected any notion that their country acted as an invader—either in the 1860s or again a century later. By the time that military dictatorships ruled both nations in the 1960s, these diverging interpretations had become firmly ossified in the political imaginary of each country. A Brazilian surveillance report in 1969 described Paraguay's opinion of the border as "entirely absurd, a perversion of legal-historical fact . . . by a pseudo-geographic worldview."[16] Paraguayan leaders, in contrast, considered their stance to be "completely solid" and ridiculed Brazil's assertions that the border had been "definitively and fully demarcated since 1872."[17] In the context of these long-standing differences of interpretation, both nations began exploring the possibility of developing the Paraná's hydroelectric potential.

Turning a Vision into Reality

Interest in the hydroelectric potential of the Guaíra waterfalls existed for most of the twentieth century. The first major discussion occurred at the Seventh International Conference of American States, held in Montevideo in 1933, where the nations of the River Plate basin (Uruguay, Argentina, Paraguay, Bolivia, and Brazil) signed an agreement concerning navigation, irrigation, and the potential development of the various tributary waters of the basin. This declaration, though nonbinding, stipulated that in order to pursue any development project, a country would have to obtain prior consultation from its neighbors.[18] In Brazil the 1933 agreement did not result in new policies until the 1951 creation of the Interstate Commission of the Paraná-Uruguay basin (CIBPU, Comissão Interestadual da Bacia Paraná-Uruguai), a collaboration between the governments of the seven southern and central-southern states.[19]

Spurred by CIBPU, the presidencies of Juscelino Kubitschek (1956–1961), Jânio Quadros (1961), and João Goulart (1961–1964) oversaw Brazil's first wave of hydroelectric development, with over two hundred big dams constructed in the 1950s and 1960s.[20] These initiatives helped expand Brazil's electric capacity by a yearly average of roughly 10 percent between 1956 and 1965.[21] During this period, Brazil's leaders commissioned a second wave of hydroelectric surveys, overseen in 1961 by the Centrais Elétricas de Urubupungá, S.A. (CELUSA). This initiative explored potential dam projects in the center-south region, particularly the Tietê, the Grande, and the Paranapanema Rivers where a series of proposed dams would have produced a cumulative total of nearly twenty-three million kilowatt-hours. Compared to the eventual site of Itapu, these projects would have been far more cost-efficient, as their closer proximity to São Paulo and Rio de Janeiro would have drastically reduced transmission costs. However, geopolitical strategy motivated the development goals of Brazil's government as much as energy production or logistical efficiency. Both the Goulart regime and the subsequent dictatorship soon discarded these early proposals in order to redirect attention to the Brazil-Paraguay borderland.

Although the legal jurisdiction over this frontier had been contested since the late nineteenth century, the geopolitics of the early 1960s elevated the debate into open hostilities. In March 1962 Brazil's government hired the engineer Otávio Marcondes Ferraz to conduct the first detailed survey of the large-scale hydroelectric potential of the area surrounding the Guaíra waterfalls.[23] Marcondes Ferraz proposed a dam built exclusively in Brazil's territory, just to the north of the Guaíra Falls; this strategy would preserve the majestic cascades and completely avoid Paraguay's portion of the Paraná River. The proposed dam would include twenty-one turbines with an energy potential of ten million kilowatts and an annual output of sixty-seven million kilowatt-hours, nearly three times Brazil's consumption in 1960.[24] If realized, Marcondes Ferraz's proposal would have nullified Stroessner's development goals in the region.

Understandably concerned, Paraguay's chancellor, Raul Sapena Pastor (head of the Paraguayan Ministry of Foreign Relations), wrote a letter to Francisco San Tiago Dantas, Brazil's minister of foreign relations, asserting Paraguay's legal claim to the waters of the Paraná. Sapena Pastor expressed his worries over Marcondes Ferraz's project and insinuated that if Brazil moved forward with its plan to build a dam without Paraguay's consent and participation, it would "deteriorate the cordial and fraternal relations that unite our peoples and our governments."[25] Additionally, he mentioned the need to respect the ongoing work of the Joint Border Commission—a group comprising engineers and civil authorities from both countries. Since its creation in 1934 this commission had conducted dozens of border surveys, and in 1962 it undertook a lengthy project that mapped ten thousand geographic border points through the Mbaracajú Mountains extending into the Paraná River a few kilometers above the Guaíra Falls. Sapena Pastor argued that the border's full demarcation had to occur before any hydroelectric development could take place. With this perspective, Paraguay immediately ratified the 1962 work of the Joint Border Commission; Brazil never did.[26]

Six months after Sapena Pastor's initial letter, he received a reply from Afonso Arinos de Melo Franco, Brazil's ambassador in Asunción. Melo Franco stated that Paraguay had no legal basis for claiming that the twenty kilometers of land west of the Paraná River remained undemarcated, although he did note that the Goulart government was open to discussing the possibility of Paraguay taking part in a potential future hydroelectric project.[27] In response, Sapena Pastor declared that pending the demarcation of the border through the Mbaracajú hills, neither country could develop the energy at Guaíra. Doing so, he warned, "would seriously threaten the relationship" between the countries.[28] In September Brazil's president, João Goulart, dispatched his minister of mines and energy, Oliveira Brito, to Asunción to deliberate with Paraguayan authorities. At this meeting Stroessner first used a phrase that he would frequently repeat in the years to come, telling Brito that "we don't want a single millimeter [of land] that is not ours, but neither will we cede a single millimeter that belongs to us."[29] Both parties felt encouraged by the discussions, and Brito even held a press conference in which he spoke lavishly of the Brazilian government's interest in a joint project on the Paraná River.[30]

In this emerging climate of cooperation, Goulart and Stroessner met on January 19, 1964, on Goulart's Três Marias farm in Mato Grosso. The two presidents spoke for six hours in a mood Goulart described as "very cordial and very affectionate." Stroessner, for his part, called it "an historic meeting, with tremendous importance for the future relations of both nations."[31] A Brazilian press release observed that "the thinking of both men was perfectly aligned, with complete and mutual respect."[32] Given the political context at the time, this meeting might have seemed impossible: Goulart was a leftist social reformer, and Stroessner a military dictator at the head of a violent regime. Yet the two leaders had found common ground in their mutual desire to harness the industrializing power of the Paraná River.

Goulart's vision for a border dam differed drastically from that of the dictatorship that eventually made the project a reality. After his meeting with Stroessner, Goulart described Paraguay's participation as "a sincere, total, and absolute collaboration"—a concession that Brazil's dictatorship, soon after overthrowing Goulart, would make only as a nominal diplomatic gesture.[33] Goulart also mentioned Argentina and Uruguay as consumers of the dam's energy, an indication that he saw a hydroelectric project as a means to strengthen the geopolitical unity of the Southern Cone.[34] As this chapter will reveal, Brazil's military government used Itaipu for the exact opposite purpose and instead saw a binational dam as a way to enhance its own power at the expense of neighboring countries. Moreover, rumors suggested that Goulart would fund the dam with loans from the Soviet Union—surely incensing the anticommunist sectors in Brazil already plotting a regime change.[35]

The United States also opposed Goulart. Although the US government did not have a direct hand in the eventual Brazilian coup, it did systematically undermine Goulart's presidency—what historian Phyllis R. Parker has called "the Quiet Intervention."[36] Looking through the prism of the Alliance for Progress, both the Kennedy (1960–1963) and Johnson (1963–1969) administrations saw Brazil as essential to winning the Cold War in Latin America. As noted in a 1963 State Department memo, "If U.S. policy fails in Brazil, it will become extremely difficult to achieve success elsewhere in Latin America."[37] Yet Goulart remained a steady thorn in the side of US interests as he renewed diplomatic relations with the Soviet Union and resisted John F. Kennedy's efforts to isolate Cuba from the rest of the hemisphere.[38] Moreover, Goulart's brother-in-law, Leonel Brizola, the governor of Rio Grande do Sul, nationalized the US company International Telephone and Telegraph.[39] As Goulart continued to unveil increasingly progressive policies—including a vision for large-scale agrarian reform—the United States closely monitored the possibilities for military intervention. On the cusp of the 1964 coup, the US secretary of state, Dean Rusk, informed Lincoln Gordon, the US ambassador in Brazil, of the commitment to seeing the overthrow of Goulart's "communist dominated dictatorship."[40]

The 1965 Border Conflict and the Contentious Roots of Itaipu

Late in the night of March 31, 1964, a military coup overthrew Goulart and established a dictatorship that ruled Brazil for twenty-one years. Even though many of the newly installed military leaders had good relationships with Stroessner, the aftermath of the coup yielded no progress on a development project in the Paraná borderlands. The hesitation from Brazil's dictatorship likely stemmed from concern over the promises that Goulart had recently made to Stroessner. Unlike Goulart, Brazil's military had no desire to extend equal participation to Paraguay. The regime change in Brazil quickly diverted the diplomatic inroads made over the previous five years.

Almost a year after Brazil's military seized power, actions by the Stroessner dictatorship set in motion a cascading series of events that engulfed both nations in a geopolitical standoff lasting fifteen months. On March 21, 1965, a group of nearly a hundred Paraguayans gathered along the shores of the Paraná River. This contingent included high-ranking figures from the Stroessner regime, various government authorities, and a large group of schoolchildren. In the shadow of the Guaíra waterfalls, they raised the Paraguayan flag, sang the national anthem, and gave rousing speeches about the pride and sovereignty of their nation.[41] In response, Brazil sent a detachment of soldiers to occupy the exact same spot and in late October arrested a group of Paraguayan officials. In a series of tense diplomatic exchanges and maneuvers over the next fifteen months, the Brazilian military negotiated a resolution that quelled the border conflict while also guaranteeing that the resulting development project would satisfy its geopolitical ambitions. On June 22, 1966, the foreign ministers of both countries signed the Act of Iguaçu, an agreement that marked the first official step toward what became the Itaipu Binational dam.[42]

More than just a prehistory to Itaipu, the border conflict became an arena through which each country sought to redefine its place in the changing landscape of Latin America. For Paraguay, the standoff offered a chance to shed its image as a defeated nation. Exactly a hundred years after the start of the War of the Triple Alliance, the Stroessner dictatorship resuscitated a debate over the Treaty of Loizaga-Cotegipe that had dismantled his country. Thus, for Paraguay, challenging the border stipulations of the 1872 treaty became a way to challenge the legitimacy of the war itself and an opportunity to rewrite a century of its haunting legacy. The Stroessner regime also used the 1965 border conflict to rally domestic support against foreign aggression while also promising economic development in the form of an eventual hydroelectric project.

The Brazilian government, in contrast, used the 1965 crisis to test the limits of its own power during the earliest phase of the dictatorship. The military regime had governed Brazil for less than a year when Paraguay staged its flag-raising ceremony in Guaíra, and the ensuing conflict marked the regime's first real venture into foreign politics. During the infancy of its dictatorship—and with the potential of a massive hydroelectric dam looming as motivation—the Brazilian regime saw the border conflict as a chance to assert its geopolitical and economic dominance. By strong-arming Paraguay and refusing to capitulate on its interpretation of the border, Brazil's government succeeded in elevating its own status while diminishing that of its neighbors. Despite the language of equal cooperation with Paraguay, Brazilian leaders had always seen the dam through geopolitical lenses. In this context, all decisions related to a form of manifest destiny known as *Brasil Grande* that for most of the twentieth century had envisioned the political and ideological ascension of Brazil as a global power.[43] Brazil's dictatorship saw its moment of greatness at hand, and winning the border conflict became a fundamental step forward.

The Border Takes Center Stage

On March 20, 1965—the day before the contingent of Paraguayans gathered near Guaíra—General Stroessner personally visited the border. According to Paraguay's minister of the interior, Stroessner wanted to "survey and measure the geopolitical potential of the area" and left instructions to assemble the local population in order to inform them of "our frontier divisions and our rights [in] the region."[44] The following day, nearly a hundred Paraguayans gathered along the shores of the Paraná for the flag-raising ceremony that would prove so controversial (figure 1.1). In the speeches that followed, one speaker declared that "Paraguay would recuperate this territory that was stolen from [us] after the War of the Triple Alliance."[45] Three Brazilian citizens who lived nearby witnessed these actions, and one ran home to get a camera. Once the Paraguayans had left, all three Brazilians went to the nearest military office to hand over the film negatives and give official testimony to what they had seen.[46]

A few weeks later, Colonel Octávio da Silva Tosta, as head of the National Security Council's Special Border Commission, visited the region to plan Brazil's response. Accompanied by a handful of engineers and a local guide, Tosta spent the afternoon surveying the region, and in a move that reflected the back-and-forth gamesmanship at the heart of the border conflict, he conducted a small ceremony in the precise spot of Paraguay's recent actions.[47] On this visit Colonel Tosta began formulating what became known as Operation Sagarana, a secret collaboration among Itamaraty (Brazil's Foreign Ministry), the army, and various government ministries. Scholars have never before studied this project, and its examination here affords unprecedented insight into the logistics of how Brazil developed its presence along the border.[48]

With the explicit goal of occupying the region, Operation Sagarana sought to link the frontier zone to the adjacent Brazilian states of Paraná and Mato Grosso. Operation Sagarana's program of building military barracks and establishing new towns and agricultural colonies represented the first concerted effort by any Brazilian government to stake a physical claim to this stretch of

FIGURE 1.1 Paraguay's flag-raising ceremony on March 21, 1965. Major Emilio Meza Guerrero addresses the crowd along the border. Photo courtesy of the *Revista do Clube Militar*, Rio de Janeiro.

the border. Although the frontier zone had held symbolic importance since the late nineteenth century, few initiatives had established any permanent physical authority. After his initial field visit, Colonel Tosta returned to Rio de Janeiro and presented his report to the National Security Council. He finalized the details of Operation Sagarana in meetings with General Artur da Costa e Silva, the minister of war, and Vasco Leitão da Cunha, the minister of foreign relations.[49] With the operation's framework in place, the government authorized the deployment of Brazilian troops to the exact location where the Paraguayans had held their ceremony.[50]

Two months later, on June 17, a detachment of one sergeant and seven soldiers crossed the Paraná River and set up camp just south of a small outpost known as Porto Renato (figure 1.2).[51] For Paraguay's leaders, this "act of aggression" constituted a complete violation of its territorial sovereignty.[52] The Brazilian regime, in contrast, considered Porto Renato within its national boundaries and thus saw Paraguay's previous actions in March, and not its own movement in June, as the *actual* invasion. The Brazilian government claimed that it had sent the detachment only to protect against terrorism and contraband operations along the border.[53] Over the course of the following

FIGURE 1.2 Brazilian detachment in Porto Renato on June 18, 1965. Photo courtesy of the *Revista do Clube Militar*, Rio de Janeiro.

year, Brazil routinely downplayed both the size and importance of these soldiers, referring to the group as nothing but "a tiny detachment" or describing their presence as merely "symbolic."[54] Internal documents indicate otherwise. In his capacity as head of the National Information Service, João Baptista Figueiredo—who later became Brazil's last military president—would write that the dictatorship aimed explicitly to "counteract Paraguay's growing presence in the region."[55]

News of Brazil's garrison in Porto Renato quickly made its way to Asunción, where Paraguayan authorities began to apply diplomatic pressure for the removal of the troops. Chancellor Sapena Pastor met routinely with Jaime Souza Gomes, the Brazilian ambassador in Asunción, and even General Stroessner made personal appeals to his colleagues in Brazil. Having made little progress in Asunción, Sapena Pastor traveled to Brasília in early July to speak directly to Brazil's foreign minister, Juracy Magalhães.[56] For nearly two months, the Brazilian regime gave no response, nor did it officially acknowledge it had even sent troops across the Paraná River. On September 1 Brazil's president, General Humberto Castelo Branco, finally sent a letter to Stroessner in which he stated that the group in Porto Renato "cannot represent anything inconvenient or harmful for either country, and that its presence can by no means indicate a strategy of pressure, coercion or repression on the part of the Brazilian Government."[57] Nowhere in his note did Castelo Branco refer to the appeal to have the troops removed. The dismissive tone of this letter must have incensed Paraguay's leaders—one report noted that Stroessner felt "totally unsatisfied"—and the Paraguayan Ministry of Foreign Relations spent the next three weeks preparing a lengthy response.[58] This marked the beginning of a back-and-forth exchange between the foreign ministries that one Paraguayan official referred to as "a veritable paper war."[59] As this conflict unfolded in the sphere of diplomatic communication, it also began to materialize in tangible ways along the border itself.

Jockeying for Control of the Border

In the middle of October, Paraguay's Foreign Ministry received reports of Brazilians constructing barracks, roads, and even an airstrip on the lands adjacent to Porto Renato—the early results of Operation Sagarana. Alarmed, Chancellor Sapena Pastor wrote to Ambassador Souza Gomes hoping that Brazil would confirm its increased presence along the border. Expressing his disappointment in how unresponsive Brazil had been over the previous month, Sapena Pastor indicated that he had just commissioned a group of important Paraguayan authorities to visit the "undemarcated zone."[60] On the morning of October 21, 1965, exactly seven months after Paraguay's previous trip to the border region, five men boarded a plane in Asunción and, after landing on an empty road because of a lack of airstrips, drove in a jeep to the Brazilian detachment. This group consisted of Pedro Godinot de Villare, the undersecretary of foreign relations; Carlos Saldívar, the chancellor's legal advisor; Emilio Meza Guerrero, the army major shown in figure 1.1 giving a speech at the March 21 flag-raising ceremony; Conrado Pappalardo, Stroessner's chief of staff; and an accompanying photographer. The group arrived in Porto Renato in the early afternoon and began taking pictures of the newly constructed facilities along the western shore of the Paraná River. A truck carrying Brazilian soldiers quickly appeared and detained the group for several hours.

What happened next depends on the perspective of the storyteller, as each government presented a version for the sake of its own geopolitical objectives. The importance of these actions, however, lies not in distilling the exact course of events; rather, it rests in how these competing stories came to be retold in each country. The Brazilian regime tried to downplay the events of October 21, framing the whole ordeal as a misunderstanding. This response attempted to de-escalate the situation while also delegitimizing Paraguay's claims in the borderlands. In contrast, outrage erupted in Paraguay. As Paraguayans commemorated the hundredth anniversary of the start of the War of the Triple Alliance, this new Brazilian "invasion" signaled a modern call to arms.

In interviews from 2015, the only two still-surviving members of the arrested Paraguayans, Carlos Saldívar and Conrado Pappalardo, offered their versions of what took place. Both men recall that the Brazilian sergeant refused to provide a reason for their detention. Saldívar remembers feeling particularly anxious because, to him, the previous months "had felt like a war. . . . [W]e knew what had happened [in the War of the Triple Alliance], and our arrest could have started another one."[61] Above all, Pappalardo remembers when Meza Guerrero refused to surrender his gun. Trying to de-escalate the situation, Pappalardo told his compatriot, "Emilio, my dear friend, hand over your pistol to this sergeant, and tomorrow I'll buy you five new ones back in Asunción." At this point, according to Pappalardo, Brazilian reinforcements arrived in the form of an army major, a captain, two lieutenants, and a company of "heavily armed soldiers" who assumed "combat positions" and treated them with "total incivility."[62] A Paraguayan press release emphasized these details, accusing Brazilian authorities of "mistreatment."[63] For the remainder of the afternoon, the Paraguayans sat outside—on tree stumps, according to Saldívar—until the commander of Brazil's southern army arrived and gave the authorization to release the five men.[64]

In the Brazilian embassy's recounting of these events, "the Paraguayan commission was never at any point arrested," and the matter simply involved needing to wait until the proper authorities arrived.[65] Brazil's narrative claimed the following sequence of events. When initially approached by the Brazilian soldiers, the Paraguayan authorities declined to give their names, and when instructed to hand over their photography equipment, Meza Guerrero refused and acted in an increasingly threatening manner. The Brazilian sergeant told the photographer to stay put until the commanding officer, Captain Gildon Pinto de Madeiras, arrived. Meza Guerrero asked whether they were being arrested, and the sergeant told him no, that only the photographer needed to wait in custody. According to one version disseminated in the newspaper *Jornal do Brasil*, at this moment the Paraguayan authorities voluntarily "turned themselves in" as an act of solidarity with their detained photographer.[66] When Captain Madeiras arrived, he instructed the Paraguayans that they could not take photographs of Brazil's military presence and, moreover, that they had intruded two kilometers into Brazilian territory. Outraged at the suggestion that this land belonged to Brazil, Meza Guerrero drew his gun and threatened to "send an armed squadron of Paraguayans to encircle the Brazilian soldiers." The situation quickly de-escalated once Meza Guerrero handed over his weapon. According to the *Jornal do Brasil*, "everything ended with a perfect understanding, with normal farewells," and Meza Guerrero even extended a cordial invitation to the Brazilian officers to spend the December holidays with their families in Asunción.

Whereas the early months of the border standoff had mostly taken place in the realm of interembassy communications, the Porto Renato incident attracted widespread media attention and inaugurated the battle for public opinion that played out over the following year. Paraguay in particular seized on this new theater of conflict and routinely portrayed Brazil as the aggressor. According to anthropologist Christine Folch, the Paraguayan public saw Brazil's presence in Guaíra as "nothing less than a provocation to war and an affront to Paraguay's national sovereignty. Speeches and letters to the editor in repudiation of Brazilian aggression were an almost [. . .] daily feature in October and November 1965."[67] News of the October 21 arrests circulated widely and sparked debate over the possibility of international mediation with Argentina, Uruguay, and even the United Nations as potential arbiters.[68]

On November 24, Stroessner had two different meetings with foreign leaders to discuss the simmering border conflict. First, he spent the late morning with Dean Rusk, the US secretary of state, who was on his way back from giving a speech in Rio de Janeiro. The transcript of this meeting reveals the depths of Stroessner's desire to be respected by world leaders: after emphasizing how well his soldiers had done in supporting the US invasion of the Dominican Republic, Stroessner complained that Paraguay had received far less economic aid than other Latin American countries. He then boasted that many foreign dignitaries, including French president Charles de Gaulle, "had assured him that he was a great president presiding over an exemplary government." Stroessner ended the meeting with an appeal that bordered on neediness, imploring Rusk to give Paraguay "more attention at the top and more favorable treatment in general."[69] Despite the United States' positive leanings toward Paraguay—Richard Nixon would later praise Paraguay "for opposing communism more strongly than any other nation in the world"—the meeting with Secretary Rusk left little doubt about Brazil's status as the preferred partner of the United States.[70]

In the afternoon Stroessner met with his former colleague, the Brazilian general Golbery do Couto e Silva.[71] Couto e Silva was one of the most influential officials of Brazil's military regime and also the ideological architect of what would soon become the dictatorship's Doctrine of National Security. Formed during his tenure at the Higher War College, Couto e Silva's vision for the DSN included theories of war, Brazil's potential as a world superpower, and a development model that combined Keynesian economics and state capitalism.[72] A hydroelectric dam on the Paraná River promised to deliver new energy that could power the DSN's goals for a new era of industrialization. Additionally, Couto e Silva surely saw the Guaíra standoff as a perfect opportunity to fulfill the idea of *fronteiras vivas* (living borders). Linked also to the ideology of Brasil Grande, the concept of fronteiras vivas saw the development of Brazil's borders as essential to its global prowess—in the sense of both physical fortification and also Brazil's geopolitical ascent beyond the boundaries of its nation-state.[73] Under Couto e Silva's guidance in the 1960s, these development ideologies eventually made the Itaipu dam the paragon of state development.

While politicians and military officials worked behind the scenes, popular forces began to mobilize their own responses. On November 27, the youth sections of the Revolutionary Febrerista and Christian Democrat opposition parties organized a demonstration in Asunción. In defiance of Paraguay's Law No. 294 that prohibited almost all forms of public protest, the crowd wound its way through the city center, stopping only at targeted locations. Protesters burned a Brazilian flag in front of the Commerce Office of the Brazilian embassy, threw Molotov cocktails through the windows of various Brazilian-owned business, lit smoke bombs across from the Center for Brazilian Studies, and painted graffiti on the walls of the Brazilian Military Offices proclaiming: "Paraguay sí, bandeirantes no: fuera los mamelucos" ("Paraguay yes, invaders no: out with the bastards"). As mentioned earlier, bandeirantes were participants in the seventeenth-century slaving raids that extended not only into the Brazilian hinterland, but into colonial Paraguay as well; and *mameluco*—an ethnic label derived from *mamluk*, the Arabic word for an overlord or soldier of enslaved origin—referred to the offspring of a European and an Amerindian. In using these terms, the protesters linked Brazil's actions at Guaíra to the centuries-old violations of Paraguay's sovereignty and its people. As anti-Brazilian unrest continued to spread across Asunción, police descended on the protesters, dispersed the crowd violently, and arrested fifteen students.[74]

Stroessner attempted to spin the protests into a sign of his government's popularity. Over the following months, a specific narrative circulated in the state-sponsored media, suggesting that for the first time since Stroessner took power in 1954, all political factions in Paraguay could unite around a common cause.[75] The opportunity to deflect criticism toward an external target allowed Stroessner to declare, "All the sectors of public opinion in Paraguay have expressed their outrage at the occupation of the non-demarcated border zone by Brazilian forces. All of the centers, associations, clubs, students . . . the unions, [the] cultural, social, and political groups, the veterans . . . the Army Reserves, everyone without exception has spontaneously denounced the hostile attitude [of Brazil]."[76]

Yet the Asunción protest showed that the situation was far more complicated than Stroessner's grandstanding suggested. The students not only denounced the Brazilian occupation but also the complicity of Stroessner himself. As a high school student during the demonstration, Ricardo Caballero Aquino remembered a central rallying cry of the protest: the dictatorship had sold out the Paraguayan people by allowing Brazil to take over Guaíra. Caballero Aquino recalls speeches from that day in which student leaders spoke of how Stroessner had gone to military school in Rio de Janeiro in the 1940s and had "been in love with Brazil ever since."[77] Stroessner did, in fact, study in

Brazil and maintained close ties with the Brazilian military. Keenly aware of this situation, Brazil's Foreign Ministry sought to exploit Stroessner's need to balance "his personal feelings with the official stance of the Paraguayan government."[78] Despite Stroessner's declarations of Paraguay's unity against the border occupation, he appeased Brazil at key moments. Less than a week after the anti-Brazilian student protests, the Stroessner regime officially apologized to the Brazilian government and offered full compensation for the damages incurred.[79]

Tensions continued to mount, and according to Mario Gibson Barboza, the newly appointed ambassador in Asunción, 1966 began in a climate of "enormous difficulty. Brazil found itself on the brink of war with Paraguay. . . . The conflict was strong and violent, the impasse deep and insurmountable . . . and all over the great problem of sovereignty, that magical word for which people kill and are killed."[80] Seeking to win the support of the international community, Paraguay's Ministry of Foreign Relations began sending out copies of its previous communication with Brazil to embassies and foreign ministries all over the world.[81]

In February Chancellor Sapena Pastor wrote to Ambassador Gibson Barboza to express his "energetic protest" in light of news that Brazil had built roads along—and potentially across—the border and also that Brazil's presence in the region now included a battalion of over six hundred men. Comparing multiple versions of this letter offers a window into the minutiae of the border conflict. Although Brazil eventually received a polished and fully edited copy of this letter, rough drafts can be found in the archive of Paraguay's Ministry of Foreign Relations. In several instances the original draft referenced the waterfalls as "los saltos" (the falls) only to have handwritten notes in the margins change the wording to "el salto" (the fall).[82] This inconsistency suggests that even within the government, great attention was given to putting forth a unified message. With so much depending on each country's ability to defend its particular view of the border, even the slightest mistake could prove disastrous.

With funding from the Ministry of War and Itamaraty, the early stages of Operation Sagarana built up Brazil's presence along the border. After the detachment of troops in June fulfilled the first objective of occupying the region, Operation Sagarana moved to its second phase and constructed multiple airstrips, a vast network of roads, multiple housing complexes, and electric power lines that connected Porto Renato to the city of Guaíra. Additionally, Colonel Tosta used his connections with the Brazilian Institute for Agrarian

Reform to help secure land titles throughout the region. These holdings eventually accomplished the longer-term goals of building schools, hospitals, and residences to support an expanded military population.[83] While both governments jockeyed for political and diplomatic leverage in the ongoing border debate, Operation Sagarana steadily reinforced Brazil's physical claim to the area.

In early March Brazil's National Security Council (CSN, Conselho de Segurança Nacional) convened at the Palácio Laranjeiras in Rio de Janeiro. Bringing together President Castelo Branco, his entire cabinet, and every high-ranking government minister, this CSN meeting focused exclusively on the border conflict with Paraguay.[84] In the lead-up to this gathering, the National Security Service—a branch of the military's secret police—had submitted a report about a Paraguayan plot to incite rebellion among the border population. The lead investigator, a Colonel Moreira, suggested that once the border communities rose up, Paraguayan-trained guerrilla soldiers would "infiltrate Brazilian lands and massacre the soldiers posted in Porto Renato in order to 'cleanse their national honor.'"[85] No uprising ever occurred, and Brazil's top leaders probably never saw Paraguay's army as a credible threat. But the unfolding situation represented more than just potential border violence. At one point President Castelo Branco observed that the Guaíra conflict had serious implications for all of South America, emphasizing above all that Paraguay played an essential role in limiting the hegemony of Argentina.[86]

In the CSN debate over how best to handle the border conflict with Paraguay, the minister for mines and energy, Mauro Thibau, suggested that Brazil simply build a smaller-scale hydroelectric project exclusively within its own territory. Thibau saw the current proposal for a dam at the Guaíra Falls as unnecessary, stating that a lower production of four or five million kilowatt-hours would provide more than enough to satisfy the nation's energy needs. The minister of planning, Roberto de Oliveira Campos, immediately voiced his agreement and suggested a series of three interconnected small dams as another viable option.[87] After these statements, however, the idea of a scaled-down project received no further attention, and the meeting returned to its goal of figuring out how to take advantage of the ongoing border conflict to build the most powerful hydroelectric dam possible. The two ministers in charge of Brazil's energy and engineering sectors clearly objected to the idea of what would become Itaipu, yet the commanding military leaders seemed indifferent to the exact details of Brazil's energy needs. Rather, they aimed to put into practice the ideology of Brasil Grande. Not only would a massive dam bring symbolic prestige on a global scale, but its inclusion of Paraguay as a geopolitical pawn would help redraw the boundaries of power relations in the Southern Cone.

The changing geopolitical landscape impacted all governments in the region. In Paraguay the Stroessner regime sought to leverage its position between Brazil and Argentina—both geographically and politically—to increase its own economic standing. A report from the US embassy in Asunción observed that "to bring pressure on Brazil . . . Paraguay is now playing up improved relations with Argentina."[88] This eventually led Stroessner to negotiate a deal with Argentina for a second binational dam on the same Paraná River, a project that resulted in the Yacyretá hydroelectric station some five hundred kilometers downstream of the future Itaipu site. Paraguay thus played into the rivalry between Brazil and Argentina to stake a claim to two different hydroelectric projects along its borders. For Argentina, competition over the Paraná River belonged to what the Argentine diplomat Juan Archibaldo Lanús referred to as the "hydroelectric saga."[89] Along with threatening Argentina's own energy projects further downstream, a Brazil-Paraguay dam would cut off Argentine shipping and commercial lines to São Paulo through the Paraná-Tietê River systems. More conspiratorially, Argentina would also claim that Brazil could use a dam as a "water bomb" to flood Buenos Aires.[90] Despite its efforts, the Argentine government could not slow Brazil's encroaching influence, either along the Paraná River or throughout the Southern Cone.

Support from the US government helps explain Brazil's willingness to antagonize neighboring countries. At an economic forum held in Buenos Aires, Paraguayan delegates approached Lincoln Gordon, the former ambassador to Brazil and then assistant secretary for inter-American affairs, to discuss the border conflict at Guaíra. Gordon acknowledged that he had indeed received all of the documents sent by Paraguay over the previous year—none of which had received an official response—but indicated "that it would be very difficult for Brazil to remove its military forces." Moreover, he voiced concerns about a "smear campaign" in the Paraguayan media against Brazil. Although Gordon implied that his government sided with Brazil in the border conflict, he did convey US interest in the prospect of a hydroelectric dam built jointly by Paraguay and Brazil.[91]

During this impasse, both governments continued to lobby potential allies and rally domestic support. In early April Stroessner gave a lengthy speech to Paraguay's House of Representatives denouncing Brazil's invasion of Guaíra and its failure to honor the legal and moral codes of "pan-Americanism that serve as the foundation of cooperation, solidarity, and friendship amongst the peoples of this hemisphere." His description of Brazil as an imperialist nation was juxtaposed with his characterization of Paraguay as a "generous, welcoming, and heroic" country that harbored neither "a domineering spirit nor greed."[92] The rhetoric of this speech echoed almost daily in the pages of Paraguay's newspapers. *Patria*, the official print organ of Stroessner's Colorado Party, ran a monthlong series of articles titled "Guairá in the Spotlight of America."[93] Even opposition newspapers got swept up in the wave of anti-Brazilian nationalism; *El Pueblo*, a paper connected to the Revolutionary Febrerista Party, changed its masthead to proclaim, "The Guairá Falls Are and Always Will Be Paraguayan."[94] International media also provided coverage, including the *New York Times* and the *Washington Post*, and other large dailies in Mexico, Chile, Venezuela, Panama, and Argentina.[95]

In Brazil, Foreign Minister Magalhães consistently made brash and often belittling statements about Paraguay. In response to Paraguay's Chancellor Sapena Pastor having called Brazil "aggressive and expansionist," Magalhães publicly said, "All of the Americas are well aware of the situation of our two governments and know which of the two must resort to fabricating artificial storylines."[96] Behind the scenes, the Brazilian regime also sought to undermine the Paraguayan dictatorship. After rumors emerged in May of a possible coup attempt against Stroessner, an Itamaraty report expressed the position that "this situation can, at the moment, act in our benefit by creating a favorable environment for the meeting [with Paraguay] that is currently being planned."[97] Although Brazil's military regime considered Stroessner an important ally, it appears likely that the threat of a coup in Paraguay—or even just the veneer of political instability—represented a powerful leverage point while negotiating the terms of a hydroelectric project.

The Act of Iguaçu and the Birth of Itaipu

The first official proposal for a binational meeting came in late April from Chancellor Sapena Pastor, with the caveat that Paraguay would attend only if Brazil's government agreed beforehand to withdraw its troops from Porto Renato.[98] Itamaraty agreed in principle to the idea of a border summit but refused to meet Paraguay's conditions. On June 3 Sapena Pastor sent word to Brazil's embassy in Asunción that "after much reluctance" the Paraguayan government consented to a meeting on the terms set out by Magalhães. The two governments then agreed to meet two weeks later, with negotiations taking place in the Paraguayan city of Puerto Presidente Stroessner in the morning before moving across the river to Foz do Iguaçu for the afternoon session.[99] On June 21, representatives from both countries met in the border region for two intense days of negotiations that produced the Act of Iguaçu, a relatively short document laying the framework for a binational dam on the Paraná River.[100] Brazil's delegation consisted of twenty-three men from various ministries within the military regime. Paraguay's contingent counted twenty men in similar positions—including all four of the political figures who had been arrested by Brazilian troops the previous October.[101]

The meeting got off to a rocky start when Paraguay's delegation insisted on the creation of a neutral border zone and a fifty-fifty split of all energy eventually produced; these were the exact criteria Brazil had refused throughout the preceding months. Brazil argued that a neutral frontier zone would set a dangerous precedent by which any neighboring country could, in theory, then challenge its borders.[102] This stalemate carried on into the afternoon, and at one point Sapena Pastor insinuated that both governments needed to reassess the treaty of 1872. Magalhães replied that a treaty could only be renegotiated by another treaty or by a war, and since Brazil refused to discuss a new treaty, he asked whether Paraguay was willing to start a war. Taken aback, Sapena Pastor asked whether the Brazilian minister was threatening Paraguay. Magalhães said that he was simply trying to have a realistic conversation based on facts.[103]

At this peak of tension, both parties agreed to end the day's negotiations and reconvene the next morning. Privately, Magalhães commented that this impasse might prove insurmountable.[104] Before leaving, however, Sapena Pastor and Magalhães exchanged proposals from their respective delegations. Each group deliberated deep into the night and returned the following morning with nearly identical documents. The main differences concerned two items that, as will be shown below, became the most important. The entire second day focused on the phrasing of these two articles.

The relative ease with which the second day progressed suggested that Magalhães's previous "threat" of war had simply been a negotiating strategy. Brazil's posturing over these two days—and its geopolitical bullying in the preceding years—served to speed along the deliberations. At almost every step, the Brazilians controlled the tone of the debate, and in the end they secured an agreement stacked in Brazil's favor.

At seven in the evening on June 22, in the presence of both delegations and various reporters, Magalhães and Sapena Pastor signed the final document.

It consisted of eight articles, with numbers 3 and 4 being the critical pair that had demanded so much attention. Article 3 stated that Brazil and Paraguay agreed to jointly explore the hydroelectric potential of their shared waters; the Paraguayan delegation celebrated this recognition of equal access to the Paraná River as its greatest accomplishment.[105] Article 4 was the most controversial part of the final agreement. Although it proclaimed that the energy produced would be "divided equally between both countries," it also stipulated that each nation maintained the right to buy the other's unused portion "at a fair price." With a fraction of the population and energy needs of Brazil, Paraguay would never use its 50 percent share. Paraguay initially suggested selling its leftover energy "at cost price" but gave in when Brazil threatened to end negotiations during the afternoon of the second day.[106] As we shall see later in this chapter, Brazil's insertion of the intentionally vague "fair price" clause guaranteed it would reap tremendous profits from the Itaipu dam.

The final text also included a single memorandum. This document declared that although Brazil remained firmly convinced of its territorial rights as granted by the treaty of 1872, it would remove its troops from the border as a sign of goodwill. The very next paragraph stated that Paraguay also maintained its interpretation of the treaty of 1872 and asserted its own sovereign claim to the region occupied by Brazil's military. What appears to be a fundamental paradox—both countries using an alleged peace treaty to codify the exact reasons that nearly brought them to war—perfectly embodies the border conflict itself. Each government made public gestures of cooperation only because this facilitated the development of a hydroelectric project. Yet neither changed its ideological approach, and the underlying issues continued to fester for years.

The signing of the Act of Iguaçu invoked a sweeping discourse of unity. Magalhães proclaimed that the agreement dissolved the tensions that had "sullied the long-standing friendship of Brazil and Paraguay" while also strengthening the pan-American community by promoting "the peace and progress of our entire continent." Sapena Pastor congratulated all involved for "finding solutions to the most difficult problems facing the relationship between Brazil and Paraguay in the 20th century."[107] Newspapers in both countries disseminated this triumphant narrative. In Asunción, *La Tribuna* celebrated the "positive and eloquent" results of the meeting, and Rio de Janeiro's *O Globo* remarked on the unprecedented exchange of peaceful negotiations that paved the way to construct the world's largest dam.[108] These symbolic achievements, however, would repeatedly be tested.

Less than a week later, an article in *O Globo* reported that Brazil had honored its agreement by beginning to withdraw its soldiers from Porto Renato.[109] If true, this would have indicated Brazil's genuine interest in opening a new chapter in its relationship with Paraguay. Yet the Brazilian regime had made no such efforts, and the detachment remained firmly entrenched along the border. By September Paraguay's government had grown so frustrated that it sent Sapena Pastor to New York to speak at the General Assembly of the United Nations to denounce Brazil for reneging on its promise. In response, Brazil said that although most of its troops had been removed, one sergeant and one corporal remained to guard the barracks and "dissuade contraband activities."[110]

Only in early December, nearly eighteen months after its soldiers first arrived in Porto Renato, did Brazil finally withdraw its military forces. Yet the troops were simply replaced with customs officials.[111] Brazilians continued to occupy the same buildings and housing units, only now with civilian border officials rather than military personnel.[112] On December 3, a ceremony in the courtyard of Porto Renato's barracks commemorated the compound's rebranding as a customs outpost. In a symbolic twist to the Paraguayan ceremony that had sparked the border conflict some twenty months earlier, a lieutenant lowered the Brazilian flag and handed it to the new head of the customs administration, who then rehung it and raised it once again (figure 1.3). In his concluding remarks, Colonel Tosta thanked the soldiers for their service and declared that "from this moment onward, a different arm of the nation will be responsible for the daily raising of this flag so that Brazil's sovereign presence is always known in this corner of our territory."[113]

Brazil's government did not remove its troops before making one final deal it had sought for years: uninhibited access to the fertile agricultural lands of eastern Paraguay. In his analysis of the Paraná borderlands, R. Andrew Nickson writes that "in exchange for the withdrawal of Brazilian troops from the Falls, agreed in the Act of Iguazu, the Paraguayan Government removed existing restrictions on Brazilian colonization."[114] Specifically, the Stroessner regime repealed the 1940 Agrarian Statute that prohibited the sale of land to foreigners within 150 kilometers of the border. Although this law had previously been circumvented—Brazilian farmers had trickled across the border for decades—its abolition allowed the open sale of land. Brazilians began to flood into Paraguay's eastern frontier, setting off a wave of agricultural migrants known as *Brasiguaios*—a central narrative in chapter 6 of this book. Brazil's maneuvers during the border crisis therefore secured not only geopolitical prestige and

FIGURE 1.3 Flag ceremony to inaugurate Porto Renato's transition from a military outpost to a customs office, December 3, 1966. Courtesy of the *Revista do Clube Militar*, Rio de Janeiro.

access to unprecedented hydroelectric energy but also a monopoly on what became a thriving agricultural enclave. By refusing to remove its troops unless Stroessner granted unfettered access to new lands, the Brazilian government satisfied the goals of both Brasil Grande and fronteiras vivas by expanding its reach even deeper into Paraguayan territory.

With the border zone now officially demilitarized, Brazil and Paraguay embarked on the precipitous task of actually building their dam. In February 1967 the governments established a binational group called the Joint Technical Commission to oversee all engineering and logistical details of the project's construction. Similar to the statements made after the signing of the Act of Iguaçu, the creation of the Joint Technical Commission elicited wide praise. Magalhães saw this as "the start of this great enterprise. . . . It will initiate a plan of action and collaboration that, if done efficiently, will bring about the ultimate goal: the common good."[115] These public celebrations again glossed over the actual state of affairs along the border.

The relationship between Brazil and Paraguay operated at two distinct levels. Publicly, both countries respected their binational agreements and the sovereignty of their neighbor, yet each nation continued to pursue its own territorial claims by building houses, roads, and other infrastructure along the border.[116] This contradiction produced various new moments of conflict. In July 1967 Paraguay's ambassador brought allegations that a group of Brazilian soldiers had forcibly expelled local Guarani families. Not only did the troops allegedly displace an entire community, but they did so after having ventured into Paraguayan territory.[117] Actions such as these reinforced the belief among Paraguayans that Brazil remained an untrustworthy enemy. And in Brazil a rumor circulated that some Paraguayan nationalists planned to "recover" the border zone. According to a secret CSN report submitted in August 1968, this plot would take place in 1970 as a way to honor the hundredth anniversary of the end of the War of the Triple Alliance.[118] No such event ever occurred, but a climate of mutual distrust and deep animosity continued to permeate the Brazil-Paraguay border.

One of the most persistent and bizarre issues concerned an observation pillar overlooking the fifth waterfall. Originally erected by Brazil in the 1930s, the pillar was graffitied, knocked over, or removed at various points in 1969. In each instance the Brazilian government restored it to its previous condition only to see it defaced once again (figures 1.4 and 1.5).[119] The controversy over this otherwise meaningless concrete post revealed how each country continued to cling to its interpretation of the border. For the Brazilian government,

FIGURES 1.4 & 1.5 The observation point above the fifth waterfall (left) and a close-up of the observation pillar after being knocked down (right). Photos courtesy of the Arquivo Nacional, Brazil.

the pillar symbolized how the border had definitively been outlined for nearly a century, and in the words of one report, it functioned as "very visible proof of the imaginary line that defines the international border."[120] The unknown perpetrators, for their part, most assuredly viewed the marker as an affront to Paraguay's sovereignty.

In April 1969 representatives from Brazil, Paraguay, Argentina, Uruguay, and Bolivia met in Brasília to sign the Treaty of the Plate Basin. This broad agreement established a multilateral basis for the "rational development and physical integration" of the rivers and tributaries that formed the greater Plate basin.[121] The treaty also provided the framework for regional collaboration that helped facilitate the eventual creation of the Itaipu Binational Corporation. A year later, the Joint Technical Commission oversaw the signing of the Cooperation Accord between Eletrobras and the National Electricity Administration, the federal energy agencies for Brazil and Paraguay, respectively.[122] This accord marked the first tangible step in the design and implementation of what became Itaipu. With a geopolitical conflict still lingering, the commission hired two "neutral" engineering firms to conduct the initial surveys: International Engineering Company (from the United States) and Interconsult-SPA (from Italy). In February 1971 the firms oversaw a new study of the potential designs and locations for the dam. These measurements involved aerial photography, bathometric and topographic surveys, hydraulic and sedimentary readings, and a series of other specialized procedures. Four task forces also examined the difference in electrical frequencies between Brazil and Paraguay, the technical details of constructing large-scale turbines, the potential risks of building on particular portions of the Paraná River, and the ecological effects of the project. By October 1972 these results yielded fifty different design proposals for ten different locations. After debating the fifty plans, the governments of Brazil and Paraguay officially chose the Itaipu proposal in January 1973.

The Treaty of Itaipu

The lead-up to the Treaty of Itaipu differed drastically from what occurred with the Act of Iguaçu in 1966. At that earlier time, the preceding border conflict meant that the bulk of the actual negotiations took place over the two tense days of in-person meetings. By 1973, in contrast, almost all of the groundwork had already been laid, by the initial 1966 act, by the various international summits, or through the work of the Joint Technical Commission.[123] The official deliberations still remained, but for all intents and purposes the Treaty of Itaipu was firmly agreed on long before presidents Emílio Médici and Alfredo Stroessner met in Brasília to sign it on April 26, 1973. The ease with which this treaty came into being resulted from a deeply contentious fifteen-year process of border standoffs and geopolitical posturing. So although the final "negotiation" lacked the drama of its 1966 predecessor, the Treaty of Itaipu functioned as a more benign culmination of an earlier and highly controversial history.

Compared to the rather concise Act of Iguaçu, the expansive 1973 Treaty of Itaipu consisted of twenty main articles complemented by three lengthy appendixes. Despite its size, the treaty had two main objectives: to codify the engineering details proposed by the Joint Technical Commission the previous January, and to establish the bureaucratic contours of the dam's governing body, the Itaipu Binational Corporation. The treaty stipulated that Itaipu Binational existed under the auspices of international public law, with guaranteed equity between both member nations. It entailed a two-tier governing structure, with the administrative council handling all political and bureaucratic components and the executive directory in charge of the technical and business side. Because Itaipu was intended as a fully binational project, all departments had to count equal representation from both Brazil and Paraguay. This included the highest leadership positions: two executive directors would jointly oversee Itaipu's major developments.

A few smaller items tucked into the final appendix held the greatest geopolitical significance. Section 3 of appendix C outlined the financial details for how Brazil and Paraguay would share Itaipu's energy.[124] Honoring the agreement made in the 1966 Act of Iguaçu, the 1973 treaty maintained that both countries retained equal right to the energy. The 1973 document, however, stipulated that all unused energy be sold to the other member nation at a far-below-market fixed price of US$300 per gigawatt-hour. By comparison, Argentina and Paraguay agreed during this same period to a price of US$2,998 per gigawatt-hour for the Yacyretá dam. More shocking still in the case of Itaipu, neither country could modify the price for fifty years, not even to account for inflation. Additionally, financial transactions would use "the currency available to the Binational," which in practice meant Brazilian cruzeiros. Paulo R. Schilling (an economist) and Ricardo Canese (an engineer) argue that the 1973 treaty served to entrench Paraguay's dependency on Brazil by pegging a substantial portion of its gross domestic product to the Brazilian currency. The treaty also effectively forced Paraguay to spend the money it received on Brazilian import products, the simplest way to spend the cruzeiros it received from the Binational Corporation.[125]

The power that Brazil had wielded over Paraguay throughout the preceding fifteen years paid huge dividends both geopolitically and financially. This begs the question as to why the Paraguayan government accepted Brazil's terms. The geographer J. M. G. Kleinpenning contends that Stroessner's acquiescence emerged from a keen awareness of Brazil's military, political, and economic power—a geopolitical dominance on display throughout this chapter.[126] Supporters of the treaty also point out that far from "exploiting" Paraguay, Itaipu represented a fair partition of energy and resources given the upfront contributions made by each nation. Because the Paraguayan government did not have sufficient capital in 1973, the Bank of Brazil loaned US$50 million for the launching of Itaipu Binational.[127] Moreover, Paraguay would only ever use roughly 5 percent of the electricity generated by Itaipu.

No matter how uneven the conditions, Paraguay's participation in the Itaipu project promised unprecedented growth and prestige for the small, landlocked nation. One month after the treaty's signing, for example, Chancellor Sapena Pastor declared in a speech to the economics graduates of the National University, "Itaipu is not a business deal, neither for Brazil nor for

Paraguay. It does not matter whether we obtain millions of dollars from it. Our objective is not its economic output, the objective is national development, the development of Brazil, the development of Paraguay. If it brings a flow of dollars into the national treasury, that is a secondary consideration, since what Itaipu is going to generate, first and foremost, is development."[128]

As had become customary, politicians and the mainstream press praised the Treaty of Itaipu while a steady stream of criticism from below called attention to many of the document's more problematic aspects. The most negative responses came from Paraguay, where outrage at the treaty focused on the financial repercussions. The Christian Democrat Party declared the 1973 treaty even worse than the concessions made at the end of the War of the Triple Alliance, writing, "We have just witnessed the most deafening failure of Paraguayan diplomacy in its history. In 1870, we were defeated after a heroic resistance, but at least we were able to negotiate with pride." Moreover, the Paraguayan government had sold out its own people: "The miniscule price at which we must sell our energy is absurd. The fifty years of this price fixing is nothing short of cowardly."[129] Demonstrations in Asunción denounced Stroessner's "betrayal," and Paraguayans living in Buenos Aires threw eggs and painted graffiti on the walls of the Brazilian embassy.[130]

Anger at the 1973 treaty also came from Argentina, where the government became increasingly worried that Itaipu would jeopardize the Corpus hydroelectric dam planned for a lower portion of the Paraná River.[131] An editorial in the Argentine newspaper *Mayoria* compared the relationship between Brazil and Paraguay at Itaipu with that of Panama and the United States at the Panama Canal, asking, "How true can a friendship be between a country with 3 million inhabitants and its neighbor with 80 million?"[132] On two occasions, the Argentine government took its case against Brazil to the United Nations.[133]

Despite these nodes of opposition, the proposed dam received mainstream admiration as a modern marvel of the twentieth century. Stroessner declared that "Itaipu is a sign of our sovereign and fraternal destiny," and further offered that Itaipu would function as the "morale boost" to guide Paraguay to a new level of prosperity.[134] The headline in *Patria*, a major Paraguayan daily, stated that "Itaipu represents the superstructure of the future."[135] Particularly in Brazil, the celebratory narrative focused on how Itaipu would benefit the entire hemisphere. In a speech to Congress, deputy Amaral de Souza described Itaipu as "the beginning of future initiatives that will bring together and unite the nations of a new Continent, it is the start of a new phase in the relations between Latin American peoples, defined by reality, without political or ideological prejudice, and devoted exclusively to the economic, social and cultural development of a vast and extensive region, whose population aspires to, and demands an exit from its unjustified underdevelopment."[136]

Over the following years, popular forces and critics of the dictatorship repeatedly challenged Itaipu's triumphalist narrative. Yet even in 1973, before construction crews had begun the colossal task of building the dam, a significant change had already taken place. For fifteen years the dictatorships of Brazil and Paraguay had jockeyed not only for control of the waters and lands that made up their shared border but for the right to define the border itself. On paper, Itaipu's importance lay in its status as the largest hydroelectric dam in the world, a feat of engineering brilliance that could produce enough energy to modernize two countries. Yet, in practice, the events and the debates over what would become the Itaipu dam helped crystallize new and increasingly uneven power relations throughout the region.

During the infancy of Brazil's dictatorship, its leaders stood firm against the demands of both Paraguay and Argentina, helping launch Brazil's ascent as the Southern Cone's major power. By seeking to fulfill the development ideologies of Brasil Grande and the DSN—with the support of the US government— the Brazilian dictatorship gained control of the waters of the Paraná River and the lands of eastern Paraguay. This process brought Paraguay into Brazil's sphere of power while simultaneously minimizing the influence of Argentina. And although Paraguay was stigmatized as a secondary nation stuck in Brazil's shadow, its actions at Guaíra guaranteed that it would benefit greatly from new sources of hydroelectric energy.

The same unflinching approach that Brazil's dictatorship relied on during the border crisis with Paraguay continued to guide its actions for years to come. The preceding geopolitical conflict helps contextualize the actions taken by the military government in the late 1970s and early 1980s against the farming communities that mobilized against Itaipu. A decade before the dictatorship contended with grassroots opposition in the western Paraná countryside, it first had to deal with foreign leaders who also saw the borderlands as key to their own nation's prosperity. The geopolitical standoff between Brazil and Paraguay thus served as a precursor to a new, more localized battle. Rather than confronting a neighboring military regime, the Brazilian dictatorship now faced off against thousands of rural communities living in the shadow of Itaipu.

CHAPTER 2

The Project of the Century and
the Battle for Public Opinion

Following the 1973 Treaty of Itaipu, western Paraná witnessed the development of two processes that fundamentally altered the region's physical and social landscape. As workers broke ground on the monumental task of building the world's largest dam, so too began the expropriation procedures for tens of thousands of rural Brazilians living in the flood zone. The dictatorship praised Itaipu's construction as a beacon of national strength that would legitimize state power domestically and strengthen Brazil's prestige globally. Itaipu's leaders and their patrons in the military regime routinely referred to the dam as the Project of the Century. Protecting this triumphalist image required the Itaipu Binational Corporation to clear the surrounding area in an orderly manner, and military authorities developed a public relations campaign to speed along the expropriations. Along with seeking to thwart any resistance from local communities, Itaipu's concern with its public image reflected a fundamental issue for the dictatorship in the 1970s: how to navigate the increasing calls for democracy while maintaining its perceived legitimacy as the caretaker of Brazil's future.

With the military beginning to make public gestures toward an eventual transition to civilian rule, Itaipu oversaw a local form of the same public gesticulation. Using a blend of paternalism and misdirection, Itaipu administrators framed displacement as a unique opportunity for farmers to get paid for their land and use the money to improve their lives. For both the dictatorship and Itaipu, these narratives suggested that Brazilians should not only comply with official policy but do so with gratitude.

The families facing displacement, however, found little reason to be thankful for Itaipu, and even fewer examples of the Binational's supposed "fair, Christian, and just" treatment.[1] With Itaipu's flood looming as a constant reminder that their homes would soon disappear underwater, farmers had to contend with expropriation policies they considered unfair and illegal. The struggle in western Paraná initially formed as an effort by farmers to receive more money for their soon-to-be-flooded lands. Yet in the process of seeking better expropriation packages, the fight expanded to include broader demands for political and agrarian rights. As pro-democracy forces throughout the country mobilized to turn public opinion against military rule, the fight at Itaipu grew to symbolize the emerging struggle between the grassroots opposition and the dictatorship. In the uncertain yet auspicious context of democratization in the 1970s, the unfolding rural conflict at Itaipu became both a product and an emblem of the country's complex political transition—what historian James Green calls Brazil's "slow-motion return to democracy."[2]

This chapter follows events in the Paraná borderlands from the 1973 Treaty of Itaipu through the birth of the Justice and Land Movement (MJT) at the 1980 protest camp in Santa Helena—the first of two such encampments that marked the MJT as a campaign of national significance. At one level, events during this time revolved largely around questions of expropriation: how would Itaipu clear the region in order to begin constructing the dam, how much money would the farmers receive, and where would the displaced communities go? Yet these issues also contributed to a deeper conflict, wherein the battle for public opinion about the dam served as a proxy for the clash over the legitimacy of military rule itself.

Given that so much of Itaipu's importance derived from the symbolism it projected within Brazil and abroad, the government sought to erase any outside influence that could potentially tarnish the dam's image. Especially after the worldwide oil crisis of 1973, military leaders pointed to Itaipu's hydroelectric energy as a sign of their government's forward-thinking vision for modernization. For the dictatorship, the dam's material and symbolic importance became increasingly acute in the late 1970s—the exact period when rural groups began mobilizing in western Paraná. Amid escalating calls for a civilian regime, the military considered Itaipu a monument to its rule that would endure even after a potential democratic transition. With the threat of a regime change, Itaipu stood as a permanent legacy to be protected at all costs.

Nearly a decade's worth of internal documents offer an inside view into how Itaipu administered its expropriations. This previously unstudied material stands in stark contrast to the benign image put forth by Itaipu's public relations campaigns. When it came to protecting its interests, the Binational Corporation proved efficient and highly structured, directing propaganda blitzes and targeted expropriations with few apparent difficulties. Yet internal reports reveal pervasive disorganization in implementing policy and honoring the promises made to displaced families. Working within a massive corporation explains, in part, the mismanagement toward local communities. But as will be shown throughout this chapter, the neglect—and outright abuse—of families in western Paraná resulted from the dictatorship's broader political agenda. Considering Itaipu's budget of US$20 billion, the farmers' goal of receiving a few thousand dollars more for each family would seem manageable. For military leaders, however, the question of financial compensation became secondary. Instead, they refused to meet the farmers' demands in order to protect their vision for Itaipu and, in turn, their own image as the rightful rulers of Brazil.

Moreover, as farmers mobilized to remain in the region, Itaipu increasingly sought to deflect their efforts by arguing that relocation outside of Paraná remained the only viable solution. Itaipu claimed to explore every possibility of finding new lands nearby. As we shall see, however, administrators worked behind the scenes as part of a larger national strategy of using private colonization companies to resettle farmers on new agricultural projects in the faraway corners of Brazil, especially in the Amazon.

Against the backdrop of political changes at the national level—from *distensão* (political decompression) in 1974 through the start of abertura in 1979—this chapter traces the formation of the farmers' movement as it confronted Itaipu's expropriations and the agrarian policies of the military regime. Understanding how the Itaipu dam fit into the ideology and hierarchy of the dictatorship enables a thorough examination of the wider implications of the rural struggles in the Paraná borderlands. The centrality of Itaipu helps reimagine the dam as a form of what sociologist Gay Seidman calls "authoritarian industrialization."[3] Similar to how the military's rapid industrialization schemes led factory workers to mobilize beyond the shop floor and toward a broader set of political goals, so too did the process of confronting Itaipu— a paragon of the technocratic, modernization-obsessed regime—help rural Brazilians articulate an expanding vision for a democratic future.

This chapter begins with a description of Itaipu's first director, the hard-line General José Costa Cavalcanti, and of the military's security structures that helped oversee the dam's development. The dictatorship's presence at Itaipu became especially relevant as the farmers' movement tapped into opposition struggles taking root throughout the country. This chapter then proceeds along a three-tiered narrative focusing on the policies of Itaipu, the early phases of rural mobilization, and the evolving dynamics of Brazil's political landscape.

In the 1970s western Paraná experienced a profound and swift transformation. The changes wrought by Itaipu's construction forced local communities to either abandon the region or join together to defend their homes and their hopes for a more democratic Brazil. Those who opted to stay helped lay the groundwork for a struggle whose demands for land and justice resonated throughout the country.

Itaipu and the Logic of Brazil's Dictatorship

In 1974 the task of choosing Itaipu's first director fell to Brazil's newly—and indirectly—elected president General Ernesto Geisel. Upon taking office, Geisel initiated a policy of political decompression known as distensão that aimed to reintroduce certain democratic rights in a process that would be "slow, gradual, and secure."[4] Geisel's distensão implied that the military would eventually release its grip on power, meaning that his choice of Itaipu's director carried the added responsibility of protecting the dictatorship's long-term vision for its much-heralded Project of the Century. Because of the dam's location in Foz do Iguaçu, the political powers of Itaipu's director carried particular weight: in 1968 the military had designated Foz do Iguaçu as one of Brazil's sixty-eight "national security zones," which canceled all direct elections for local office and essentially created semi-autonomous legal districts.[5] This national security zone meant that the already powerful position of Itaipu's director included the added dynamic of working in a region legislatively separate from most of the country.

For the director of Itaipu, Geisel appointed General José Costa Cavalcanti (figure 2.1), a career military officer and a principal conspirator in the 1964 overthrow of president João Goulart. Yet Cavalcanti actively opposed the military's first postcoup president, the soft-line General Humberto Castelo Branco. Subsequently, Cavalcanti helped orchestrate the successful 1967 candidacy of General Artur da Costa e Silva, under whom he served as minister of mines and energy. Having established himself as a key player within the hard-line faction of the military, Cavalcanti then partook in the 1968 coup-within-a-coup that consolidated the dictatorship's repressive regime. On December 13, 1968, Cavalcanti and sixteen other military leaders signed into law Institutional Act No. 5, the draconian measure that legalized and regulated torture while giving the president the power to close Congress and strip politicians of their mandates. Cavalcanti also helped secure the presidency of General Emílio Médici (1969–1974), who oversaw the most violent phase of Brazil's dictatorship—a period known as the *anos de chumbo* (the years of lead). Médici promoted Cavalcanti to minister of the interior, where he over-

FIGURE 2.1 General Alfredo Stroessner (center) and the two directors of Itaipu, the Paraguayan Enzo Debernardi (left) and the Brazilian General José Costa Cavalcanti (right), May 30, 1980. Reproduced from *Relatório Anual*, Itaipu Binational, 1980.

saw major infrastructure projects like the Trans-Amazonian Highway and also the persecution of numerous guerrilla and revolutionary groups.[6] As a key member of the military hard-liners, Cavalcanti's background in policing the Brazilian countryside made him an especially appealing candidate for Itaipu's first director. In the context of distensão and the uncertainty it implied for the military's monopoly on power, Cavalcanti became responsible for constructing a dam that would secure the legacy of the dictatorship long after any potential return to democracy.

Along with the leadership of Cavalcanti, the military regime maintained control over Itaipu through the Special Committee of Security and Information (AESI, Assessoria Especial de Segurança e Informação).[7] During its twenty-one years in power, Brazil's dictatorship relied heavily on similar committees (*assessorias*) to gather information on businesses, public enterprises, and, above all, universities. Unlike most other assessorias, however, AESI not only conducted surveillance but also investigated and prosecuted any potential crimes or threats. It stayed in constant coordination with the National Information Service, the government intelligence agency that historian Alfred C. Stepan has described as a primary conduit for Brazil's most concentrated period of repression.[8] The eyes, ears, and arms of AESI proved especially important in the coming years when the government contended with opposition groups and the growing profile of the farmers' movement.[9] Whether by gathering information on local church leaders, infiltrating meetings, physically confronting protesters, or gathering evidence to falsely prosecute dissident journalists, AESI functioned as the dictatorship's de facto presence at Itaipu.

The military's authority in the region allowed it to oversee the development of Itaipu, to monitor contraband along the border, and also to keep tabs on any "subversive" activity. This mounting presence had the unintended consequence of raising the political consciousness of local communities. In almost all interviews, participants in the farmers' movement remembered the mid-1970s as a period when people had to communicate in coded messages and travel circuitous routes to avoid detection. Whereas certain rural groups had not previously come into direct contact with the military regime, the development of Itaipu helped amplify the realities of authoritarian rule in the Paraná countryside.

Building the Project of the Century

The creation of the Itaipu Binational Corporation in May 1974 set in place the legal and administrative structures to begin the dam's construction. Building the largest dam on the planet demanded a workforce of unprecedented size: over 35,000 workers from Brazil and Paraguay took part throughout the nearly twenty years of construction, with a peak of almost 31,000 workers employed in 1978 alone. The overwhelming mass of these workers migrated from outside the region, leading to massive growth on both sides of the border. In Brazil, western Paraná's population rose from 56,000 in 1974 to over 250,000 less than six years later. Likewise, the Paraguayan city of Puerto Presidente Stroessner (later renamed Ciudad del Este) boomed to over a hundred thousand inhabitants, making it the second-largest city in the country.[10] At its height, Itaipu poured an average of 300,000 cubic meters of concrete a day—enough to build a twenty-story building every fifty-five minutes. When primary construction ended in 1984, the Itaipu dam stretched nearly five miles across and contained enough iron and steel to build 380 Eiffel Towers.[11]

FIGURES 2.2 & 2.3 Left: The Paraná River in 1975 prior to construction. Right: Itaipu's progress in 1977. Reproduced from *Relatório Anual*, Itaipu Binational, 1975 and 1977, respectively.

Although the dictatorship cited these impressive statistics to bolster its prestige, the ongoing construction had a very different set of consequences for local communities. Beginning in the mid-1970s, long before the flood engulfed the surrounding region, construction of the dam disrupted local markets, blocked trade routes, and reoriented labor demographics (figures 2.2 and 2.3). Combined with a particularly destructive frost during the harvest of 1975, the early phases of displacement saw agricultural production in the region drop by over 200 million kilograms.[12] Even before the region disappeared underwater, Itaipu caused significant financial challenges that helped motivate the farmers' struggle for fair expropriations.

The decline of farming outputs in western Paraná marked the end of the region's short but successful status as a thriving agricultural center. Extensive farming in the Paraná borderlands had begun only in the 1950s. Triggered by an exhaustion of land under coffee cultivation in the neighboring state of São Paulo, thousands of farmers pushed westward and settled on some of the country's most fertile soils. For the most part, these families descended from European immigrants who came to Brazil in the early decades of the twentieth century. A contemporary report described the influx of new settlers into the region: "In truth . . . none of them were born here. They are Brazilian, yes, but born in Rio Grande do Sul. They are gauchos. Their parents and grandparents, when they arrived in Brazil, came from Germany, Italy, or Poland."[13] The European background of this initial wave of settlers projected a sense of respectability and legitimacy that, in the eyes of mainstream society, differentiated them from the region's ethnically mixed peasants and indigenous families.

The early Euro-descendant settlers helped establish an agricultural sector in western Paraná that by the early 1970s accounted for 98 percent of the region's overall economic activity. The area had become a booming farming zone within the span of only a few generations—a brief success story that dissipated with the rise of Itaipu.[14] On the Brazilian side of the Paraná River, Itaipu flooded 780 square kilometers (111,332 hectares) of land, or roughly 14 percent of the entire region.[15] The majority (91 percent) of the inundated area was classified as rural, with an average of fifteen hectares per property, hinting at the propensity toward small- and medium-scale farming in the region. These statistics, however, only account for those with legal land titles. As will be shown, the flood also displaced thousands of landless peasants, squatters, day laborers, and indigenous people.

It is helpful as well to describe what was actually farmed in the area.[16] The three main crops in the Paraná borderlands were soybeans, corn, and coffee, with secondary products of wheat (mostly as a winter harvest), beans, and manioc (a staple for landless farmers, as it could feed them and their livestock). Smaller commercial activities also included eggs, chickens, and fruit, all of which tended to be produced by those living closer to cities, for ease of transportation. The difference between landed and landless peasants related less to which crops were grown, as both groups drew from among the same items listed above; instead, the main difference concerned *how much* they grew, as having more land enabled one to grow more and to diversify production. Although subsistence farming was the primary focus for both landed and landless alike, the larger the plot of land, the greater the chance of producing a surplus to sell in local and regional markets. Moreover, owning land also allowed for the use of heavy machinery, wherein a property deed could serve as collateral for a bank loan. In particular, access to machinery facilitated the production of soy and corn, the leading cash crops at the time. Although landless farmers could, in theory, use their work contract (if they had one) as a lien for a bank loan, such instances were not common. The Avá-Guarani, for their part, grew corn, manioc, sweet potatoes, peanuts, beans, squash, tobacco, and assorted fruits.[17] In the years after Itaipu's flood, subsistence farming—along with access to hunting and fishing—became increasingly precarious for the

indigenous community, and they came to depend heavily on foodstuffs provided by the federal government.

Between the signing of the 1973 Treaty of Itaipu and the reservoir flooding in October 1982, the question of land in the western Paraná borderlands
pivoted around the dual processes of expropriation (the transfer of landownership from individuals to Itaipu Binational) and indemnification (the actual
payment for the properties). Brazil's Constitution of 1967 provided the main
legal framework, as Article 157 required the government to pay "a fair price"
for expropriations made in the name of the public interest.[18] At key moments
in the evolution of the farmers' movement, certain groups—particularly the
landless—pushed for "land-for-land," in which the government would relocate displaced communities on nearby lands rather than offering money.[19]
This strategy would have required the government to expropriate lands from
large landholdings and redistribute them among the general population—and
thus represented a larger structural change. As such, Itaipu's leadership and
its allies in the dictatorship consistently relied on the Constitution's financial
definition of expropriation to dictate the terms and long-term consequences
of their interactions with displaced farmers.

The Initial Phases of Expropriation

Toward the end of 1973, Itaipu undertook a preliminary census of the surrounding lands and determined that the flood would impact around 42,000
people; as shown in the introduction, that figure left aside as many as 6,000
landless Brazilians. Itaipu's survey identified 8,257 indemnification cases for
legally owned properties—6,658 in rural lands and 1,599 in urban areas. This
represented 11 percent of the population in the eight affected municipalities
and 45 percent of the active workforce.[20] As news of the flood spread throughout the region, many farmers decided to leave Paraná altogether, marking the
start of a mass exodus from what had become one of Brazil's most productive
agricultural zones. A large portion of these farmers, those who came to be
known as *Brasiguaios*, chose to cross the border into Paraguay. For those who
stayed in western Paraná, the experience of expropriation depended heavily
on where they lived, what their social background was, and whether or not
they held legal title to their land.

The first wave of indemnifications took place from 1974 to 1976 and covered the "priority area" that included the construction site, the administrative

buildings, and the workers' housing complexes. Most of the priority area was located in Alvorada do Iguaçu, one of the region's wealthier municipalities. Residents of Alvorada do Iguaçu, for example, owned an average of sixty-two hectares per property, over four times the size of the landholdings in the surrounding "reservoir area."[21] In dealing with this community of large landholders, while trying to create a favorable public image, Itaipu handled these early cases with almost no conflicts. Unlike the rampant disorganization that soon defined the expropriations of the nearby small farmers, Itaipu established clear procedures for the priority area.[22] In certain instances Itaipu even advanced the payment packages for property owners in Alvorada do Iguaçu.[23] And although regional land prices in the mid-1970s fluctuated between Cr$25,000 and Cr$30,000 (roughly US$4,300) per *alqueire*, residents of Alvorada do Iguaçu received substantially more.[24] In one case from 1974, Itaipu expropriated a single property for over Cr$2.5 million, or US$340,000.[25]

Itaipu's approach to Alvorada do Iguaçu was also racialized. Of the initial 151 expropriated properties, 110 belonged to farmers who came from Brazil's southern states, which had largely Euro-descendant populations. The respect given to these Brazilians differed from the treatment of the poorer and darker-skinned communities that would take part in the mobilizations against Itaipu later in the decade. In its survey of the priority area, Itaipu noted that "the farmer from the South comes to this region with spirit, skill and courage to settle; while the majority of the rest (those from Minas Gerais and the Northeast) arrive here and almost always become day laborers or squatters."[26] While many northern migrants did, in fact, become precarious rural workers, the coded assumption of their lack of spirit, let alone their skills, helps explain Itaipu's reluctance to meet the demands of the nonwhite marginalized farmers—or to even recognize them as a legitimate social force.

The efficiency of the Alvorada do Iguaçu expropriations did not, however, guarantee the long-term success of its inhabitants. A 1981 article provides the personal account of Clôvis Melo, a farmer from Alvorada do Iguaçu who was among the first to receive indemnification. According to the story, in 1975 Melo sold his eight alqueires of first-rate land to Itaipu and bought a modest house fifteen kilometers outside of Foz do Iguaçu. But he could not keep up with his mortgage payments and faced ongoing unemployment in his new urban surroundings.[27] Melo's account hints at one of the many problems confronting farmers in their interactions with Itaipu: even those compensated for their lands had to then decide where to relocate. Melo migrated to a growing urban center, where jobs became increasingly scarce as construction on the Itaipu dam attracted unprecedented numbers of workers. Later groups of indemnified farmers, having perhaps heard stories similar to Melo's, opted to stay in the countryside and fight to maintain their rural livelihoods.

The Importance of Public Opinion

Once Itaipu completed expropriations in the priority area in early 1976, attention shifted to the more problematic reservoir area. With the flood scheduled for 1982, Itaipu planned to finish all remaining expropriations between 1978 and 1980. As part of this overly ambitious timeline—the deadline got pushed back numerous times—Itaipu embarked on a publicity campaign to win over public opinion and convince farmers to accept its proposals.[28] Acquiring lands in a timely manner would help deter any local resistance while also speeding along construction. Itaipu distributed posters throughout the region designed to reassure local communities (figure 2.4). One leaflet proclaimed, "You, too, will help build Itaipu, the world's largest hydroelectric dam. Itaipu will acquire land for a fair price, which is to say that the payout will correspond not only to the value of the land itself, but also to the benefits that can be attached to the land."[29] Despite these statements, Itaipu consistently offered below-market prices. Other campaign materials appealed to the personal anxieties of those facing an uncertain future. One poster (figure 2.5) told farmers, simply, "Stay calm." Another presented Itaipu as the farmers' key to a life of tranquility: "With this money saved you will never need to work again."[30] Itaipu also hired celebrities like the singer Teixeirinha, the radio personality Zé Béttio, and the actor Lima Duarte to participate in the publicity blitz. Interviews also aired on local television with farmers talking about how Itaipu had paid them handsomely for their lands.[31] The public relations campaign could also be fun and playful: one advertisement claimed that the ice used in just one hour to produce the concrete for Itaipu could chill all of the Brahma beer in Brazil.[32]

As much as Itaipu tried to glorify the expropriation process, problems simmered from the outset. As early as January 1975, newspapers reported that farmers were already demanding more money for their lands.[33] Additionally, a Foz do Iguaçu city councilman named Evandro Stelle Teixeira denounced Itaipu for evaluating lands within his city's boundaries as rural rather than urban, a designation that limited expropriation prices. Teixeira placed these issues in the larger context of Brazilian politics by saying, "At this moment

FIGURES 2.4 & 2.5 Examples of Itaipu's public relations campaign. Left: "Itaipu pays the fair price." Right: "Stay Calm." Photos courtesy of Guiomar Germani.

when President Geisel sets an example to initiate open dialogue within the Executive Office, Itaipu Binational remains deaf and unmoving to the plight of those who seek nothing more than what is fair and just."[34]

Itaipu's strategy also included a process of targeted expropriations intended to isolate individuals and dissolve local communities. Miguel Isloar Sávio, a rural organizer in the region, noted that "Itaipu unleashed a psychological war," stripping communities of their ability to collectively resist.[35] Pastor Werner Fuchs, the most active religious leader in the fight against Itaipu, remembers that upon entering a new region the Binational would first indemnify markets, pharmacies, and schools, forcing the inhabitants to travel upward of twenty kilometers for basic necessities.[36] This not only complicated the routines of daily life but diminished a town's ability to organize a collective response. The removal of basic infrastructure also devalued the surrounding properties, thus allowing Itaipu to continue offering low land prices.[37] Especially during the early years before a protest movement took shape, rural inhabitants often had little recourse but to accept the offer made to them. One farmer gave the following rationale for agreeing to Itaipu's proposal:

> I was forced to accept because, first off, everyone in the town had to leave so I was left alone with no resources and no markets to buy or sell; second, there was great pressure from the Itaipu representatives, who said that if we didn't accept, the case would be brought to court; third, those who didn't accept right away would only get another offer much later and the price of the available lands for us to buy would have risen. For fear of going to court and of not being able to find good lands to buy later on, [it] made a lot of people sign unfair deals.[38]

Such descriptions expose the realities behind Itaipu's publicity campaign. At almost every stage of its development, Itaipu's leaders consistently told the public of their commitment to indemnify farmers in a "fair, Christian, and just" manner. Archival and anecdotal evidence show that Itaipu rarely adhered to these standards. As the injustices continued to mount, local communities began to respond.

The Progressive Church and the Formation of Rural Mobilizations

The earliest initiative to organize the farmers came from the Catholic Church. Beginning in the 1960s, progressive sectors of the Catholic Church had helped lead social movements throughout Latin America, offering a social justice–based form of church participation that condemned underdevelopment and state violence. By the early 1970s, this social current culminated in the doctrine of liberation theology.[39] In Brazil the Pastoral Land Commission (CPT, Comissão Pastoral da Terra) played a key role in rural campaigns across the countryside. Created in 1975, the CPT existed as a branch of the National Conference of Brazilian Bishops, a Catholic organization, though many of its members in local struggles belonged to the Evangelical Church of the Lutheran Confession.

The CPT made the fight at Itaipu one of its central campaigns when it established a state headquarters in Paraná in 1976. The following year, it opened a new office in the town of Marechal Cândido Rondon—one of the areas slated for flooding. Over the next five years, the CPT served as the most outspoken and consistent ally of the region's displaced farmers. Although the religious leadership's insistence on peaceful tactics at times conflicted with the demands of local communities, the initial fight against Itaipu resulted almost entirely from the organizing efforts of the CPT.

Similar to how progressive religious groups operated throughout Brazil, the CPT began its involvement at Itaipu through the creation of ecclesial base communities (CEBs, *Comunidades eclesiais de base*) that sought to raise consciousness about agrarian issues and political rights. In the mid-1960s, CEBs emerged in Brazil and—led by priests, pastors, nuns, bishops, and laypeople commissioned by the Church—helped establish a wide network of grassroots groups over the following decade. Political scientist Scott Mainwaring argues that the CEBs in Brazil contributed some of the most innovative work of the progressive Church in all of Latin America, emphasizing in particular their role in encouraging opposition to the military regime.[40] In western Paraná the CEBs originally formed as Bible study groups but soon shifted focus almost entirely to the farmers' standoff with Itaipu. Father Edgard Raviche recalled that by the end of the 1970s, the CPT had successfully organized some three hundred CEBs in Paraná.[41]

The CEBs became especially important sites of mobilization in light of the dictatorship's close relationship with existing rural unions. In the 1970s many of Paraná's rural unions had been dismantled and rebuilt, often to support policies like the military's rural welfare program, the Rural Assistance Fund. Historian Cliff Welch argues that although the embrace of the Rural Assistance Fund expanded union membership by providing benefits like medical care, it nonetheless transformed organized labor into "a creature of the military regime" where corruption became a common trait among the co-opted leadership.[42] According to Silvênio Kolling, these pro-government rural unions strongly disliked the movement at Itaipu, often belittling the farmers as *pelegos*—a somewhat surprising use of the term for "scab" or "strikebreaker," as it was normally reserved for pro-company workers and union officials.[43] More than just filling a void of rural organizing, religious organizations also provided political cover for dissidents. Aluízio Palmar stands as a striking example. A former member of MR-8, the 8th October Revolutionary Movement, Palmar was imprisoned by the dictatorship in the late 1960s and released into exile in 1971 as part of an exchange for the kidnapped ambassador of Switzerland. When Palmar sneaked back into Brazil later in the decade, the CPT hired him as a community organizer, thus allowing him to operate politically in a way that would have been impossible otherwise.[44]

As we shall see, religious figures had a complex role at Itaipu. Their approach to rural communities often bordered on paternalism, and leaders like bishop Olívio Fazza attempted to silence calls for more direct action. The CPT wielded tremendous influence over the direction of the farmers' demands, and at key moments its commitment to peaceful protest stifled the potential for an escalation of tactics. The CPT also received criticism for not having done more to organize the neighboring indigenous communities.[45] Despite these limitations, the Church proved indispensable in the emergence of an organized resistance movement (figure 2.6).

As religious leaders began to organize in the Paraná borderlands, local politicians also lobbied Itaipu. In 1976 the mayor of Marechal Cândido Rondon wrote to Itaipu asking for clarification on when expropriations would begin and whether roads in the region would remain in operation throughout the expropriation process.[46] It appears that Itaipu refused to provide this information, since only a few years later the city's mayor again requested an explanation on the same set of issues.[47] Itaipu's silence forced local governments throughout the region to make similar appeals. The mayor of Paraíso do Norte asked the Binational's legal director, Paulo da Cunha, for a map and timeline of the expropriations, and wondered whether there existed any forum for farmers to raise their concerns.[48] Many communities had no means to present their questions directly to Itaipu, and a coalition of Paraná deputies sent a petition expressing concern that "the farmers have not yet received any concrete information about how and when they will receive compensation." Additionally, the deputies requested that Itaipu allow representatives from local communities to participate in the evaluation of their own lands, "so that the farmers know that somebody is fighting for their rights and to guarantee that they are receiving fair prices for their lands."[49]

As concerns over Itaipu's expropriations continued to grow, farmers held their first large-scale event. On March 31, 1978, a few hundred people gathered in Marechal Cândido Rondon. This assembly resulted in an initiative called the Noah's Ark Project.[50] Seeking to save the farmers from the flood of Itaipu, the project declared:

> Without calling into question the importance of an enterprise like Itaipu for the Nation, we concern ourselves with mankind. After 30 years of pouring sweat into these lands, the settlers, at great pain, succeeded in creating a commercial infrastructure; they succeeded in building their homes, in educating their children, in organizing themselves into religious and social

FIGURE 2.6 Ecumenical service at the Santa Helena encampment, July 1980. Photo courtesy of Guiomar Germani.

communities. These settlers now confront having to leave for strange and distant lands to start all over again. They deserve our attention, our respect, our efforts.[51]

Formed initially by twenty groups from the neighboring municipalities of São Miguel do Iguaçu, Santa Helena, and Marechal Cândido Rondon, the Noah's Ark Project provided a foundation around which the displaced communities began to organize, framed by the biblical imagery of Noah's ark. Religious leaders explicitly called for the movement to adopt a respectful and peaceful strategy.[52] The Noah's Ark Project maintained that local farmers did not necessarily object to the construction of the dam but rather to Itaipu's expropriation policies. This approach helped counter statements from Itaipu's supporters who claimed that the mobilized farmers did not care about the needs of their country. One conservative politician recalled that the farmers wanted to stop Itaipu from being built because they believed "Brazil didn't need the [dam's] energy."[53] In contrast, a displaced farmer remembered that "nobody refused to give up their land. . . . Everyone gave their land for the progress of Brazil because [the country] needed energy. The problem was the price."[54] At a time of transition and uncertainty, both sides defended their positions with a rhetoric of patriotism and civic duty. The farmers presented their demands as an extension of their hard work and sacrifice in the region. Marcelo Barth, one of the most visible and outspoken leaders of the budding movement, proclaimed at the 1978 meeting:

> The farmers are tired of being treated like animals in Brazilian society. We have tended these lands for many years. We confront an aggressive and hostile backlands full of beasts and poisonous snakes. There were no roads or bridges, no schools or businesses. There were no clubs or churches to pray to God, who made this earth for all men. We have all of this today thanks to our unbreakable will and the cost of our own sweat. If we could gather all the drops of the sweat that we shed, we would make a new lake, not Itaipu, but a salted lake, full of illusions of a dignified and humane future.[55]

Stories such as Barth's helped nudge public opinion away from Itaipu's propaganda campaign. In May 1978 Itaipu invited twenty-four pastors and priests to visit the dam—the first official meeting between the Binational and representatives of rural communities.[56] After a tour of the construction zone, Itaipu employees showed the visitors a video about the dam's progress and gave a presentation on the timeline and criteria for how expropriations would proceed in the years to come. The majority of the clergy's questions centered on why the early land payments had been so low. Others spoke about the farmers' desire to receive new lands in nearby regions. In response, Itaipu's representatives declared that local land markets made it almost impossible to relocate families within Paraná and emphasized instead the availability of cheaper lands in other states throughout Brazil. As we shall see, these gestures toward land outside of Paraná—primarily in the Amazon and the northeast—would soon become Itaipu's unofficial relocation policy.

In the meantime, the communities facing displacement continued to mobilize. The early phases of collective action attracted a wider audience, and the mainstream press also began to cover the struggle against Itaipu. The São Paulo-based Folha da Tarde ran an article titled "Itaipu: A Nightmare for Farmers," and the Folha de São Paulo—Brazil's largest daily paper—reported that six thousand families still awaited indemnification.[57] As the farmers' notoriety grew at the national level, the movement's first milestone took place on October 16, 1978. Nearly 1,500 farmers convened on the patio of a Catholic church in Santa Helena, and after a round of opening remarks, the attendees split into smaller groups to discuss the following questions: What are three or four problems relating to Itaipu that led you to come to this assembly? How would you like these problems to be resolved? How can we proceed from these suggestions?[58] The farmers were aware of likely government surveillance, and so these breakout groups assembled by region in order to separate out any unknown people. One farmer remembered that this security measure left nearly a dozen men standing alone, indicating the military's intent to infiltrate the gathering.[59]

After a few hours, the smaller groups reconvened and held a general assembly that debated and finally approved a document to send to Brazil's president, General Geisel. Known as the Santa Helena Letter, this declaration served as a springboard for the growing mass movement.[60] The Santa Helena Letter provided a list of fifteen demands that included a price increase to Cr$100,000 (US$5,170) per alqueire for all types of land, the resettlement of families in nearby areas, and the indemnification of all members of a community at the same time. Another item demanded that farmers without legal title to their property still receive a minimum of 50 percent of the land's value.[61] Although the concern for landless farmers dissipated at key moments over the next three years, its inclusion in the Santa Helena Letter reflects the broader demands of the movement's earliest phase. Along with crafting the Santa Helena Letter, the assembly elected a commission of twenty-five farmers and three church leaders who soon traveled to Foz do Iguaçu and met with the minister of mines and energy, Shigeaki Ueki. Hoping to placate the farmers, Ueki promised to open an office of the National Institute for Colonization and Agrarian Reform (INCRA, Instituto Nacional de Colonização e Reforma Agrária) in Foz do Iguaçu—a promise the government never kept.[62] While the Santa Helena assembly and its resulting document failed to bring about any immediate changes, it marked the start of a movement capable of collectively forming a list of wide-reaching demands. The ability to mobilize and gain meetings with government authorities also meant that those in power began to take the farmers more seriously.

Transitions at the national level added to the importance of the Santa Helena actions. The first fissures in Brazil's dictatorship appeared in the mid-1970s, initiating a breakdown in political control that historian Maria Helena

Moreira Alves views as the process through which "people began to lose their fear of the military government."[63] Early on, this momentum coalesced around an amnesty campaign that sought the return of exiled dissidents and the reinstatement of those who had lost their jobs and political rights.[64] Grassroots mobilizations continued to pressure the dictatorship as student protests in 1977 and the reemergence of a strong union movement further motivated activists throughout Brazil. Beginning in 1978, a wave of militant labor strikes in São Paulo's industrial "ABC" region marked the arrival of Luiz Inácio "Lula" da Silva as a national opposition figure. In total, the ABC strikes counted the participation of over four million workers.[65] Across the country, Brazilians forged new ways to challenge the dictatorship's legitimacy. These opening spaces of negotiation between popular and state forces helped condition the events taking place in the shadow of Itaipu.

Despite these reemerging nodes of political dissent, the realities of life under dictatorship persisted. Especially in regions like western Paraná, the political freedoms opened by the distensão (and later the abertura) in cities like Rio de Janeiro and São Paulo often arrived much later, if at all. During this regionally uneven process, the farmers at Itaipu nonetheless cultivated unique forms of political consciousness. This resulted largely from two processes. First, the history of rural struggles predating 1964 gave certain communities a politicizing experience independent of the official opposition struggles taking shape in urban centers. Second, the geopolitical importance of the Itaipu dam meant that the dictatorship maintained an extremely close watch over all grassroots actions in the surrounding region. As such, farmers confronted firsthand the mechanisms of Brazil's national security state. In the early years of the movement (1975–1980), repression and surveillance forced people to hold meetings in secret, communicate in coded messages, and travel circuitous routes to avoid detection. Silvênio Kolling, a local farmer, remembered it as a time when "we couldn't have open meetings, because Institutional Act No. 5 was still in place and we couldn't even park our cars near the place where we would gather."[66] According to Pastor Fuchs, farmers constantly feared infiltration from the state police, the army, the National Information Service, and Itaipu's security forces.[67] Documentary evidence reveals that all of these agencies did, in fact, keep close tabs on the movement. Because farming communities in the Paraná borderlands had little prior contact with the dictatorship, this surveillance had a profound and unintended consequence. Carlos Grillmann recalled that by asking questions like "Why do we have to meet in secret?" farmers began to form larger questions about why they did not have other freedoms and rights.[68] The experience of confronting Itaipu thus added a tangible awareness of life under dictatorship.

In the increasingly politicized struggle, politicians also began to speak out in support of the farmers. In an address to the Paraná Legislative Assembly, the pastor and recently elected state deputy Gernote Kirinus declared that rural communities "are making a patriotic sacrifice by shouldering the serious problems emanating from this Pharaonic project. We must turn our attention away from the outrageous megalomania that is feeding this source of national vanity, and concentrate instead on . . . the rights of our state's inhabitants."[69] The theme of sacrifice resonated strongly in the afflicted communities. According to a congressional speech by Paulo Marques, representatives of Itaipu had told a farmer that "for this dam to be built, someone has to be sacrificed for the good of Brazil." Marques relayed the farmers' full testimony to Congress, which included the following exchange:

> But why must we be sacrificed? We have been here for ten, twelve, twenty years digging, planting, sowing, paying taxes, contributing to the greatness of these lands, and now they tell us we must be sacrificed. As if our calloused hands were not enough, our curved spines, our wrinkled faces; as if it weren't enough that we had to watch our wives cry for lack of food, for lack of medicine. . . . And now we must be sacrificed. They don't even have the guts to admit that farmers won't receive enough money to buy new lands and that we will be sent to INCRA's lands in god-knows-where. So after all that we've already gone through, we now wait for jungles, wild animals, mosquitoes, malaria, sickness, and perhaps death itself.[70]

The early months of 1979 saw a sequence of victories and potential setbacks for the quickly growing farmers' movement. In January Itaipu agreed to a 40 percent increase: its first-ever price concession.[71] Seeking to temper any sense of popular triumph, Paulo da Cunha, the Binational's legal director, attributed the raise not to pressure from the farmers but rather to an effort to remain consistent with changes in the land's market value. Da Cunha claimed that the increase allowed Itaipu to more efficiently administer 250 indemnification contracts per month to meet its goal of completing all compensation agreements by 1980.[72] Two months later, President Geisel signed a decree that marked the lands around Itaipu as belonging to the "public utility" and gave the Binational Corporation sole jurisdiction in the indemnification process— previously, government agencies like the Ministry of the Interior or INCRA had administered these policies.[73] For the farmers who already considered

Itaipu to have abused its powers over the local population, this decree likely provoked even more anxiety.

Motivated by these recent events, over three thousand people gathered for an assembly in Santa Helena on April 7 in the movement's largest action yet. Journalists from *O Estado de São Paulo*, *O Globo*, *Veja* (Brazil's largest weekly magazine), *O Jornal do Brasil*, and numerous local and state outlets attended the meeting.[74] After labor leaders and bishops gave opening speeches, over fifty farmers took the microphone to voice outrage and frustration. Stories included Itaipu paying unequal amounts for identical plots of land, the Bank of Brazil taking illegal commissions on land-sale transactions, and an Itaipu employee asking to borrow one farmer's land deed to make a photocopy but then refusing to return it unless the farmer signed a sale contract.[75] Similar tales of mistreatment circulated throughout the region. An extreme example claimed that Itaipu officials set a house on fire to get a family to vacate the property.[76] Whether or not this event actually happened matters less than the meanings attached to such stories by local communities. A less visible form of abuse related to Itaipu's proposed timeline. One farmer remembered the frustration of being strung along:

> The pattern was always the same: Itaipu would say that they were coming but never did! Every day of our lives, every night, during all those years it was the same torment. You can't make any plans because soon enough you'll get paid and will have to leave. That might seem easy, but after a year, and then after another year, all that waiting is so exhausting that eventually you're ready to leave everything behind and leave, just to free yourself of that torment.[77]

In the late afternoon at the Santa Helena meeting, the assembled farmers discussed and voted on ten specific demands. The resulting statement called for Itaipu to immediately begin an expropriation process in accordance with the laws of public well-being; for a statewide agrarian reform program that worked directly with local communities; for a minimum price for all land compensation of Cr$100,000 per alqueire; and for the indemnified to receive a one-year grace period to pay off existing mortgages.[78] The document framed these demands as a natural extension of their rights as Brazilians, citing the Constitution's guarantee of the "inviolable rights to life, liberty, property, and security."[79] As people throughout the nation reasserted their vision for a new democratic society, farmers in western Paraná made similar claims to their own rights as citizens.

This evolving set of demands and its coverage in the national media elicited a response from Itaipu's director, General José Costa Cavalcanti. Within a few days of the Santa Helena assembly, Cavalcanti sent a lengthy note to various state deputies, newspapers, and the farmers' allies emphasizing that Itaipu was "doing everything possible to benefit the expropriated, giving them the humane and Christian treatment that they deserve."[80] Addressing the main demand of receiving more money, Cavalcanti claimed that Itaipu simply paid according to evaluations done by private companies the previous year—a claim that would be disproved in 1981 when a government agency determined that Itaipu paid far below market value.[81] Cavalcanti also sidestepped the farmers' desire to stay in Paraná by claiming that the responsibility for resettlement lay solely with INCRA. He did note, however, that Itaipu had provided a list of seven private companies with available land and encouraged farmers to choose freely among them.

Despite Cavalcanti's attempts to project a calm demeanor, internal documents suggest otherwise. A confidential AESI report described the Santa Helena meeting as "a political event carefully prepared to have national and international effects. The display of democratic freedoms provides a favorable climate for other opposition movements." From Itaipu's perspective, the farmers' actions posed a threat that could reverberate far beyond western Paraná. As described in the AESI memo, the movement had "the possibility to negatively influence both the internal and external politics of Brazil."[82]

At the end of May, Cavalcanti consented to give his first public interview, meeting with the journalists Juvêncio Mazzarollo and João Adelino de Souza from the Foz do Iguaçu newspaper, *Hoje*. As we shall see in chapter 5, Mazzarollo was the journalist whom Cavalcanti helped imprison two years later for his coverage of Itaipu's standoff with the farmers. In the middle of 1979, however, before Mazzarollo helped establish the dissident newspaper *Nosso Tempo*, the government did not yet consider him a threat. In the interview Cavalcanti discussed a wide range of topics, including Paraguay's involvement with Itaipu, the status of the dam's construction, and the legitimacy of the farmers' demands.[83] When asked about the displaced families, Cavalcanti framed them as an unfortunate yet necessary reality: "Of course we feel bad seeing these farmers leave their lands, but Brazil needs this energy, it would not be possible for Brazil to survive the next decade without the energy of Itaipu."[84] And when pressed about offering below-market expropriation payments, Cavalcanti claimed that the Binational simply could not afford to pay more: "We want to construct Itaipu as cheaply as possible and we cannot pay for the land at a price above what it's worth."[85]

Coming from the director of a project with a budget that would stretch to nearly US$20 billion, these statements likely rang hollow to families seeking an increase of roughly US$5,000 each.[86] Moreover, Cavalcanti's public statements contradicted those he made privately. In 1978 he noted in confidential settings that Itaipu already planned on paying up to Cr$100,000 per alqueire—four times the farmers' minimum demand.[87] This raises the question of why Itaipu acted so disingenuously in forcing the farmers to struggle for price increases that the Binational was already willing to concede. Itaipu's importance derived in great measure from the image of strength it projected for the government, which became increasingly relevant as opposition forces began to chip away at the dictatorship's monopoly on power. Whether it be raising wages for industrial workers on strike or giving more money for lands to be flooded, the military regime likely saw any form of financial concession as an inherently political concession. To increase payments to farmers, therefore, would grant popular forces a semblance of political legitimacy. Although Itaipu had internally agreed to increase expropriation prices, its refusal to do so publicly reflected the dictatorship's determination to maintain an impression of complete control.

The interview with Cavalcanti eventually pivoted to the dam's construction, and Mazzarollo mentioned reports of workers forced into grueling conditions with shifts of up to fifteen hours straight. Cavalcanti denied these accusations, yet similar claims consistently dogged Itaipu, as innumerable workers died while building the dam. While it is impossible to know the exact number of workplace fatalities—estimates range from Itaipu's official number of 149 to as high as 1,000—its symbolism among the local populations is clear.[88] One article from 1981 described the construction site as a "concentration camp," and to this day people remember Itaipu as a dam "built with concrete and blood."[89] Despite Cavalcanti's efforts, the realities of what transpired in both the construction zone and the surrounding countryside provided a counterpoint to the public image that Itaipu sought to cultivate.

Support for the farmers continued to increase over the next few months, highlighted by a speech in late June by Sérgio Spada, a Foz do Iguaçu city councilman. In response to the bad publicity, da Cunha issued a press release declaring that Itaipu is always "in defense of the farmers' legitimate rights, in their treatment, and the search for viable and fair solutions. [. . .] Itaipu strives for an expropriation policy defined by the Christian approach of always helping those around us."[90] Such statements aimed to convince the public that Itaipu was doing everything within its power to process the expropriations in a fair and timely manner. However, internal documents again depict Itaipu's handling of the expropriations as highly disorganized and shrouded in secrecy.

Although da Cunha's press release described Itaipu as "totally transparent" in its indemnification policies, the Binational prohibited its employees from divulging information regarding expropriations to anyone other than the individuals involved on a case-by-case basis. Even then, farmers could only learn the details of their particular case once it had been processed and approved by the Binational's regional headquarters and its local secretary.[91] More than just a lack of transparency, documents from Itaipu's legal office reveal an unclear chain of command, constantly shifting regulations, a mishandling of budget deficits, and rampant inefficiency in the actual processing and paying of land expropriations.[92] One report spoke of a "troubling pattern" of land-sale contracts ruined by coffee stains.[93] Even leaving aside the larger political explanations for the mistreatment of local communities, the level of internal disorganization meant that Itaipu's actions could likely never match its rhetoric.

In the unfolding battle for public opinion, Itaipu brought a group of state deputies to tour the construction site prior to the completion of the Paraná River's diversion canal. One of the visitors, Nelton Friedrich, noted that such an invitation never could have occurred earlier in the decade—a type of progress he attributed to the increase in popular pressure during the early phases of Brazil's political reopening. Friedrich nonetheless saw the visit as a gimmick to deflect criticism, stating that "Itaipu is using an old American trick of trying to convince people through their eyes, which is to say with grandeur, with numbers, trying to gloss over the vision of politicians."[94] Around this time Itaipu conceded a new round of price adjustments by instituting a 17.8 percent raise to adjust the base value for "top-quality" lands to around Cr$100,000. In private, Itaipu described the update as necessary to "avoid the great discrepancies that caused so many problems in the ongoing process of expropriations."[95] Despite these changes, it appears that Itaipu still used various tactics to avoid paying the money as promised. An AESI memo from November 1979 described a series of complaints that Itaipu had sent its employees to coerce families into signing contracts, and also outright refusals to deliver compensation by the agreed-on deadlines.[96]

With each passing month, the specter of the planned 1982 flood drew ever closer, and pressure mounted to find a solution before the region disappeared underwater. Toward the end of 1979, finding common ground seemed highly improbable. In fact, INCRA even warned Itaipu's leaders that failure to update their policies could "create a climate of revolt and social unrest" throughout the region.[97] Itaipu ignored these words of caution and did little to adapt its actions to the changes taking root in western Paraná and throughout the country.

The Start of Abertura and a New Era of Opposition in Brazil

As the impasse between Itaipu and the farmers moved toward its eventual tipping point at the 1980 Santa Helena encampment, popular forces continued to gain traction at the national level. Mobilizations like the amnesty movement and the student and labor strikes of the late 1970s had already succeeded in advancing opposition to the dictatorship. Even before the new president, General João Baptista Figueiredo (1979–1985), inaugurated the abertura program, grassroots actions had injected opposition campaigns with the confidence to defend the goals of a democratic Brazil. As a result, these popular struggles helped pave the way for the legal and legislative components of democratization that would soon be codified in the abertura.

At the end of Geisel's presidency in December 1978, the government allowed Institutional Act No. 5 to expire, thereby ending the law that had justified torture and the rampant suspension of political rights. The act had embodied the dictatorship's national security state, and its repeal signaled an important step in Brazil's wayward return to democracy. General Figueiredo assumed the presidency in March 1979 and initiated the official policy of abertura under the auspices of pacifying the elite opposition in order to guarantee that any transition away from military rule would occur "with greater stability and wider support."[98] During his first six months in office, Figueiredo oversaw the passage of two laws that suggested the beginning of a more democratic Brazil. In August the Amnesty Bill authorized the return of Brazilian exiles and allowed suspended politicians to regain their rights. Although the law represented an important step of democratization, it also reflected the underlying—and still unresolved—negotiations between opposition groups and hard-liners within the military regime. Exiles could return to Brazil, and persecuted public employees regained their posts, but members of the military also received blanket pardons for any alleged participation in torture or repression. Then in October the Party Reform Bill abolished the two state-created political parties, the Alliance for National Renovation (ARENA, Aliança Renovadora Nacional; the government party) and the Brazilian Democratic Movement (MDB, Movimento

Democrático Brasileiro, the "loyal" opposition party). The Party Reform Bill still placed obstacles in the path of opposition parties.[99] James Green argues that the bill was Figueiredo's response to a fear that the MDB might win a majority in Congress and in key state legislatures: "It was a divide-and-conquer strategy directed toward splintering the legal opposition."[100] Moreover, the abertura reforms continued to be shaped by, and largely for, the benefit of urban elites.

Scholars have tended to reproduce this official view of the abertura. Bernardo Kucinski has described the abertura as a controlled process that "reaffirmed the Brazilian political tradition of conciliation among elites."[101] Similarly, Elio Gaspari views the transition as an effort by forward-thinking generals like Ernesto Geisel and Golbery do Couto e Silva to reclaim Brazil from the "disorder" of the military hard-liners.[102] And Scott Mainwaring and Donald Share categorize Brazil as an example of "transition through transaction" where elites controlled the timing and mechanisms of political change.[103] To be sure, the actions of urban elites fundamentally advanced the return of civilian rule. Yet examples like Itaipu demand that scholars explore the processes that played complementary—if not entirely independent—roles in pushing democratization forward. Although Brazilian elites passed laws to end the dictatorship, their policies took shape in relation to an environment of grassroots battles waged across the country.

Despite the limitations of both the Amnesty and Party Reform Bills, they nonetheless created new tools for the exercise of political rights and facilitated the legal and legislative reopening of Brazilian society. In particular, the formation of new political parties allowed opponents of the military to build a broad coalition of pro-democracy forces. Localized conflicts like the farmers' movement in western Paraná became new avenues for the growth of nationwide opposition. As the direction of Brazil's transition toward civilian rule continued to fluctuate, the fight at Itaipu offered an example of rebuilding a culture of democracy at the local level.

At the end of 1979, the CPT produced a document that offers a clear window into how social movements engaged with the national rhetoric of abertura. Titled "You and Hydroelectric Dams" ("Você e as hidroelétricas"), the CPT publication served as a guide for its members in how to organize a series of community meetings. The first gatherings included Bible study groups framed by questions intended to help participants infer religious lessons about collective struggle and injustice: "Who in our region is Goliath, and who is on the side of David?" and "In your life, who could be a Moses figure, and who plays the role of Pharaoh?"[104] After these initial meetings, the pamphlet instructed CPT members to discuss workers' rights in general, and the farmers' movement at Itaipu specifically. From there, the document launched into a full analysis of the ABC industrial strikes and asked farmers to consider, "What lessons can we take from the example of the São Paulo workers?"

Over the arc of fifteen pages, this CPT guidebook connected stories from the Bible, the fight at Itaipu, and national events like the ABC strikes. The document concluded by asking participants to reflect on the following ideas: "After seeing these examples, can you still say that farmers and workers are capable of nothing? It is now the time for us to prove that we are all like them. We also have these abilities, and together can be a great force. What are you doing to help build this great force, to be worthy of our rights and those of all workers?"[105]

In the early months of 1980, many of the tensions of the national abertura existed at the local level in western Paraná. At the same time that various opposition groups supported the farmers' movement, pro-military forces also spoke out in favor of Itaipu. The vice president of the Paraná Legislative Assembly, an ARENA deputy named Tércio Albuquerque, vilified the rural protesters as "demagogic and futile."[106] According to an AESI security report, Albuquerque then sent a personal letter to General Cavalcanti saying that "although he could not act as Itaipu's official spokesperson [in the state assembly] he vowed to always stand up against any antagonistic politicians."[107] Such statements expose the contradictions between the rhetoric of abertura and the reality of how it actually unfolded: despite the political and electoral reforms taking root nationally, supporters of the dictatorship continued to cite grassroots movements like those at Itaipu as evidence of the chaos plaguing Brazil. According to this logic, the subversion incited by the farmers in western Paraná proved that the country still required military rule to maintain order, especially in this region where a potential return to democracy could cripple the government's ability to deliver the economic promise of the world's largest hydroelectric dam. In the years to come, pro-military and pro-Itaipu forces invoked this narrative to push back against the farmers and against the abertura more broadly.

By March tensions on the ground grew to the point that INCRA again sent Itaipu the same warning as six months earlier: change your actions or risk creating "a climate of revolt and social unrest."[108] At this moment the CPT invited a bishop named José Brandão on a speaking tour to share his recent experience with communities similarly displaced by the Sobradinho hydroelectric dam in the northeastern state of Bahia.[109] Brandão gave a speech in which he denounced the president of Brazil, criticized capitalism and the mainstream media, and urged the farmers to take a bold stand against Itaipu. As Pastor

Fuchs later recalled, "With each phrase [from Bishop Brandão], the anxieties of people fell away little by little."[110] Soon afterward, the farmers' movement began discussing potential strategies for achieving their demands, including a march on Brasília and the construction of a roadblock on the highway linking Foz do Iguaçu and Paraná's capital city of Curitiba.[111]

Although these actions never took place, the farmers made it known that their patience had run out. In late June the MJT sent a statement to Itaipu and various government ministries declaring that rural communities were prepared to enact radical and even violent strategies as "a last resort" in response to Itaipu's "refusal to solve these problems."[112] The letter noted that land values had risen to over Cr$180,000 while Itaipu kept its prices below Cr$120,000, and that 2,500 families still awaited expropriation. Considering that the Binational's deadline for paying all indemnifications loomed less than six months away (it had recently been extended to December 1981), this meant that many in the region faced the possibility of leaving their lands without receiving any financial compensation.

With the flood looming, the farmers, emboldened by the political developments taking place throughout Brazil, soon took decisive action. In the lead-up to the movement's first direct action—a land encampment in front of Itaipu's regional office—a final effort attempted to peacefully engage Itaipu and the national government. Farmers sent a petition with over 1,200 signatures to General Cavalcanti and to various federal offices. The document noted that although the movement had thus far been guided by the concern of religious leaders with "just and harmonious solutions for the rural class," an emerging sentiment of "anguish and revolt [was now] readily found among the affected populations."[113] As had occurred over the previous five years, authorities ignored the farmers' demands. This time, however, Itaipu's obstinacy sparked a new phase of rural mobilization that culminated in a pair of land encampments in 1980 and 1981. This escalation of strategy put the farmers directly in the path of Itaipu's forward progress and thrust the MJT struggle into the national spotlight.

In the years to come, the fight at Itaipu reflected Brazil's complex path away from military rule. By denouncing Itaipu's expropriation policies, the farmers helped redirect public opinion away from the triumphalist image the Brazilian government sought to project on a global scale. And in framing their demands as part of the broader struggle for democratic freedoms, the movement tapped into a surging grassroots opposition across Brazil. Yet, as we shall see, even within the rural movement only certain sectors of the countryside could access the benefits—both material and ideological—of the official democratic transition. As the MJT leaders helped turn the fight at Itaipu into a referendum on the legitimacy of dictatorship, the region's landless and indigenous communities remained marginalized and overlooked. In the years to follow, rural communities in western Paraná confronted both the structures of military rule and the inequalities long entrenched in the Brazilian countryside. As described in the following chapter, the land encampments at Itaipu amplified these rural conflicts and rural livelihoods to unprecedented levels.

CHAPTER 3

The Double Reality of Abertura

Rural Experiences of Dictatorship and Democracy

In a little-known 1983 documentary, *Os desapropriados* (The expropriated), Marcelo Barth describes the sense of despair that led him and his fellow farmers to escalate their fight against Itaipu in July 1980. The decision to set up a land encampment outside the Itaipu Binational Corporation's regional office in Santa Helena marked the official beginning of the Justice and Land Movement (MJT). In his interview with the filmmaker Frederico Füllgraf, Barth noted:

> The Justice and Land Movement was practically born out of desperation, it was a shout of anguish from people who had to leave but who received [no money] to actually do so. . . . So some of us yelled, "We are going to occupy these offices to see if they finally pay us." . . . Because we saw that it just couldn't go on any longer, it wasn't enough to complain, have a few protests, go on marches. That wasn't enough. We had to do something serious, we had to stay there with our agony on full display, because if we didn't then we would never, ever solve anything.[1]

The land encampment at Santa Helena lasted fifteen days and served as a test of both the farmers' resolve and the degree of dissent the dictatorship would allow. This initial protest brought scores of new members into the MJT and introduced their demands to a national audience. Eight months after Santa Helena, the MJT staged a second encampment directly in front of the dam's construction site in Foz do Iguaçu, at which point the escalating drama at Itaipu began to occupy headlines in Brazil's largest newspapers. The increased attention helped catapult the lives of farmers in western Paraná into national debates over land, development, and democracy. This chapter traces the evolution and internal dynamics of the MJT, using the period between the initial land encampment in 1980 and the flooding of the Itaipu reservoir in 1982 to illuminate the overlapping history of agrarian struggles and political opposition at a critical juncture in Brazil's path away from dictatorship.

Over the course of the two protest camps, the MJT forced Itaipu to substantially increase land prices, gained a national spotlight, and received solidarity from unions, politicians, and civic groups across the country. When Itaipu dispatched hundreds of heavily armed soldiers to block the farmers' encampment at Itaipu, journalists and political figures questioned the dictatorship's commitment to its own policy of abertura—the ostensible transition to democracy. With global attention cast on the dam's construction, protesters evoked the symbolism of the all-powerful Itaipu repressing the humble farmers of Paraná, an image popularized in the slogan, "Are Itaipu's guns the symbol of the abertura?"[2]

Yet the farmers' standoff was more than just a local expression of a national reawakening. It took place in a region separated both geographically and politically from major urban centers. In interviews then and now, many MJT participants used the terms *Itaipu* and *government* interchangeably, indicating that Itaipu became a stand-in for the dictatorship itself. Moreover, the region's proximity to two neighboring countries also ruled by military regimes (Argentina and Paraguay) produced a steady transborder flow of exiles and opposition forces. Numerous farmers referred to the fight against Itaipu as a sort of political classroom where rural communities learned to defend both their rights to land and their rights as citizens. So rather than serving as a passive setting on which the Brazilian state could imprint its grand development schemes, the borderlands of western Paraná incubated a distinct form of political consciousness.

The farmers' struggle is emblematic of what I conceptualize as the double reality of abertura. I argue that all Brazilians, regardless of their background, lived in a world of double abertura: the official one they understood to be dominant elsewhere and the one they experienced as their own reality. At the level of consciousness and its relationship to social movement organizing, people constantly compared their own lived version of abertura to what they thought—or were made to believe—was happening in other parts of the country. This double reality of abertura meant that although the process of democratization cast a wide rhetorical net of political rights, the tangible benefits of democracy remained limited to a small sector of society. Because Brazilians of different class, ethnic, gender, and regional statuses experienced the dictatorship in particular ways, the transition to democracy involved a diverse collection of memories and visions for the future.

Despite the appearance of a forward-moving and controlled abertura—a goal shared by military and civilian elites alike—the path to democratic rule remained highly problematic. To be sure, the limitations of abertura applied to nonelite *urban* Brazilians as well as those in the countryside; Bryan McCann's study of favela (shantytown) movements in Rio de Janeiro, for example, traces the legal, racial, and spatial inequalities confronting the urban poor in the late 1970s and early 1980s.[3] But a rural perspective like that at Itaipu brings out an even greater contrast between the normative progress of abertura and the realities that nonetheless persisted. As such, a view from the countryside offers an especially compelling point of entry for understanding the grassroots experience of democratization. Catalyzed by the presence of Itaipu and the absence of a meaningful abertura from above, members of the MJT mobilized around their own notions of political rights and justice. The gulf between the electoral and political reforms of abertura and the long-term needs of rural communities helps explain why groups at Itaipu fought for demands that went beyond the immediate challenges posed by either the dam or the official timeline of military rule.

The competing realities of abertura meant that even within a grassroots movement like the MJT, only certain livelihoods came close to attaining mainstream legitimacy. As the 1982 flood inched steadily closer, a contradiction took root between the MJT's egalitarian claims and its hierarchy that existed in practice. The internal dynamics of the farmers' movement highlights one of the core theoretical contributions of this book: the dialectic of land and legitimacy. Although rural Brazilians of various backgrounds took part in the MJT, only the whiter, title-holding men were able to translate their fight for land at Itaipu into any semblance of a long-term solution. This dynamic was also conditioned by ethnic and gender constructions, yet I argue that the experience of displacement at Itaipu was defined primarily by one's relationship to land.

Those who legally owned their soon-to-be-flooded lands were far more likely to have their demands met by the authorities—and to become seen as legitimate participants in Brazil's resurfacing culture of democracy. Those who did not hold the deed to their land, in contrast, found themselves increasingly excluded from the MJT and, by extension, from the opportunity it opened to perhaps overcome a status of invisibility in the countryside.[4] The inability of the MJT to advocate equally for all displaced communities shows that the competing realities of abertura were not simply a product of whether one belonged to the elite or not. Rather, any number of deeper-rooted issues contributed to what democratization—and its limitations—could look like. In the rural case of Itaipu, the most significant factor was one that had persisted long before the dictatorship seized power in 1964: land, and its impact on a person's perceived sense of legitimacy.

In this chapter I analyze both the progress of the MJT and the extent to which its focus on financial expropriation cast aside those with diverging relationships to land. In the Paraná borderlands, this primarily meant the marginalization of the Avá-Guarani Indians and the region's landless peasants, the histories of whom are the focus of chapters 4 and 7, respectively. For now, an overview of each group offers a starting point for understanding the complexities of the MJT. The minutes of general assemblies, interviews with surviving participants, and the dictatorship's own surveillance reports reconstruct the development of a heterogeneous and often inconsistent movement. This chapter also considers the role of the religious groups, especially how certain clergy helped stymie a growing demand of "land-for-land" that envisioned a more radical agrarian program. Although it presented itself as a harmonious counterpoint to the injustices of the military regime, the MJT also exhibited traits that perpetuated long-standing and localized forms of inequality.

This chapter concludes with an analysis of two seminal events that took place toward the end of 1982: the flooding of the Itaipu basin and Brazil's first direct elections under the dictatorship. Over the course of two weeks, beginning on October 13, a landscape of lush farmlands supporting thousands of families disappeared under twenty-nine billion cubic meters of water. The dam's reservoir became an enduring legacy of military rule, a dramatic physical marker that persisted into democratic Brazil. The permanence of the flood stood in contrast to the national elections that took place the following month. On November 15 all legally recognized parties put forth candidates for every office except the presidency. Nearly fifty million Brazilians went to the polls, and observers celebrated the election as a triumph of the abertura. The plight of the displaced farmers, however, and the stagnant return of political rights for marginalized people—both rural and urban alike—showed that the official gains of the abertura could not fully erase the ongoing realities of living in authoritarian Brazil.

The Santa Helena Encampment: "A Laboratory of Consciousness"

As shown at the end of chapter 2, farmers had discussed directly confronting Itaipu throughout 1979 and into the early months of 1980. After weighing other options, the farmers' movement planned a July 1980 protest in front of Itaipu's regional office in Santa Helena, a relatively small but centrally located town. On Friday, July 11—three days before the encampment began—local leaders cautiously distributed information among the surrounding communities. Plans for the camp reflected the heavy influence of the movement's religious leaders: no alcohol or weapons would be allowed, and in the event of outside provocation, the protest would remain nonviolent.[5] Over the weekend, news of the encampment traveled by word of mouth, as organizers hoped to avoid tipping off Itaipu and the police. Churches offered an especially efficient venue, as priests and pastors used their pulpits at Sunday mass to urge families to gather the following day in Santa Helena.[6]

Early in the morning on July 14, farmers began arriving from all over the region. People descended on Santa Helena on trucks and by foot, and brought food, equipment, household cooking and cleaning supplies, tents, and banners. Local radio stations reported the news, and word spread quickly throughout the surrounding area.[7] Within a few hours, almost two hundred people had gathered directly in front of Itaipu's offices; the number would grow to nearly a thousand by the afternoon. Late in the morning, the camp's first general assembly opened with the singing of the national anthem and a speech by Barth. Speaking from an improvised stage on an elevated truck bed, Barth declared, "The farmers are waking up and through the strength of unity assert the right to land, [and] the right to fair compensation when the government demands our land. . . . We will show that we are a respectful people, disciplined, full of love for peace and justice." Barth called for the support of unions, churches, and civil and military authorities, declaring, "Politicians! You have a choice. We want to know who is with the people and who is against the people."[8]

By calling out politicians and offering them a choice to join the movement, the MJT positioned itself within Brazil's increasingly polarized political climate. Supporting the farmers meant supporting justice and the rights of average citizens. To stand with Itaipu, in contrast, acted as an implicit endorsement of the authoritarian status quo. Following Barth's speech, farmers read an open letter denouncing the government and Itaipu for subjecting rural families to "many years of psychological pressure."[9] The letter also outlined the initial six demands of the encampment, including a 100 percent increase in compensation for land expropriations, additional price readjustments every ninety days, and distribution of new lands nearby in Paraná. Pastor Werner Fuchs, a select group of farmers, and two state deputies then went inside the Itaipu building to deliver the complete list of demands to Paulo da Cunha, the Binational's legal director.

Itaipu listened to the farmers' appeals for nearly four hours. Regarding the primary demand of a 100 percent price increase, da Cunha reportedly said that Itaipu had already allotted 6 percent of its total budget for land expropriations and that if that number increased according to the farmers' wishes, the added financial burden would slow the dam's construction.[10] Da Cunha implied that the farmers' goals, if met, could halt the progress of Itaipu and, by extension, that of Brazil as a whole. In the battle for public opinion, both sides wanted to show their devotion to the country. Against claims that it did not care about the energy needs of Brazil, the MJT invoked the same patriotic rhetoric used by Itaipu's supporters to present its own members, and not the government, as the true defenders of the country's well-being. This reveals another layer in the contested domain of what development meant at Itaipu. More than a question of which side supported or opposed the Itaipu dam, the conflict tested the legitimacy of competing visions for the progress of the nation.

As negotiations took place inside Itaipu's offices, hundreds of families continued to arrive outside. One farmer told a journalist that the gathering crowd "was ready to pour out every last drop of their blood to defend their right to land." In another interview an older man shared, "It's sad to remember how we had to fight to settle these lands. First against the *índios*, then the squatters, and then with [the government]. I saw my dad lose his life having sacrificed for our right to work these lands . . . and [now] Itaipu appears and suddenly kicks everyone out."[11] These sorts of attachment to land suggest more than just the personal history of a given farmer and his family; they hint at the deeper conflicts among the region's various rural communities. By alluding to the índios and squatters as previously vanquished foes rather than potential allies, this landed small farmer reflected the challenges inherent to finding common cause among diverse populations in the countryside.

The deliberations inside lasted through the early afternoon, at which point da Cunha declared that his office needed upward of two weeks to prepare a thorough solution. The farmers and their allies informed the crowd outside of the stalled negotiations. Upset at the suggestion of waiting two weeks for a response, the assembly voted to give Itaipu until the following afternoon to provide a clear plan for meeting their demands (figure 3.1).[12] After the vote the farmers began preparing to spend their first night in camp. According to Pastor Fuchs, only in the closing hours of that first evening did farmers begin to

FIGURE 3.1 General assembly at the Santa Helena encampment, July 1980. Photo courtesy of Guiomar Germani.

fully understand the scope of what lay ahead: "Itaipu promised us a response the next day, but we were left waiting. So we stayed there for fifteen days, and while waiting we learned how to make our encampment without having a [planned] idea of what it would look like."[13]

The next morning, Brazilians in western Paraná and throughout the country awoke to news of Santa Helena. A state paper, *O Paraná*, had a front-page headline declaring "Farmers Prepare for Battle," and major national outlets like *O Globo* and *Jornal do Brasil* also provided coverage.[14] These articles offered connections between Santa Helena and the political changes swirling throughout Brazil. A quotation from state deputy Nelton Friedrich, for example, placed the camp squarely within the national fight for democracy: "What is happening here is an example of the social injustices that are being committed throughout Brazil. The farmers want only that which is their right."[15]

While waiting for the second day's follow-up meeting with Itaipu, the camping farmers settled into what quickly became the normal routine during the fifteen days at Santa Helena. Events started at ten in the morning with a minute of silence, the singing of the national anthem, and an ecumenical service, followed by the day's first general assembly. Every afternoon the camp split into study groups, and in the early evening farmers discussed their problems during the day's second general assembly.[16] Different committees oversaw camp guidelines, finances, media outreach, food and provisions, sound equipment, and artistic activities (figures 3.2 and 3.3). Security groups not only protected against outside agitation but also monitored the actions and morale of the campers, giving particular attention to keeping alcohol from entering the protest.[17] The encampment's sound system—dubbed "Justice Radio"—played news briefings, speeches, and a variety of musical and artistic performances.[18] Roughly two thousand people took part in the protest during the daytime, with about two hundred people camping overnight.[19]

On the second day of the encampment, negotiations continued between farmers and representatives from Itaipu and the Paraná government. Claudio Pizzato, a local lawyer who acted as the MJT's legal representative, described the atmosphere of the meeting and recalled "the fear of the [farmers] in negotiating against the power and the grandeur of Itaipu Binational. . . . Imagine, four farmers in front of ten lawyers, in front of engineers, in front of government ministers; [Itaipu] negotiated from that position, and they could do whatever they wanted."[20] After nearly six hours of deliberations, da Cunha's team agreed to concede on almost all of the demands. The lone exception was the farmers' most important item: a 100 percent price increase.[21] Encouraged by the concessions yet still frustrated by the Binational's unwillingness to bend on the 100 percent increase, the protesters voted that evening to maintain the encampment until Itaipu met all of their demands.[22]

As the impasse began to solidify, each side took measures to strengthen its position. Da Cunha left Santa Helena to travel to São Paulo and Rio de Janeiro to debrief with the high administration of Itaipu.[23] The MJT, for its part, maneuvered to increase public pressure on the Binational. Some farmers discussed the possibility of staging a hunger strike—a strategy that never took place but that nonetheless attracted plenty of media attention.[24] At the same time, the encampment voted to add new items to their list of demands, most notably that Itaipu fully compensate the landless for the value of the

FIGURES 3.2 & 3.3 Farmers at the Santa Helena encampment, July 1980, with signs
that read (above) "The price of peace: Justice and land" and (below) "Itaipu: Global
attraction [but] crucifixion for Brazilians." Photos courtesy of Guiomar Germani.

lands they worked.[25] Although the defense of landless farmers dissipated over time, its inclusion here indicates that, early on at least, the encampment did endeavor to support as large a coalition as possible.

The Santa Helena protest saw a massive outpouring of solidarity from political and civic groups. By the fifth day, representatives from thirty-one labor unions had personally moved into the encampment, and the heads of seventy-one federations representing over 350,000 workers had signed a document of solidarity.[26] Over the course of the camp's fifteen days, the farmers received letters of support from over two hundred groups throughout the country and even from neighboring Paraguay.[27] These included some of Brazil's most prominent opposition groups: the Metallurgical Workers of São Bernardo (leaders of the ABC strikes), the National Union of Students, the Committee for Amnesty, the Brazilian Lawyers Association, and the archdiocese of São Paulo.[28] One such declaration from Manaus proclaimed, "From the distant Amazon, we raise our voice of protest against the crimes of a dictatorial government against a defenseless people, and we send our total support to the cause of these people who, with full lungs, call for justice."[29] Rather than naming Itaipu specifically, the letter from Manaus directed its call for justice against the national government, a refraction of the national fight for democracy present in much of the solidarity given to the farmers.

Politicians also vocalized their support. In a congressional speech, Paraná senator Leite Chaves declared that "all of the opposition groups in this country . . . must denounce the injustices being committed by Itaipu Binational." The state deputy Nelton Friedrich explicitly connected Santa Helena to the suffering of all Brazilians under dictatorship: "[The farmers] are being political, yes, in the highest sense of the word. But it is necessary to help us discuss and clarify for all involved the situation created by the Binational's authoritarian leaders and by the technocrats that aim to usurp all political legitimacy."[30] This question of political legitimacy helps explain why the farmers' movement became so significant. More than just a protest against a state-run corporation like Itaipu Binational, the MJT articulated a growing vision of land and agrarian-based democratic rights.

The year 1980 was both a turning point and a moment of uncertainty in the evolution of the abertura. As shown in chapter 2, the ABC strikes of 1978–1980 had fundamentally advanced labor militancy, but a subsequent economic crisis cut into the recently won wage gains and slowed the momentum of the radicalizing union movement.[31] And although the reform packages of 1979 had opened the door for structural changes to Brazil's political system, opposition parties and the return of political rights still faced numerous obstacles. In this moment of transition, the protest at Itaipu offered a space where rural Brazilians and their allies could learn to put dissidence into practice.

At Santa Helena the dictatorship closely monitored the farmers and the increasing presence of opposition figures. Recently declassified documents show that the National Intelligence Service (SNI, Serviço Nacional de Informações), the Ministry of War, the Federal Police, and Itaipu's own Special Committee of Security and Information (AESI) kept a close eye on the protest. These agencies reported on daily events and speeches from the encampment, compiled personnel files on the leadership, and noted the appearance of any union leader, politician, or other "radical elements."[32] It appears that the military regime did infiltrate the MJT, showing that the movement's modest security measures could not keep away the penetrating reach of the dictatorship. A telling example comes from an SNI report on a gathering at the house of Father Valentin dal Pozzo on July 22. The meeting, attended by high MJT leaders (Pastors Fuchs and Kirinus, the farmers Marcelo Barth and Ari Konrad, and state deputy Friedrich), focused on deciding which new strategy the encampment should adopt in its second week. Suggestions included a march on Foz do Iguaçu and an intimation that the movement "needs a martyr."[33] Reports like these indicate that the dictatorship considered the MJT enough of a threat to warrant its infiltration.

The expansion of political consciousness within the Santa Helena camp offers evidence of the double reality of abertura. Having experienced few of the tangible benefits of the official abertura, farmers in western Paraná linked their fight for land at Itaipu to some of the most prominent opposition campaigns of the time. Interviews suggest that the farmers viewed the Santa Helena camp as "our ABC." By regarding their fight against Itaipu as an altered or analogous version of the broader struggle to end the dictatorship, many of the farmers felt as though they were directly participating in the struggle for democratization. Barth argued that the courage displayed by the farmers came from both the despair at their own circumstances and the political changes taking root throughout Brazil: "The ABC strikes had happened just a year before, and that gave us strength to confront the military."[34] By invoking the meanings of political legitimacy and resituating them in the western Paraná borderlands, farmers at Itaipu showed that rural communities in a tucked-away corner of Brazil could make their own stand against the dictatorship.

At times, such political views caused tension within the MJT. In particular, certain religious leaders sought to keep the movement focused on the demands for land and justice. Pastor Fuchs recalled that whenever farmers mentioned "our ABC," he would correct them by saying that, unlike the militancy of the ABC labor strikes, the protest at Santa Helena was not political: "We had to teach the farmers that [the camp] was not a strike, because they weren't seizing a factory or anything. What we were doing was a movement, so we had to help them respect the Justice and Land Movement properly."[35] Fuchs's statement suggests that the political consciousness of some farmers had surpassed the goals of the MJT leadership. During the fifteen days of protest at Santa Helena and throughout the following year, the radicalizing demands of many farmers helped propel the MJT further into the struggle to shape the national abertura. These competing views also exacerbated internal tensions between different sectors of the movement.

A diverse cross-section of rural Brazil participated in the Santa Helena camp, although media portrayals and participant memories often underrepresented this fact. Albano Melz, a landowning farmer, recalled that only southerners (meaning white Brazilians) took part in the protest.[36] Adil Fochezatto, a farmer of Italian origin, made similar remarks and also noted that very few people in the protest did not have legal title to their lands—a selective omission of the camp's landless workers.[37] In contrast to these observations, a tenant farmer of mixed indigenous and Afro-Brazilian origin named Itamar da Silva remembered clearly that Santa Helena drew "people from all over Brazil."[38] Material evidence from the camp offers perspective on the diverging memories of its participants. A young graduate student named Guiomar Germani served as the camp's secretary, setting up a tent in which she registered all participants.[39] According to Germani's record keeping, the encampment included people from across Brazil and brought together day laborers, landowners, peasants, and even some indigenous families: "This showed that in the region there weren't just the descendants of Italians and Germans, but there were many [from the state of Minas Gerais] and people from the northeast, people who had previously migrated to Paraná and had worked on the larger farms, and that now had nowhere to hide from [Itaipu's] waters. People even came secretly at night from Paraguay."[40]

Photographs of the camp further reflect the racial diversity at Santa Helena (figure 3.4). This serves as a counterpoint to the media's dominant portrayal of the MJT. Under the headline of "Above All, a Love for Land," an article in the *Folha de São Paulo* described the farmers as a humble and hardworking immigrant enclave: "The majority of them descend from Europeans, and came up from Rio Grande do Sul and Santa Catarina in search of fertile lands, they still have heavy accents and a healthy appearance, they fight to maintain their lifestyle and are respectful of their heritage—characteristics that differentiate them from the other popular movements sprouting up in recent years throughout Brazil."[41] The description of this "respectful" form of protest exposes another fragility of the abertura, wherein the Santa Helena protesters and sympathetic media outlets knew that to win over public opinion the farmers could not represent a threat to the established social order. Too much unruly protest, especially if led by ethnically diverse Brazilians, could undermine the prospects of a controlled democratization. As Brazilians throughout the country debated notions of citizenship and equality, the protesters on the front lines against Itaipu Binational—and by extension the military regime—were most often presented as humble, Euro-descendant people.

The distortion of the camp's ethnic composition belongs to a longer history of how racial and regional power dynamics have developed in Brazil. In her study of race and nation in São Paulo—Paraná's neighbor to the east and, historically, its greatest influence—historian Barbara Weinstein argues that regional identities functioned as a racialized category that "could be mobilized to legitimate narratives of modernity and backwardness."[42] By privileging the perceived whiteness of Brazil's southern states, a "regional discourse formed the basis for a national project that implied a hierarchy of regions."[43] In the early twentieth-century process of nation building, this regional hierarchy entrenched a long-standing social and geographic divide through which whiteness became both a prerequisite and an implicit synonym for political legitimacy. During the abertura in the early 1980s, Brazilian elites attempted to transition to a new political system without fundamentally changing the established social order. In this context, race and regionalism mattered immensely, and although exercises of renewed democratic rights were increasingly tolerated, threats to Brazil's deeply rooted social fabric were not.

Similar patterns emerged in the representation of the camp's gender dynamics. Women actively participated in the Santa Helena protest, yet the media only gestured to them as secondary members in charge of keeping house in the camp. In large part, this reflected the limited roles that the MJT's all-male leadership gave to women. But similar to how political legitimacy was reserved for "white" Brazilians, so too did citizenship function as a mas-

FIGURE 3.4
Members of the MJT
at the Santa Helena
encampment,
July 1980. Photo
courtesy of Guiomar
Germani.

culine construct. With so much media attention focused on the fight at Itaipu, the MJT camp reinforced traditional gender dynamics.[44] Chapter 7 will go into greater detail on the marginalization of women within these rural campaigns. Women played fundamental roles in the Santa Helena camp's ability to sustain itself for over two weeks. Wives, mothers, and sisters made the daily trek from the encampment back to their homes to tend the crops, feed animals, look after the children, and maintain the farms that the protesters were fighting to preserve.[45] Media portrayals, however, almost never included women; those that did tended only to reinforce the image of women as caretakers. A *Jornal do Brasil* article described one set of women as the literal nourishers of the Santa Helena camp: "A group of mothers brought their children, and during the afternoon, began to breast-feed them in hastily made tents set up next to trucks parked along the outskirts of the camp."[46]

For an average Brazilian following the events at Santa Helena, the news depicted the protesters as ethnically white, male, and respectful farmers. This portrayal—both from the media and within the MJT itself—ignored the reality of how the encampment included both women and men, and counted people from a wide spectrum of ethnic and regional backgrounds, many of whom sought a more confrontational approach and long-lasting change.

As the encampment stretched into its final week, the standoff with Itaipu centered almost exclusively on the price of land expropriations. Itaipu maintained that it could not pay more than Cr$140,000 per alqueire—the equivalent of roughly US$2,600 at the time. The farmers, however, claimed that inflation had pushed prices as high as Cr$240,000, or about US$4,500.[47] Documentary evidence from within Itaipu complicates the Binational's public statements. In a confidential letter to General José Costa Cavalcanti, da Cunha wrote on June 20, 1980—a few weeks *before* the start of the Santa Helena camp—that Itaipu already planned on implementing a new price adjustment in the coming months.[48] Additionally, once the encampment began, Itaipu's executive office acknowledged privately that because "land prices in the region rose substantially," there was now a need to bring its offers within the range of Cr$180,000–Cr$220,000.[49] Itaipu never publicized these internal admissions, insisting instead that land prices could not increase. The MJT thus mobilized for something that Itaipu had already planned on conceding, suggesting that the authorities had nonfinancial reasons for refusing to meet the farmers' demands.

This disjuncture stemmed from the dictatorship's need to retain control—or at least the perception of control—in the process of abertura. By 1980 opposition forces had achieved certain political freedoms, but the regime was determined to maneuver the transition with as much authority as possible. As such, Itaipu became an arena of the struggle over power, political legitimacy, and the consequences of democratization. In the context of the Santa Helena camp, this meant securing the long-term viability of the Itaipu dam while also protecting the dictatorship's public image. As national media outlets chronicled the standoff at Santa Helena, the Binational and its allies in the military likely felt compelled to take an even stronger stance against the MJT. The question of land prices did not get settled until April 1981, when, at the height of the subsequent Foz do Iguaçu encampment, an independent government report stated definitively that the Binational paid far below market value.[50] Until then, the conflict remained a series of back-and-forth allegations.

Nearly two weeks into the encampment, the MJT benefited from the July 25 celebration of Brazil's annual Day of the Farmer. Delegations from all over western Brazil converged in Santa Helena, and the concentration of some eight thousand demonstrators brought widespread media attention.[51] With the nation's eyes on the encampment, pressure bore down on Itaipu. On July 26 da Cunha presented Itaipu's updated offer of a 65 percent price increase, to a median price of Cr$200,000 per alqueire—far less than the 100 percent demanded by the MJT. Farmers rejected the proposal that same night at the encampment's general assembly.[52] The members of the MJT appeared steadfast in their refusal to make concessions, but unless they backed up their speeches with new actions, a continued stalemate seemed unavoidable.

Sensing the need to intensify the pressure on Itaipu, the MJT debated proposals to meet with the president of the republic, to block the entrance to Itaipu's main construction zone, and to occupy all three of Itaipu's regional offices in Foz do Iguaçu, Santa Helena, and Marechal Cândido Rondon (figure 3.5).[53] In the end, the general assembly voted unanimously to march on Foz do Iguaçu.[54] Once the movement alerted Itaipu of its plans to march on the dam's headquarters and construction zone, General Cavalcanti finally agreed to meet with the farmers' leadership. In his analysis of the Santa Helena camp, Juvêncio Mazzarollo believed that Cavalcanti feared the possibility of thirty thousand Itaipu construction workers—many of whom objected to their own workplace conditions—mobilizing in solidarity with the MJT.[55] On the morning of the MJT's scheduled meeting with Cavalcanti, the encampment woke up to see that during the night Itaipu employees had covered the entire camp with thousands of leaflets titled "A Message from Itaipu to Farmers in the Surrounding Area." An attempt to stem the camp's rising momentum, the pamphlet urged farmers to "make a deal with Itaipu" and to "not get involved with agitation. . . . Only you know how to best defend your [family's] personal interests." In response, the farmers collected the scattered papers and set them ablaze in a ceremonial bonfire.[56] Meanwhile, representatives of the MJT met in Foz do Iguaçu with General Cavalcanti and numerous Itaipu administrators.[57]

Late in the evening of July 28, Pastor Fuchs telephoned from Foz do Iguaçu announcing that the MJT had secured numerous concessions, including an almost 85 percent price increase. At a general assembly the following morning, the farmers voted to demobilize their encampment. While framing the victories at Santa Helena as a first step in a potentially longer battle, MJT leaders distributed a document justifying the end of the encampment. These included a price increase between 80 and 85 percent, depending on the quality of land; the

FIGURE 3.5 Discussion among MJT leaders at the Santa Helena encampment, July 1980. Photo courtesy of Guiomar Germani.

guarantee that 80 percent of lands would be qualified as "first rate"; a readjustment of prices every ninety days; compensation for roads and electrical lines; payment within fifteen days of a contract's signing; the ability to plant and harvest crops until April 1982; and a weekly report from the Institute of Land and Cartography (ITC, Instituto de Terras e Cartografia) on land sales in Paraná.[58]

In a sign of the uneven representation of all the region's farmers, the MJT made an additional gentleman's agreement with Itaipu to compensate the landless farmers "at a fair price" for the properties they worked.[59] The MJT and Itaipu never formally signed this agreement, and the unrealized progress of the landless farmers remained a lingering problem. Despite falling short of winning certain demands like a 100 percent price increase and having wheat mills and gasoline stations compensated, the MJT declared its fifteen-day occupation a major success. It had forced Itaipu to make concessions to the farmers' movement while also swaying public opinion. This development proved especially important the following year when the MJT staged its second encampment at Foz do Iguaçu.

In the days to come, the MJT received hundreds of congratulatory letters and phone calls.[60] Newspapers throughout Brazil reported on the end of the encampment with headlines such as "Fearing a March [on Foz], Itaipu Backs Down" and "Farmers Decide to Accept Itaipu's Proposal."[61] Most media coverage seemed favorable to the MJT, although a number of articles outlined Itaipu's rationale for having made so many concessions. One such report cited Itaipu's claim that the price increase had nothing to do with pressure from the MJT; rather, it stemmed from a normal adjustment to account for the previous year's successful harvest.[62] When asked whether the encampment had played any role in Itaipu's price increase, General Cavalcanti said that the movement had no influence at all, adding, "We were not concerned with anything other than the values [of land markets]."[63] Within the Itaipu leadership, however, decisions had proven far more complicated. In an executive meeting right before the final agreement, General Cavalcanti had cautioned that if Itaipu did not change its expropriation policies, the agitation could soon spread across the river to Paraguay.[64] Cavalcanti's private statement and the context of what transpired at Santa Helena strongly suggest that Itaipu's concessions resulted directly from the pressure applied by the MJT.

The MJT's leadership sought to keep the farmers active in spite of the encampment's demobilization by saying that the struggle would continue until the last person received fair compensation. A description of the final day of the Santa Helena camp conveys a dual sense of exhaustion and optimism: "And so, on the afternoon of July 29, the tents were taken down. The farmers' faces were tired from days of no sleep, but they showed a happiness from a great victory won through the unity of all involved and from the solidarity they received. Everyone is hopeful that their suffering and their struggle will help other comrades, and above all, will show the authorities that they must always act justly in all that they do."[65]

How exactly should one interpret the Santa Helena encampment? It was not the first land encampment in Brazilian history, nor was it the longest or the most successful. The farmers also avoided physical repression like that experienced by other land movements under the military regime. During the same period that the MJT staged its protest camps against Itaipu, another land occupation took place at Encruzilhada Natalino, less than five hundred kilometers to the southeast of Foz do Iguaçu. Unlike the relative "civility" witnessed at Santa Helena, Encruzilhada Natalino included constant physical confrontation. Angus Lindsay Wright and Wendy Wolford describe the attacks on the camp: "jailing people, administering beatings, stabbing people with bayonets, burning down shacks and threatening people with further violence and death."[66] The comparison of these two land encampments sheds light on the specific dynamics of the Santa Helena protest, in the sense of both who the MJT targeted and what kinds of rural Brazilians led the movement.

Whereas Encruzilhada Natalino confronted private land estates, the Santa Helena camp formed in opposition to the Itaipu dam. For Brazil's dictatorship, so much of Itaipu's importance lay in its global image. The international attention that it garnered meant the military regime could not easily use violence against the farmers at Santa Helena. Hence, the government acted with a level of caution and feigned a respect that was never extended to movements taking place further from the public gaze. In this sense, the MJT greatly benefited in confronting such a significant appendage of the dictatorship. Moreover, the Encruzilhada Natalino encampment was composed exclusively of landless peasants, day laborers, and sharecroppers. Although these same demographics existed at the Santa Helena camp, the mainstream perception showed the MJT as a movement of property-owning small farmers who cared little about the type of structural agrarian reform in question at Encruzilhada Natalino.

Local communities learned a variety of lessons at the Santa Helena camp. Those who saw the need to push beyond the MJT's more "respectable" strategies became frustrated by the protest's limited victories. This dissatisfaction continued to develop, both at the second MJT encampment a year later and in the subsequent creation of an independent landless movement. But Santa Helena also marked an escalation of rural political consciousness. The pastor and state deputy Gernote Kirinus believes that only at the encampment did local communities fully lose faith in Itaipu and the government; until that time, many people were still waiting to see whether the authorities might honor their promises.[67] Before Santa Helena, the fight against a core element of the military regime remained somewhat abstract. As Silvênio Kolling noted, Santa Helena became "a laboratory of consciousness. [Before it] we didn't know the size of the monster."[68] The camp provided a fundamental experience in political participation that nourished a sense of collectivism in the region. In the words of one participant, the Santa Helena encampment served as "a big political classroom." He explained, "The fact that you brought so many people together when normally those sorts of gatherings would be repressed and their leaders thrown in jail, and to actually have a movement that resisted, well that was the practice of democracy. Not a [form of] democracy that was permitted or authorized by the government, but a democracy that was won by the force of our own movement."[69]

"The Guns of Itaipu": Repression and Politics at the Foz do Iguaçu Encampment

The relative calm after the Santa Helena camp lasted less than a month. On August 26 the leaders of the MJT again met at Itaipu's headquarters in Foz do Iguaçu to denounce Itaipu for not honoring its agreements.[70] The main objections related to delays in payment and miscalculations of land quality. The Santa Helena camp had secured Cr$200,000 per alqueire, but only for "first-rate" lands, and the farmers believed that Itaipu was purposefully unde-revaluating lands in order to keep prices down.[71] Along with the issue of land prices, another point of contention concerned resettlement within Paraná. Itaipu again deflected responsibility to the National Institute for Colonization and Agrarian Reform (INCRA) while encouraging farmers to relocate to projects in faraway states like Mato Grosso, Bahia, and Amapá.[72] The only option within Paraná, an area called Arapoti, was not yet ready to receive settlers.[73] Although farmers like Marcelo Barth stressed the need to maintain pressure and to consider taking drastic action—proposing in one speech that the MJT occupy nearby lands—the movement staged no new actions through the remainder of the year.[74]

Tensions resurfaced early in 1981. With the flood less than two years away, Itaipu had processed only 60 percent of the indemnification cases. Moreover, the price adjustments won at Santa Helena could not keep pace with Paraná's soaring real estate prices. At the end of the Santa Helena protest, Itaipu agreed to pay an average of Cr$200,000 per alqueire. Soon thereafter, however, land in western Paraná cost anywhere between Cr$500,000 and Cr$700,000.[75] These land prices resulted in large measure from overspeculation. According to an exposé in *Nosso Tempo*—the local political weekly run by the previously mentioned Juvêncio Mazzarollo—the publicity from the Santa Helena encampment enabled land speculators to increase prices the moment that Itaipu announced a new agreement.[76] This made it nearly impossible for farmers to stay in Paraná. With little regulation of the regional land market and with INCRA urging farmers to resettle in northern colonization projects, MJT farmers again found themselves in a precarious situation.

On March 16 an article published in *Time* magazine cast an unprecedented and entirely negative spotlight on the Itaipu dam. Under the title "Big Profits in Big Bribery," the article reported allegations of corruption in Latin America, Africa, and the Middle East. The report claimed that European electric companies had paid upward of US$140 million in kickbacks to win contracts with Itaipu.[77] This was not the first—or last—report of corruption at Itaipu, but given its origin in a prominent US news outlet, the claim immediately launched a scandal in Brazil.[78] *O Estado de São Paulo* translated and published the article as its front-page headline the following morning.[79] At a moment in Brazil's abertura when opposition forces were looking for any chance to chip away at the military's power, they could point to bribery as further proof the country needed a regime change.[80] For those following the farmers' struggle in western Paraná, the *Time* article symbolized a parallel injustice: one headline declared "140 Million Dollars in Bribes to Itaipu Technocrats While Eight Thousand Families Fight for Fair Compensation."[81] Whereas the MJT protests had helped sway public opinion within Brazil, the allegations of corruption in *Time* now projected a negative image at a global level. Determined to protect the legacy of the dam, Itaipu issued a press statement denouncing the allegations as completely baseless. General Cavalcanti personally wrote multiple letters to the editor of *Time* seeking to provide similar clarification—none of which were ever published.[82]

Coincidentally, on the same day as the *Time* article's publication, farmers in western Paraná organized a general assembly in the town of Itacorá. The meeting's purpose was to decide whether to march on Foz do Iguaçu to set up a second encampment inside the Itaipu construction site. Organizers told families to prepare for weeks or even months of protest and also discussed possible solidarity actions with construction workers. With over 1,500 people in attendance, the assembly voted nearly unanimously to march on Foz do Iguaçu the next morning.[83] *Nosso Tempo* reported that once Itaipu found out about the farmers' decision, it immediately sent representatives to a few farmers with improved contracts to back its claims of having paid fair prices since the Santa Helena encampment.[84] The leaders of the MJT saw this as an attempt to bribe farmers into not marching on Foz do Iguaçu. Itaipu's efforts appeared to have little effect, and the farmers prepared to march on the dam the following morning.

Although it had been discussed over the preceding years, this strategy had never crystallized into action. On the eve of the march, a sense had arisen among protesters that something profound awaited. As one observer noted: "Itaipu's behavior will inevitably change, and its image will never again be the same. Itaipu never could have imagined that it would have experienced this disgrace. Brazil and the whole world will now see [Itaipu] for what it really is."[85]

Early in the morning on March 17, nearly eight hundred people left Itacorá to make the hundred-kilometer trip to Foz do Iguaçu. After arriving on the outskirts of the city at around nine in the morning in a caravan of cars, trucks, and tractors, the group walked the remaining five kilometers on foot.[86] As they approached the entrance gates, the crowd saw their path blocked by a sizable police force. Marcelo Barth later recalled that "from a distance, we saw soldiers, with guns pointing at us, and they even had a water cannon [and tear gas]. But we showed up ready to defend what was ours."[87] Over the next hour, a tense standoff ensued between farmers wanting to march onto the construction site and security forces determined to repel the crowd.

With the late-morning sun bearing down—temperatures that day surpassed a hundred degrees Fahrenheit—the crowd approached the gates chanting "Justice, justice, justice." Speaking through a megaphone, General Junot Rebello Guimarães demanded the farmers leave the premises and relocate to a nearby church.[88] Behind Rebello Guimarães stood dozens of state troopers and nearly a hundred agents of Itaipu's private security force. Less than ten meters from the entrance gates and roughly five hundred meters from the Binational's central offices, the farmers demanded safe passage and a meeting with Itaipu's executive committee. Rebello Guimarães replied that any attempt to pass the gates would be met with physical force. This was not an idle threat as, according to one news article, the state secretary of public safety had authorized the soldiers to physically suppress the farmers if necessary.[89] Tensions continued to mount, and as recounted by a *Nosso Tempo* journalist, a farmer at the front of the crowd unbuttoned his shirt, bared his chest to the soldiers, and dared them to shoot.[90]

Shocked at the display of repressive force before them, the protesters shouted statements like "How can you have armed police like this? It's a shame for Itaipu and for the whole country" and "We are the ones that feed these people, and this is how we are received, with bayonets and machine guns?"[91]

After nearly thirty minutes of back-and-forth exchanges, the MJT leadership decided to forgo its plan to march on the construction site and instead set up an encampment along the adjacent fork in the road. This location became known as the Field of Shame (Trevo da Vergonha), an area in front of the entrance gates that placed the protest in full view of anyone visiting the hydroelectric project. Situated along Highway BR-277 (the regional access point to the Pan-American Highway), the encampment was also visible to drivers going to Paraguay, tourist buses, and commercial vehicles.

Similar to the media coverage at the start of the Santa Helena camp, newspapers quickly announced the events unfolding in Foz do Iguaçu. In this instance, however, the press focused largely on the specter of violence. One headline (figure 3.6) wrote in capital letters "ITAIPU RESISTS WITH GUNS," while another reproduced an increasingly popular phrase among the farmers and their allies: "Are the guns of Itaipu the symbol of the abertura?"[92]

While setting up the Foz do Iguaçu encampment, farmers distributed leaflets with the demands made at the Itacorá meeting. The document included calls for land prices between Cr$500,000 and Cr$600,000 (roughly US$7,500) per alqueire and for INCRA to be more efficiently involved. And similar to the wide scope projected at the outset of the Santa Helena camp, the leaflets also declared support for the various communities facing displacement. The MJT demanded an immediate solution to the plight of the landless communities and made gestures of solidarity to both the nearby indigenous community and the families impacted by Itaipu on the Paraguayan side of the river.[93] At the start of such an important protest, this document reflected the MJT's need to appeal to a broad support base. As was the case at Santa Helena, the concern for nonlanded farmers faded away over the course of the protest.

In the ongoing battle for public opinion, Itaipu evidently felt that its show of force had allowed the farmers to win too much sympathy. When the protesters awoke on the second day, they noticed that the police patrolling the entrance gates no longer had guns or bayonets.[94] Despite this veneer of decreased security, the farmers employed the same measures developed at Santa Helena. The camp again held daily meetings to identify potential undercover agents, and it even created a chain of command in case the dictatorship disappeared any MJT leaders.[95] The farmers also developed a network of committees to organize all aspects of camp life. In light of the extreme heat, the delivery of fresh water became an especially important task. Early in the encampment, Foz do Iguaçu's mayor, Colonel Clóvis Cunha Vianna, ordered soldiers to cut off the farmers' water supply. Aluízio Palmar remembered the politicizing effect of these actions: "When the camp's water was shut off, the farmers knew that it was the dictatorship that was cutting them off."[96] Other responsibilities included food preparation, sanitation, and the shuttling of families back and forth from their farms. Yet even these collaborative actions revealed some of the fissures within

FIGURE 3.6 *Nosso Tempo* headline: "Itaipu Resists with Guns," March 18, 1981.

the MJT. Pastor Fuchs remembered how the food brought to the Foz do Iguaçu camp laid stark the differences between the landed farmers and the peasants: "When people brought food from home to share, the property-owners brought a lot of meat—beef, pork, and chicken—but the squatters and the sharecroppers brought almost nothing but manioc."[97] So despite the overall solidarity displayed at Foz do Iguaçu, the fault lines of the movement were visible on a daily basis.

Media coverage—either unaware of or unconcerned with the MJT's internal tensions—offered admiring accounts of the camp's organization and cohesion. Headlines called readers' attention to how the farmers had created "a mini-city" and "an evolved society."[98] In a striking example, the largest newspaper in the state, *O Estado do Paraná*, mimicked Itaipu's triumphalist slogan—the Project of the Century—to call the Foz do Iguaçu protest "the encampment of the century."[99]

After four days, General Cavalcanti invited five representatives from the MJT to a meeting in the Binational's central office. Cavalcanti presented Itaipu's offer of an 80 percent price increase, which would bring the average compensation package to around Cr$380,000—roughly Cr$200,000 less than the farmers demanded.[100] Speaking to reporters afterward, Cavalcanti declared that Itaipu would not raise its current offer and that the Binational had "no desire to negotiate with the farmers; we simply wanted to present our position."[101] A general assembly that evening rejected Itaipu's proposal. After the vote, the MJT issued a press release chastising Itaipu for refusing to hold open and honest dialogue and called on "the authorities and the Brazilian nation as a whole for support in the defense of our rights."[102]

That same afternoon, two other events underscored the encampment's expanding influence. First, Leonel Brizola, the former governor of Rio Grande do Sul and head of the Brazilian Workers' Party (PTB, Partido Trabalhista do Brasil), visited the camp. One of the most visible and outspoken critics of the dictatorship, Brizola had recently returned from exile. In a speech to the encampment, Brizola promised to intercede on behalf of the farmers by discussing their situation the following week with the minister of justice.[103] The second event took place in Brasília, where leaders of the Indigenous Missionary Council held a press conference "accusing the federal government of committing a crime against the Guarani" families facing displacement at Itaipu.[104] Despite the indigenous invisibility perpetuated by both the military regime and social movements like the MJT, the press conference showed how pro-indigenous groups capitalized on the momentum generated by the Foz do Iguaçu camp to also call attention to their own parallel demands.

During the opening weeks of the camp, more than a dozen politicians, primarily from the opposition Brazilian Democratic Movement Party (PMDB, Partido do Movimento Democrático Brasileiro), gave solidarity speeches in Congress and the Senate. A particularly revealing speech came two days after the initial standoff at the entrance gates, when Paulo Marques (PMDB-Paraná) addressed the Chamber of Deputies in Brasília and vilified Itaipu for sending machine guns and crowd-dispersing water tanks to confront farmers whose calloused hands produced the nation's food supplies. Marques noted that perhaps this violent show of force was the actual symbol of the abertura and declared that it only served as further "proof of the government's false intentions" in the alleged opening of democracy.[105] The outpouring of criticism sparked counterresponses from supporters of the military regime. For example, deputy Jorge Arbage (from Pará, a member of the Democratic Social Party, or Partido Democrático Social) proclaimed that, contrary to media reports, the government had done nothing to "usurp the rights of small farmers"; in his speech Arbage also dismissed recent criticism from the PMDB as mere opportunism in light of the corruption allegations published in *Time*.[106] Whether for antidictatorship forces seeking to call attention to an example of injustice or for supporters of the military determined to slow down the process of abertura, the events at Foz do Iguaçu became a topic of national debate.

At the state level, Paraná governor Ney Braga announced that his office would officially act as a mediator between the MJT and Itaipu. Citing the need to keep as many farmers as possible within the state, Braga declared that he would speak directly with General Cavalcanti, a close friend from their days in the military. More important, Braga also announced he would commission the ITC to conduct an independent report on land prices in western Paraná.[107] Although Braga did not formally take the side of the farmers, his intervention signaled a significant change. Braga was a decorated major in the armed forces, he had been a prominent member of the pro-regime Alliance for National Renovation (ARENA) Party, and he had been appointed—via indirect election—as Paraná's governor in 1978. It is difficult to imagine Braga showing any degree of support for a grassroots struggle earlier in the period of military rule. But by 1981 Brazil's political landscape had shifted enough that he could, even if minimally, intervene on behalf of the farmers' movement.

Similar to the gestures of solidarity at Santa Helena, the Foz do Iguaçu camp received a steady influx of visitors, letters, and calls for action from groups across Brazil. Various religious groups, rural and urban unions, student organizations, and civic and trade associations all sent their support. Almost all of the letters referenced the standoff at the entrance gates as an example of the government's violent disregard for the rights of average citizens. In a published statement, the archbishop of Curitiba reflected on how people throughout Brazil supported the MJT: "The Justice and Land Movement is a legitimate and peaceful response to the problems caused by [this regime]. But as shown in the declarations of solidarity from all over the country, this regional mobilization is helping the Brazilian people raise consciousness and organize themselves to fight back against the evils of our current system."[108]

The Double Reality of Politics in a Borderland

The MJT illustrated how popular struggles could tap into a national wave of political dissent to put forth local visions for democratization. Because of its location in a borderland, the movement offers a new and important case study for understanding the development of political consciousness across Brazil. Distant geographically, politically, and socially, regions like western Paraná developed in ways that often diverged from major urban areas. More than just an example of political resistance in the countryside, the MJT calls attention to the particular dynamics of the region from which it emerged.

Located far from Brazil's established political centers, the Paraná borderlands also shared a frontier with two other countries ruled by military regimes. Many exiles returned to Brazil through this border region, and the immediate proximity to Paraguay and Argentina enabled the formation of international solidarity organizations. In August 1979 Paraná played host to the first-ever meeting of Latin American Opposition, a gathering of dissident political leaders from Brazil, Paraguay, Argentina, Peru, Chile, and Mexico. The meeting took place in the state capitol of Curitiba, organized in part by Gernote Kirinus—a leading ally in the farmers' fight at Itaipu. Key speeches were delivered by Paraguay's Domingo Laino (the main critic of the Stroessner regime) and two eventual presidents of Brazil (Fernando Henrique Cardoso and Luiz Inácio "Lula" da Silva); a statement was also read on behalf of Hugo Blanco, a leader of the Peruvian peasant movement. According to one report, the meeting sought to put forward a collective approach to "the question of democracy, which is today the central political problem of the continent as it is being suffocated by military dictatorships."[109] Such an event likely could not have taken place at this time in cities like São Paulo or Rio de Janeiro. It is doubtful whether so many of Latin America's top opposition figures would have been able—or even willing—to assemble so close to the heart of a military regime.

The political momentum generated in the region by this initial meeting continued in subsequent years.[110] A telling example comes from the Foz do Iguaçu congress refounding the PTB, headed by Leonel Brizola. Along with denouncing the military regime, the PTB rooted its appeals in the region's political and social landscapes. In his closing speech, Brizola referred to the lack of local elections in Foz do Iguaçu as emblematic of the political injustices suffered throughout the country. And when he spoke about the future of a democratic Brazil, he celebrated the local farming communities and emphasized that "only agriculture can save our country."[111] Western Paraná was both a place where rural people earned their livelihoods and a porous borderland where politics easily became internationalized. And although the dictatorship saw the region as a source of untapped natural and geopolitical power, it also became a space where opposition movements saw an opportunity to build democracy.

Paraná's rural communities connected their fight against Itaipu to the advances of the abertura that they understood to be taking place elsewhere. Brazilian elites at the time—and many scholars since—often described Brazil's return to democracy as an urban process pushed forward by mainstream politicians and established social movements.[112] Yet the characteristics of this borderland helped incubate an antidictatorship movement rooted in localized struggles for land. In seeking to understand Brazil's era of military rule, scholars must begin to widen their lens, not only to groups like the MJT but also to the various regions that conditioned the emergence of new political actors.

Politicians, for their part, looked to the farmers' standoff at Itaipu as both a new example of political participation and a mass cluster of potential votes. Although the national security zone of Foz do Iguaçu precluded local elections for mayor, by 1980 elections had returned for regional positions in city councils and the state assembly. For opposition parties, grassroots movements like the MJT could translate into a local electorate to help rebuild a national presence. This was especially the case with the PMDB. Barely two weeks after the Santa Helena encampment, the party distributed leaflets outlining the efforts of various senators and deputies who had given speeches, marched in the streets, and defended the rights of farmers. The document stated that the PMDB "has always fought against the exploitation and injustice of Itaipu. [The party] was there from the very beginning."[113] Itaipu's supporters claimed that the PMDB selfishly used the struggle in western Paraná to further its own political agendas. A confidential SNI report observed that opposition politicians became increasingly active in the farmers' movement only "to elevate their names in the media and to secure political debts for eventual electoral campaigns."[114] Similarly, the executive committee of Itaipu Binational referred to PMDB politicians as "professional agitators."[115]

While Itaipu administrators and their allies in the dictatorship likely used these labels as a means to undermine the legitimacy of the MJT, it is significant that people on the ground also noticed the opportunism of certain supporters. One farmer recalled that "politicians had their interests, they wanted our votes, so that's why they fought with us."[116] The returned political exile Aluízio Palmar and a clergyman, Father Edgard Raviche, similarly expressed that many politicians got involved with the MJT in order to earn credibility and votes.[117] These political undertones also extended into the realm of national politics as both Itaipu's director, General Cavalcanti, and Paraná's governor, Ney Braga, were considered potential presidential candidates. With their sights set on the presidency, each man had to approach the standoff at Itaipu cautiously. They had to avoid alienating potential future voters while also not upsetting the established political elite. As observed in the *Folha de São Paulo*, "it will not be because of two thousand farmers suffering through the drama of expropriation that Cavalcanti and Braga fall out of favor [for the presidency]."[118] Under the spotlight cast by events at Itaipu, political stakeholders at the local and national level approached the farmers' conflict with an eye toward advancing their own goals.

At the end of March, employees from the ITC conducted the survey previously requested by Governor Braga. The start of this project amplified the demands of farmers who wanted to be given access to new lands rather than receive money from Itaipu. Because the Brazilian Constitution required all expropriations to be done monetarily, the notion of land-for-land knowingly advocated a far more structural change that would require the revision of federal expropriation policy. Not only would the Constitution no longer serve as the primary legislative conduit, but the government would also have to appropriate underused landholdings to redistribute among the lower classes. This represented a direct challenge to notions of private property and Brazil's existing system of land tenure. As such, the members of the MJT who demanded land-for-land positioned themselves beyond the movement's main goal of increased financial compensation. Documentary evidence does not offer a de-

TABLE 3.1 Estimates of land values given by Itaipu, the ITC, and the MJT

LAND CLASSIFICATION	PRICE (in cruzeiros)		
	Itaipu, March 1981	ITC suggestion	Demands of MJT
First rate	360,000	491,183	600,000
Second rate	315,000	427,542	n/a
Third rate	252,000	273,897	n/a
Fourth rate	109,000	112,901	500,000

Source: Arquivo Nacional, Rio de Janeiro, AESI Report E/AESI.G/IB/BR/021/81, April 10, 1981, in SNI ACE.892/81.

finitive view on who within the MJT supported land-for-land, yet interviews and context point strongly to the region's landless families. Without legal deed to property and its attendant status of social legitimacy, these groups fought against Itaipu while also advocating a new platform of agrarian reform.

At this point in the Foz do Iguaçu encampment, INCRA had obtained lands for resettlement projects at Arapoti within Paraná, and also at Bom Jesus da Lapa in the northeastern state of Bahia. The *Folha de São Paulo* reported that when the ITC team began its work, the MJT declared that farmers would not accept lands of inferior quality and rejected the notion of being transferred to either Arapoti or Bom Jesus da Lapa.[119] A participant in the movement, Lauro Rocini, remembered that the MJT voted down the idea of land-for-land precisely because of the notion of land "inferiority."[120] As will be detailed in chapter 6, the areas deemed inferior by the MJT (Arapoti and Bom Jesus da Lapa) were the exact locations where many of the landless farmers would be resettled in the aftermath of the Foz do Iguaçu encampment.

Given the pressing time frame of the fight at Itaipu—most interviewees recalled the anxiety of the flood always looming on the horizon—it should not be surprising that the landed farmers in the MJT leadership bypassed land-for-land and opted instead to focus on financial compensation. As code for agrarian reform, land-for-land carried high political risk, and as a result, it never gained enough support to become a core MJT demand. Nearly three decades after the fight at Itaipu, Marcelo Barth described this moment with a sense of regret: "We lacked strength and courage. . . . We were tired from all the lies, all the deceit, all the things Itaipu refused us. It still makes me so sad that we couldn't keep fighting for land-for-land."[121] The failure to adopt land-for-land as a long-term strategy reflected more than just the financial priorities of the MJT; it was also a by-product of the movement's religious influence. Aiming for more structural change implied a radical approach that clashed with the leadership's insistence on incremental and peaceful goals. Pastor Gernote Kirinus remembers the landless peasants at Itaipu as the most forward-thinking but notes that the movement "abandoned" them once the landed farmers and religious leaders decided to focus only on winning a "fair price." Early in the farmers' movement, Kirinus had been encouraged by the support given to the landless. Looking back, he now thinks that the shift from land-for-land to a fair price constituted "the great sin" of the church's role at Itaipu.[122]

The ITC Report and the De-escalation of the MJT

The ITC released its report nearly a month into the Foz do Iguaçu encampment. Its findings (table 3.1) showed that Itaipu paid roughly 30 percent below the market value of land. Not only did this provide the MJT with proof of Itaipu's low payments, but the sense of victory that it gave to the landowning farmers fundamentally shifted the direction of the movement. Prior to the ITC report, the encampment saw increasing calls for more radical approaches, including land-for-land. But the news that Itaipu might have to pay higher prices pushed the MJT to press even more for financial compensation. As a consequence, the momentum for landless demands soon faded.

The ITC report included 132 surveys of land plots, 268 interviews, and 143 smaller compilations of market data. It identified Itaipu's expropriation policies as the primary cause of rising land prices but also noted the effect of a robust agricultural harvest and the devaluation of Brazil's currency. The ITC recommended that Paraná's government acquire large plots of land "that can serve not only for the resettlement of the displaced, but also as a means to regularize the regional real estate market."[123] The Foz do Iguaçu encampment celebrated the ITC findings, yet Itaipu offered no indication it would make any of the suggested changes. Director Cavalcanti addressed the report in a press conference: "The State Government has no influence in relation to Itaipu. Governor Ney Braga, a friend of mine for over forty years, warned me that he had requested [the ITC] study so that he personally could have an idea about this problem. . . . Without a doubt, ITC's charts can serve more as a parameter for adjusting future prices. . . . We will not, in the meantime, meet with any farmers."[124]

Only a few weeks earlier, the MJT had conducted a tent-by-tent survey of the camp, asking what the movement should do if Itaipu and the government continued to ignore the farmers' demands. Responses included suggestions to block all entrances to the dam with tractors, to have women and children lead an invasion of Itaipu's headquarters, to send a delegation to meet with Paraguay's dictator Alfredo Stroessner, and even to halt the construction work altogether.[125] Itaipu's security forces closely monitored this radicalizing groundswell. One report noted that "so far the Justice and Land Movement has, despite its opposition to the government, presented a peaceful character, but has recently changed its behavior [and now presents] possibilities of aggressive behavior if its demands are not met." In particular, security forces worried about backlash against the ITC report.[126] Contrary to Itaipu's anxieties, the ITC report had the opposite effect: in the aftermath of its release, the growing momentum in the camp actually *diminished*, and the mood within the MJT shifted accordingly.

From the earliest days of the struggle against Itaipu, farmers had sought the type of state support and validation evident in the ITC data. For the first time, the movement could now base its demands on findings from a government agency. Supporters celebrated this as a victory for both the MJT and the emerging power of grassroots struggles in the twilight of Brazil's dictatorship. Paradoxically, it also marked the beginning of the encampment's end. In the most immediate sense, the ITC report was just that, a report. It gave little in the way of policy recommendations and offered no strategies for improving government oversight of land expropriations. It simply stated that Itaipu paid below market value. Even if fully implemented, then, the ITC report could only mediate the present situation and offered few measures to prevent future conflicts. For the landowning farmers who comprised the movement's leadership, the ITC data confirmed that Itaipu should substantially raise its compensation. Sensing that they would finally receive more money, the MJT leadership turned its attention to getting Itaipu to the bargaining table.

After nearly six weeks of silence, Itaipu offered the first indication that it would negotiate with the MJT. On April 28—forty-three days into the encampment—Paulo da Cunha invited five farmers, their lawyer, and the president of the Justice and Peace Commission to meet in Curitiba (figure 3.7). Although they failed to reach an agreement, da Cunha did present Itaipu's offer of a 30 percent price increase and committed to meet again on May 8.[127]

At this juncture it is necessary to examine the movement's de-escalation and to ask why *this* was the moment when more radical action was voted down. The successes of both encampments had largely resulted from farmers embracing direct action. In Santa Helena the threat of a march on Foz do Iguaçu had compelled Itaipu to meet with the farmers for the first time, and the second encampment happened only when the farmers actually followed through on that initial threat. So why, as the encampment approached its third month, and when farmers were finally negotiating directly with Itaipu, did the proposal to escalate the struggle gain so little traction? The findings of the ITC report suggested that Itaipu would soon increase its compensation, and the landed farmers did not want to risk losing this opportunity. Over the previous years, MJT leaders had maintained a noticeable, albeit uneven, level of support for the landless peasants in their ranks, including occasional demands that workers receive compensation even if they had no legal deed. Yet these gestures of inclusion often came at the start of campaigns when the movement sought to expand its base and increase public pressure on Itaipu.

With a small window for winning their financial demands and with the threat of the flood hanging over them, the landed farmers pushed for an agreement. Left out, however, were those who stood to gain nothing from a victory based on the premise of established legal property. By opting to negotiate based on the terms set by the ITC, the MJT leadership foreclosed the possibility of defending the landless farmers.

Although the MJT leadership moved toward a more moderate approach, calls for direct action continued. At the camp's ensuing general assembly, a group of farmers presented a motion to preempt Itaipu's follow-up meeting on May 8 by invading the construction site on May 1.[128] The persistence of this more radical approach shows that many in the camp still hoped to force Itaipu's hand. According to the *Jornal do Brasil*, the MJT leadership struggled at this time to maintain a sense of calm among the frustrated farmers.[129] That same week, *Nosso Tempo*'s Juvêncio Mazzarollo wrote an article declaring that "Itaipu and the Government must know that whatever act of violence on behalf of the farmers . . . will be perfectly deserved and completely justified."[130] Despite this lingering undercurrent, the proposal to invade Itaipu's headquarters never gained a majority in the general assembly, and the energy behind it receded in the following days.

FIGURE 3.7 Negotiations between Itaipu (far side of table) and farmers. Reproduced from *Cadernos de Justiça e Paz*, no. 5, February 1983, 65, courtesy of the Biblioteca Pública do Paraná.

Almost two months after the encampment began, it appeared as though the MJT's strategy of peaceful protests and attempts at negotiation had reached its limits. This sense of anxiety was compounded by the fact that over 30 percent of the region's expropriations still remained unfulfilled.[131] In a climate of uncertainty, the stakes were very high for the May 8 meeting. The MJT leaders hoped to meet personally with da Cunha, but Itaipu's legal department instead presented them with a prepared statement outlining a set of conditions almost identical to those given ten days earlier in Curitiba.[132] As it had done previously, Itaipu again offered a 30 percent increase for first-rate lands. The MJT representatives returned to the encampment to decide their next move. The leaders stressed that while the movement could not claim to have completely forced Itaipu's hand, over the course of the fifty-four-day encampment it had won nearly 80 percent of its demands, and the farmers' situation "was significantly better than it had been at the start of the encampment."[133]

The following morning the farmers held a seven-hour general assembly on whether or not to accept Itaipu's proposal. In the end, twenty-four groups (each representing a different region or community) voted to approve the offer and end the encampment. Only three groups voted to maintain the protest.[134] Although available evidence does not clarify the composition of the three dissenting groups, context suggests that they were landless. With this decision, the farmers agreed to demobilize the camp the next day. Before ending the assembly, the MJT crafted a final document that chronicled the history of the two-month encampment and included a list of twelve victories. These included Itaipu's two price adjustments (yielding a net increase of 62 percent) and the promise that land indemnifications would proceed immediately, with priority being given to those who had participated in the encampment. The document ended with a declaration: "This was one step. We will always be ready to repeat our protests, whether against Itaipu or the government. . . . The Justice and Land Movement continues. It will only end when the last farmer is indemnified. Farmers united will never be defeated. The Price of Peace: Justice and Land."[135]

Press coverage proved very favorable to the farmers. Revealing the extent to which public opinion had sided with the MJT, newspapers reported on the final agreement with headlines such as "Making the Leviathan Fold" and "At Itaipu, Unity Was Strength."[136] Organizations that had lent support throughout the farmers' struggle also celebrated the MJT's victories. The Paraná Federation of Agricultural Workers (FETAEP, Federação dos Trabalhadores na Agricultura do Estado Paraná) issued a statement declaring, "This mobilization of united and organized workers, together with unions and other opposition groups, offered concrete proof . . . that only the mobilization of all [Brazilians] can secure social justice."[137] Despite this public praise, the farmers' movement had a far more complicated impact among those involved in the protest. In the aftermath of the final general assembly, *Nosso Tempo* collected declarations that reflected a wide range of perceptions on the encampment's outcome.

—Claudio Pizzato, the MJT's lawyer: "It was a partial success. We won 70 to 80 percent of what we sought when we decided to camp. The people showed that they know how to fight for their rights. [Do the victories justify the demobilization?] Yes, because we exhausted all the peaceful means.

To go beyond what we won, perhaps we would need to veer into violence, which is not the position that we take.

—Fidelcino Tolentino, state deputy from Cascavel, PMDB: "It showed that Itaipu responded to its problems with military and paramilitary actions. . . . For them, everything is war, where the dangerous element is a mobilized people."

—Werner Fuchs, pastor and CPT leader: "In the circumstances in which we fight, victories are very telling. Itaipu was [backed by] the Government, while the workers did not receive such protection. The movement served as a school for other movements that will follow."

—Osvino Murfp, farmer and member of the camp's negotiation team: "It was not time to return home, no. We needed to endure for another six months. A majority decided to leave and I will not stay here alone. But I do not feel very good leaving right now."[138]

These opinions expose the multilayered and often contradictory realities of what transpired in the MJT. As evidenced in the first three quotations, the movement won a substantial portion of its official demands and forced a powerful state enterprise to yield, at least partially, to the pressures of popular struggle. The MJT attracted the support of opposition leaders and showcased local forms of resistance that expanded on broader ideas of democratization. The MJT also confronted Brazil's armed forces and emerged relatively unscathed from a two-month standoff. In the early 1980s, proponents of the official abertura anticipated the successful conclusion of Brazil's controlled political transition. For nonelite Brazilians like those in western Paraná, however, the exact form that the abertura would take remained unclear. In their confrontation with an important branch of the dictatorship, the MJT farmers put forth an alternative vision of democratic rights. As seen in the celebratory comments above, these grassroots struggles for democracy were beginning to bear fruit.

Despite these broader implications, the comment by a disenchanted farmer that "I do not feel very good leaving right now" elicits a deeper reflection on the MJT. When the movement voted to accept Itaipu's proposal and lift the encampment, many farmers and peasants were left wanting. For the landless who did not hold any legal claim to property, Itaipu's concession of increased compensation offered no tangible victory. While the landed farmers could celebrate their win and begin looking for new land to buy, their landless neighbors—aside from the politicizing experience of mass protest—had gained almost nothing.

The divisions between the landed and landless farmers highlight the internal tensions inherent to social movements, and illuminate how popular struggles can reproduce some of the hierarchies they claim to challenge. Like all popular struggles, the MJT was a diverse coalition organized around the perception of common goals and a common enemy. When the demands of only certain members were met, the bonds that held the coalition together began to dissolve. In the end, the landed farmers and their allies controlled most of the campaign and succeeded in framing their demands within the existing system of land tenure and property rights. This strategy precluded any serious gains for the landless farmers within their ranks. This does not suggest that the leadership betrayed the movement or that Itaipu or the government manipulated MJT leaders. Quite to the contrary, as the desire for more profound change had never been embraced as a central demand. The landed farmers who held the most influence sought increased compensation for their flooded properties and, to their credit, achieved many of their goals.

That so many landless farmers even took part in a movement that rarely advocated on their behalf calls attention to the complexities of rural mobilization in Brazil. For landless workers in Paraná during the early 1980s, the MJT represented the best chance at that particular moment to overcome a particular set of inequalities. The property-owning farmers never prioritized the needs of the landless because they never intended to fundamentally alter land relations in Brazil. For landless farmers unable to sway the direction of the movement, their experience in the MJT must have been vexing. As we shall see, many of the landless who stayed in the region soon gathered the lessons of this frustration and formed an independent movement based solely on their own demands.

From the perspective of how the MJT progressed over time and which strategies it did or did not implement, the fight at Itaipu also reflects how social movements are constantly shifting alliances that can alienate their own members. After persevering under two decades of dictatorship—and having confronted other forms of repression prior to military rule—many in the MJT hoped to use more radical tactics to fight for a different political and social reality. As opposition forces throughout the country mobilized around ideas of democratization, the contours of political participation and popular protest began to shift drastically.

One of the best examples of these changes comes from an article written by the journalist Juvêncio Mazzarollo in the aftermath of the Foz do Iguaçu encampment. The essay—which, as we shall see later on, helped land him in prison—reflects on the contours of "acceptable" protest and foreshadows the more radical movement of landless workers:

> In the name of peace, many advances were lost through the simple confusion between radicalization and violence. In the first place, it must be known that a movement like [the MJT] had very little pacifism. It was a true act of war, short of actually arming itself. Peace and nonviolence do not end only in the moment when a punch is thrown or when blood begins to flow. . . . A demonstration, an encampment, the energetic protests, these are all violent manifestations and nothing pacifist. So why were only more radical attitudes put in the category of violence?[139]

Whose Abertura? The Itaipu Flood and the 1982 Elections

Only a week after the Foz do Iguaçu encampment ended, INCRA loaded the first group of farmers from western Paraná on buses and sent them on a weeklong journey to resettlement projects in Bahia. *O Estado do São Paulo* reported that all of the sixty-nine families were sharecroppers, and the majority originated from the northeast.[140] This meant that the landless, darker-skinned farmers were the first to be sent far away from their soon-to-be-flooded homes. Over the following months, INCRA relocated hundreds of families throughout Brazil.

The farmers who remained in the region confronted the reality that despite the claimed victories at the protest camp, very little had changed. Many of the same issues that had persisted for years resurfaced again, including late payments and a refusal to compensate for electrical lines and other investments as promised.[141] By the end of August, over a thousand families (out of an original total of six thousand) still awaited payment. In protest, a few hundred farmers held a rally on the site of the original encampment in Santa Helena.[142]

As had happened twice before, Itaipu pushed back the deadline for completing all expropriations, this time for an additional five months. In doing so, Itaipu allowed itself to process any remaining contracts as late as a few weeks before the flood. One of the farmers' most consistent allies, FETAEP, conducted in late June a survey of the families awaiting expropriation. The results indicate the type of farmer at the very bottom of Itaipu's priority list. According to FETAEP's survey, the average person still in the flood zone was forty years old, had lived in the region for less than five years, and lived on only five alqueires of land. Moreover, nearly 30 percent of those surveyed had originally come from central and northern Brazil.[143] These data paint a clear picture of the region's landless farmers. A letter from three sharecropper peasants to the state secretary of public safety reflects the precarity of their situation. The three men wrote, "After innumerous broken promises, we are now threatened, to the point of potential death, if we do not leave our homes before the set deadline. If we haven't left our homes yet, it is simply because we have nowhere to go." The letter ended by imploring the secretary to take action: "We trust that [you] will help us and that you will not allow more blood to be spilled. [Please do not let] violence occur yet again in this twisted world."[144]

To speed along the final expropriation cases with as little resistance as possible, Itaipu oversaw another round of public relations campaigning. The headline for a *Gazeta do Povo* article in mid-August declared "Expropriation at Itaipu Is Complete," despite the fact that as late as October the cases of over a hundred families remained pending.[145] Itaipu also aimed to strengthen its global image, as seen in an October article in the *New York Times*. Under the title "Brazil Creates a Lake, with Care for Man and Beast," the report celebrated the respectful treatment of local landscapes, writing, for example, that "Itaipu planners have evacuated 42,000 people, [and even] relocated cemeteries coffin by coffin."[146] At an internal level, Itaipu also employed several strategies to clear the region of any remaining farmers. When the Binational deployed extra security forces, it purposefully sent men with "family in those cities, and a personal stake" in avoiding conflict.[147] And in the final weeks before the flood, Itaipu allegedly resorted to using direct force. A confidential SNI report described the case of an elderly peasant who claimed that an Itaipu employee and a member of the state police had destroyed his house and his barn and torn open two hundred sacks of flour—all in an effort to have him abandon his land.[148]

As the final communities scrambled to figure out where they would go after the flood, the Sete Quedas waterfalls (detailed in chapter 1) received a great deal of attention (figure 3.8). Hoping to catch one last glimpse of the falls, forty thousand people visited Sete Quedas on its final day open to the public.[149] A grassroots environmental movement called "Adeus Sete Quedas" brought together artists, ecologists, and activists to highlight how Itaipu's flood would destroy the habitats of thousands of different species of mammals, birds, insects, and fish, while also submerging over two hundred archaeological sites dating back eight thousand years.[150] Carlos Drummond de Andrade, one of Brazil's most celebrated poets of the twentieth century, wrote an elegy to the falls, the ending of which observed:

Sete Quedas left us
and we didn't know, ah, we didn't know how to love it,
and all seven died,
and all seven lifted into the air,
seven ghosts, seven crimes
of the living who fight for a life
that will never be reborn.[151]

In the final weeks before the flood, the remaining families finally received their expropriation money and left the area. What had recently been a lively agricultural hub was now desolate; abandoned gas stations, cemeteries, churches, and half-demolished buildings dotted the landscape. One journalist wrote that the region felt as though "it suffered an aerial bombing and all the people living in the small cities below were forced to evacuate in haste."[152] *O Estado de São Paulo* ran a five-page spread titled "The Last and Sad Days of Itaipu," which described the bleak region and the sorrows of those forced to leave. Among the many inhabitants quoted in the article was Alvin Wuzke, who had lived in the town of Porto Mendes for almost two decades: "Itaipu always said that it wouldn't leave anybody in a bad situation, but it did. I have to survive, but how do I do that now?"[153]

The Itaipu flood began on October 13, 1982. Over fourteen days, twenty-nine billion cubic meters of water formed a lake that covered 1,350 square kilometers of Brazilian and Paraguayan lands (figure 3.9). The flood had originally been planned to take place over ninety days, yet heavy rains in the preceding weeks had swelled the Paraná River. The speed of Itaipu's flood, even if it had taken the full three months, can be seen as an indication of just how monumental the dam was for the military regime's self-image and its aspirations to global prestige. For comparison, the Lake Powell dam in the United States filled its lake over the course of seventeen years (1963 to 1980), and China's Three Gorges dam—which would supplant Itaipu as the largest in the world— took nearly five years (2003 to 2008) for its reservoir basin to reach full capacity. Yet Itaipu's flood was completed in a relative blink of the eye. In the span of fourteen days, a landscape of lush farmlands supporting thousands of families disappeared, lying swollen and untilled at the bottom of the reservoir.

A week after the flood, the governments of Brazil and Paraguay held an inauguration for their much-heralded Project of the Century. Over five hundred journalists, including almost two hundred foreign reporters, attended.[154] Many phases of construction still remained, and the dam would not begin to

FIGURES 3.8 & 3.9 The Itaipu flood. Left: The Guaíra Falls in December 1978, courtesy of Mario Cesar Mendonça Gomes. Right: The falls in the process of being submerged during the flood, October 1982, courtesy of the *Revista do Clube Militar*, Rio de Janeiro.

yield energy until 1984, but the reservoir flood was a colossal achievement. Not only had Itaipu Binational produced the largest artificial lake on the planet, but in harnessing and rerouting a sizable portion of the world's seventh-longest river, it had successfully completed the most challenging aspect of the dam's construction. Having overcome all manner of diplomatic, social, and environmental obstacles over the previous twenty years, the leaders of both countries could now rejoice.

Brazilian president João Baptista Figueiredo celebrated Itaipu as "a continental project. In the present atmosphere of crisis and pessimism . . . an event such as today reaffirms our confidence in humanity's strength." By gesturing to the economic crisis plaguing most of the Southern Cone in the early 1980s and also the political unrest unfolding domestically in Brazil, Figueiredo held up Itaipu as proof of his government's ability to lead the country. Paraguay's Alfredo Stroessner similarly described Itaipu as "more than just the greatest producer of hydroelectric energy in the world, [more than] a giant monument of concrete and steel. It will serve as a marvelous moral fortress, forever a symbol of unity, cooperation, and fraternity."[155] Neither leader mentioned the sacrifices made by local populations. For tens of thousands of people on both sides of the Brazil-Paraguay border, the Itaipu lake represented little more than the watery grave of their previous lives.

One of the most important political milestones of the abertura occurred one month after the flood. On November 15, 1982, Brazil held its first direct elections for national offices since 1965.[156] All legally recognized parties could run candidates for city council, mayor, state assembly, governor, Congress, and Senate.[157] Although the election did not include the presidency, it still marked a pivotal phase in the official return to democratic rule. Over forty-eight million Brazilians went to the polls, a voter turnout of roughly 83 percent.[158] As important as the electoral turnout were the results themselves: the PMDB opposition party received 43 percent of the total vote. Arguably the most symbolic result came from Leonel Brizola's election as governor of Rio de Janeiro. Alfred C. Stepan writes that Brizola's victory "represented a new stage in the evolution of the opposition."[159] The morning after the election, an editorial in the *Folha de São Paulo* celebrated a "victorious democracy," writing that November 15 offered a clear indication of "the construction of a democratic Brazil."[160] The history of Itaipu also resonated in the 1982 elections with two outspoken supporters of the farmers' movement winning prominent state-wide elections. With nearly 60 percent of the vote, the governorship of Paraná went to the PMDB candidate José Richa, who a week into the Foz do Iguaçu encampment had given a Senate speech denouncing Itaipu and the military.[161] Moreover, Álvaro Dias, one of the MJT's most consistent political allies, won a Senate seat with over 58 percent of the vote, easily beating out the sitting governor, Ney Braga.[162]

The flood and elections of 1982 provide a symbolic example of Brazil's uneven return to democracy. The celebration of Itaipu's construction effaced the severe hardships of local communities in their struggles against the Pharaonic project. And while the elections of 1982 signaled an important step toward democratization, for many Brazilians the abertura's promise of a full return of democratic rights remained a distant notion. The military did not actually cede power until 1985, and even so, not until 1989 did Brazil have a democratically elected president.[163] Like many regions across the country, western Paraná experienced a process of democratization defined not by elite policies but rather by the various microhistories within its population. Events in Foz do Iguaçu—an important border town and the home of the Itaipu dam—show how local realities often diverged from the alleged advances of the abertura from above. Scores of displaced farmers had relocated to Foz do Iguaçu seeking employment and a new life after the flood, yet the city's ongoing designation as a national security zone precluded its inhabitants from electing local candidates. This continued marginalization offers further proof of Brazil's limited transition: after suffering through the process of displacement, many now lived in a city without the same political rights that were reemerging elsewhere in Brazil.

As we shall see in the remaining chapters of this book, the traumas caused by Itaipu did not end after the flood. Because the histories of resistance and repression in the countryside had formed long before either the Itaipu dam or the dictatorship that built it, the flood was less of a rupture than a concentration of forces. As a result, these issues would continue long afterward.

CHAPTER 4

Sem Tekoha não há Tekó

Avá-Guarani Lands and the Construction of Indigeneity

This chapter marks the start of the second part of this book: each of the following four chapters traces specific histories that predated and ran concurrently with the main story of Itaipu and the formation of the Justice and Land Movement (MJT). Having already followed Itaipu's more linear narrative in the first part—from the dam's geopolitical roots through the 1982 flood—the book will now explore the overlapping chronologies that conditioned the wider experiences of life in western Paraná. These chapters challenge the assumed periodization of Brazil's transition to democracy by showing how the struggles of certain groups continued long after Itaipu's 1982 flood and the official end of the dictatorship in 1985. Chapter 5 will follow a journalist imprisoned for covering the MJT fight at Itaipu, a saga that gained international attention and reflected the regional variations in Brazil's path of democratization. Chapters 6 and 7 will then examine, respectively, the histories of settler farmers across Brazil's frontier zones and of landless peasants in western Paraná. First, however, this part opens with the present chapter on the Avá-Guarani indigenous community.

Twenty-five kilometers north of Foz do Iguaçu, the Avá-Guarani lived in an area known as Jacutinga, or Barra do Ocoí.[1] The process of indigenous expropriation at Itaipu shared certain commonalities with the adjacent farmers' movement. Both groups confronted the Itaipu Binational Corporation's evasive legal policies, the slow government response, and the looming threat of displacement. But the indigenous struggle was predicated on a distinct history of exploitation and a separate set of legal and social constraints. In fact, some of the neighboring farmers had themselves participated in the first wave of immigrant settlement that encroached on indigenous lands. The history of the Avá-Guarani exemplifies how indigenous communities in many parts of Brazil faced a complex system of marginalization, not only from entities like

Itaipu or the government but also from their non-Indian rural neighbors. By tracing how indigenous and other rural histories intersected in the fight at Itaipu, this chapter examines how constructions of race, indigeneity, and political legitimacy shaped the contours of life and popular mobilization in the Brazilian countryside.

The experiences of the Avá-Guarani and the nearby farmers were based on fundamentally different relationships to land. As previously discussed, the tension between the landed and the landless farmers reflected how the former viewed land as *individual property*, while the latter perceived land as a form of *collective rights*. The narrative of the Avá-Guarani offers a third conception: land as *a way of life*. A common refrain within the community is the concept of *sem tekoha não há tekó*—without land there can be no Guarani. The centrality of land to Guarani society is further embedded linguistically: the word for land, *tekoha*, is composed around the root *tekó*, a sociopolitical space that describes a way of being and a system of cultures, laws, and traditions. Bartomeu Melià observes that the dialectic between *tekó* and *tekoha* "simultaneously implies and produces economic and social relations and a political-religious organization essential to Guarani life."[2]

As explained by the current leader (*chomoy*) of Tekoha Itamarã, the Avá-Guarani fundamentally disagreed with Itaipu's efforts to buy, expropriate, and control land: "There is only one owner, he made the trees, the forests, the fish, and he left everything for us. For the actual owner of this land, you never paid a cent."[3] These lands formed the core of Avá-Guarani life, and their loss represented an ontological rupture far greater than that experienced by neighboring farmers. In an ethnography of the Avá-Guarani—one of the few extensive studies of the community—Maria Lucia Brant de Carvalho examines the community's social structure, its conception of land tenure, and its previous experience with encroachment from state and private initiatives.[4] Brant de Carvalho's analysis shows that the conflict at Itaipu involved much more than just a physical landscape of indigenous territory. Rather, Barra do Ocoí became a space where notions of ethnicity and power were contested and given meaning (figure 4.1).

Compared to the size of the neighboring farmers' movement and even to other indigenous struggles in Brazil, the Avá-Guarani community chronicled in this chapter was quite small. By the time Itaipu's expropriations began in the late 1970s, some twenty families (around seventy-five Avá-Guarani) lived in the planned flood zone. The point of this chapter is not the scale of the indigenous fight against Itaipu but rather the insight it offers. By historicizing

FIGURE 4.1 Members of the Avá-Guarani, Barra do Ocoí, May 1982. Photo by Maurício Simonetti, courtesy of Maria Lucia Brant de Carvalho.

the differences between the Avá-Guarani and the nearby farmers, this chapter shows how and why certain sectors of the Brazilian countryside were excluded from Brazil's reemerging democratic polity. Although the community secured material and symbolic victories, its overall situation saw little improvement in the aftermath of the Itaipu flood and the end of military rule. The case of the Avá-Guarani demonstrates how indigeneity and the contested politics of land and citizenship were fundamentally embedded in both Brazilian society and the eventual transition to democracy.

The indigenous history at Itaipu was not simply one of repression. In challenging the actions and policies of the federal government, the community and its allies won a series of important concessions. Although Itaipu and the National Foundation of Indigenous Affairs (FUNAI, Fundação Nacional do Índio) attempted to move the Avá-Guarani to an existing Indian reserve, the community demanded their own lands of greater size and quality. They eventually secured 251 hectares along the shores of the Paraná River—an area over twice the size of what the government had initially offered. In their drive for better lands, the Avá-Guarani forced the military regime to uphold its own laws, specifically the 1973 Indian Statute. Whereas FUNAI had tried to process the expropriation of indigenous lands as individual titles, the Avá-Guarani invoked the Indian Statute to win recognition of their land as communal property.

The question of collective landholding became especially important because the Avá-Guarani also had to deal with a land speculator named Nicolás Fernandes who tried to convince government authorities—and briefly succeeded—that he was part of the community and thus entitled to personal compensation from Itaipu. In the face of local opportunism and also federal policies intended to limit their access to land, the Avá-Guarani used the Indian Statute to strengthen their own collective demands.[5] A law written by the dictatorship ultimately functioned as a tool of democratization: by refashioning the meanings of the 1973 Indian Statute in the climate of the abertura, the Avá-Guarani challenged the legitimacy of government policy and also the dominant perception of indigenous communities as passive groups with no stake in the political changes taking root throughout Brazil.

As scholars like Luis Rodríguez-Piñero have shown, this was the period in which legal bodies like the International Labor Organization and the United Nations, along with nongovernmental organizations like Cultural Survival, began arguing for the need to redefine categories of ethnicity and the corresponding legal rights.[6] Amid these transnational movements to articulate and defend a platform of indigenous rights, the question of indigenous lands became fundamental. In order to preserve indigenous heritage against threats such as deforestation, mining, and "modernity" more broadly, advocates pressured national governments to demarcate and protect Indian lands. The fixing of indigenous life to a measurable stretch of territory helped cultivate a discourse of rights focused on the idea of *place*. While this shift often glossed over the fact that many indigenous groups moved about frequently—not only within the countryside but also into and between cities—the notion of place and the fight for indigenous lands offered a new strategy for the making of political claims. These global changes resonated strongly in Brazil, where the context of democratization helped give the struggle for land a distinctly political edge.

Initially, the Avá-Guarani demanded that Itaipu and the federal authorities respect the Indian Statute's definition of cultural and territorial rights. But with the impending flood and conditioned by the advancing abertura and the growth of transnational advocacy networks, the Avá-Guarani put forth an increasingly political critique. At a time when groups across Brazil were finding new ways to challenge military rule, the reassertion of indigenous identities became a political act in its own right. In standing up to a central apparatus of the military regime, the Avá-Guarani defended their rights not only as an indigenous community but as citizens of Brazil. This duality challenged the belief that indigenous groups did not belong to the Brazilian polity—what Alcida Rita Ramos has called the position of being "internal outsiders."[7] By articulating a clear attachment to the Brazilian nation, the Avá-Guarani adapted what few legal rights they had under military rule toward the promise of a new democratic society.

The parallel emergence of the MJT complicated the Avá-Guarani's struggle. To be sure, the Avá-Guarani used the media spotlight given to the farmers to spark public criticism of the government's abusive indigenous policies. Yet the MJT's leadership almost completely overlooked the Avá-Guarani. This not only precluded any chance of forming a joint struggle but also denied indigenous groups the sort of political legitimacy won by certain groups of nearby farmers. Even sympathetic media portrayed the Avá-Guarani as exotic and downtrodden others rather than as valid political actors. Because indigenous groups like the Avá-Guarani did not fit neatly into the broader standoff between democracy and dictatorship, their struggle in the early 1980s positioned them both within and beyond the abertura. For the Avá-Guarani, democratization was not a stand-alone objective; it was a vehicle to confront deeper inequalities rooted in ethnic identity and access to land.

Centuries' worth of laws and customs had discursively and politically turned Brazil's indigenous people into "orphans."[8] By defining Indianness as a temporary condition, Brazilian policy transformed individuals into wards of the state with the ultimate goal of assimilating Indians into Brazilian society. And although the association between Indians and orphans had been abandoned by the 1920s, the Indian Statute of 1973 recodified the belief that, like young orphans, Indians should remain under the tutelage of the government until they "came of age," meaning their full integration into mainstream society.[9] This approach held serious implications for the control of indigenous lands, since only legally defined Indians could access federally protected indigenous territory. As such, an acculturated—or "emancipated"—Indian became a non-Indian in the eyes of the law and subsequently lost his or her legal rights.

Indigenous policy focused largely on questions of land, and when the government stripped indigenous groups of their legal identity, it freed up previously protected lands for private and state enterprises.[10] In the 1970s and 1980s, the federal branch charged with administering these policies was the notoriously prejudiced FUNAI. Seth Garfield contends that during this period FUNAI "embodied the federal government's growing hegemony over the countryside and its efforts to foster capitalist growth and defuse social conflict through bureaucratic administration."[11] This approach was evident with the Avá-Guarani. Despite private memos discussing the indigenous community living in Barra do Ocoí, FUNAI maintained a public stance that it was unaware of the group. Only after persistent grassroots protest did FUNAI officially recognize the community. Hence, to defend their legal and territorial rights, the Avá-Guarani had to first struggle for the acknowledgment of their very existence.

Even then, the conflict extended to *how many* indigenous people lived in the region, as the authorities employed a survey intended to erase—both literally and ontologically—the status and number of Indians. Working toward the goal of diminishing the number of legally defined Indians, FUNAI used criteria with racist underpinnings to calculate the Indianness of those living in Itaipu's flood zone. Among other categories, the test evaluated an individual's skin pigment, language, clothing, and name. Scholars have called this a "perverse . . . ethnic litmus test" and a "true-false test for Indianness."[12] The survey, conducted on a single day in 1981, counted only five indigenous families even though the actual number was closer to two dozen. As we shall see, the mechanisms for how FUNAI counted Indians reflected more than just the prejudice of using physical and cultural traits to determine an individual's ethnicity. Rather, it disregarded the fundamentals of Guarani society. Many families were absent from Barra do Ocoí on the day of FUNAI's survey not because they did not live on those lands but because at that time they were living in other parts of the region.

In the triple-frontier zone of Brazil, Paraguay, and Argentina, the two main subgroups of Guarani, the Mbya and Ñandeva, lived spread out in over a hundred villages, with families often spending time in different locations for extended periods.[13] Mobility is central to the Guarani social identity. Their creation legend ties physical mobility to the essence of what makes the Guarani truly human: the Father (*Nhanderu*) carved wooden images (*yvyra*) similar to the deities and placed them "in front" (*ovai*) and "standing" (*ã*) in order to walk on Earth, an upright physical position that allows the Guarani to maintain a connection to their deities.[14] Moreover, Guarani communities lived throughout the triple-border region long before the establishment of national boundaries.

In order to process the expropriations quickly and in accordance with the federal construction of indigeneity, FUNAI and Itaipu needed to make the indigenous population seem as small as possible. With the help of allies in civil society, particularly within the progressive Catholic Church, the Avá-Guarani demanded that federal authorities recognize the true size of their community. As part of the immediate fight to win better land for relocation, the community's struggle at Itaipu also served as an attempt to reclaim the political and cultural power to define its own identity.

This chapter argues that the experiences of indigenous repression and resistance offer especially illuminating perspectives on the presumed chronology of dictatorships. The Avá-Guarani's marginalization at Itaipu resulted from forms of social and physical exclusion that predated the military regime and continued after the official 1985 transition to democracy. In her study of Mapuche Indians in twentieth-century Chile, Florencia E. Mallon shows that the start of Augusto Pinochet's dictatorship in 1973 functioned less as a breach of democracy than as the return of an earlier status quo.[15] Mallon's analysis helps reframe struggle in the Latin American countryside—especially regarding indigenous groups—as a two-tiered landscape. Linked by historical context to specific political systems, the Avá-Guarani, the Mapuche, and countless other groups experienced periods of military rule in very tangible and immediate ways. Yet the persistence of indigenous and rural repression under civilian and military governments alike shows that, although perhaps amplified during particular periods of authoritarian rule, abuses in the countryside resulted from deeply embedded realities of violence and inequality.

Before Itaipu: Colonial and Postcolonial Legacies

Unlike the landed farmers, who began migrating to the Paraná borderlands in the 1940s, Guarani indigenous groups had lived throughout the region long before the arrival of Europeans. When Spanish explorers first encountered the Guarani in the 1530s, they observed an extensive population network in the areas between the Paraná, Uruguay, and Paraguay Rivers. In the early 1600s, members of the Jesuit order began to congregate the Guarani into missions, and by the end of the seventeenth century, the region's indigenous communities were living on thirty missions spread across a geographic realm comparable to the size of modern-day California and with a population of roughly a hundred thousand.[16] When the Portuguese and Spanish Crowns expelled the Jesuits in 1759 and 1768, respectively, many of the Guarani dispersed back throughout the region and lived at the margins of the national societies that were beginning to form.

With the independence of Paraguay (1811), Argentina (1816), and Brazil (1822), conflicts arose over the territorial boundaries of the new nation-states, reaching a bloody crescendo in the War of the Triple Alliance (1864–1870). In his study of indigenous mobility, Evaldo Mendes da Silva notes that this war "caused a deep socio-spatial disorganization of the Guarani, not only because they had to leave their villages, but also because many men, including children, were forcibly recruited by local governments and died in combat."[17] Moreover, the war caused the spread of smallpox as indigenous soldiers contracted the disease on the front lines of battle and brought it home to their communities.[18] By the start of the twentieth century, the previous three hundred years of encroachment had resulted in a geographically dispersed Guarani population barely a fraction of its original size.

A series of events in the early twentieth century greatly impacted the Guarani living primarily within the national territory of Brazil. First, settler farmers and landowners fought in the Contestado War of 1912–1916, when a combination of religious millenarianism and material frustrations over access to land sparked a rebellion by local communities that was eventually put down with support from the Brazilian state and police.[19] The following decade, the famous Prestes Column rebellion passed through western Paraná, toward the start of a two-year uprising of junior army officers—known as *tenentes*—led by Luís Carlos Prestes and Miguel Costa. In September 1924 the rebels conquered the towns of Guaíra and Foz do Iguaçu, where for many months they relied on guerrilla tactics to fend off the federal troops led by General Cândido Rondon. This conflict destroyed rural *obrage* plantations that employed Guarani as Mate tea pickers, and many also fled across the Paraná River into Paraguay to escape the violence brought by the Prestes Column.[20]

Beginning in the 1940s, farmers began to arrive in the Paraná borderlands from both the southern state of Rio Grande do Sul and São Paulo to the east. These settlers seized and deforested many of the Guarani lands in order to introduce small- and medium-scale agriculture. The first forced relocation of the Avá-Guarani took place in 1953. The Indigenous Protection Service transferred part of the community to live with the Mbya-Guarani on the Rio das Cobras indigenous reserve. But the Avá-Guarani did not take to living with the Mbya, and most of the relocated families returned to their previous homes in the area of Barra do Ocoí.[21]

Over the following decades, the Brazilian government increased its presence in the border region to develop new infrastructure plans. Once the military regime took power in 1964, it brought federal indigenous policy in line with its broader ideology of national security and development. The regime dismantled the Indigenous Protection Service in 1967, restructured it as FUNAI, and placed it within the Ministry of the Interior. Seeking to further centralize the government's political and territorial power, the 1967 Constitution designated all indigenous lands as federal property.[22] With a dictatorship bent on fortifying its frontier zones and the newly created FUNAI acting as the guardian of Brazil's indigenous groups, the Avá-Guarani's homeland in the Paraná borderlands became a target of government attention (figure 4.2).

Along with the Itaipu hydroelectric dam, the region also witnessed the expansion of the Iguaçu National Park. Originally established in 1939, the park functioned as an early tool for the nationalization and development of the border region. Especially after World War II, tourism accelerated in the park, and the Brazilian government incorporated an additional 400,000 acres of land into the park. In the early 1970s, this required the removal of 447 families (roughly 2,500 people) of Euro-descendant farmers who had lived inside the park since the 1950s. To accommodate the relocation of these white settlers, the National Institute for Colonization and Agrarian Reform (INCRA) chose an area along the confluence of the Paraná and Ocoí Rivers, to be called the Ocoí Integrated Settlement Project. This decision proved highly contentious as the project included the ancestral lands of the Avá-Guarani. According to historian Frederico Freitas, INCRA knew of the existence of the indigenous community and applied enough pressure to convince some members to flee across the river to Paraguay or Argentina.[23] Those determined to stay on their lands resisted INCRA's advances, and at the end of 1975 a violent conflict set in motion a decade's worth of standoffs between the Avá-Guarani and state forces.

Newspaper coverage and oral testimonies recount the events of late December 1975, when a group of men—either the police, employees of INCRA, or hired thugs—arrived in Barra do Ocoí and set numerous houses on fire.[24] One inhabitant said that the community "had a Christmas full of fire and misery."[25] Another member recalled:

> INCRA shows up here, kicking people off their land, they scared us, threatening us, telling us to leave, setting our homes on fire, burning our crops, throwing our things onto the road, forcing us from here. . . . They threatened to shoot us in the leg, whoever didn't get up on [their] trucks. A lot of people escaped to the other village, also of Guarani, here in Paraná, or to Rio das Cobras . . . to villages in other states, in São Paulo, Rio de Janeiro. . . . Some

FIGURE 4.2 Forests and farming plots in Barra do Ocoí, May 1982. Photo by Maurício Simonetti, courtesy of Maria Lucia Brant de Carvalho.

even went to Argentina and Paraguay. FUNAI wasn't here [to protect us]. . . . The bravest stayed behind.[26]

Available documentary evidence does not prove that it was, in fact, INCRA employees who set fire to the houses. Yet in the memories of the Avá-Guarani, the blame for these actions always fell squarely on INCRA, consequently tarnishing all future interactions with the state agency. As indicated above, the fires forced many Guarani into hiding, and as many as twenty of the twenty-seven families fled the village.[27] Although some families returned in the aftermath of the fires, many never did on a permanent basis. This helps explain why FUNAI could place the Avá-Guarani's population at such a low number. Government policies thus functioned as a two-stage process to render the Avá-Guarani literally, ontologically, and ethnically invisible. First, intimidation and potentially violent directives forced families from their lands. Second, the subsequent population loss then justified the claim that the community included only a handful of indigenous people. Under the rationale that only a few "genuine Indians" lived in the area, state authorities sought to process the expropriations on a person-by-person basis, as they had done with the neighboring farmers. This individualized titling undermined the Avá-Guarani's conception of land, and the community persistently fought to have its territory recognized as shared communal property.

Around this time a man named Nicolás Fernandes (also known as Nicolau) moved into Barra do Ocoí; claiming to be a community leader (cacique), he subsequently seized control of Avá-Guarani lands. In testimonies then and now, Fernandes is referred to variably as a land speculator, a timber extractor, or a false cacique.[28] In a 2000 interview, a member of the Avá-Guarani recalled:

> A man showed up one day, saying that he was Indian also, but he actually just meant to trick the Indians. . . . The old cacique said "I don't know [that] white man, first time I've ever seen a white man here". . . . [Fernandes] even spoke a bit of [our] language, but actually he was a Paraguayan who came over and said he was going to stay with us, and he stayed. He tricked the Indians, saying "I'll be a cacique, I'm going to help you all." But . . . he cut down trees, took lands, he only destroyed. He called himself cacique but he wasn't Indian.[29]

Fernandes's ability to claim an indigenous identity represents a less common, but equally insightful, by-product of the 1973 Indian Statute. In her analysis of the statute, anthropologist Jan Hoffman French argues that while the law was intended primarily to assimilate people so that they *ceased* to be indigenous, its emphasis on self-ascription also allowed for others to claim an ethnic identification in order to *become* Indians.[30] On the whole, indigenous groups used the elasticity of this law as a tool of empowerment: communities that had been forcibly assimilated or were being threatened with assimilation could invoke the statute to reclaim the cultural and legal rights afforded to Brazil's Indians. Yet because the statute served as the primary conduit for demarcating and distributing indigenous land, it also opened the door for opportunism by individuals like Fernandes. As we shall see, Fernandes nearly succeeded in receiving government compensation for his supposed property that would be flooded by Itaipu. Only the mobilization of the Avá-Guarani kept this from happening.

At the request of Itaipu Binacional in March 1977, FUNAI began its first official study of the region's indigenous community. Called the Working Group XV, or GT for short, this commission was tasked with counting the indigenous people living within the dam's flood zone. Given twenty days to conduct its study, the GT visited three locations that might be home to indigenous tribes.[31] The GT determined that the first two, Três Lagoas and the Ocoí Integrated Settlement Project, included no indigenous elements whatsoever.[32] At the third area, Barra do Ocoí, the study group counted a total of eleven families. The GT's final report described the community as "in the process of acculturation (the children attend nearby schools) and whose subsistence is based on fishing from the Paraná River and agricultural products sown on plots alongside their homes."[33] Although the GT's description of the Avá-Guarani themselves consisted of only this one sentence, it included a more extensive suggestion for how to process the community's expropriation.

The report proposed two potential solutions for relocating the Avá-Guarani close to where they currently resided, either on a small island that would result from Itaipu's flood or along the banks of the Paraná River further upstream. Additionally, the report suggested resettling families in such a way as to "maintain the sociocultural aspect that ties them to their land."[34] The president of FUNAI wrote a letter to the director of Itaipu, General José Costa Cavalcanti, reiterating the importance of resettling the Avá-Guarani "along the shores of the [dam's] reservoir" to ensure the "survival of the socioeconomic aspects that connect them to their land."[35] Cavalcanti agreed with this proposal and offered to begin processing the transfer of a 110-hectare island for the resettlement of the Avá-Guarani.[36]

Although FUNAI and Itaipu soon abandoned this approach, it proves that both entities acknowledged the existence of nearly a dozen indigenous families—a claim the government would refute only a few years later. Moreover, the authorities agreed to relocate the families on nearby lands in immediate proximity to water, as was their custom, and in a manner that preserved the community's social and cultural foundation. Given the history of indigenous repression in the region, the measured tone of this proposal might seem surprising. Yet it must be placed in the context of the adjacent farmers' movement. In early 1977 the Binational had only recently begun to expropriate the communities living in the future flood zone, and the seedlings of an organized resistance had barely taken root. Before local farmers challenged Itaipu's expropriation policies on a mass scale, the Binational could contemplate a relatively respectful approach to the Avá-Guarani's relocation. At this early moment, Itaipu likely saw no cause for alarm in moving a handful of indigenous families a bit upstream. From the perspective of official policy, these Indians were little more than orphans who posed no real threat.

Later, the rise of an increasingly politicized farmers' movement meant that any semblance of a fair expropriation could set a dangerous precedent for the entire region. If Itaipu showed leniency to an indigenous community, what would keep MJT farmers from demanding the expansion of their own legal and political rights? This issue became especially acute as the Avá-Guarani mobilized around an indigenous identity that, contrary to government perceptions, was anything but passive or apolitical. Because the MJT had raised the stakes for Itaipu's expropriation policies, the Avá-Guarani had to work even harder to win the few concessions that the authorities had appeared willing to give them from the start.

The closing years of the 1970s saw Itaipu move toward a new plan for relocating the Avá-Guarani. Rather than use nearby lands, the Binational began transferring families to the existing Rio das Cobras indigenous reserve over two hundred kilometers east of the Paraná River. In August 1979 FUNAI loaded a portion of the Avá-Guarani on a bus and brought them to Rio das Cobras. According to witnesses, when the bus first arrived to begin the transfer, one family immediately fled across the river to avoid the relocation entirely.[37] Once in Rio das Cobras, many of the families found little reason to stay at the new reservation. One report observed that the Avá-Guarani did not enjoy being forced to cohabit on lands that belonged to the Mbya-Guarani, and soon afterward only three families continued to live in Rio das Cobras.[38] The remaining families either returned to Barra do Ocoí, where they soon confronted Itaipu, or continued even farther west and rejoined others living on the other side of the Paraná River.[39]

Over the next year and a half, the Avá-Guarani and their allies—especially the Indigenous Missionary Council (CIMI, Conselho Indigenista Missionário)— mobilized against the planned relocation to Rio das Cobras.[40] Itaipu and government authorities initially showed no willingness to meet with the community, and agreed to do so only when the MJT reached its apex at the Foz do Iguaçu encampment. As shown earlier, the fifty-four-day land encampment on the periphery of the dam's construction site brought unprecedented attention to the issue of Itaipu's expropriations, albeit in a racially sanitized manner. Although many in the MJT were blind to the plight of the nearby indigenous families, the Avá-Guarani were nonetheless able to use the spotlight cast by the farmers' movement as a platform for their own demands. During the first week of the Foz do Iguaçu encampment, CIMI issued a press statement denouncing the forced relocation to Rio das Cobras. It considered Itaipu's actions in "flagrant violation" of the Indian Statute, calling particular attention to the law's requirement that resettlement lands be of the same size and offer the same ecological conditions.[41] This statement by CIMI got traction in major media outlets. Alongside an article on the farmers' Foz do Iguaçu encampment, the *Jornal do Brasil* reported on the Avá-Guarani under the headline "Indians Are Also Protesting Itaipu."[42]

Despite entering a heightened phase of struggle against Itaipu at this exact same time, the farmers and the Avá-Guarani remained almost entirely disconnected. The indigenous community had previously attempted to link up with the farmers' MJT campaign by sending members to the 1980 Santa Helena encampment. Yet aside from a few solidarity statements at the start of the 1981 Foz do Iguaçu protest, the Avá-Guarani remained virtually invisible to the MJT.[43] As one leader of the farmers' struggle later recalled, "At that time, our understanding of the indigenous question wasn't like it is today. There were people [in the movement] who didn't even know there were índios in the region."[44] So despite capitalizing on the attention generated by the land encampments, the Avá-Guarani ended up excluded from the farmers' fight against Itaipu. Speaking in 2014, the Avá-Guarani leader Adriano Tupã Rokenji observed that in the community's attempt to make common cause with the MJT, "we were never even seen by the farmers."[45]

Two days after CIMI's anti-Itaipu press release—and likely because of it—FUNAI invited three members of the Avá-Guarani and their allies to a meeting in Curitiba. According to *O Estado de São Paulo*, FUNAI's regional director, Harry Luis Telles, opened the gathering by claiming that he was "unaware of the existence of índios in the region" and that FUNAI was under the impression that the occupants of Barra do Ocoí were not, in fact, indigenous.[46] As previously mentioned, FUNAI had explicitly discussed the indigenous group in the flood zone as early as 1977. Four years later, however, public awareness of Itaipu's expropriations forced the government to change its stance, and Telles told the Avá-Guarani that he would speak with national administrators about conducting a population survey of Barra do Ocoí. An article in *O Globo* further reported that the Avá-Guarani informed FUNAI they did not want to receive indemnification like the neighboring farmers, citing their right to lands equal to those slated to be flooded.[47] In doing so, the Avá-Guarani defended their conception of land in contrast to the experience of nonindigenous rural Brazilians and also within a legal-rights discourse.

The day after the meeting, CIMI's regional director, Wilmar D'Angelis, sent Telles a follow-up report summarizing the community's demands against FUNAI and Itaipu. Above all, the Avá-Guarani sought the "pure and simple

FIGURE 4.3 Members of the Avá-Guarani along the highway outside of Barra do Ocoí, May 1982. Photo by Maurício Simonetti, courtesy of Maria Lucia Brant de Carvalho.

application of the [Indian Statute]."[48] By grounding its claims in an existing law—one passed by the military regime in 1973—the community sought to position itself as a legitimate political force. As Brazilians of all backgrounds contested the limitations of the abertura, the Avá-Guarani sought to use a dictatorship-era law to justify their own claims to democratic rights. Concerned that the unequal treatment of indigenous communities would persist even under a new civilian government, CIMI also emphasized that the Avá-Guarani did not want to be resettled on lands belonging to other indigenous groups. D'Angelis concluded his letter by saying that forcing the community onto the Rio das Cobras reserve "represented [FUNAI's] practice of diminishing indigenous lands in the state, the region, and throughout the country." Staking their movement to an existing law while at the same time challenging the future implications of federal policy allowed the Avá-Guarani to focus on both the immediate fight at Itaipu and also the long-term need to navigate Brazil's political transitions. Although the abertura provided indigenous groups with an opportunity to raise an emerging voice of protest, it also highlighted the reality that despite a broadening rhetoric of equality, Brazil's Indians remained excluded from the national polity (figure 4.3).

Anthropological Surveys and the Politics of Counting Indians

In light of FUNAI's first public acknowledgment of the Avá-Guarani's existence, Telles held true to his word of surveying Barra do Ocoí. In late May a FUNAI employee named Célio Horst visited the community to conduct an "anthropological assessment" (*laudo anthropológico*). This survey employed a controversial methodology that revealed FUNAI's underlying approach to dealing with the region's indigenous groups. Visiting Barra do Ocoí for one day and using a metric based on "indicators of Indianness," Horst concluded that only five indigenous families lived among the community. Then FUNAI used these results to justify relocating the Avá-Guarani to the Rio das Cobras reserve. In response, allies of the Avá-Guarani invited a researcher from the Brazilian Anthropological Association (ABA, Associação Brasileira de Antropologia) to administer an alternative survey. With a methodology focused on measuring the community's own sense of ethnic and cultural identity, the ABA counted twenty-three families. But the ABA results carried far less political weight than the state-sponsored FUNAI assessment. Only after a year of grassroots mobilizations did the government finally succumb to public pressure and officially renounce FUNAI's data. This battle over the competing surveys showed the practical consequences of defining indigeneity.

On the day Horst visited Barra do Ocoí, he calculated a total of ten families (forty-one individuals) living in the community. Of the ten families, Horst determined that five were "indigenous," two were "nonindigenous," and three others were of indigenous descent but did not necessarily "self-identify as being indigenous."[49] Horst surveyed only males he considered to be the heads of families. Based on his measure of whether a given male was indigenous or not, Horst then extrapolated out the same assessment for all potential family members. Having begun with this myopic and gendered approach, Horst's subsequent use of FUNAI's indicators of Indianness further diminished the

Avá-Guaraní's population size. For each respondent, Horst filled out a chart intended to calculate his "ethnic identification." Points were assigned for fifteen different criteria, wherein 0 points represented "no characteristics," 5 meant "some characteristics," and 10 reflected "all of the characteristics." The fifteen categories included, among others, cultural elements, pigment qualities, language, historical identity, tribal identity, personal identity, art, food, and name. Anyone receiving 0 to 75 points was deemed non-Indian, and anyone receiving 76 to 150 points was considered Indian. The average total was 80 points, and no man received higher than 145—meaning that even in its most generous assessment, FUNAI did not consider a single person in Barra do Ocoí to be completely indigenous.

The logic of FUNAI's indicators implied that whoever "failed" the test was not actually indigenous and thus ineligible for government protection. Officially, the term for indigenous rights was *tutela* (tutelage), an invocation of guardianship that reinforced the notion of Indians as orphans. Removing the rights of tutela emancipated a person from the status of ward of the state. Technically, the person now enjoyed full citizenship; this supposed benefit, however, was predicated on the loss of indigenous rights. Ramos observes that the process of emancipating indigenous "orphans" specifically targeted the right to land, since "only as civil minors [were] Indians entitled to the possession of their territories."[50] By changing the legal identity of the Avá-Guaraní, FUNAI's policy attempted to annul the government's responsibility to its indigenous wards. And, most important for the immediate task of clearing Itaipu's flood zone, showing the existence of only five families of legal Indians greatly simplified the expropriation of land titles and the displacement of the entire community.

Another dynamic of FUNAI's survey relates to Nicolás Fernandes, the "false cacique." According to the Avá-Guaraní, Fernandes "manipulated" and "influenced" the survey, allegedly telling Horst how to classify members of the community.[51] *O Estado de São Paulo* reported this story under the headline of "FUNAI Went to See Indians but Only Spoke with a *Grileiro*"—a Brazilian insult meaning "land thief."[52] What is perhaps most fascinating about Fernandes's story is that after years of pretending to be Avá-Guaraní, the self-described Indian chief dictated FUNAI's survey so that he and his family would be categorized as *non*-indigenous. His actions appear directly linked to Itaipu's expropriations. At the time of Horst's visit, Fernandes had amassed over twenty-five hectares of land in Barra de Ocoí, nearly a third of the community's total holdings.[53] Under the Indian Statute, if Fernandes were to be labeled indigenous, it would entitle him only to land rights and not to any financial compensation. Moreover, it would require him to relocate to a new indigenous reserve with the rest of the community. So whereas identifying as Indian had helped Fernandes take over indigenous lands, he then opted to discard his previously assumed identity in hopes of being compensated financially on an individual basis as Itaipu had done with the nearby farmers. Because of the pushback from the Avá-Guarani, Fernandes appears to have unceremoniously left the community—without financial compensation. From this point forward, he falls out of the historical record. Yet in the ensuing debates over the exact number of Indians living in the flood zone, Fernandes remained a symbol of the problematic effects of government attempts to define and enforce indigeneity.

As it happens, FUNAI had begun using the indigenous indicators only four months before Horst's visit to Barra do Ocoí.[54] Along with the Avá-Guarani, FUNAI used the criteria to measure the Wassu and Tingui tribes in the northeastern state of Alagoas. Compared to the two cases in Alagoas, the public criticism sparked by the Avá-Guarani had the largest impact in national debates. In the aftermath of the Horst report, activists and academics denounced FUNAI's methods as an attempt to diminish indigenous lands. In an interview that made the front page of the *Folha de São Paulo*, the president of the ABA, Eunice Durham, stated that FUNAI's indicators "don't hold up to any serious scientific analysis" and that some of the criteria were "dangerous, fascist and racist."[55] Durham, a professor of social anthropology at the University of São Paulo, said the government had never consulted the scientific community and that none of the FUNAI employees who formulated the criteria had any qualifications for working with indigenous groups.[56] At a national meeting of indigenous organizations in September, a press release condemned the criteria as "a new attack from official indigenous policy seeking the compulsory emancipation . . . [to deny Indians] their collective ownership of land."[57] In its November 1981 news bulletin, CIMI criticized FUNAI for allowing a maximum of only ten days to complete a survey and for not requiring its employees to justify the points given for each indicator.[58] Another anthropologist described the indicators as "political tools to suppress indigenous demands" that allowed FUNAI to "wash its hands" of helping the Avá-Guarani.[59] These sorts of responses eventually forced FUNAI to abandon its policy. In the fallout from this negative attention, FUNAI did not subject any more communities to the indicators of Indianness.

In the interim, however, Horst's survey still stood as the government's official assessment. In an effort to counter FUNAI's measurements, CIMI contacted the

ABA about having one of its anthropologists produce an alternative survey. A month after Horst's initial visit, the ABA sent Edgard de Assis Carvalho to conduct a study of the community's social conditions and the "cultural modalities through which they express a Guarani ethnic identity."[60] Carvalho observed a total of twenty-three Avá-Guarani families, all of whom, in contrast to FUNAI's claims, he categorized as indigenous. Carvalho found that although only nine families were currently living in Barra do Ocoí, fourteen other families also belonged to the community: along with the three families who had stayed in Rio das Cobras after the initial 1979 transfer, two others were living in the Santa Teresinha region and nine more on the Paraguayan side of the Paraná River. The ABA report ended by urging the government to uphold the 1973 Indian Statute and, at the very least, to respect the cultural history of indigenous groups and recognize their right to ethnic self-identification.[61] In spite of the ABA research, FUNAI still showed little willingness to change its position.

By underrepresenting the Avá-Guarani, the government could more easily circumvent the federal Indian Statute and thus avoid designating the land as official Indian territory. Because the Indian Statute required indigenous lands to be expropriated as communal territory—one of the Avá-Guarani's central demands—the government aimed to minimize the number of "Indians" actually living in Barra do Ocoí in order to process the expropriations on an individual basis. Horst's findings also diverted attention away from two other violations of the Indian Statute: FUNAI's proposed transfer to Rio das Cobras did not have the legally mandated presidential decree, nor did it provide lands of equivalent size or ecological conditions. Finally, the survey criteria helped legitimize official responses to the rise of politicized rural movements in the region. As early as 1977, Itaipu and FUNAI had considered moving the Avá-Guarani to nearby lands along the Paraná River, but as rural communities fought for fair expropriations, the government could not be seen as making any sort of concession. The results of Horst's survey provided important justification for this strategy. Writing to Itaipu's director in September 1981, the director of FUNAI declared that in light of the recent indigenous "identification," the government no longer needed to resettle the Avá-Guarani on nearby lands.[62] With survey results now showing only a handful of indigenous families in the flood zone, FUNAI and Itaipu seemed determined to process their expropriations as strategically and invisibly as possible.

The selective use of so-called expert knowledge is evident in cases around the world. In his study of the World Bank, Michael Goldman traces the suppression of research findings relating to a hydroelectric project in Laos during the 1990s. The original pair of anthropologists hired to survey the area recommended that populations near the proposed dam site be labeled "indigenous people" rather than "ethnic minorities," but they received administrative pressure to remove the term "indigenous . . . for fear that the classification would require that the project fall under the Bank's Operation Directive on indigenous people, which could further postpone it." When the anthropologists refused to change their findings, a new consultant was brought in who quickly concluded that the various communities belonged to a single ethnic group—"a melting-pot culture"—that could not only survive but actually benefit from displacement and resettlement.[63] Whether by international organizations like the World Bank or federal bodies like FUNAI, so-called scientific knowledge can be strategically deployed to justify and advance any number of hegemonic interests.

Over the remaining months of 1981, the Avá-Guarani and their allies continued to mobilize for Itaipu to acknowledge their full population and to implement policies that respected their legal rights. The Avá-Guarani repeatedly attempted to get clarification on the status of their expropriations; although the government had internally decided to transfer the Avá-Guarani to Rio das Cobras, the community received no notice of this plan. In early December 1981, after six months of silence, Avá-Guarani leaders wrote a letter to the president of FUNAI defending the lands that had belonged to them "since time immemorial." The flood loomed some ten months away, and the community felt anxious to receive an official proposal for where they would go.[64] After two more weeks with no response, three Avá-Guarani traveled to Brasília to deliver the letter in person, where FUNAI's president, Colonel Paulo Moreira Leal, finally agreed to a meeting. On hearing the Avá-Guarani's demands, Leal said that FUNAI would conduct a survey of possible lands available and promised to send an official proposal within thirty days.[65] The meeting in Brasília also convinced Leal that, contrary to the Horst report, the three people he spoke with were, in fact, indigenous. With this firsthand evidence, Leal mentioned a willingness to "revisit" the previous survey.[66]

As FUNAI prepared its first official offer, media outlets throughout Brazil increased their coverage of the indigenous struggle. Regional newspapers offered extensive descriptions of the Avá-Guarani, painting a tragic picture of a helpless people facing the loss of their homes.[67] National media focused more on the implications for the progress of Itaipu, giving special attention to a potential lawsuit proposed by CIMI that threatened to halt construction on the dam.[68] In response, Itaipu's legal office issued a public statement clarifying that it had not made an offer to the Avá-Guarani because the Binational had to first wait for FUNAI to fulfill its responsibilities.[69] Given that Itaipu had recently emerged from its standoff with the MJT, its deflective language—and its willingness to pass blame to FUNAI—was surely a tactic to avoid further negative publicity.

In the midst of these battles for public opinion, Itaipu presented the community with its first official proposal. In the middle of December, one day before FUNAI's self-imposed deadline, representatives from Itaipu made an offer of roughly a hundred hectares of land. The plan called for Itaipu to expropriate twenty hectares of an adjacent farm and to allow the Avá-Guarani to use an additional eighty hectares of the so-called security line (*faixa de segurança*), the thin strip of land that would border the shores of Itaipu's reservoir. Allies of the community saw this as an important first step, even if only because it proved that, contrary to previous claims, Itaipu could find available lands nearby.[70] Additionally, the offer conceded to the community's refusal to live on the Rio das Cobras indigenous reserve. But the Avá-Guarani still saw many flaws in the proposal. The security line was only three hundred meters wide, and because of the planned flooding in the Itaipu reservoir, the Avá-Guarani could not plant crops or build homes on the eighty hectares of land.[71] Moreover, the Avá-Guarani would not actually hold legal domain to land in the security line, as it would still technically belong to Itaipu Binational. The indigenous community would essentially rent their lands from Itaipu—one critique declared that territory "lent to the Indians today could be taken right back tomorrow."[72] Itaipu's offer represented another disjuncture between hegemonic and indigenous notions of landownership.

The issue also remained of how many community members FUNAI recognized as indigenous and thus entitled to take part in the relocation process. Despite Leal's statements the previous month, FUNAI had still not reviewed its survey. Even if accepted, the hundred-hectare proposal would apply only to the original five families that FUNAI had defined as indigenous.[73]

After receiving Itaipu's offer, a group of Avá-Guarani leaders went to see the proposed lands for themselves. The community rejected the offer and sent the director of Itaipu and the president of FUNAI a detailed letter—signed with the thumbprints of six indigenous leaders—outlining why they refused to live on the hundred-hectare site. The Avá-Guarani remained convinced that the government still did not understand them or their culture, above all because the land had almost no trees. If transferred, the Avá-Guarani would need trees to build new houses. Moreover, a lack of trees meant a lack of firewood, and some members worried that they might freeze to death on Itaipu's proposed lands.[74] In the letter, community leaders wrote, "The Guarani cannot live in clearings, he loves forests where there are animals, and birds, and our way of life is that. The Guarani system is to live where there are trees. . . . This land of Itaipu is okay to plant, but it's not good for the Guarani, it has no forest, and it is very little land. You must keep searching for a forested place."[75]

Newspapers quickly picked up the story of the Avá-Guarani's rejection. A regional paper, the *Folha de Londrina*, outlined the problem of having "only 20 functional hectares and 80 hectares that are useless" and even mentioned the allegations against FUNAI and the Military Police of having set fire to Avá-Guarani houses in the mid-1970s.[76] A week later, the national *Folha de São Paulo* ran a two-page spread explaining why the community refused to live in an "unknown and barren area."[77] The report exoticized the indigenous group, as the opening three paragraphs romantically described an Avá-Guarani religious ceremony and a picture caption read, "Threatened with losing their lands, the indigenous can now only look to their gods." This characterization implied that the Avá-Guarani had no recourse other than their own spirituality and deprived the community of the material and political status needed to overcome the challenges ahead. Otherwise well-intentioned allies also put forth this same image of a noble people fighting for the lands of their ancestors. *Nosso Tempo*, the Foz do Iguaçu–based newspaper and outspoken critic of Itaipu, gave voyeuristic exposés to help readers "learn about the lives of the Avá-Guarani."[78] In the context of abertura, portraying the community as passive and apolitical denied it the type of legitimacy recently extended to the region's landed farmers.

In early 1982 Itaipu dispatched officers from its Special Committee of Security and Information (AESI) security force to compile a confidential assessment of Barra do Ocoí. The report concluded that the indigenous community had thirteen families totaling seventy-one people with at least another nine families currently in other parts of the region, including in Paraguay.[79] This population count confirmed the ABA survey and the Avá-Guarani's own claims. In the ongoing battle over ethnic representation, this recognition, even if only made in private, showed that the Avá-Guarani had created fissures in official constructions of indigeneity. The AESI survey also called Itaipu's policies "socially traumatic" and observed that with the flood barely six months away, the conflict imposed "a considerable psychological pressure" on the community.[80] Internally at least, it appears that Itaipu acknowledged its problematic approach to the Avá-Guarani. Despite this private recognition,

Itaipu maintained a public position that sidestepped its role in the suffering of indigenous communities.

The growing awareness of the Avá-Guarani struggles, both in the realm of public debate and perhaps even from within Itaipu, resulted in a second proposal. The revised offer included 105 hectares, with 62 hectares of forested land.[81] Community representatives again went to evaluate the area, and again they rejected Itaipu's offer. Whereas the previous reasoning had focused on the land's logistical faults—too small and not forested—the second rejection criticized the government's ignorance of indigenous culture and its violation of federal law. In a letter to the president of FUNAI, eight leaders of the Avá-Guarani declared:

> It's as if Itaipu didn't understand our letter from February 5, where we explained that we would only leave our land for another area that has conditions for us to continue our way of life. This land offered by Itaipu is much too small for the Guarani to live. . . . It's as if Itaipu doesn't know the law. . . . We know that FUNAI is responsible for helping indigenous communities, so we don't understand why it isn't defending our rights. . . . It's not our wish to leave here, but we are forced to by the [Itaipu] project of this government. It's this same government that made the law guaranteeing our rights as índios, and it created FUNAI to enforce that same law. So why, then, does FUNAI not uphold the law?[82]

Previously, the Avá-Guarani had aimed their demands at either FUNAI, Itaipu, or INCRA. Although directly linked to the central state, these organizations stood only as branches of the military regime. In contrast, this second rejection pointed directly at the government for building a project that would destroy their homes, for passing a law it failed to uphold, and for creating a federal agency that did not honor its mandate of protecting indigenous communities. Defending both their territorial rights as indigenous people and their legal rights as Brazilians became a means to reclaim political agency from an authoritarian government. Having seen their earlier claims to cultural rights make relatively little progress, and likely attuned to the growing political rhetoric of the abertura, the community now framed its struggle as a matter of democratic principles. These claims suggested that if the military regime truly deserved to govern Brazil, it had to respect the rights and aspirations of indigenous communities. Failing to do so, according to the Avá-Guarani, implied that perhaps the government had already lost its legitimacy to rule.

As it had done in February, the *Folha de São Paulo* ran an extensive report on the rejection of Itaipu's newest offer. Similar to its previous coverage, the article employed a romantic narrative describing the community as an "ancient, proud, and strong people." The story included a picture of a stoic indigenous woman carrying her baby. Yet the report also reproduced verbatim the majority of the Avá-Guarani rejection letter.[83] The increasingly political tone of indigenous demands now reached readers of one of Brazil's largest daily papers. Through these public channels, Brazil's Indians broadcast their voice into the ongoing debates of the abertura. Despite the romanticized portrayals, the escalating coverage nonetheless elevated the community's national profile.

In late April Itaipu made a third offer, of 190 hectares.[84] Several aspects of the new proposal came closer to meeting the community's demands: it contained almost twice the land of the second proposal, included nearly 160 hectares of forest, and bordered the shores of the Itaipu reservoir. Although encouraged by the updated offer, the Avá-Guarani rejected it for not demarcating the land as communal holdings.[85] Having won concessions from Itaipu regarding the parameters of the land itself, the Avá-Guarani now sought to reverse the government's attempts to process all land titles as individual holdings. The Guarani saw communal territory as both a pillar of their way of life and a legally protected right. Knowing that the flood would soon force them to abandon their homes, the Avá-Guarani fought to make sure that their new lands would at least belong to the community as a whole.

Five years after Itaipu first approached the subject of indigenous expropriation and after nearly a year and a half of evasive public statements, it appeared that the Binational might finally come to terms with the Avá-Guarani. On the heels of its standoff with the farmers' MJT and with the flood triumphantly planned a few months later, Itaipu seemed eager to resolve its indigenous problem. The *Folha de São Paulo* noted that an agreement with the Avá-Guarani would allow Itaipu to "escape from one of its greatest sources of criticism in recent years."[86]

A series of meetings in early May finalized the details of the resettlement. First, a lengthy negotiation took place on May 7 at Itaipu's regional office in Curitiba, with representatives in attendance from Itaipu, INCRA, FUNAI, CIMI, the Justice and Peace Commission, and the National Indigenous Action Association. Although no members of the community participated, their allies read a letter on their behalf explaining why they had refused the recent proposal. The subsequent discussion revolved around the question of having all land recognized for "communal use" and the nullification of the five individual deeds from the original FUNAI survey.[87] The government met both of these demands: INCRA agreed that all relocation lands legally belonged to the entire community, and FUNAI stated that it would disregard the 1981 Horst findings. This concession further implied that the government would offer a larger area of land to accommodate the increased number of families.[88] Although this first round of deliberations did not produce a signed agreement, Itaipu pledged to hold a follow-up meeting and bring a new offer directly to the community in Barra do Ocoí.

On May 12 four representatives from Itaipu and two each from FUNAI, CIMI, the Justice and Peace Commission, and the National Indigenous Action Association convened in Barra do Ocoí to meet with the Avá-Guarani. The new proposal called for 251 hectares of communally recognized land situated twenty-five kilometers away, along the shores of the future reservoir.[89] Itaipu also agreed to pay Cr$2.2 million in accordance with the Indian Statute's laws of expropriation. After hearing the details of this proposal, the community discussed it among themselves and with their supporters. In the end, the community chose to accept the offer.[90] The decision was not unanimous, as some members still considered the land insufficient. Others also worried about Itaipu distributing the compensation money through FUNAI rather than paying the community directly—ostensibly so the government could supply "the basic needs of the índios," such as food and agricultural tools. The Avá-Guarani ultimately based their decision on the urgency of the impending flood and opted to accept the proposal in order to begin preparing the next harvest on their new lands.[91]

A Reluctant Relocation

On June 7 a fleet of government trucks transported nineteen families from Barra do Ocoí to the new lands twenty-five kilometers away. Teodoro Tupã Alves remembers the experience: "It was like a tragedy because a peaceful community was destroyed, it was a psychological tragedy. . . . So many people were born there and lived there, you know, and you never imagine that any of this would happen, without any hope. For us the future was never going to be this, it would be something else, always getting better, always having a more relaxed life. But the opposite happened. Losing our lands, losing our freedom."[92]

A series of issues continued to plague the community long after the relocation. During the flood in October 1982, the reservoir came higher than anticipated, making it nearly impossible to grow crops on the partially inundated lands. Moreover, a government initiative to increase the local fish population outlawed all fishing activities in the Itaipu lake. A report later observed that the Avá-Guarani suffered from so much hunger they considered cutting down their trees to sell as timber in order to buy food.[93] In a sign of the community's desperation, it debated cutting down the same forested lands that had served as the centerpiece of its earlier demands.

The Avá-Guarani never did cut down their trees, but in the long run their livelihoods never drastically improved. In the aftermath of the 1982 resettlement, the community continued to pressure Itaipu and FUNAI for more resources and larger tracts of land. A rise in conflicts between indigenous communities and neighboring farmers exacerbated these problems, as did the contamination of indigenous farmlands by chemical runoff from nearby agricultural estates.[94] The situation worsened as the community increased in size, both by normal population growth and through the return of Guarani families living in other parts of the border region. After over a decade of lobbying, Itaipu conceded to creating a second area for the Avá-Guarani, and in 1997 FUNAI transferred thirty-two families to a 1,700-hectare site known as Tekoha Iñetete. By 2007 nearly 130 families were living on the reserve, requiring the transfer of twenty-eight families onto 240 hectares of adjacent land in a newly created third community called Tekoha Itamarã (figure 4.4).

The specter of Itaipu looms large in the collective memory of the Avá-Guarani. To this day, community members still point to Itaipu as a source of their poverty. Yet many people also look back on the fight in the late 1970s and early 1980s as a formative process for learning how to make themselves socially and politically visible in the public eye. A community leader, Adriano Tupã Rokenji, recalled, "At first we didn't know anything about [Itaipu] . . . but we learned how to work with CIMI, we learned how to use the newspapers to get our rights. We found lawyers to explain what Itaipu was doing. We learned how to get our rights."[95]

The name Itaipu actually comes from the Guaraní language. Meaning "the rock that sings," Itaipu had long been the name given by Indians to a set of rocky outcrops in the middle of the Paraná River. For an overlapping series of geographic and geopolitical reasons, the governments of Brazil and Paraguay chose the portion of the river that the Guarani called Itaipu as the site of the future hydroelectric complex. In a symbolic twist of linguistic appropriation, Itaipu's 1982 flood destroyed the surrounding indigenous lands. Although the rising waters of Itaipu's reservoir permanently engulfed "the rock that sings," the legacy of indigenous struggle remained. These issues continued well after

FIGURE 4.4 A member of the Avá-Guarani community in Tekoha Itamarã, 2014. Photo by author.

the transition to democratic rule, illuminating the contradictions of the abertura process and the extent to which constructions of ethnic exclusion exist deeply within the fabric of the Brazilian polity.

The Avá-Guarani's conflict at Itaipu was predicated on a much larger history of repression. Similar to other indigenous groups throughout Brazil and across Latin America, the community had long confronted land encroachment and coercion from federal authorities. For generations this violence reinforced the Avá-Guarani's status of social invisibility. Only when placed in the crosshairs of a massive development project did the Avá-Guarani's conception of land and identity become an obstacle for the Brazilian state. In the context of national debates over the contours of democracy and citizenship, a small indigenous community accessed grassroots networks to amplify its demands. As groups like the Avá-Guarani embraced a growing sense of ethnic and political empowerment, the federal government sought to reinforce the tutela system of marginalization, only now with new mechanisms. Seeking to diminish the physical and symbolic presence of Brazilian Indians,

FUNAI's survey functioned as a tool to control the parameters of indigeneity. The grassroots response to FUNAI, however, shows how racist, exclusionary practices like the indicators of Indianness actually served to energize indigenous movements in Brazil. In the controversy over counting Indians at Itaipu, the actions of the Avá-Guarani and their allies forced FUNAI to abandon the survey. Yet the reversal of one authoritarian policy could not undo Brazil's embedded politics of indigeneity.

In an attempt to gain legitimacy, the Avá-Guarani put forth an alternate framework of indigenous rights that appealed to the government's own legal structures. Despite the context of abertura, the Avá-Guarani's demands for land, cultural rights, and legal equality reflected a vision for indigenous life unmoored from whether a military or civilian regime governed Brazil. As a movement that existed both within and beyond the climate of abertura, indigenous struggle in this period did not fit neatly into the struggle between dictatorship and democratization. This helps explain why indigenous groups like the Avá-Guarani were excluded by the regime and by most mainstream opposition forces—with the notable exception of progressive sectors of the Catholic Church. By seeking to defend their dual rights as indigenous people *and* citizens of Brazil, the Avá-Guarani challenged the contours of Brazil's democratic transition. Although often portrayed as apolitical actors in their fight at Itaipu, they refused to be cast aside as helpless and socially invisible orphans. And in the face of federal policy intended to erase their ethnic and literal presence, the Avá-Guarani won a series of concessions from branches of an authoritarian regime. In doing so, they challenged the prejudice of both the government and the region's nonindigenous rural workers.

Throughout this process and in the decades that followed, the community was exoticized and set apart from the Brazilian polity. The persistent marginalization of the inhabitants of Barra do Ocoí further proves that the advances of the abertura remained limited to only certain sectors of Brazil. While negotiations between elites yielded amnesty and party reform laws, indigenous groups like the Avá-Guarani defended their lands and livelihoods from a variety of government and nonstate threats. And as millions of Brazilians reclaimed the streets and the factories as spaces of democratization, racist federal policies attempted to count and categorize Indians in a way that rendered them invisible. Despite these constraints, the Avá-Guarani articulated an ethnic identity based on a particular relationship to land and its corresponding legal rights. Although this approach never fully achieved a sense of mainstream political legitimacy, it positioned them to directly confront, and to make inroads into overcoming, the dominant construction of indigeneity in Brazil.

Even in Brazil's largest effort to date to account for the brutality and violence of its authoritarian past, the repression of indigenous groups remains categorically overlooked. The 2014 National Truth Commission (CNV, Comissão Nacional da Verdade) confirmed 343 cases of murder or forced disappearance committed by agents of the military regime and revealed the pervasive use of torture and illegal imprisonment.[96] These categories of state-sanctioned violence correspond most closely with the way scholars and human rights activists tend to analyze periods of political violence. As we have seen, however, violence under an authoritarian regime did not only result from the direct actions of the dictatorship. To the CNV's credit, the report did detail less official forms of repression, including against urban workers, militants, the LGBT community, and university students. Additionally, the CNV determined that under the dictatorship and in the preceding decades (1946–1988) at least 8,350 Indians were killed. Despite the inclusion of indigenous deaths—which the CNV recognized as only a partial total—these cases of violence were not included in the main body of the report. Rather, the section on indigenous repression exists as a thematic appendix, coming after the final conclusions and recommendations. And whereas the CNV provides a detailed biography and, when available, a picture of each of the 343 certified victims of state violence, the appendix on violence against Indians includes few individual names or personal details.

Fifty years later, the official victims of the military dictatorship are memorialized as people, each with a family and a story to tell. Brazil's Indians, in contrast, remain almost entirely unidentified. While compiling evidence of abuses against indigenous groups poses a challenge, the structure of the CNV itself reinforces the dual existence of Brazil's Indian communities. Visible at times, indigenous groups are confined to a secondary status, remaining just beyond society's collective gaze.

CHAPTER 5

The Last Political Prisoner

Borderland Elites and the Twilight of Military Rule

In October 1982 Juvêncio Mazzarollo was not among the throng of Brazilian and international journalists descending on western Paraná to cover the Itaipu flood. Rather than reporting on the culmination of a story he had written about for years, Juvêncio—as is the Brazilian custom, he was commonly known by his first name—sat in a jail cell some six hundred kilometers away. Four months earlier, a military court had found him guilty of violating the National Security Act (LSN, Lei de Segurança Nacional). As the cofounder and lead writer for the Foz do Iguaçu–based *Nosso Tempo*, Juvêncio was sentenced for allegedly using his newspaper to incite subversion. These charges, however, appear to have been little more than a manufactured cover. Juvêncio was thrown in prison for two escalating reasons: first, he wrote a series of exposés on the corruption of local officials; and, second, he became the most consistent media ally of the farmers' movement against the Itaipu dam.

Juvêncio remained in jail until April 1984, long after the dictatorship had released all the other journalists and major political opponents it had imprisoned. In the supposed twilight of abertura, Juvêncio won his freedom only when an international solidarity campaign—coupled with his own staging of two hunger strikes—forced the government to grant his release. Even after journalists and political dissidents of much wider acclaim had been liberated, this writer at a relatively tiny borderland newspaper stayed behind bars. Of the thousands of Brazilians jailed by the dictatorship, a small-time journalist born and raised in the southern countryside transformed into an unexpected symbol of democratization. On the cusp of the official return to civilian rule, and magnified by the spotlight on the Itaipu dam, Juvêncio earned the notorious distinction of "the last political prisoner."

This chapter chronicles Juvêncio's trial and imprisonment. Having shown throughout this book how the Itaipu dam served as a testing ground for public opinion and political legitimacy, we can now trace these issues through their most headline-grabbing example. While the Justice and Land Movement (MJT) had received national attention, the story of Brazil's last political prisoner reached global audiences; Amnesty International, for example, took up Juvêncio's imprisonment as a major campaign. It is telling that in terms of public awareness, the plight of a journalist *covering* the struggles of rural Brazilians eclipsed that of the protagonists of the original story. This is not to take away from Juvêncio's commitment to the farmers' movement or his role within the national fight for democracy. Instead, his transformation from an ally of the MJT to a stand-alone symbol of opposition reflects the complex nature of legitimacy and visibility during the abertura. Juvêncio's position as a journalist—and the privilege conferred through his southern Brazilian, European heritage—enabled him to attain recognition beyond anything achieved by the displaced farmers.

Juvêncio's story also sheds light on the experience of elites, a dynamic of the abertura that might otherwise get overlooked in a grassroots history of Brazil's dictatorship. Previously in this book, the elites in question have mostly been the leaders of Brazil's dictatorship or the high administrators of the Itaipu dam. While national officials did play an important role in the saga of Juvêncio's imprisonment, this chapter will focus on elites at the local level, specifically a judge and a few politicians and midlevel army officers. Because it took place in western Paraná, the case of Juvêncio offers an especially compelling insight into a certain type of authority: borderland elites. By virtue of their positions linked to the dictatorship, these officials—referred to interchangeably in this chapter as *elites* or *authorities*—were members of Brazil's elite classes. Yet their location in a border region left them slightly askew of the policies enacted by the central military regime. For two decades under dictatorship, local and regional power dynamics became entrenched in particular ways across Brazil. As such, when the process of abertura disseminated outward from Brasília, local elites like those in western Paraná continued to act as though unbeholden to the parameters of democratization.

By exploring the logic of why these borderland elites imprisoned Juvêncio, this chapter shows how the double reality of abertura did not exist only for marginalized groups. Rather, it applied to all Brazilians, including military officials and their political allies. Similar to the farmers, Indians, and peasants living in the flood zone, elites in Brazil also experienced a doubling wherein their own perspective on democratization did not align with the official stages of the abertura. Yet unlike the displaced communities reimagining a democratic future, the double reality for elites at Itaipu was seen through a rearview mirror: local elites initiated a criminal trial against Juvêncio to safeguard the privileges they had become accustomed to over the previous two decades. In areas like western Paraná, local authorities often considered themselves above the process of abertura they saw unfolding in major cities. Against a backdrop of Brazil's official transition to democracy, elites such as those in Foz do Iguaçu operated within a competing reality that sought to reverse even the limited goals of the abertura.

Juvêncio was imprisoned when his stories about local corruption and his denouncements of Itaipu drew the ire of the military elite in Foz do Iguaçu, especially the city's mayor, Colonel Clóvis Cunha Vianna; an army officer named João Guilherme da Costa Labre; and a military judge, João Kopytowsky. For these men who felt immune from the process of democratization they saw happening elsewhere, Juvêncio's repression served as an attempt to exercise their quickly fading power. In concert with national leaders determined to protect the triumphalist image of the Itaipu dam, these borderland elites showed a willingness to repress Brazilian citizens in spite of—or, more likely, because of—the official progress of abertura. With a potential democratic return looming ahead and with the dam almost ready to begin producing energy, it became increasingly important for the military regime to maintain its impression of control. In the aftermath of the 1982 flood, the battle for public opinion in western Paraná shifted from the MJT to Juvêncio's imprisonment.

As was the case with other aspects of the dictatorship's actions at Itaipu, the repression of Juvêncio had the unintended consequence of amplifying dissent rather than silencing it. Amid a resurgent national push for democracy, opposition groups throughout Brazil rallied around the writer who, they claimed, was unjustly imprisoned for writing about the abuse of power and the mistreatment of displaced farmers. From late 1980 through the middle of 1984, Juvêncio went from being a largely unknown journalist to a rallying point for Brazilian democracy. In the twilight of military rule, Juvêncio emerged from the shadow of the Itaipu dam to become known throughout the country and across the globe as the last political prisoner in Brazil (figure 5.1).

Before he helped start *Nosso Tempo*, Juvêncio had already publicly criticized Itaipu Binational in several articles on the dam's construction and, most important, in a book on the early stages of the MJT.[1] In anticipation of *Nosso Tempo*'s inaugural issue in December 1980, Itaipu's internal security warned the executive committee that "subversive" materials would soon circulate throughout the region.[2] Itaipu's worries appear trenchant; from its beginning,

FIGURE 5.1 Starting in February 1984, *Nosso Tempo* printed a running tally of the length of Juvêncio Mazzarollo's imprisonment.

Nosso Tempo wrote extensively on charges of corruption among local military leaders and the ongoing farmers' struggle.

The cover of *Nosso Tempo*'s first issue depicted a naked man, hands tied together, hanging upside down by his ankles while men in overcoats held him in place and burned his face with a cigarette (figure 5.2). With this reference to the military's infamous torture method called the "parrot's perch" (*pau de arara*), *Nosso Tempo* alleged that Foz do Iguaçu's military police had committed torture against local citizens. In their reporting Juvêncio and his co-authors identified only one individual by name: the city's head judge, João Kopytowsky.[3] This judge was among the three local elites who interrogated Juvêncio less than five months later, setting in motion his arrest and eventual imprisonment.

In its third issue, *Nosso Tempo* printed a three-page story about the failures of Foz do Iguaçu's mayor, Colonel Cunha Vianna. Writing that *Nosso Tempo* did not want to "only be an organ of news, but also an active participant in municipal life," Juvêncio organized a roundtable discussion to talk about Cunha Vianna that gave the impression of an incompetent mayor with no support from the general population.[4] Within days Cunha Vianna personally contacted *Nosso Tempo* and demanded an interview.[5] Juvêncio took advantage of this opportunity and confronted Cunha Vianna about the mismanagement of public

Ano I - No. 1 - Foz do Iguaçu, de 3 a 10/12/1980

Nosso tempo

CR$ 20,00

FÁBRICA DE CONFISSÕES

FIGURE 5.2 The cover of *Nosso Tempo*'s first issue, December 3, 1980.

funds, the prioritization of Itaipu at the expense of Foz do Iguaçu residents, and the fact that his status as mayor came via federal appointment rather than a direct popular vote.[6] Despite Cunha Vianna's efforts to improve his public image, the interview portrayed him as an out-of-touch military politician. A series of subsequent articles continued to denounce the local government. In February *Nosso Tempo* obtained and printed a letter signed by the mayor authorizing the illegal seizure of the property and assets of a local citizen.[7] Two weeks later *Nosso Tempo* reported that Cunha Vianna had submitted a request to change his official title from colonel to mayor, a development that *Nosso Tempo* mocked under the headline "Is the Mayor Embarrassed of Being a Colonel?"[8] Until this point Juvêncio and his newspaper had denounced local elites for torture, corruption, and a disregard for average Brazilians. None of these articles had appeared to incite any immediate repression or intimidation. That changed in March 1981 when *Nosso Tempo* began covering the farmers' encampment in front of Itaipu.

By the time of *Nosso Tempo*'s launch in December 1980, the MJT had already staged its first protest camp at Santa Helena. The farmers' campaign soon accelerated in March 1981 with the start of its second encampment on the periphery of Itaipu's entrance gates. As farmers mobilized against Itaipu, Juvêncio and his newspaper became the movement's most outspoken media ally. For the government, Juvêncio's earlier denouncements presented a problem at the local level, but the national attention brought by the farmers and the centrality of Itaipu to the dictatorship pushed Foz do Iguaçu's military elite to silence *Nosso Tempo*.

On April 6, 1981—three weeks into the MJT encampment—Juvêncio was putting the final touches on that week's issue when an unknown man in a dark suit and tie knocked on the door of *Nosso Tempo*'s office. The stranger introduced himself as a member of the Federal Police and presented a summons for Juvêncio, who then spent the rest of the day nervously awaiting further instructions. At four in the afternoon, security forces arrived to escort him to the Federal Police station.[9] Upon his arrival, police placed Juvêncio in a room with Judge Kopytowsky, Mayor Cunha Vianna, and Colonel Labre. According to Juvêncio, the interrogation quickly proceeded into a series of insults aimed at himself and the work of *Nosso Tempo*, with the land encampment serving as a major focal point: "The farmers displaced by Itaipu had camped in Foz do Iguaçu and the situation in the city was extremely tense. [The farmers] asked for help and Colonel Labre refused. [*Nosso Tempo*] provided total coverage of the farmers' movement."[10] The authorities criticized Juvêncio's editorial line and threatened him with legal action if the newspaper continued its coverage.[11]

No official accusations were filed that evening, but three days later the government indicted Juvêncio and his two coeditors, Aluízio Palmar and João Adelino de Souza, for having violated Article 14 of the LSN. Article 14 made it a crime "to make public, through any means of mass communication, untrue or biased information, or true information in a partial or distorted manner, in such a way as to create or attempt to create hostility against the constituted authorities."[12] The Fifth Regional Military Tribunal oversaw the investigation and summoned all three editors to the Foz do Iguaçu police station to provide statements. With official charges lodged against them, the editors of *Nosso Tempo* used the pages of their newspaper to denounce the Brazilian state and defend their freedom of expression. A subsequent editorial observed, "After [reading] the revelations that we are going to make here, whoever still [believes in] the open investigation into this newspaper [under] the National Security Act, is either crazy or consciously swallowing lies."[13] In reaction to his arrest, Palmar stated simply, "What kind of abertura is this?"[14]

Three months into the investigation, Juvêncio and his colleagues won a significant but fleeting victory. On July 22, 1981, a judge from the Fifth Regional Military Tribunal in Curitiba rejected the original charges against the three editors.[15] Considering that a guilty verdict under Article 14 of the LSN carried a sentence of up to two years in prison, the writers of *Nosso Tempo* saw this as a potential turning point. Their sense of triumph, however, dissolved less than two months later with a new set of allegations. This time, only Juvêncio was charged, setting in motion his imprisonment the following summer.

Singling out Juvêncio because of his "dangerousness" (*periculosidade*), this second round of charges accused Juvêncio of violating the same LSN Article 14 from the first arraignment but also included alleged violations of Articles 33, 36, and 42.[16] Combined, the charges against Juvêncio carried the possibility of a twenty-year prison sentence. Whereas the earlier charges related to general events and perceptions—an ambiguity that helped lead to their rejection two months earlier—the indictment against Juvêncio now focused specifically on an article he had published in a July issue of *Nosso Tempo* titled "You Can't Milk a Dead Cow." Although the article in question denounced the military government and called for the return to a democratic society, it was no more incendiary than any of his previous writings.[17] Nevertheless, the authorities cited the "Dead Cow" article as enough evidence to accuse Juvêncio of engaging in "violent and direct acts against the regime of the constitutional authorities, seeking to incite true subversion."[18]

What can one infer from the military's second round of charges against Juvêncio? Was his article so radical that it merited a criminal investigation? An overview of other newspapers during this period reveals that Brazilian journalists repeatedly challenged the military regime and suffered little to no repression. One example comes from 1978, a year before President João Baptista Figueiredo officially inaugurated the policies of abertura and four years before Juvêncio's imprisonment. Investigating the story of a bomb that had exploded in the offices of the daily newspaper *O Estado de São Paulo* ten years prior, a journalist at *Repórter* named Luiz Alberto proved that military forces had committed the attack and then covered up their actions. Neither Alberto nor his paper received any persecution for revealing state violence.[19] According to Joan R. Dassin, the most important test of press freedoms during this period came during the 1981 Riocentro bomb plot, a plan by the military's ultraright faction to incite a countercoup to reverse the abertura. In response to Riocentro, "new techniques of investigative reporting were developed on the spot," and one Brazilian journalist claimed that the press "passed with flying colors as the story was kept alive."[20]

The dictatorship did little when journalists revealed government bombings, but the regime threw Juvêncio in jail when he denounced the Foz do Iguaçu military elite and became a leading disseminator of news on Itaipu. Contrary to the official charges against the "Dead Cow" article, Juvêncio's imprisonment resulted from the overlapping interests of local and national elites during one of the most delicate phases of Brazil's transition away from military rule.

Freedom of Expression on Trial

Juvêncio's trial started on November 11, 1981, and did not conclude until June 27 of the following year. Journalists from two of Brazil's leading daily newspapers, *O Globo* and *O Estado de São Paulo*, attended the trial and kept the country informed of its proceedings.[21] This media presence shows that although Juvêncio initially was one of the only voices covering the farmers' movement against Itaipu, by the time of his trial—and largely because of it—the story had evolved into a national topic. The trial offered a showcase of the dictatorship's stand against oppositional forces in the waning years of military rule, and it drew widespread interest from those who recognized its implications for the progress of abertura.

Juvêncio's defense lawyer, Rene Dotti, cited *Nosso Tempo*'s coverage of the Itaipu conflict to argue that rather than advocating seditious politics, the newspaper simply took the side of a popular social movement. As reported by *Nosso Tempo*, of all the questions raised during the trial, the question of Itaipu was "amply exposed. The movement of the farmers dispossessed by Itaipu was the most profoundly analyzed."[22] This strategy sought to justify Juvêncio's articles by showing that public support for social movements like the farmers' struggle had become increasingly acceptable by this stage of the abertura. Juvêncio's defense portrayed him not as a subversive, but as a concerned Brazilian citizen during this era of national transition. The complicity of local elites also loomed large. During the trial Dotti argued that Juvêncio's repression resulted from "a personal grudge on the part of Colonel Labre."[23] Supporters outside of the courtroom shared this opinion as well. In a speech to the national Chamber of Deputies, Osvaldo Macedo (Brazilian Democratic Movement Party [PMDB], Paraná) declared that Colonel Labre only cared about "satisfying his own personalistic desires." Macedo called on the President Figueiredo and the deputies in attendance to defend Juvêncio and to honor the meaning of democracy, concluding, "The law is the law. But a colonel is nothing more than just a colonel."[24]

The context of the Itaipu dam reveals the full magnitude of Juvêncio's ongoing trial. As shown earlier, around this time Itaipu's leaders had to deal with the fallout of the *Time* magazine allegations of corruption. With their public image in doubt on the global stage, Itaipu executives became increasingly anxious about Juvêncio and his escalating calls for more direct action from the protesting farmers. Confidential records show a meeting on July 14 between Itaipu's legal director, Paulo da Cunha, and the Ministry of Justice.[25] These talks decided that the National Information Service (SNI) would gather information to build a case against the newspaper, and also that Itaipu's director, José Costa Cavalcanti, should engage the federal courts with the long-term goal of charging *Nosso Tempo*'s editors under the LSN.

In the aftermath of the farmers' Foz do Iguaçu protest camp, Juvêncio had written a pair of articles—analyzed at the end of chapter 3—that justified a more confrontational strategy in the standoff with Itaipu. These appeals for more radical tactics likely compelled the authorities to take decisive action.[26] A series of SNI memos sent directly to Cavalcanti over the following month called for swift legal action if *Nosso Tempo* did not soften its political tone. These exchanges emphasized that Itaipu was carefully monitoring a potential trial through Cavalcanti's close connection to the regional superintendent of the Federal Police.[27] Additionally, of the forty-one agenda items at Itaipu's 1981 year-end legal conference, the issue of Juvêncio was the only one marked "confidential" and "off-the-record," suspiciously leaving no details as to what exactly Itaipu's leaders had discussed.[28] Finally, the minutes of a classified meeting reveal that on the whole Itaipu considered its public relations campaign successful, noting a clear decrease in "criticisms of the Itaipu project." The sole exception, however, was *Nosso Tempo*, whose writers continued to publish articles that remained "insulting and provocative to government authorities and entities, [particularly] Itaipu Binational."[29] So while Itaipu and its collaborators in the dictatorship celebrated an improved public image, Juvêncio lingered as a persistent problem.

After nearly seven months of trial, the court gave its verdict at two in the afternoon on June 27, 1982. On charges relating to Articles 14, 36, and 42 of Brazil's LSN, the court found Juvêncio not guilty. But on the charge under Article 33, he was found guilty and sentenced to one year in jail.[30] Whereas the other three articles dealt with inciting subversion in the general population, Article 33 pertained to "offending the honor or dignity" of government authorities.[31] Juvêncio's sentencing under Article 33 thus offers surprisingly candid proof that Juvêncio's repression resulted largely from the vendetta of local military elites.

According to those present at the trial, the reading of the guilty verdict brought a stunned silence to the courtroom. When a lieutenant colonel asked the public to clear the room, a few people in the gallery began to cry. Juvêncio remained seated for nearly an hour before three federal agents escorted him to a nearby police department and to the Piraquara prison later that night.[32] Juvêncio, a man whom colleagues described as "shy, but courageous," went to prison for criticizing a government that, in theory, had already begun transitioning to a free and open democracy.[33] A *Nosso Tempo* editorial emphasized the contradiction between the veneer of an official reopening and the imprisonment of a journalist: "Nepotism, corruption, and theft are all being discussed daily by the press and by honest politicians without being punished. Juvêncio Mazzarollo, who dared denounce all of this, is behind bars" (figure 5.3).[34]

The outpouring of support for Juvêncio paralleled the accelerating opposition movement nationwide. The Freedom for Juvêncio Mazzarollo Committee formed within twenty-four hours of the guilty verdict, and the following morning the Paraná Student Union organized a demonstration in the state capital of Curitiba.[35] Marching through the city, protesters waved signs and

FIGURE 5.3 Poster, Freedom for Juvêncio Mazzarollo. Courtesy of the Mazzarollo family.

distributed pamphlets denouncing the verdict as "a violation of the freedom of the press and expression." By that same afternoon, graffiti spread across Curitiba and Foz do Iguaçu declaring "Down with the National Security Act! Free Juvêncio!" and "No More Dictatorship! Freedom for Juvêncio!"[36]

Juvêncio's imprisonment became emblematic of the larger struggle to end military rule, as letters of solidarity poured in from all over Brazil identifying him as a symbol of the fight for democracy. After Juvêncio had been in prison for five months, the prominent opposition lawyer Dalmo Dallari visited him and commented, "Mazzarollo, condemned by the LSN, is an active participant of the Brazilian political process, and his courage is being admired throughout Brazil, having his name transformed into a banner for those who want democratization in the country."[37] The National Labor Front similarly declared, "His imprisonment is even more proof that what is being called abertura is little more than a series of superficial acts to impress the international community."[38] A pamphlet put out by the Workers' Party (PT, Partido dos Trabalhadores) calling for a general strike on October 25 listed freedom for Juvêncio as the third demand—behind a denouncement of antiwage laws and unemployment, yet before union rights and direct elections.[39] In many ways, Juvêncio's saga had become synonymous with the broader arc of national opposition struggles.

As the abertura continued along its curvy path, Juvêncio's prospects of freedom suffered a serious setback. Approaching the end of his initial one-year sentence, Juvêncio appealed for release on parole in September 1983. In response, the Supreme Military Tribunal voted 7–4 to instead *increase* his sentence by an additional two years.[40] This ruling had a tremendous impact on Juvêncio, in terms of both his political convictions and his own psychological well-being. As he revealed in a personal letter, "I am just now starting to realize how serious my situation is. . . . It feels almost impossible to find any optimism about the future. What I see happening in Brazil is catastrophic. We are lost."[41] This experience and feeling of hopelessness stayed with Juvêncio for the rest of his life. His widow, Vilma Macedo, believes that his time in prison left profound scars on his soul, relating that Juvêncio once confided to her, "Whenever I wake up, sadness is already waiting for me."[42]

The increase in his sentence forced Juvêncio to confront a reality he had perhaps not yet fully considered. Rather than succumb to his newfound feelings of despair, he decided to take action. Emboldened by the contrast between his own repression and the abertura freedoms he perceived beyond his prison walls, Juvêncio staged a hunger strike. He went on strike October 23, 1983, writing that the authorities had "stupidly [robbed] me of my life for futile reasons. Nothing, absolutely nothing justifies such a severe punishment. I can no longer allow—by the ethical duty and through the body that God gave me—fascist inquisitors to make me into the grass on which they feed their sadism and that they carry out, at my expense, the role of oppressor for all society. . . . I have already suffered enough. The situation is unbearable. This must finally end."[43]

The hunger strike attracted national media attention and placed enough pressure on state authorities that Paraná's senator, José Richa, publicly declared his intent to intercede at the federal level.[44] Along with informing the nation of his personal struggle, Juvêncio sought to use his hunger strike as a means to protest the LSN and the continued existence of a repressive Brazilian state. Global human rights groups soon picked up the story of Juvêncio's hunger strike. Amnesty International mobilized a letter-writing campaign that sent thousands of letters from all over the world to Brazil's president, the minister of justice, and the minister of the interior.[45] And the Committee to Protect Journalists paired Juvêncio's case with a campaign to free Ranka Cicak, a Yugoslav journalist imprisoned for her criticism of the former president Josip Broz Tito.[46]

After sixteen days without food, Juvêncio ended the hunger strike, writing that it had served its purpose of bringing attention to his cause. Moreover, he reemphasized the ideology driving his actions, writing that "the right to information belongs to everyone; no man is free if he lacks the right to say and know the truth; no country is free when there is a law that punishes those who denounce a crime but does not punish the real criminals."[47]

By early 1984 Juvêncio's situation remained unchanged; although the abertura seemed to advance at the national level, he was not yet free. His patience depleted, Juvêncio decided to again take direct action. He began a second hunger strike on March 23, exactly a year and a half after his first day in prison. Claiming with "absolute certainty" that he was the victim of a terrible injustice, he vowed to only feed himself again as a free man: "Freedom or death. It is my choice. . . . I hope to survive, but that is now in the hands of Justice in which, despite everything, I am still required to trust."[48]

The second hunger strike mobilized an unprecedented showing of support across Brazil and beyond. The Board of Supervisors in Foz do Iguaçu voted unanimously to approve a motion of solidarity, declaring that "Juvêncio did nothing more than denounce corruption and take the side of the less fortunate." Members of Paraná's Legislative Assembly sent a commission to Brasília to lobby national authorities and redress the "national shame" unfolding in their state. The National Conference of Brazilian Bishops used its connections to rally support and attention. Brazil's most militant labor organization, the Unified Workers Central, circulated petitions demanding his release. Students throughout Brazil held rallies, and eight teenagers in Curitiba staged their own hunger strike in solidarity. And as far away as London, journalists and students at the British Communication School held assemblies and erected a protest camp.[49]

The message delivered by Juvêncio's second hunger strike resonated with a population exhausted by twenty years of dictatorship. To the delight of the embattled journalist and his supporters, the Supreme Court freed Juvêncio on April 6, 1984, ten days into his hunger strike. In a decision with clear implications for the future direction of Brazil, in the end the Supreme Court, a federal body, overturned the original sentence handed down by the military tribunal. The transition to civilian rule did not occur until the following March (in 1985), and direct elections for the presidency did not return until 1989. But Juvêncio's release in 1984 signified an important phase in Brazil's democratic opening. Sentenced in 1982 by a military tribunal, Juvêncio won his freedom two years later from a civilian court when a national solidarity movement

FIGURE 5.4 Juvêncio Mazzarollo arriving at the Foz do Iguaçu airport after his release from prison. Courtesy of the Mazzarollo family.

turned his prison sentence into a banner for Brazilian democracy. Juvêncio saw his repression as symptomatic of the suffering shared by all Brazilians, writing, "My freedom was a victory for all. It was a victory of the people and of Justice."[50] *Nosso Tempo*'s headline proclaimed "Vencemos"—"We Won." Newspapers across Brazil carried the message of Juvêncio's release, and hundreds of supporters gathered outside of his Curitiba prison to commemorate the conclusion of a long campaign that until that moment had provided very few moments worth celebrating.[51]

Writing as a liberated journalist for the first time in nearly two years, Juvêncio credited the solidarity movement for winning his freedom. He praised the efforts of opposition forces in Foz do Iguaçu, across Brazil, and throughout the world, saying that it was only through grassroots mobilization that "the last political prisoner in the country could leave from where, in justice, he should never have entered" (figure 5.4).[52]

Juvêncio was not a typical opposition figure. He grew up poor on a farm in Santa Catarina and worked as a field hand until going to university, where he trained to be a teacher. When he eventually made his way to Foz do Iguaçu to work as a journalist in the late 1970s, few could have guessed that this soft-spoken man of humble beginnings would gain international fame as the last political prisoner of Brazil's dictatorship. But his efforts to start a newspaper in Foz do Iguaçu at such a pivotal moment—for both the construction of the Itaipu dam and the official course of the abertura—set him on an unforeseen path.

Juvêncio's story offers two important insights. First, it opens a window into the experience and motivation of elites at a local level. While national leaders like President Figueiredo made gestures, even if just nominally, toward a peaceful transition of power, regional authorities did not necessarily follow suit. They had enjoyed relative autonomy throughout the previous two decades of military rule, and their attachment to power was not easily relinquished. Local elites like Mayor Cunha Vianna and Judge Kopytowsky were fully aware that their high commanders in Brasília and Rio de Janeiro publicly supported the policies of abertura; yet these authorities in Foz do Iguaçu repressed Juvêncio as if democratization had not yet reached their corner of Brazil. Their role in protecting the interests of the Itaipu dam surely gave them an added sense of immunity from the official process of abertura. In the early 1980s, Juvêncio and the Foz do Iguaçu elite inhabited the same city at the same time, yet their actions existed within entirely competing realities. This duality could not exist for long. As seen in the outpouring of solidarity to free Juvêncio, the opposition struggles throughout Brazil mobilized in hopes that their visions for democracy might soon become the dominant reality.

And, second, Juvêncio's saga as the last political prisoner expands on the underlying question of public opinion and legitimacy, perhaps in somewhat unexpected ways. If it seems as though this chapter has diverted our attention from the displaced communities to focus instead on the plight of one man, that is precisely the point. That is what happened in western Paraná. The original issue that landed Juvêncio in jail—the fight for land and justice at Itaipu—was soon overtaken by the story of the journalist imprisoned for writing about the farmers. On the heels of a movement that pitted a diverse array of rural Brazilians against the dam and the dictatorship, a new narrative took its place. To be sure, public opinion had largely taken the side of the farmers in their standoff against Itaipu, yet when the protest camp ended, and especially after the 1982 flood, the farmers no longer occupied headlines with the same frequency. The defense of rural livelihoods—a deeply complex task, as we have seen—proved far less palatable to mainstream audiences than the defense of an innocent journalist. Once the Itaipu dam no longer served as a common enemy for the farmers and their political allies, opposition forces found fewer reasons to mobilize around the plight of rural Brazilians. Juvêncio, in contrast, resonated as a clear symbol of Brazil's fight for democracy. As a prisoner, Juvêncio stood as proof of the dictatorship's insincere commitment to handing over power, and as a journalist, his writings embodied the growing call for a new political order. In both senses, Juvêncio achieved a level of visibility above anything reached by the nearby farmers.

For understanding the constructions of legitimacy in the Brazilian countryside, it is fundamental to see how the marginalization of rural groups can emerge from allies in civil society. Although of rural origins himself, Juvêncio did not spend his years in prison as the son of farmers but as a journalist. That distinction increased his profile within Brazil and connected him to a global network of activists. And his European heritage made it even easier for him to become a face of antidictatorship campaigns. As we shall see in the remaining chapters of this book, the visibility attained by Juvêncio, and to a lesser extent that of the landholding farmers he wrote about, contrasted starkly with the perception of illegitimacy projected onto the rural migrants and peasants displaced by Itaipu.

CHAPTER 6

"Men without a Country"

*Agrarian Resettlement and
the Strategies of Frontier Colonization*

We were all tricked with photographs, and with color images.... I was
tricked. They told us that here we'd have everything, cars, medicine,
schools, all that. What happened? All that we got, with all their promises,
was sickness, death, and despair in the middle of this jungle.
—FARMER INTERVIEWED IN FÜLLGRAF, *OS DESAPROPRIADOS*

The above quotation comes from a 1983 interview with a farmer who, after
being displaced by the Itaipu dam, relocated to a government-sponsored
agrarian colony in the Amazon. The man and his family joined the thousands
of rural people from western Paraná who resettled in various colonization
projects throughout Brazil. This process occurred while tens of thousands
more followed a similar pattern westward across the border in Paraguay. His
feelings of deceit and despair reflect a common narrative from those on the
front lines of the military's incursions into new frontier zones—both within
Brazil and on foreign soil. This chapter takes a step back from the rural mobilizations and political protests to examine the Itaipu dam's importance for
the dictatorship's policies of agricultural and territorial expansion. The construction of Itaipu and its eventual flood triggered two major demographic
shifts: the migration of Brazilians into Paraguay (those who came to be known
as *Brasiguaios*) and the resettlement of displaced farmers into the far reaches
of Brazil. Through these rural population shifts, Itaipu helped extend Brazil's
territorial reach westward into Paraguay and north and northeastward into
its own internal frontier zones.

For the Brazilian government, Itaipu provided a political entry point to
Paraguay while creating a massive physical presence directly on the border
itself. As shown in chapter 1, the 1960s frontier conflict at Guaíra not only
secured Brazil near-unilateral control of the eventual hydroelectric project
but also forced the Paraguayan regime to change its border policies. As part

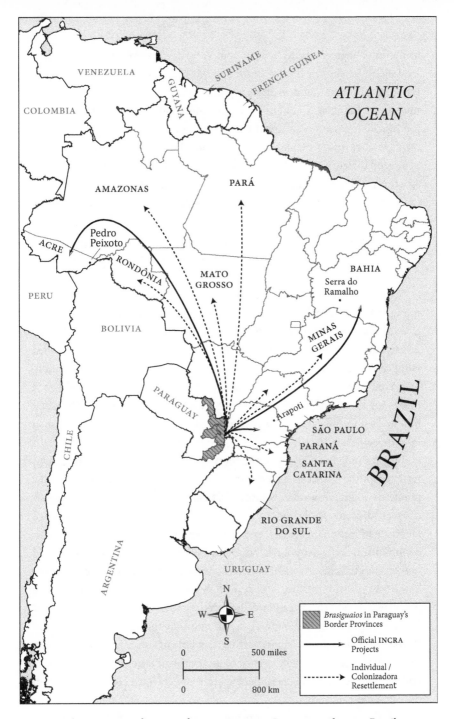

MAP 4 The trajectory of migrant farmers to eastern Paraguay and across Brazil.
Courtesy of Gabriel Moss.

of the initial agreement to build Itaipu, Paraguay had to legalize the sale of land along its eastern border to foreigners. The dam opened the floodgate for rural migration, and in the early 1970s, Brazilians began relocating en masse into Paraguay's eastern border region. With the frontier now open, the Brazilian government urged its citizens to cross into Paraguay with the promise of cheap, available, and fertile lands. For the expansionist ideology of Brazil's dictatorship, Itaipu served the dual function of erasing border restrictions and creating a new wave of potential migrants; many of the Brazilian farmers displaced by Itaipu had little recourse but to relocate to nearby Paraguay. Brasiguaio enclaves thrived to the point that by the late 1990s an estimated 450,000 Brazilians were living in eastern Paraguay—representing 60 percent of the region's population and nearly 10 percent of Paraguay's entire population.[1]

When Brazilian-run soy plantations began to thrive in Paraguay during the 1980s and 1990s, Brasiguaios became synonymous with wealthy and exploitative agriculture barons. Yet historically the majority of Brazilian immigrants in Paraguay have been small-scale farmers. Like many of their impoverished Paraguayan neighbors, these Brasiguaios faced constant marginalization. Triggered by the Itaipu dam, Brasiguaios functioned as agricultural shock troops for Brazil's dictatorship. They were pushed across the border to settle new lands only to be discarded once a new class of Brazilian elites established booming agribusinesses.

By reframing Brasiguaio immigration within the logic of Itaipu, this chapter exposes the extent to which territorial expansion and a desire to incorporate new agricultural lands formed a distinct part of the military's development ideology. As previously discussed, Brazil's dictatorship relied on a Doctrine of National Security (DSN) that combined developmentalism, anticommunism, and a geopolitical vision of the country's ascension as a world power. The concept of fronteiras vivas (living borders) served as a centerpiece of the DSN, envisioning Brazil's sphere of power to include any territory where its citizens lived. The question of borders became especially important for Latin American military regimes in the 1960s, as the specter of the Cuban Revolution made all rural zones seem susceptible to guerrilla insurgency. The DSN sought to increase the presence of the Brazilian state in these vulnerable regions while offering material benefits to dissuade local communities from potential radicalization.

Rural Brazilians acted as the primary conduits of the border-expansion process. With government promises of land, infrastructure, and an improved livelihood, unprecedented numbers of farmers left for distant agrarian projects. Many scholars discuss agriculture as a colonization tool *within* Brazil, above all in the Amazonian regions where the military regime incentivized the relocation of millions of farmers. Yet few have analyzed the similar processes that took place *beyond* the country's own borders. The case of Itaipu shows how the strategy of frontier colonization developed as an internal and an external process. Borders, in this sense, served as both physical and ideological spaces that could fulfill the military's geopolitical ambitions. By reframing the narratives of Brasiguaios and northern resettlement as parallel components of the same history, we see how rural landscapes—and the importance of land more broadly—played a fundamental role in the development policies of Brazil's dictatorship.

The second narrative of this chapter relates to how the Brazilian government sought to relocate the displaced farmers in so-called colonization projects. The Itaipu dam must be analyzed in the context of the military's 1964 Land Statute that, among other goals, aimed to uproot farmers in southern and northeastern Brazil and resettle them along the central-western borderlands and in the Amazon basin.[2] This policy sought to plug the country's vast frontiers, considered "paths of penetration" vulnerable to foreign threats, while simultaneously expanding modernized agriculture into new regions.[3] The dictatorship's agrarian technocrats and development planners viewed these farmers as an easily deployable source of agricultural labor. Much like how the government used Brasiguaios to shore up Brazilian influence across foreign borders, it also sent peasant farmers into Brazil's backlands to settle regions long considered internal frontier zones.

Despite statements that Itaipu tried to resettle the displaced farmers on nearby lands, documentary evidence shows a concerted program of sending the region's more marginalized communities to northern agricultural colonies. This process was carried out jointly by Itaipu, private colonization companies (*colonizadoras*), and the National Institute for Colonization and Agrarian Reform (INCRA). The government's focus on northern relocation helps explain why, despite having a budget that swelled to nearly US$20 billion, Itaipu resisted increasing its expropriation prices. Chapters 2 and 3 argued that, in part, the posturing over land prices resulted from the military regime's attempt to navigate the abertura while retaining a maximum perception of power over opposition forces. The present chapter shows how the low prices also satisfied the dictatorship's goals for agrarian colonization: offering below-market compensation packages—or, in the case of landless peasants, no compensation at all—precluded many from staying in western Paraná. As a result, rural families had few options but to accept a relocation to new agricultural colonies.

The peasants, day laborers, and sharecroppers sent to INCRA's relocation projects belonged to the poorest subset of the western Paraná countryside. With no legal property, the landless farmers were the last people accounted for in Itaipu's expropriation process. Moreover, they represented the region's most recent wave of migration, having arrived in the previous decade, largely from the central and northern states of Minas Gerais and Bahia. This stood in contrast to most of the Euro-descendant farmers, who came from southern states in the 1950s and 1960s. At Itaipu many of the white landed farmers received financial indemnification and bought new properties throughout southern Brazil, often through colonizadoras approved by INCRA. But the younger, darker-skinned peasants had neither the explicit (financial) nor implicit (racial) attributes that served as criteria for staying in southern Brazil. With the goal of northern frontier settlement, the government saw a clear logic and justification in relocating poor migrants who had relatively recently left their previous homes. In the aftermath of Itaipu, all of the displaced families experienced varying degrees of trauma; even the farmers who found new lands nearby in Paraná still confronted profound material and personal hardships. Yet only landless communities had to relocate to government-sponsored projects thousands of kilometers away.

In the end, farmers uprooted by Itaipu went to three main resettlement colonies: one in the Amazonian region of Acre, one in the northeastern state of Bahia, and another within Paraná. The Brazilian government and Itaipu originally intended a much higher rate of resettlement, but they ultimately sent less than 10 percent of the estimated forty thousand displaced people to these three projects. The relatively small percentage of displaced farmers who wound up in agricultural colonies—at least compared to the number originally envisioned by authorities—resulted from the Justice and Land Movement (MJT) and its public pressure to receive lands nearby. But the success of the MJT did not cover all participants. The landless farmers sent to the colonies suffered tremendously as they confronted unfamiliar lands, often without the government services promised to them. Some settlers died from diseases and unsanitary conditions, most lacked adequate nutrition, and many others left the projects after only a few years.

This chapter links numerous processes that unfolded simultaneously, showing how the mobilizations of farmers against Itaipu overlapped with the development and agricultural goals of the Brazilian state. As farmers organized in western Paraná to defend their visions of land and justice, the military regime initiated policies to dissolve local land conflicts while deploying mass numbers of rural Brazilians across international and internal borders. For the government, the harsh conditions awaiting these settler farmers proved inconsequential compared to their role in laying the groundwork for Brazil's expanding agricultural reach. Seen together, the dual narrative of Brasiguaios and northern colonization reveals Itaipu's role in the physical and conceptual construction of frontiers. At the nexus of state development and agrarian expansion, the Itaipu dam served as a central arc in the territorialization of Brazil.

The title of this chapter comes from how the term *Brasiguaio* first came into public usage. At a 1985 community meeting, a Brazilian peasant living in Paraguay told the Brazilian congressman Sérgio Cruz, "I mean to say that we don't have rights as Paraguayans because we aren't Paraguayan; we don't have rights as Brazilians because we abandoned the country. But tell me something: in the end, who are we?" In response, Cruz declared, "You are Brasiguaios, a mix of Brazilians with Paraguayans, men without a country."[4] The notion of existing as people without a country helps explain the history of these two groups of settlers. In both cases, the federal government deployed and essentially abandoned rural Brazilians in frontier zones. So although their bodies and labor helped consolidate a Brazilian presence in new territories, rural communities were rendered invisible and isolated from this expanding state. Moreover, the reference to all Brasiguaios as *men* without a country further obscured the presence of women; as was the case with female participation in the MJT protest camps, women migrated, worked, and sacrificed alongside their male family members. Both within and across Brazil's borders, women—and rural women in particular—experienced several levels of invisibility.

As described above, Brasiguaios felt excluded from both Brazil and Paraguay. The internal settlers, for their part, faced the added challenge of feeling rejected by Brazilian society despite living within its national boundaries. The lack of the promised infrastructure in frontier colonies suggested that the military regime saw these rural Brazilians not as citizens worthy of rights and protections but as an easily discardable resource. Whether they had moved across foreign borders or within Brazil's own territory, the migrant farmers displaced by the Itaipu dam—an already marginalized sector of society— experienced new forms of invisibility that left them even further excised from the national polity.

As discussed in the introduction to this book, Rob Nixon has argued that nations are built not on a common idea of belonging but through the active unimagining of certain communities.[5] The history of Brasiguaios and settler farmers builds on Nixon's thesis: the ability of a nation to *conceptually* unimagine certain sectors of its population is linked to its ability to *physically* displace people far from the public eye. As with most large-scale development projects, the unimagining produced by Itaipu extended well beyond the flood zone. What makes Itaipu an especially compelling case is that the conceptual and physical unimagining of communities in western Paraná pushed them across foreign and domestic frontiers. Rendered invisible by their own government, these "men without a country" experienced displacement as a long and complex process, and the traumas of Itaipu's flood often continued into the challenges of frontier life.

Brasiguaios and the "Occupation" of Eastern Paraguay

The 1966 Act of Iguaçu catalyzed Brasiguaio migration and allowed Brazil's dictatorship to take a two-pronged strategy for settling the border region. First, foreigners could now legally purchase Paraguayan frontier lands, leading to a steady stream of Brazilians across the border. Second, the construction of the Itaipu dam in the 1970s left thousands of rural Brazilians with no land and very little money. Uprooted from their homes, many displaced Brazilians had few options but to resettle in Paraguay. One migrant recalled:

> I came to Paraguay because my property along the Paraná River was flooded; when Itaipu was built all of our lands were flooded. And since we were a large family, we were left with very little since the price that they paid us was not equivalent to the real value of the land, but rather to their own estimations. . . . Since we had little money and the land [in Paraguay] was cheap and had lots of timber, we decided to leave for Paraguay.[6]

With Paraguay's frontier zone now open, the Brazilian government actively encouraged its citizens to move across the border. Newspapers and radio stations in southern Brazil broadcast propaganda encouraging settlement in Paraguay. These ads focused largely on the low cost of land, ranging anywhere from one-sixth to one-tenth of the price in Brazil.[7] With funding from the World Bank and the Inter-American Development Bank, Paraguay's government instituted tax programs in the border region to incentivize migration. Along with favorable credit rates, eastern Paraguay offered the added bonus of zero income tax and a minimal—and rarely enforced—land tax. Brazilians further benefited from the lack of an export tariff, meaning that all production on Paraguayan lands flowed back to Brazil untaxed. Smallholders in Brazil became very receptive to their government's publicity campaign and often saw Paraguay as a land of opportunity (figure 6.1). As Gerd Kohlhepp observes, migration to eastern Paraguay not only offered farmers the prospect of higher-quality lands but also included "the added allure of social mobility in a nascent border community."[8]

Take, for example, the case of one Brazilian who relocated to Paraguay in 1977. After selling his 17.5-hectare plot of land to Itaipu for Cr$520,000—roughly US$37,000—he moved to Paraguay and bought 75 hectares for only Cr$230,000, around US$16,000. With the remaining profit, he bought a house, planted twenty-five hectares of soybeans, and still had a bit left over to buy a tractor the following year.[9] This type of story most assuredly spread through rural Brazil and motivated thousands of farmers to seek new opportunities in Paraguay. In turn, the number of Brasiguaio settlers increased dramatically. As late as 1969, there had been fewer than 11,000 Brazilians living in eastern Paraguay; once Itaipu's expropriations began, less than a decade later, that figure jumped to nearly 150,000.[10]

Migrant farmers rarely achieved the sort of success promised by government bulletins and colonization companies. One account observed that many Brazilians in Paraguay "don't have any hope of acquiring land" and were living as either itinerant day laborers (boias-frias), landless peasants, or farmers with miniscule tracts of land.[11] Most Brasiguaios had to navigate illegal land contracts, a corrupt agrarian bureaucracy, and the threat of expulsion from their recently acquired lands—almost exclusively to make room for a new class of Brazilian soy magnates. Even on foreign soil, many Brasiguaios continued to face the same issues that had led them to leave their home country in the first place.

Although Brasiguaio settlement seemed to favor the Brazilian state, it also served the interests of Paraguay's dictatorship. Determined to "modernize" the countryside, Alfredo Stroessner saw the type of subsistence and small-scale agriculture practiced by the indigenous and peasant communities as limiting the country's productive capacity. The Paraguayan regime thus considered Brasiguaios a valuable import to bring new technologies, agricultural know-how, and access to capital.[12] When asked about the growing presence of Brazilian farmers, Alberto Fernandez, a captain in the Paraguayan army and director of a private land settlement company, proclaimed, "We're simply doing what Brazil already did when it stimulated the arrival of Italian, German, and Japanese settlers to its country."[13] Under the auspices of the Institute for Rural Well-Being in the mid-1960s, the Paraguayan government sold off

FIGURE 6.1 *Brasiguaio* farmers harvest mint in the Paraguayan border department of Alto Paraná in the early 1970s. Reproduced from Szekut and Eremites de Oliveira, "'Aquí todos somos migrantes,'" 340.

state-owned lands to high-ranking officials and politicians, who frequently auctioned them off to Brazilian colonists.[14] Local elites, including members of the military and state functionaries, capitalized on opportunities in a poorly regulated environment. Nepotism became especially rampant in the early years of border settlement, as well-connected bureaucrats received privileged jobs in charge of land speculation and distribution. One report claimed that "those in charge of controlling and taxing the area quickly became millionaires, or basically that instead of actually administering, all the officials charged taxes however they pleased without drawing up any legal documents."[15] In this manner, the collusion of state and local elites exacerbated an unequal form of land distribution throughout the border region.

Although a small subset of migrants benefited from the expanding foreign enclave, most Brasiguaios confronted a series of lingering problems. Government employees, for example, forced many farmers to pay exorbitant amounts of money to receive their migration papers. In the words of one observer, the settlers "lived between illegality and permanent extortion from the Paraguayan authorities."[16] Large numbers of Brazilian immigrants also struggled to gain legal ownership of lands they bought either from the Paraguayan state or through colonizadora companies in Brazil. One such company, Industrial Mbaracayú s.a., allegedly sold properties to nearly eight thousand Brazilian families only to then deny them the actual land deed.[17] A *Folha de São Paulo* article explained that 70 percent of Brazilians living in Paraguay did not have the legal title to their lands and were instead forced to work as tenant farmers, sharecroppers, or itinerant day laborers.[18] Another article cited an example from the Paraguayan municipality of Puerto Sece, where four hundred Brasiguaio families had paid four times for the same land to four different administrators.[19] Despite the promises of a better life, many farmers found themselves, in the words of one headline, living "in a Paraguayan hell."[20]

Given the challenges faced by the initial wave of immigrants, and their role in laying down the first roots of what later became a thriving soy monopoly, the early Brasiguaios served as a form of agricultural shock troops. Simply put, they were mobilized and exploited in order to clear lands, settle farms, and establish a base from which larger development could take hold. Like the farmers displaced by Itaipu and sent to faraway resettlement projects, Brasiguaios functioned as a deployable agrarian tool for the expansion of Brazil's territorial influence.

In Brazil both the dictatorship and opposition forces made explicit links between Brasiguaios and the northern resettlement projects. In 1973 Brazil's surveillance agency, the National Information Service (SNI), commissioned a confidential survey of settler farmers in Paraguay. The report asked Brasiguaios why, given the challenges of life in Paraguay, they did not simply go to the new agricultural colonies in the Amazon. Some claimed that the cheap lands kept them in Paraguay, while others told of hearing stories that Brazilians who went to the Amazon died of yellow fever and had been "completely abandoned" by the Brazilian government.[21] This survey shows that Brazil's military regime knew of the Brasiguaios' hardships and, moreover, that the government attempted to keep sending these farmers to regions that aligned with national interests. Critics of the dictatorship also held up the mistreatment of Brasiguaios as proof of the injustices of military rule. At a transnational meeting of Latin American opposition groups, the assembly denounced "the predatory occupation of a new political and agrarian frontier, like what already happened in western Paraná and which is [also] happening again in the Amazon."[22] Whether they moved across international borders or within Brazil's own frontier zones, settler farmers factored into the policies and resulting criticisms of Brazil's dictatorship.

Advances in agricultural technologies accelerated the settlement of Paraguay's border region and triggered new conflicts among local communities. The biggest influence came from the introduction of mechanized soybean cultivation in the 1970s.[23] Because the industrialized production of soybeans required relatively low amounts of manual labor, small- and medium-scale farmers could expand their lands under cultivation without needing to hire more workers. This facilitated a new wave of land grabbing by Brazilian farmers that further marginalized local Paraguayans. In response, Paraguayan peasants formed the Agrarian Leagues, a grassroots campaign that government authorities saw as a threat to national security. In many instances, the Stroessner regime deployed the army to expel the peasant collectives. In one example from 1970, Paraguayan soldiers forcefully removed and set fire to the houses of 1,300 families in the border municipality of Yhú in order to confiscate their lands.[24] Once the state kicked out local Paraguayans, military personnel seized the lands and sold them off as private holdings—often to Brazilian colonists.

For their role in territorial colonization, Brasiguaios incurred the hostility of local communities. Paraguayan peasants denounced Brazilian migrants as "colonizers, invaders and destroyers of nature and of Paraguayan culture."[25] In rural Paraguay, Brasiguaios became the symbol of the so-called Brazilian invasion. In a 1977 news article, a local farmer described the devastation brought by Brazilian immigrants: "The small homes [of Paraguayan farmers] are being destroyed. They'll be built again, but only to be torn apart again. The whole thing keeps repeating."[26] The nature of frontier expansion meant that even if many of the early Brasiguaios came from similar socioeconomic backgrounds as Paraguayan farmers, they nonetheless contributed to a process of displacement and repression. These settlement patterns formed an ongoing cycle in the reorientation of eastern Paraguay. As more small-scale Brasiguaios settled in Paraguay, their presence pushed out local farmers, whose subsequent mobilizations stood as justification for the government to further appropriate peasant lands. As soy grew in importance and as land consolidated in the hands of a new rural elite, small farmers—Brazilian and Paraguayan alike—lost their lands at an increasing rate. One Brazilian settler told the *Folha de*

Londrina that despite owning his farm in Paraguay for fifteen years, he was expelled to make room for a new plantation, declaring that the border region now belonged "in the hands of the big landowners, and [us smallholders] won't last very long."[27]

These new agricultural oligarchies were composed almost exclusively of Brazilians. In an underlying paradox of Brasiguaio immigration, Brazilians living in Paraguay wound up expelled by their own compatriots. As we shall see at the end of this chapter, the mistreatment of Brasiguaios did not only occur on foreign lands. When migrants began returning to Brazil in the early 1980s, their fellow citizens routinely treated them as unwelcome pariahs. The countryside they had left behind in the previous decade was in a process of transformation, and they again found themselves in the middle of agrarian struggles that extended from western Paraná throughout the far reaches of Brazil.

Brazil's Internal Frontiers

The start of Brasiguaio immigration in the early 1970s occurred as the Brazilian dictatorship initiated one of the most ambitious state-run development programs in the country's history. Anna Luiza Ozorio de Almeida calls the 1970s the "Decade of Colonization," highlighting the Amazon frontier in particular for receiving almost three million people.[28] The desire to settle Brazil's frontiers existed for most of the twentieth century. In the influential 1935 book *Projeção continental do Brasil*, the army captain Mário Travassos charted Brazil's territorial expansion and rise to continental supremacy. Along with urging national development toward the resource-rich lands of Bolivia, Travassos saw the domination of the Amazon as key to Brazil's hegemony in South America.[29] Travassos's views had lasting effects on Brazil's geopolitical policies. His writings greatly influenced General Golbery do Couto e Silva— the dictatorship's leading ideologue in the 1960s and 1970s—and also paved the way for a series of initiatives prior to the military taking power. The presidency of Juscelino Kubitschek (1956–1961) erected the new national capital inland at Brasília, which the Brasília-Belem Highway then connected to the Amazon. Advances in transportation technologies allowed the Brazilian state to more easily access and develop the Amazonian regions long considered Brazil's last frontier.

Northern development accelerated greatly after the military regime took power in 1964. Under the DSN, military leaders gave unparalleled attention and resources to Brazil's borders with neighboring Latin American nations and also its own internal "backlands." The dictatorship saw agriculture as a tool of frontier colonization that could resolve land conflicts in central and southern Brazil. Ozorio de Almeida argues that territorial expansion in the 1970s offered "a way to circumvent the land problem, taking the landless to frontier regions and leaving property structures in the rest of the country untouched."[30] Other scholars observe that the resettlement process "represented a path of least resistance" to address the lack of land reform in Brazil.[31] Moreover, the northward agricultural expansion provided a vehicle for establishing a government presence to protect against guerrilla insurgencies like the Araguaia War in the northern state of Goiás in the early 1970s.[32]

In June 1970 Emílio Médici, the dictatorship's fifth military president, announced plans for the construction of the Trans-Amazonian Highway and the National Integration Plan (PIN, Plano de Integração Nacional). The PIN aimed to settle a hundred thousand families in Brazil's northern regions by the middle of the decade.[33] In the words of one government report, the PIN sought to "mark, by the presence of Brazilian men in Amazonian lands, the conquest for themselves and for their country, of that which always belonged to them, so that no one would ever dare to contest them on this objective."[34] Although the PIN never fulfilled its ambitious goal of relocating a hundred thousand families, it nonetheless provided the financial and political impetus for a massive demographic shift.

Table 6.1 shows the changes in rural population by region in the 1960s and 1970s, reflecting the trend toward northern colonization. After seeing the country's largest rise during the 1960s, the southern states then experienced the sharpest decline in the following decade. Rural population loss in the south and southeast occurred as the north and northeast became the only regions in all of Brazil where the number of rural inhabitants increased during the 1970s. The effect on the southern countryside especially impacted the state of Paraná. After seeing a net growth of almost 1.5 million people in the 1960s, Paraná's rural population then dropped by nearly 1.3 million a decade later.[35] These shifts also resulted from a steep rise in rural-to-urban migration brought about by the introduction of mechanized agriculture and the subsequent loss of farming jobs. In the context of this changing countryside, the construction of the Itaipu dam and the displacement of tens of thousands of people presented the government with a large pool of potential migrants for its goals of northward expansion.

Itaipu's leaders and federal authorities had been operating behind the scenes since the mid-1970s to send farmers to the northern colonization proj-

TABLE 6.1 Changes in rural population by region

REGIONS	1960–1970	1970–1980
North	383,076	924,532
Northeast	1,945,981	957,853
Center-west	720,432	−178,430
Southeast	−1,224,574	−1,963,936
South	1,826,351	−2,023,200
Brazil (total)	3,651,266	−2,283,181

Source: Ozorio de Almeida, *The Colonization of the Amazon*, 18.

ects originally envisioned by the PIN. For many years, the farmers' movement at Itaipu delayed the efforts to simply ship farmers northward. On the eve of the Foz do Iguaçu protest camp in March 1981, many of the displaced families still had no idea where they would relocate. For the landed farmers who soon won increased compensation packages and could afford to buy new lands, the issue of resettlement proved less troublesome. But the region's landless peasants, sharecroppers, and day laborers now anxiously focused on whether the government would provide new lands, where these potential lands would be located, and what type of life awaited them on these settlement projects.

The fact that a relatively low number of the displaced ultimately went to these agricultural colonies—less than 10 percent of those living in Itaipu's flood zone—resulted from the MJT's campaign to win higher land prices, which allowed farmers to find new lands nearby. Many bought new property within the state of Paraná. Others left for Paraguay or purchased land in states throughout Brazil, including Rio Grande do Sul, São Paulo, and Minas Gerais, among others.[36] Yet the negotiations between Itaipu and the farmers' leadership left thousands of landless Brazilians with neither a compensation package nor a promised relocation site. Barely two weeks after the Foz do Iguaçu protest demobilized, the government began a yearlong process of resettling the region's landless families. In total, authorities sent nearly four thousand people displaced by Itaipu to three main colonization projects (Table 6.2). Far

TABLE 6.2 Statistics on three main resettlement projects

	SERRA DO RAMALHO	PEDRO PEIXOTO	ARAPOTI
State	Bahia	Acre	Paraná
Distance from Foz do Iguaçu	2,200 kilometers	3,700 kilometers	700 kilometers
Size of project	257,000 hectares	296,243 hectares	3,876 hectares
Number of Itaipu settlers	72 families	191 families	401 families
	399 people	1,193 people	2,390 people
Average land claimed	20 hectares	19 hectares	10 hectares

Source: Itaipu Binational Documentation Center, "Desaproriações, área do reservatório (margen esquerda)," 1983 report, 4148.187–195.

from the idyllic conditions depicted by federal authorities, the relocation sites contained lands ill suited for farming, and the projects' lack of infrastructure resulted in problems of disease and malnutrition. The remainder of this chapter explores the history of how farmers who had already experienced the traumas of displacement now confronted an additional set of challenges in the resettlement colonies.

From its inception, the MJT demanded new lands within Paraná. Largely resigned to the eventual flooding of their own lands, the MJT farmers lobbied Itaipu and INCRA to acquire nearby properties for displaced farmers. In response, Itaipu made a series of public statements attempting to deflect criticisms by showing that it did "everything possible to benefit the expropriated" and that the military regime remained committed to "giving [farmers] the humane and Christian treatment that they deserve."[37] Claiming to have fully explored the options of finding nearby lands, Itaipu declared it nearly impossible to relocate families within Paraná. Extensive documentation from within Itaipu, however, disproves the statements that land within Paraná simply was not available.

Throughout the entirety of its standoff with the mobilized farmers, Itaipu said that it was working closely with the federal government to find a solution that would satisfy the displaced farmers. Yet from the very beginning of the expropriation process, Itaipu's behind-the-scenes deliberations suggest the Binational had only briefly explored the possibility of finding new lands within Paraná. Documentary evidence also reveals the underlying motivation to send the farmers far from their flooded homes. In the middle of 1978, Itaipu began discussing the situation of the displaced farmers with INCRA, the government branch legally responsible for the farmers' relocation. Very quickly it became clear that INCRA had little desire, and even fewer resources, to process the situation at Itaipu. In particular, INCRA cited its previous difficulties in relocating farmers displaced by the Sobradinho dam in the northeastern state of Bahia.[38] On the heels of INCRA's reluctance, Itaipu's leaders began to shift their attention toward colonization projects in the north.

The correspondence archive of Itaipu's executive office shows that around this time the Binational received numerous proposals from different colonizadoras. These colonizadoras boasted of their successful track record in building agricultural colonies in regions throughout Brazil, especially in the Amazon, and even mentioned their influence in passing land laws favorable to new projects.[39] The Sinop Company, for example, described its ability to help colonize the Amazon and made an explicit appeal to the development goals of the military regime, writing, "We must send Brazilian settlers to the regions that make up [the nation's] 'geo-economic and demographic' holes."[40] These letters seemed to accelerate the pursuit of northern projects, leading Itaipu's director, General José Costa Cavalcanti, to observe that "the participation of private initiatives . . . will help solve the situation of families that must be resettled."[41] The Binational soon brought in private corporations and government authorities to help plan the northward relocation.

Despite the inclination to send farmers to northern settlement projects, an underlying dynamic of racial and class disparity still meant that certain sectors of the displaced could stay in Paraná. At a December 1978 meeting in Rio de Janeiro between the leaderships of Itaipu and INCRA, General Cavalcanti stated that "men accustomed to working the fertile lands of Paraná are not prepared to go to the Amazon." Itaipu's legal director, Paulo da Cunha, elaborated by declaring that the small amount of land that *was* available in Paraná should go to the older farmers "who do not have the courage to confront a new region."[42] The history of settlement in Paraná meant that the older farmers had almost all migrated from the southern states of Rio Grande do Sul and Santa Catarina, while the younger ones had more recently come from Minas Gerais and Bahia. This acted as a thinly veiled acknowledgment that the older, whiter, and title-holding settlers could stay nearby, while the younger, darker-skinned, and poorer farmers should be sent to the government's frontier projects. As shown earlier, supporters of the farmers' movement often invoked this same racialized narrative to argue that the Euro-descendant families should remain in Paraná. With both the federal government and sympathetic politicians implying that material and social attributes should determine which farmers could stay in Paraná, it became even harder for the region's landless families to avoid the northern agricultural colonies.

At a follow-up to the previous gathering in Rio de Janeiro, representatives of eight different colonizadoras met with Itaipu and INCRA to discuss the role of private companies in relocating the displaced farmers.[43] Along with setting in motion the eventual choice of the three main government-run resettlement projects, this meeting offers further insight into the logic of the military regime's agrarian policies. General Cavalcanti opened by welcoming the colonizadora directors, many of whom he considered friends from his tenure as minister of the interior. Having collaborated with these companies on previous projects in the Amazon, Cavalcanti reiterated that he "always had more faith in private initiatives than in the abilities of government agencies." Cavalcanti and his colleagues then outlined the logistics of how the colonizadoras could work in tandem with INCRA to relocate the farmers, discussing details of the communities themselves and the timelines for relocation and financial payments.

In the years to follow, many expropriated farmers heeded INCRA's publicity campaign and purchased lands, through colonizadoras, in projects throughout Brazil. Although the private projects did not necessarily offer better conditions than those eventually found at INCRA's three relocation sites, the choice to even pursue the colonizadora option remained available only to those who received financial compensation from Itaipu. Beginning in 1979, Itaipu disseminated widely a list of colonizadora projects approved, and ostensibly regulated, by INCRA. Speaking with politicians and media outlets, Itaipu repeated its preference for paying the farmers and giving them the "right to choose freely" from various options on the open market.[44] Private companies made these same claims and sought to capitalize on the uncertainty pervading the entire borderlands. One company told the São Paulo–based *Jornal da Tarde*, "If farmers don't want to go to Paraguay, they still can't stay in Paraná. . . . The North of the country has the benefit of larger tracts of land at competitive prices."[45] This echoed the colonization strategy initially used to attract settlers to Paraguay, as the promise of cheap lands surely resonated with impoverished rural

Brazilians. Publicity for northern projects described the benefits and services awaiting farmers. All of the INCRA-approved private projects would supposedly include roads, schools, hospitals, churches, banks, and the infrastructure to give "farmers and their families the support necessary [to maintain] a community-centered life."[46] But like the experience of Brasiguaios across foreign borders, the farmers within Brazil soon learned firsthand that the reality of frontier life rarely aligned with its idyllic representation.

Throughout the end of 1979 and into 1980, the question of relocation remained a core pillar of the fight against Itaipu. In a letter to the president of Brazil and to the ministers of agriculture and the interior, the farmers demanded resettlement options within Paraná.[47] When the MJT officially formed at the Santa Helena land encampment in July 1980, the protest's first public statement attacked the government's relocation policies: "They want to expel us to Paraguay or to the Amazon. Because with the money they've offered we'll never be able to buy new lands here in the region, and for the resettlement in Paraná, which is our greatest desire, absolutely nothing has yet to be done. . . . WE WANT LAND IN PARANÁ. DO NOT EXPEL US. WE WANT TO PLANT AND HARVEST, BUT ONLY IN PARANÁ."[48]

As discussed in chapter 3, the demands relating to agrarian reform and "land-for-land" within Paraná faded away during the fifteen-day Santa Helena encampment. As the protest gained greater support and mainstream political traction, the movement's leadership of landed farmers and religious allies focused on the issue of expropriation prices. The MJT opted to mobilize for financial compensation rather than land-based demands, and the final agreement with Itaipu dealt almost exclusively with how much Itaipu would pay for different plots of flooded land.[49] In the face of government programs determined to send them away, the resettlement colonies became increasingly likely destinations for the region's peasant farmers, who had seen the possibility of winning nearby lands dissipate at the Santa Helena camp.

Barely two months after the Santa Helena protest, Itaipu announced that settlers could now leave for the colonization sites.[50] One was the Serra do Ramalho project in the northeastern state of Bahia. And in a slight concession to the farmers' long-standing demand, INCRA established a second colony called Arapoti in the northwestern interior of Paraná.[51] Although Arapoti satisfied the farmers' demand to receive land within Paraná, it suffered from the same lack of resources as the northern colonization projects. With the Bahia and Arapoti colonies ready, Itaipu and INCRA explored options for other relocation sites, giving particular consideration to lands in Mato Grosso and Minas Gerais.[52] In the end, however, the government chose a third project called Pedro Peixoto in the Amazonian state of Acre, one of the northernmost regions of the country, situated over four thousand kilometers from western Paraná.

Resettlement Projects

Between May 1981 and June 1982, INCRA transferred 3,982 people from their homes in western Paraná to the three resettlement projects (figure 6.2). For the relocation process, the government provided Cr$40 million of financing, fifty INCRA employees, and the use of 136 buses and 219 trucks.[53]

The projects in Bahia and Acre were the first to receive farmers displaced by Itaipu. These initiatives originally began in 1975 and 1977, respectively— well before the dam's expropriation conflict became a national issue.[54] But it was only in the immediate aftermath of the MJT that INCRA began sending hundreds of Paraná families to these sites thousands of kilometers away. The first caravan to Serra do Ramalho in Bahia departed less than ten days after the end of the Foz do Iguaçu protest encampment. A few weeks later, buses began taking farmers on the weeklong drive to Acre. Critics saw this as a strategy to further clamp down on the grassroots mobilization that had recently taken place in front of Itaipu's construction site. Pastor Werner Fuchs, a leader of the farmers' movement, characterized the immediate northern resettlement as an effort "to empty western Paraná of its current social tension."[55] In the aftermath of a popular struggle that challenged the legitimacy of military rule, the government seemed eager to prevent future protests by sending away thousands of peasants and small farmers.

Similar to how Brasiguaio immigrants served to establish a Brazilian presence in Paraguay, so too did the northern settler farmers clear the way for what became booming industries of cattle ranching and timber extraction. The farmers displaced by Itaipu similarly functioned as agricultural shock troops for the dictatorship's frontier policies—both by staking a physical claim to an unfortified border and by opening up new regions through agricultural expansion. Marianne Schmink and Charles H. Wood observe that under military rule, "developmentalism became firmly joined to the national security doctrine. The fusion of the two produced a distinctive perspective that informed every aspect of the military's behavior in Amazonia."[56] Opponents of these policies viewed northern settlement as little more than an attempt to exploit farmers. Speaking later at a national meeting about agrarian

FIGURE 6.2 Settlers arrive at the Arapoti colonization project, 1981. Courtesy of INCRA, state office, Curitiba, Brazil.

colonization, Pastor Hans Train denounced the government for prioritizing private commercial interests over the well-being of rural Brazilians: "The current form of colonization is little more than land speculation, and does not seek [to actually] settle men on these lands. The farmers are thrown into unknown regions, in the middle of the jungle, without technical support or infrastructure. There, they clear the lands as best as they can and later are forced to leave again. Then the large companies come in and take over."[57]

In order to arrive at the northern agricultural colonies, the farmers first endured a nine-day bus ride (figures 6.3 and 6.4). One woman remembered that the drive to Acre made almost no stops on its four-thousand-kilometer journey, and that INCRA did not have enough food for all of the families onboard.[58] The lack of supplies en route to the colonization projects foreshadowed the conditions awaiting farmers on their arrival. Within only a few months of

FIGURES 6.3 & 6.4 Left: Road to Acre, May 1983. Right: A family displaced by Itaipu who had been living in Acre for two years. Screenshots from *Os desapropriados*, documentary film directed by Frederico Füllgraf, 1983.

settlement in Acre, *O Estado de São Paulo* reported that Paraná settlers had contracted malaria, measles, and hepatitis. Because INCRA had not provided the promised building materials for constructing houses, families were living in canvas tents that left them exposed to the elements. Many people became ill, including an eight-year-old child who died of malaria.[59] Another farmer explained, "Nobody had any way of going to see a doctor, you practically died on the way there. [We had to walk] for twenty kilometers."[60] Other media outlets reported on the high price of food, a pervasive lack of drinking water, and INCRA's inaction on resolving these issues.[61] For its inability to manage the northern agrarian projects, INCRA earned the dubious nickname of Instituto que Nada Conseguiu Realizer na Amazônia (Institute That Managed to Accomplish Nothing in the Amazon).[62] Public officials also spoke out against the agrarian colonies. Acre's secretary of agriculture denounced the imposition that the federal government had placed on his state, and noted that "farmers are going hungry, they don't have medical care or schools, and suffer intense bouts of malaria that's affecting 40 percent of people."[63]

The opening of this chapter quoted a farmer as saying, in part, "I was tricked . . . All that we got, with all their promises, was sickness, death, and despair in the middle of this jungle. And nothing else, nothing else."[64] After already experiencing the hardships of displacement, the former Paraná farmers now living in the north felt betrayed, both by Itaipu for not having made available better lands and by INCRA for giving a false idea of life in the colonies.

The realities of these projects reveal a core contradiction in state-directed frontier colonization. This chapter has made clear that government leaders could mobilize mass numbers of potential settler farmers, whether by force (displacement) or appeal (propaganda). Yet life in the agrarian colonies suggests that the federal government cared far less about actually governing them. By essentially abandoning the farmers, the Brazilian state did more than just fail to uphold its social and legal contract. The near-total neglect of northern settlers constituted the practical effect of being unimagined, and served to keep the landless peasants invisible within the Brazilian polity. Some farmers indicated that the original trauma of the Itaipu flood was partially offset by knowing that their sacrifice for the dam would help Brazil enter a new era of prosperity. The frontier experience, however, left the settlers further isolated from the Brazilian nation that Itaipu would help construct. So despite living within Brazil's national boundaries, these settler farmers had become "men without a country." They were visible substantively, yet invisible in the national imaginary.

The Arapoti Colony: "A Rural Favela"

The federal government registered Arapoti as a state-run agrarian project in early August 1981, and the first farmers arrived at the end of September. By June 1982, four months before Itaipu's flood, INCRA had completed the resettlement for all 2,400 of the project's inhabitants. Similar to the demographics of the northern settlers, peasants constituted the majority of Arapoti settlers, with 77 percent of the colony categorized as tenant farmers (*arrendatários*).[65] Located in northeastern Paraná—within a day's drive of Foz do Iguaçu, the state capitol of Curitiba, and also the city of São Paulo—Arapoti nonetheless suffered from rampant food shortages and a lack of basic infrastructure. Even without the north's malaria-plagued jungles and despite its closer proximity to urban areas, Arapoti still posed numerous challenges that paralleled those in Bahia and Acre. One farmer recalled the poor quality of land and the inadequate housing provided by INCRA:

> We wanted to come here to look at the lands and Itaipu didn't want anyone [to do that.] They told us that the land would be good for planting, but when we arrived it wasn't like what they said. And even the houses

don't have enough space for beds, because [they're] really small, with eight people in a house that's 2.5 by 5 [meters]. We can't be here, we have to leave. In the end, almost everyone is trying to leave.[66]

In September 1982 the deputy Gernote Kirinus (from the opposition Brazilian Democratic Movement Party, or PMDB) gave a speech in the state Legislative Assembly denouncing INCRA for abandoning four hundred families who had just suffered through "the social destruction caused by Itaipu." Kirinus claimed that federal authorities had failed to process the legal titles for the resettlement plots and that the farmers now confronted "misery" and "a delirious hunger" owing to an inability to grow food on the arid lands.[67] In the following months, regional newspapers offered headlines such as "Arapoti Is Living a Cruel Existence" and "Displaced Western Farmers Are Starving in Arapoti."[68] Many families struggled to survive financially, as unproductive harvests forced some to either chop down what few trees they possessed (to sell as firewood) or take out loans. These financial difficulties and the lingering specter of hunger left many farmers looking for a way to leave the project— though INCRA's contracts made it exceedingly difficult to sell their land.[69]

The situation became especially unstable toward the end of 1982, in the months immediately following the Itaipu flood. As discontent grew within Arapoti, government authorities actually decreased their support of the farmers: INCRA reasoned that by providing food supplies to underwrite the farmers' unsuccessful harvests, it had steered them away from the project's goal of self-sufficiency.[70] In December the government cut off all food donations to Arapoti. This action heightened the growing conflict, with one report noting a fear of potential looting in nearby supermarkets. Only a few days before Christmas, INCRA finally allowed a shipment of three thousand kilograms of food that provided rice, beans, oil, salt, and sugar.[71] In the aftermath of this tension, the Paraná state government conducted a survey of Arapoti. The report observed that families had initially arrived "without the minimum resources necessary to survive, [that] the lands were in terrible condition," and that almost everyone lacked critical nutritional support. Moreover, the project had poor sanitation conditions and little access to water.[72] Although the government never admitted so publicly, the report concluded that along with pervasive unemployment in the region, the principal cause of Arapoti's problems "was a lack of integrated planning" between INCRA and the local municipal authorities.[73] Based on these findings, INCRA introduced new plans to increase food support, offer technical agriculture courses, extend electric

FIGURE 6.5 Arapoti settlers and INCRA officials, 1981. Courtesy of INCRA, state office, Curitiba, Brazil.

power lines and roads, and improve the project's medical facilities and its schools (figure 6.5).

This renewed commitment from INCRA appears to have produced few tangible results. By the middle of the following year, national media outlets provided extensive coverage of the deteriorating conditions at Arapoti.[74] In July 1983 the *Folha de São Paulo* ran a lengthy exposé titled "Ex-Farmers from Itaipu Are Now Going Hungry on Arapoti."[75] The article claimed that a significant portion of the project's 425 families were suffering from hunger and that most people were surviving on provisions supplied by the local government. The report described farmers as living in makeshift plastic tents rather than wooden houses, and numerous interviews elaborated on the "psychological problems" and "trauma" caused by going into debt to cover bad harvests.

The four schools within Arapoti were chronically underfunded and did not provide enough of the legally mandated school lunches—the main reason students attended, since they had almost nothing to eat at home. One resident observed, "We never could have imagined being in a situation like this. We had good land [before Itaipu]. And all of a sudden we're tossed onto lands that produce nothing. . . . INCRA totally abandoned us."[76]

Similar to the negative attention from the previous December, the national exposure of Arapoti spurred an internal investigation, this time conducted by the dictatorship's main intelligence agency, the SNI.[77] Along with describing the project's glaring logistical problems, the study also found that because of Arapoti's small and unproductive land plots, many farmers had left the project to seek work in nearby towns as itinerant laborers. This led to an increasingly negative perception of the farmers within the surrounding populations; inhabitants of nearby towns referred to people from Arapoti as "INCRA's hobos" (*vagabundos*) or "INCRA's slum dwellers" (*favelados*). Despite INCRA's stated mission of supporting rural Brazilians, its failed programs helped push farmers toward a life of urban poverty. Like the Brasiguaios in Paraguay and the settlers in northern Brazil, the families of Arapoti were left ungoverned by federal authorities.

The SNI report also reflected the unfolding political climate of abertura. While acknowledging Arapoti's problems of poverty and hunger, the SNI noted that these issues had only gained wider public awareness during the recent election period, "when the project became a center of attention for [candidates] who offered improvements in exchange for votes."[78] Because political candidates appealed to Arapoti's struggling farmers, the SNI report framed the demands of rural communities as the result of manipulation by opposition forces rather than as worthwhile claims. As they had during the 1980 and 1981 land encampments, government authorities continued to deny farming communities the political legitimacy required to overcome the hardships created in large measure by the policies of the military regime itself.

In the following years, as Brazil navigated the final phases of a return to democratic rule, conditions at Arapoti crumbled even further. Some families lost their lands when they defaulted on bank loans—money borrowed in part to cover costs incurred owing to the lack of government support.[79] The dry, unproductive lands continued to provide underwhelming harvests, and according to some inhabitants, INCRA failed to implement any long-term structural improvements.[80] By the end of 1985, some six months after the dictatorship officially handed over power to a new civilian government, Arapoti had become, in the words of one politician, "a rural favela."[81] Agricultural failures and unemployment had brought about a level of poverty that sparked petty and violent crimes, including five homicides. Nearly a hundred families illegally broke their contracts with INCRA to abandon Arapoti. Those who stayed demanded that the government find them new lands, a form of re-resettlement for farmers who had already gone through multiple stages of displacement and relocation.

Never to Return Home

The desire to abandon Arapoti underscores the enduring problem for farmers who after being uprooted by Itaipu tried to migrate elsewhere: the irreversible nature of the flood meant that even those able to leave resettlement initiatives had few options for where to go next. With their original lands underwater, many migrant farmers, having lost confidence in federal authorities to provide adequate alternatives, either continued to struggle in their current situation or joined a growing trend of rural-to-urban migration and entered the informal economy in nearby cities. The growing population of itinerant day laborers further stigmatized farmers within Paraná society. The families sent to Bahia and Acre confronted an even harsher reality. Not only did they suffer from a similar lack of government support and bleak economic prospects, but they did so in inhospitable environments thousands of kilometers from their previous homes. Most did not have the financial means to leave, and after a drawn-out process of resettlement, many likely stayed in the north simply because they had no other choice.

The challenges of returning home extended equally to the Brasiguaio farmers in Paraguay. The early 1980s saw the first concentrated examples of return migration to Brazil. This trend resulted largely from land conflicts in which rural Paraguayans began occupying Brazilian-owned properties.[82] Compounded by the financial hardships faced by the average Brasiguaio, the backlash from local communities persuaded many to yearn for a return to Brazil. José Raimundo, a sixty-eight-year-old Brazilian immigrant living in eastern Paraguay, described his disenchantment with life as a Brasiguaio: "Everything was an illusion. Now I only want to sell my five alqueires and return to die in [Brazil]."[83] But the process of coming home was far from simple. Upon their return to Brazil, many farmers were shunned and seen as unwanted outsiders by political authorities and the landed elite, who feared that Brasiguaios would return in large numbers to disrupt the labor market.[84] With no legal title to lands in Brazil, many returning Brasiguaios encountered the same challenges of unemployment and urban poverty facing the farmers who had abandoned the Arapoti colony.

The experiences chronicled in this chapter show that the hardships triggered by the Itaipu dam were not confined to the flood zone or its immediate surroundings. Instead, they extended outward across Brazil's frontiers, both foreign and internal. In Paraguay, Brasiguaio communities following the allure of cheap and fertile lands confronted a corrupt agrarian bureaucracy and animosity from distraught local Paraguayans. Within less than a decade, many Brasiguaios saw their new lands taken over by wealthy Brazilians who then established large-scale soy plantations. In Brazil, thousands of farmers displaced by Itaipu journeyed north to INCRA's colonization projects. Once there, they encountered barren lands, diseases, and a chronic lack of state support. In both cases the farmers were fundamental to the dictatorship's territorial ambitions, yet they rarely received government support or recognition. As an unimagined community tasked with laying the groundwork for national expansion, these settlers were left to toil as people without a country.

As the poorest sector of the western Paraná countryside, these communities had few avenues for contesting the development policies of the Brazilian state. Around this same time, however, the plight of landless peasants increasingly became a national issue. Conditioned by a history of rural struggle that predated the military regime, landless Brazilians used the context of abertura in the early 1980s to mobilize against the sorts of policies that allowed the government to exploit Brasiguaios and settler farmers with no consequences. In the aftermath of the struggle at Itaipu, landless workers regrouped to lead a new charge for agrarian reform in Brazil. After generations of being overlooked and delegitimized, the formation of landless movements elevated the visibility of rural livelihoods to unprecedented levels. As the abertura neared its official completion, the ongoing repression—and growing mobilization—of landless Brazilians offers important insight into the limitations of the democratic transition looming ahead.

CHAPTER 7

Land for Those Who Work It

MASTRO and a New Era of Agrarian Reform in Brazil

In late 1974 *O Estado de São Paulo* observed that the "largest remaining concern in the future flood area has been solved." Under a headline of "[The] Landless Will Be Compensated," the article reported that Itaipu would pay 50 percent of the land value to those without property deeds.[1] For the thousands of landless families living in the western Paraná borderlands, this news offered the first public reassurance that Itaipu would include them in the expropriation process.[2] Even if the dam would irreversibly flood their homes, receiving partial financial compensation might offer them the chance to relocate on nearby lands. But Itaipu never paid the landless, neither at that moment in 1974 nor in the decade to come.

In a larger sense, this neglect was systemic. For generations, the countryside's poorest inhabitants had received few, if any, benefits or recognition from the Brazilian government. But the exclusion of landless families in Itaipu's expropriations was also shaped by the actions of their own rural neighbors. Because most of the farmers in the Justice and Land Movement (MJT) focused on winning higher prices for their legally owned properties, the initial campaign against Itaipu largely silenced the voices of the landless. Misled by the government and overlooked by a grassroots struggle that claimed to defend them, the landless soon mobilized for a farther-reaching vision of agrarian rights. Although the hierarchies reproduced within the MJT precluded the landless from gaining the same level of visibility as their landholding neighbors, the movement at Itaipu nonetheless provided an opening to bring the long-standing struggle for land into a new era. Propelled by their experiences both at Itaipu and in the decades beforehand, and seeing none of their most pressing needs reflected in the official abertura, landless workers in western Paraná escalated their demands and their strategies. This fight for land and legitimacy reemerged in force during the waning years of Brazil's dictatorship, and it would continue long after the transition to civilian rule.

This chapter traces the history of the landless campaign that formed in the aftermath of the conflict at Itaipu, a group known as MASTRO—the Landless Farmers Movement of Western Paraná (Movimento dos Trabalhadores Sem Terra de Oeste do Paraná). It was established in July 1981, barely two months after the MJT demobilized at the Foz do Iguaçu protest camp. Rallying around the slogan "land for those who work it," MASTRO fought for the rights of landless Brazilians. While most of the MJT farmers had focused on financial compensation, the new landless movement sought to achieve larger goals of agrarian reform and the redistribution of land. This ideological shift translated into a diverging set of strategies. The earlier fight chose to stage encampments on the periphery of Itaipu's offices; MASTRO, in contrast, led occupations on private and state-owned lands in which hundreds of individuals took up residence on abandoned and underused properties.

Between 1981 and 1984, MASTRO counted almost ten thousand members and served as a central organizer of the 1984 founding conference of the Landless Workers Movement (MST), which has since become one of the largest social movements in the Western Hemisphere. Along with offering an overlooked prehistory of the MST, this chapter discusses the implications of MASTRO's emergence from the initial fight at Itaipu. Moreover, it argues that the vision of land as a collective right positioned landless Brazilians to confront the immediate realities of military rule while also seeking a more visible presence in a potential democratic future.

This chapter focuses on six land occupations in western Paraná that began in 1983 and 1984. In the first three cases—on the Padroeira, Três Pinheiros, and Anoni farms—MASTRO played a supporting role. It then served as the primary organizer for the remaining occupations: of the Cavernoso and Mineira farms and of a forest reserve belonging to Itaipu Binational.[3] Four of the six occupations witnessed physical repression from either state troopers (who beat, tortured, and harassed the occupiers) or hired gunmen (responsible for two murders). The occupations lasted anywhere from a few weeks to multiple years, and two of them ultimately secured the legal titles to the lands in question and became official settlement communities known as *assentamentos*. Although MASTRO participated primarily in these six occupations, at least seven other actions occurred in western Paraná during this same period.[4] The concentration made the region one of the leading centers of landless mobilization in Brazil and helps explain why the MST held its founding conference in the nearby city of Cascavel.

In Brazil, as throughout Latin America, the countryside included a wide range of groups from different regional, class, and ethnic backgrounds. With

MAP 5 Land occupations by MASTRO in 1983–1984 and other historical markers in western Paraná. Courtesy of Gabriel Moss.

distinct histories of migration and labor, and drawing from personal interactions with both the Brazilian state and neighboring citizens, rural communities were never monolithic. Variations across the Brazilian countryside enabled groups to form distinct relationships with their landscapes. In practice, these conceptions of land tenure led to what I theorize as the dialectic of land and legitimacy. Land expresses material connections such as title holding, longevity of occupation, and improvements made, as well as deeper cultural values. Combined, the material and cultural meanings of land impact the perceived legitimacy of rural communities, both for how rural groups see themselves and also for how they, in turn, are seen by mainstream society. In the case of the Itaipu conflict, the title-holding small farmers considered land to be *individual property*, while the Avá-Guarani viewed land as a *way of life*. The history of MASTRO offers a third perception: land as a basis for *collective rights*.

Compared to the earlier conflict at Itaipu, the landless movements of the early 1980s represented an entirely distinct challenge to the status quo. Although the MJT encampments brought negative attention to Itaipu and the military regime, its leadership kept the movement within the existing boundaries of private property law. The focus on financial compensation meant that once the government negotiated a settlement—and especially after Itaipu's 1982 flood—the movement no longer posed a concerted threat. In contrast, because the landless movements occupied private property and fought for the redistribution of land, they confronted waves of repression that rarely occurred in the more visible arenas of democratization. At Itaipu the idea of land as property was seen as a legitimate-enough claim to insulate the MJT from overt physical attacks. For groups like MASTRO, the defense of land as a collective right provoked violent reactions.

In 1983 and 1984, two peasant farmers were shot to death during land occupations organized by MASTRO, and hundreds more were physically expelled from their homes. To be sure, violence against rural communities has predominated throughout Brazilian history. Peasant movements had existed long before military rule in the 1960s, but grassroots landless struggles—those with no explicit political affiliation—only began to organize at a national level in the context of abertura in the late 1970s and early 1980s. With a regime change looming on the horizon, the prospect of an autonomous and unified rural campaign helps explain why these new challenges to private landholdings incited violence from elite forces, both hired gunmen and state troopers alike.[5] Despite occasional news coverage, landless occupations and the subsequent violence took place far from the public spotlight. The relative isolation of these events sets them apart from the far more visible actions at Itaipu and also from the paradigmatic antidictatorship struggles like the ABC labor strikes or the Diretas Já (Direct Elections Now) campaign. As millions of people in Brazilian cities denounced military rule with relatively little fear of reprisal, thousands of impoverished families occupied remote areas of the countryside under constant threat of attack. While acknowledging that urban protests also dealt with serious challenges before and after democratization, this chapter examines the implications of violence against rural mobilizations.

The repression most commonly associated with Brazil's dictatorship was committed in the late 1960s and early 1970s by members of the military and the police. In almost all cases, this violence took place in cities. Yet the attacks on landless Brazilians in the 1980s were carried out to a large extent by gunmen and thugs hired by elite landowners. This form of nonstate violence shows the extent to which repression in the countryside under the dictatorship was both endemic (emerging from a longer history prior to the regime) and normalized (emerging from a culture of impunity codified by the regime). In both senses, violence under military rule was never contained to the immediate structures of dictatorship. As such, it would continue even after the 1985 transition.

The landless group MASTRO arose directly from the MJT campaign at Itaipu. Its main leaders had participated in the fight at Itaipu, and its initial membership drew from communities in the flood zone that received no compensation money and refused to be relocated to faraway agrarian colonies. Although its steady growth in the early 1980s brought in thousands of new members who had not been among those displaced by the dam, MASTRO was, at its core, a by-product of the MJT. The fight at Itaipu provided more than just solidarity networks and a ready supply of potential members: for landless families who took part in the MJT, the experience of confronting a central appendage of the dictatorship served as an incubator of political consciousness. One man remembered the earlier land encampments as "the start of the fire that ignited everything, we didn't worry anymore. The people saw that they had rights."[6] Similarly, a former leader of MASTRO recalled that Itaipu provided a catalyst for agrarian reform since it created a "no-alternative" situation for thousands of people with no other recourse after the 1982 flood.[7]

Despite its immediate connections to the fight at Itaipu, MASTRO's ideological roots reached further back to regional peasant and squatter movements prior to the dictatorship. These earlier struggles from the 1940s through the 1960s included uprisings within the state of Paraná and also the creation of rural organizations like the Movement of Landless Farmers (MASTER, Movimento dos Agricultores Sem Terra) in the southern state of Rio Grande do Sul. The history of MASTRO thus provides an important link between predictatorship rural mobilizations and the post-abertura growth of the MST.

This chapter does not claim that MASTRO was the sole vehicle for keeping alive the lessons of previous struggles in the countryside, as numerous movements under military rule also mobilized in defense of rural Brazilians.[8] In particular, the National Confederation of Agricultural Workers made agrarian reform its *bandeira de luta*, or rallying flag.[9] As we shall see, rural unions grew at unprecedented rates under the dictatorship and won substantial benefits for their members—an impressive feat given the context of military rule. But the focus on wage increases and social welfare programs kept the rural union movement within a specific set of goals that did not always advocate for landless or precarious workers like those in MASTRO. Federal labor policies also made it difficult for rural unions to represent anyone not employed full-time in agriculture, effectively precluding membership for most landless and precarious workers. Moreover, rural unions tended to promote a form of *trabalhismo* (laborism) that moved away from the *agrarismo* (ruralism) of earlier peasant movements to instead seek the sorts of financial and social service demands sought by urban workers. With no formal affiliation to organized labor or political parties, and as a movement that emerged from the emblematic fight against the Itaipu dam, MASTRO offers a compelling and underexplored case study for the meanings of land and mobilization in modern Brazil.

Legacies and Memories of Peasant Action

The history of land struggles in Paraná developed in tandem with the state's patterns of migration and the expansion of agrarian capitalism. Settler farmers first arrived in the region during the late 1930s as part of the March to the West initiated by president Getúlio Vargas.[10] Sparked by high coffee prices and declining agricultural yields in the neighboring state of São Paulo, Paraná's population grew from approximately 1.2 million in 1940 to almost 7 million three decades later. This demographic expansion placed added pressure on the availability and price of land. From 1940 to 1960, the total amount of lands under cultivation nearly doubled, and the per-hectare price of land rose from Cr$98 in 1940 to Cr$674 in 1970.[11] To incentivize the settlement of western and northern Paraná, the state government offered unoccupied public lands with relatively little taxation or oversight. However, the end of Vargas's Estado

Novo (New State) regime in 1945 saw a new governor take power in Paraná who shifted course by distributing massive amounts of public land for the creation of private estates. In response, the newly displaced farmers led a wave of direct action.

The most prominent of these early conflicts was the so-called Porecatú War, which lasted from 1949 to 1951. In the countryside near the town of Porecatú, hundreds of local families confronted the wealthy Lunardelli family over the right to nearly a hundred thousand acres of land. With the support of militants connected to the Peasant Leagues (the rural branch of the Brazilian Communist Party), the farmers faced off in a violent standoff with the Lunardellis' hired gunmen, resulting in numerous deaths on both sides of the fighting.[12]

Six years later, the region also witnessed the Squatters Rebellion in the city of Francisco Beltrão, some two hundred kilometers east of the future Itaipu dam site. For the month of October 1957, landless workers seized control of the city and demanded the government expropriate the lands of several estates.[13] Covered at length in regional and national news outlets, the Squatters Rebellion expanded on the momentum generated by the Porecatú War to establish a precedent of Paraná as a space of radicalized landless mobilization.

For some rural Brazilians who would later belong to MASTRO, these earlier events served as personal and collective referents. Nildemar Silva, a leader of MASTRO in the early 1980s, holds strong memories of his family's participation in the Squatters Rebellion. Silva saw the uprising as more than just an example of peasant radicalization: it was a victory that allowed landless farmers to remain in the region at a time of changing land relations and the rise of large agro-estates:

> That history of rebellion and of the settler resistance that my family was part of, it was also very present, yeah, [in MASTRO]. We learned that the resistance would help us continue that process of struggle. Because if our families hadn't resisted in the 50s, we definitely would've been expelled to other regions. . . . [And for MASTRO,] people couldn't take it anymore, they had nothing left. And I think that with the construction of Itaipu, [it connected to] the Squatters Rebellion, with the resistance in southern Brazil, with the Porecatú War. I think that everyone was looking for the confidence to organize as families and to fight and make occupations to guarantee our rights.[14]

Earlier landless campaigns beyond Paraná also inspired MASTRO; the most influential of these was MASTER, formed in Rio Grande do Sul in the early

1960s. With the support of Leonel Brizola, the state's populist governor, MAS-TER led a series of land occupations between 1962 and 1964, when the military coup resulted in the imprisonment or exile of many rural leaders.[15] Gabriel Ondetti credits MASTER with popularizing the strategy of direct occupations and establishing the social identity of the landless rural worker that allowed future movements to take on their "most massive organized expression in the smallholder-dominated areas of southern Brazil."[16] In the years leading up to the military's 1964 coup, MASTER brought unprecedented attention to the issue of landlessness and set in motion the ideology and the naming of MASTRO in the early 1980s.

Militant rural movements in the 1950s and 1960s had presented a growing challenge to the landed elites' stranglehold on political and economic power in the Brazilian countryside. Pushed forward by this grassroots pressure, president João Goulart advocated for rural workers and displayed a willingness to enact structural agrarian reform. According to historian Cliff Welch, the combination of popular militancy and support from Goulart provoked fear among large-scale farmers and other elites, providing an impetus for them to support the 1964 coup.[17] With the start of military rule, a new wave of repression swept over the Brazilian countryside.

In the infancy of Brazil's dictatorship, the government followed through on its anticommunist rhetoric by taking a hard-line approach to dealing with potential rural unrest. At the national level, this manifested as a prolonged effort to root out any seeds of guerrilla warfare, such as the Araguaia War in the early 1970s, when ten thousand soldiers fought against roughly sixty guerrilla fighters in the northern jungles of Goiás.[18] Along with overt state actions, the repression of Brazil's countryside also included the normalization of local-level abuses. The use of hired thugs known as *jagunços* or *grileiros* was already a long-standing tactic of landed elites seeking to force peasant farmers off their land. Yet the violent displacement of rural families appears to have accelerated under military rule. In western Paraná, for example, armed men consistently harassed and beat landless peasants, threatening to shoot them or burn down their houses. The holdings of the Public Archive of Paraná, specifically the secret police files of the Department of Political and Social Order, offer numerous cases of hired jagunços attacking small-scale farmers every year between 1969 and 1973.[19] In certain instances, local politicians allegedly paid the assailants.[20]

In the repressive climate of authoritarian rule from 1964 to 1985, the rural trade union movement paradoxically grew to over nine million members, making it the single largest category of organized workers in all of Brazil and one of the largest labor groups in all of Latin America. The expansion of rural unions in Brazil stands in contrast to what occurred in neighboring Latin American countries during their respective dictatorships. Before the 1973 coup of Augusto Pinochet, for example, Chile had 850 rural unions with roughly 250,000 members. By 1981 that number had dropped to 348 unions and 27,000 members.[21] In Brazil the rise of unions linked closely to programs initiated by the dictatorship itself, above all the Rural Assistance Fund, which empowered rural labor unions to offer medical care and social services in the countryside.[22] As shown in chapter 2, although the fund delivered tangible benefits to rural workers, it also helped co-opt union leadership and bring them under the patronage of the military regime. Despite the advances of rural unions, their connections to the dictatorship obviated a deeper challenge to the legitimacy of military rule.

Once opposition forces began to loosen the military's grip on power in the mid-1970s, grassroots rural movements, much like civil society more broadly, began to reassert their demands. As discussed earlier, peasants staged a land occupation in 1979 on the Natalino farm in the state of Rio Grande do Sul.[23] The protesters stood firm and eventually won the appropriation of 1,870 hectares of land for over 160 families. Similar occupations occurred throughout southern Brazil in the early 1980s, suggesting the emergence of landless workers as an increasingly visible sector of the population and a renewed social force.

Progress and Limitations within the MJT

Although the MJT largely overlooked the landless farmers within its ranks, the movement's leadership did include landless demands at key moments in the fight against Itaipu, most notably at the start of every new initiative or protest. When the MJT published its first major declaration in October 1978—an open letter to Brazil's president Ernesto Geisel—the fifteen-point list included that "squatters receive at least 50 percent of the land's value, in accordance with the initial promise of Itaipu Binational."[24] Perhaps this inclusion resulted from the young movement needing to attract as many people as possible, or maybe farmers were simply more optimistic early on that they could achieve a wider range of goals. Similar gestures were also made toward the demands of the landless at the onset of the Santa Helena and Foz do Iguaçu camps in July 1980 and March 1981, respectively. In each instance, over the course of the protest, the MJT leadership redirected its goals, and the concern for landless workers declined.

A turning point in the silencing of landless voices came during the 1980 land encampment at Santa Helena. During the MJT's negotiations with Itaipu, the group's leaders decided to stop pushing for the demand of land-for-land that would have given displaced families new tracts of land instead of financial compensation. One MJT member, Carlos Grillmann, recalled the decision to change course:

> Well that was a huge compromise [*uma troca grande*], it was an issue that in the end lost a lot of internal support. Because it had been a political question and when money gets involved it's complicated to keep the struggle. And there was also the question of urgency and needing to bow to the situation, because the [Itaipu] project was about to come, it was almost done. And that land-for-land also needed more time, to see if maybe with a slower expropriation process. But maybe if the movement had started a few years earlier, say four or five years before . . . it would've been enough time to go more into that, but there wasn't enough time. It was too fast.[25]

In the end, the 1980 Santa Helena accord between the MJT and Itaipu made no mention of the landless.[26] Although the MJT leadership secured a "gentleman's agreement" to compensate the landless at "a fair price," no deal ever materialized.[27] In the aftermath of these decisions, landless workers continued to face marginalization from Itaipu, from the Brazilian government, and from within their own movement.

This process of social silencing took place for two main reasons. The first relates to the immediate context and contingencies of the MJT: as Itaipu's flood loomed closer, pressure mounted on the MJT to achieve the largest number of victories for the largest portion of its membership. Landed farmers who took part in the MJT and received financial compensation from Itaipu echoed this sense of urgency. Adil Fochezatto, for example, said, "We had to accept because we had no other option, the water was going to rise and [Itaipu] would have kicked us out anyways."[28] Similarly, Dona Suita recalled that "if we didn't leave really quickly, the water would have taken everything, even us."[29] The smaller size of the landless sector, in terms of both numbers and influence, likely induced the MJT leadership to focus on more attainable goals that would benefit a greater number of people.

The second reason is more endemic. The diverging perceptions of land as individual property versus a collective right helped determine which demands were seen as valid and thus prioritized within the MJT. Many of the property-owning farmers justified their actions as a defense of the lands they had purchased and invested money in over many years. In the initial fight against Itaipu, these landed farmers often told stories about how their families had arrived in the region, bought land, cleared the forest, and settled a previously barren and wild landscape—selectively blind to the existence of nearby indigenous communities. Dona Suita spoke about her family's motivation for taking part in the MJT: "We bought it and paid for it. If it had been a question of land invasions, that's one thing, but we had bought [our land]."[30] By this logic, those who did not own their land had no legitimacy to take a stand against Itaipu.

In the context of abertura, the dialectic of land and legitimacy helps explain how these contrasting conceptions of land tenure shaped the political trajectory of the displaced communities. With support from national opposition forces, the farmers' movement at Itaipu attained a growing political profile. Although the abertura broadened the MJT's reach and helped expand the political consciousness of its members, the attention it received changed the scope of the fight at Itaipu. With the eyes of Brazil fixed on farmers in western Paraná, it became politically risky for the MJT to advocate the sort of structural agrarian reform that would have benefited the landless. Instead, at a time when Brazilians throughout the country were testing the limits of political legitimacy, the MJT leadership focused its demands on the immediate question of financial indemnification. The climate of abertura helped frame the MJT as a legitimate struggle of downtrodden farmers confronting an unjust appendage of the military government. The movement's leadership and allies likely feared that a change in narrative could lose the battle for public opinion and jeopardize the prospects of winning tangible victories.

The landless experience within the MJT also invokes a second concept articulated throughout this book: the double reality of abertura. On the one hand, participation in the fight at Itaipu encouraged landless farmers in western Paraná to see their vision for the future as part of the abertura's broader rhetoric of democratic rights. On the other hand, their continued marginalization—from both mainstream society and existing rural movements—presented a far different reality. When the MJT reached an agreement with Itaipu in May 1981, the landed farmers could celebrate the 62 percent increase in land prices as a political victory for popular struggle. The landless, however, gained neither financial benefits nor an increased foothold in Brazil's slowly widening polity.

Despite the limits placed on landless demands in the MJT, members of MAS-TRO still look back positively on the initial fight at Itaipu. One tenant farmer stated, "The main thing Itaipu taught us was the capacity that us peasants have to resist."[31] One woman connected the MJT protests to the rise of popular struggles, saying, "The Santa Helena encampment [in 1980] was the seed of everything, that's where it all started and the encampment was where the Church got involved and where the farmers learned to fight."[32] These sorts of positive attachments did not form only in hindsight; during the MJT's campaign at Itaipu, some groups already recognized the potential for a larger and more direct movement. After visiting the government's proposed Bahia resettlement project in August 1980, Marcelo Barth and Ari Konrad reported back to the MJT about the deplorable conditions found in the northeast and stressed the need to take extreme action if Itaipu continued to ignore their demands:

> We consider our expulsion from western Paraná an undeserved and distant exile; the lands for sale [here] in the region are reaching absurd levels; we know that there are enough areas of land in this region to resettle all of us; we demand the immediate appropriation of this area, and that the same law be used that authorized the President of the Republic to decree the [initial] expropriation of our lands. We will wait only 30 days for a satisfactory response; at the end of that time we will occupy the lands of our own choosing . . . [even] if it becomes necessary to occupy with force.[33]

Although the MJT rarely included these approaches in its official declarations—Barth and Konrad's position was not taken up by the general assembly—the demand for land expropriation and the willingness to stage occupations existed as a consistent, if often overshadowed, undercurrent. And in the aftermath of the initial fight, when Itaipu no longer served as the main enemy, a new movement emerged that expanded on the lessons of previous struggles.

The Creation of MASTRO

Although evidence cannot be found to confirm the exact date when MASTRO formed, a lengthy article in a July 1981 issue of *Nosso Tempo* discussed MASTRO as a newly created organization, describing a movement determined to bring about an agrarian reform that was "total, complete, immediate." Denouncing the expulsion of smallholders, MASTRO blamed the government for concentrating land in the hands of the elite through a process of "directed colonization." Along with demanding access to land, MASTRO identified the presence of agro-industries as another key source of problems, displaying an awareness of "the enemy" that included Itaipu, the government, and also private enterprise in general.[34] A selection from MASTRO's anthem reflects the direction and character of the fledgling movement:

So much land abandoned / Beautiful land unplanted
So much land in few hands / So many people who have nothing
Sacred calloused hands / Whose table lacks bread.[35]

Barely two months removed from the Foz do Iguaçu encampment, this new campaign served as both a continuation of and a challenge to the conflict at Itaipu. Although MASTRO grew to include those who had no immediate connection to Itaipu, it emerged directly from the MJT campaign. The three people most active in the new landless movement had all participated in the fight at Itaipu: Celso Anghinoni, Darci Appio, and Aristeu Elias Ribeiro. And in an interesting twist to the depoliticizing effect of religious leadership in the Itaipu protests, Pastor Werner Fuchs and Father Adriano Van de Ven also played fundamental early roles in establishing MASTRO and expanding its membership base. Having learned from the experience at Itaipu, where a connection to national politics limited the movement's ability to escalate, landless farmers envisioned MASTRO as an autonomous organization with no political affiliation. Rather than a central leadership, local committees elected rotating representatives to coordinate with groups throughout the region.[36] In theory, MASTRO existed as a leaderless movement. One participant, Afonso Camer, remembers how peasant farmers drew lessons from rural struggles throughout Brazilian history, mentioning specifically the 1897 Canudos War between federal troops and a community of northeastern settlers in the interior of Bahia: "Canudos became a very interesting history [for MASTRO], where Antonio Conselheiro was a leader that brought together a bunch of people. But when the leader died, the movement ended. So that was the risk . . . if they kill the leader the movement goes away."[37]

In practice, however, MASTRO never quite existed as a leaderless movement. Along with the larger roles played by the above-mentioned individuals, the group also received logistical support from branches of the Syndicate of Rural Workers in São Miguel do Iguaçu, Santa Helena, and Medianeira.[38] As Pastor Fuchs recalled, "rural unions were a sort of umbrella, but not the principal driving force of MASTRO."[39] In particular, Miguel Isloar Sávio, the president of the São Miguel do Iguaçu branch, became one of MASTRO's most visible organizers when the group began staging land occupations. The goal of remaining unaffiliated with unions and political parties, regardless of its implementation, underscored the effort to create a more responsive organization that could defend the interests of landless Brazilians regardless of the changing political climate.

The first regional assembly of MASTRO took place on September 2, 1981, gathering roughly sixty people in the town of São Miguel do Iguaçu, some forty kilometers east of Foz do Iguaçu.[40] Within a month of the first regional meeting, MASTRO grew to include 1,780 registered members in twenty-two groups across three municipalities in western Paraná. As MASTRO continued to expand, both the Federal Police and the National Information Service (SNI) began to monitor the group.[41] This surveillance suggests that with the struggle at Itaipu essentially over, concerns over rural unrest in the Paraná borderlands now shifted to the threat of landless mobilization.

A survey of MASTRO conducted in 1982 provides a closer look at the organization's membership.[42] Although it counted only 688 of the over 6,000 members enrolled at that time, the survey sheds light on the movement's general demographics. The overwhelming majority of MASTRO members (96 percent) were male, 69 percent were married, and the average age was thirty-five. Survey respondents reported twenty-one different categories of employment, most commonly day laborer (29 percent), squatter (17 percent), informal worker (15 percent), and sharecropper (11 percent). In another sign of MASTRO's broad reach, smaller sectors also included fisherman, domestic worker, and waiter. In terms of education, only 16 percent of respondents had completed primary school, and 14 percent were illiterate. The final category of data concerned region of origin. Most came from the southern states of Santa Catarina and Rio Grande do Sul (combined 53 percent), with the remaining members from an additional eleven states throughout Brazil, including Paraná, Bahia, Ceará, São Paulo, Sergipe, Pernambuco, and Minas Gerais. From this survey we can construct the picture of an average MASTRO member as a young adult male, married and likely with children, with little if any education, and having immigrated from either the southern countryside or the northern regions of Brazil. The demographics of this survey did not differ drastically from the participants in the previous MJT, likely because many of the more ethnically mixed landless families had already been sent north to the agrarian colonies. Compared to the farmers in the MJT, one fundamental characteristic distinguished the MASTRO members: whereas those who received financial indemnification from Itaipu had owned an average of fifteen hectares of land, farmers in MASTRO were almost exclusively landless.[43]

The campaign for agrarian reform initiated by MASTRO took place in the context of a drastically changing countryside. Throughout the 1970s export crops had largely displaced food crops, and farming had become increasingly industrialized. The mechanization of agriculture in Paraná, for instance, led to a growing reliance on tractors and a new focus on single-crop production. In 1970 there were roughly 18,000 tractors on Paraná farms; by 1980 that figure had more than quadrupled to over 79,000.[44] During the same period (1970–1980), almost 100,000 rural properties disappeared in Paraná, via either state expropriations or the consolidation of agricultural estates.[45] The mechanization of agriculture, the decrease in farming jobs, and the rise of rural-to-urban migration also made it harder for labor unions in the countryside to maintain their membership base and influence. With a precarious rural labor market and with less land available for small- and medium-scale agriculture, Brazilians like those in MASTRO felt compelled to raise the stakes—and the methods—of their actions.

In early 1982 the scope of MASTRO's meetings began to change. Government surveillance reports suggest that MASTRO started to discuss which farms in the region could be sites for occupation. According to state security forces, MASTRO had researched potential properties to target and knew, for example, how many brothers of a particular family owned a farm in Santa Helena, when they had inherited it from their father, and exactly how many hectares they controlled.[46] Members of MASTRO did not stage any land occupations until the following year, but their preparations to do so less than six months after the movement's creation show them taking the initiative. As the group held internal discussions about larger protests, it also began appealing to national politicians. A letter to federal senators in February 1982 outlined four main goals: land in Paraná, new policies to protect the legal and contractual rights of rural workers, better availability of farm credits and loans, and new systems for acquiring land.[47] With the November 1982 elections on the horizon—one of the most tangible advances yet of the abertura's official transition to civilian rule—it appears likely that although unaffiliated with any political party, MASTRO nonetheless saw the utility in using political allies and the context of democratization as a way to garner support and media attention.

By May MASTRO had become a full-fledged movement with over 6,600 members.[48] Earlier government surveillance had tended to provide only basic details, but the organization's continued growth seemed to provoke a new sense of alarm. Along with chronicling when and where MASTRO held its meetings, an SNI report offered three broader conclusions: "MASTRO has energized the hope for resettlement within the region of western Paraná. The movement can spread to other cities, increasing the risk of the invasions already being planned. [And] the movement has political and electoral connotations, undermining the public image of the government."[49] A similar SNI memo described MASTRO as "a movement conditioned to be used by subversive organizations to create centers of agitation in the countryside."[50] As democratization loomed on the horizon, MASTRO represented a form of grassroots dissent that helped add an agrarian vision of rights into the wider political climate.

Over the following months, MASTRO increased its presence in what was quickly becoming a national landless movement. First, the group held its largest event to date, convening over four thousand people in the town of Medianeira and crafting a declaration titled "The Shout of the Landless" ("O Grito dos Sem Terra").[51] In emphasizing the need for access to land, the document called for MASTRO to join similar movements across the country and begin occupying the lands of unproductive farms. Three weeks later, MASTRO hosted a three-day meeting, again in Medianeira, that included seventy representatives from throughout Brazil. According to Bernardo Mançano Fernandes, this was Brazil's first major convening of landless peasants.[52] On the heels of these two summits, MASTRO then served as one of four co-organizers for the First National Landless Meeting in the central state of Goiás.[53] As MASTRO made alliances and established a presence at the national level, it also continued working toward its goal of obtaining land in Paraná.

While still preparing for potential land occupations, MASTRO accelerated its campaign of engaging with public officials. In early August 1982, representatives met in Curitiba with the interim governor of Paraná, José Hosken de Novais of the Brazilian Democratic Movement Party (PMDB), who had assumed office when the sitting governor, Ney Braga, began his campaign for senator. In his conversations with MASTRO members, Hosken de Novais promised to work with the Institute for Lands and Cartography (ITC) to evaluate the demands of the landless. Moreover, the governor pledged to "spare no effort in seeking a solution to the farmers' problems."[54] Three weeks after meeting the governor, MASTRO also sent a delegation to Brasília to meet with the minister of land affairs, Danilo Venturini.[55] In light of these appeals, the National Institute for Colonization and Agrarian Reform (INCRA) made its first official gesture to MASTRO, offering access to resettlement plots in the Amazonian states of Acre, Romaira, and Mato Grosso.[56] At a general assembly later in the month, delegates rejected INCRA's proposal, emphasizing the movement's central goal of winning land in Paraná. More encouraging news arrived in the form of the ITC report that Governor Hosken de Novais had commissioned, which outlined 507,000 hectares of land that the government could appropriate.[57]

The different positions of the ITC (a branch of the state government) and INCRA (a federal body) reflected the disjointed path of democratization and its relationship to grassroots forces. By acknowledging the availability of over half a million hectares, the ITC appeared more responsive to the demands of local communities—at least compared to its federal counterpart INCRA. The mounting pressure from below accelerated after the elections of November 1982, when a resurgence of opposition swept candidates into office across the country. As mentioned in chapter 3, this included Paraná's new governor, José Richa, who had been a vocal supporter of the MJT farmers' movement at Itaipu. Less than a month after the elections, INCRA began to shift its approach. While still emphasizing the policy of northern settlement, INCRA informed MASTRO of a proposal to relocate two thousand families within Paraná over the course of the following year.[58] In the postelection advance of opposition groups, INCRA's proposal suggested that government officials were beginning to take landless demands more seriously—or, at the very least, that they saw the need to placate a growing social movement.

Regardless of which scenario—or a combination of the two—was more likely, MASTRO's influence continued to spread. This growth is further seen in an internal report from José Guilherme Cavagnari, INCRA's regional director. Along with noting the existence within Paraná of almost 200,000 families of "day laborers, sharecroppers, [and] tenant farmers," Cavagnari discussed the advances made by MASTRO: "Over the last year this behavior has gained strength such that if their demands are not satisfied, new 'movements' will form [and] protests will become more frequent and radical . . . with threats to invade private lands."[59] Echoing the ITC results, Cavagnari wrote that Paraná contained up to 500,000 hectares of underused land (*vazios de produção*) and that the government could expropriate as much as 100,000 hectares of that total.[60]

Another of Cavagnari's observations hinted at the extent to which the climate of abertura had instilled an anxiety about popular forces. The report urged INCRA to "equip labor unions such that they can assume the role of selecting and controlling the 'organized movements.' . . . Here the understanding is implicit that the surplus of nonorganized farmers can accelerate new imbalances between [the government's] attention to their demands and new social conflicts."[61] As previously discussed, such statements resulted from the government's close relationship with mainstream rural unions. Yet in the abertura landscape of the early 1980s, MASTRO proved more autonomous than national unions like the National Confederation of Agricultural Workers. In fact, the group's determination to remain independent of political and labor organizations led to instances of tension with neighboring rural unions. One state report observed that these conflicts occurred because landless movements and formal labor unions tended to attract a different membership base.[62] Celso Anghinoni, a leading member of MASTRO, recalls that once the group began its land occupations, certain sectors of the union movement withdrew their support.[63] In the context of abertura, rural Brazilians continued to engage and challenge one another over the role of the countryside in Brazil's looming democratic future.

In a year-end overview of MASTRO, the Pastoral Land Commission's *Poeira* newsletter noted that 1983 would become "the year of popular movements, of neighborhood associations, of agrarian reform movements in the countryside. . . . All this because the political climate of abertura, the staging of elections and the victory of the opposition . . . make possible this popular mobilization."[64] This resurgent momentum of grassroots protest continued into the early months of 1983 and helped MASTRO organize its largest actions yet.

From Encampments to Occupations

By April 1983, roughly eighteen months into MASTRO's existence, the landless farmers of western Paraná appeared to have lost any remaining confidence in the state and federal government to intervene on their behalf. Although MASTRO emerged from the comparatively peaceful encampments at Santa Helena and Foz do Iguaçu, the group now used direct occupations to confront the deeply rooted inequalities facing its members. The shift in tactics also reflected a shift in ideology: while the MJT encampments had operated within existing property laws, the MASTRO occupations aimed to put forth a new system of land tenure. This distinction again underscores the dialectic of land and legitimacy, with particular weight on the legal components of how legitimacy was understood and enacted. Luis Pozzolo, a member of MASTRO who also took part in the earlier MJT struggles, remembers a clear contrast between the two movements: "The fight against Itaipu was different, yeah because it was already defined, there was a demand [for a better price] that was negotiated. So the [MASTRO] occupations were more complicated. They were against the law, what we were doing was against the law." Reflecting the vision of land as a collective right, Pozzolo added that contrary to claims by newspapers and government critics, MASTRO's actions did not constitute a land *invasion* but rather a land *occupation*, stating that "an invasion is you taking something that isn't yours, an occupation is retaking something that was robbed, because the large estates were all stolen. . . . Who actually invaded was that big [landowner]."[65]

Beginning in 1983, MASTRO took part in six land occupations, the first three in a supporting role and the subsequent three completely under its own leadership. Nildemar Silva looks back on the start of these occupations as a moment when rural communities learned how to mobilize together: "To win that right to land, to get a settlement, the families had to make an occupation, they had to stay united. . . . The movement began to understand that it was possible to defend our rights if we were organized, and that [happened in] the occupations."[66]

The participation of MASTRO in these actions started on April 13 when nearly five hundred people occupied unused lands on the Padroeira farm in the town of Matelândia (figure 7.1).[67] Although not the sole instigator of the occupation—peasants employed on the farm served as the lead organizers—MASTRO contributed logistical support and helped attract public attention.[68] According to the occupying families, the state government had intended to expropriate the farm in the 1970s, but it had remained private property of the Minolli family. In the early 1980s, tenant farmers discovered that the son of the farm's owner had filed a claim against his father to win full ownership for himself. While the son's claim proceeded in court, the workers planned their occupation and even hired a lawyer to file their own claim to the unused land.[69] The landless farmers thus capitalized on a family's internal dispute to seek possession of a portion of farmland that the government had previously failed to expropriate.

Over the first month of the occupation, public opinion shifted toward the peasant farmers. On April 28 the mayor of Matelândia released a statement of support for the landless families, and the following month the state secretary of public safety expressed sympathy for the occupation and promised to "keep the peace." Paraná's ITC director also stated that the only solution was for INCRA to take control of the disputed lands and then transfer them to the occupying families.[70] These declarations, however, did not guarantee government action. Claus Germer, the newly appointed state secretary of agriculture and a key ally in the earlier fight against Itaipu, sidestepped the demands of the Padroeira occupiers by saying that his office could not process any land expropriation; that power, Germer noted, lay with INCRA at the federal level.[71]

FIGURE 7.1 The April 8, 1983, cover of *Nosso Tempo* announces the land occupation on the Padroeira farm in Matelândia. Of note, even supportive media outlets described MASTRO's actions as invasions rather than occupations.

In the face of government inaction, landless farmers continued to pressure authorities by directly agitating for agrarian reform.

Six weeks into the Padroeira occupation, MASTRO held a general assembly ten kilometers away in Medianeira. The meeting brought together over three thousand people, including representatives from INCRA, the diocese of Foz do Iguaçu, the local town council, the ITC, and several rural unions.[72] Early in the meeting, the representative from INCRA, Maria Angela Somero, addressed the crowd and outlined a proposal for resettlement in the Amazon. After years of demanding access to land within Paraná, the workers in Medianeira roundly denounced INCRA's offer. The meeting eventually approved a resolution with four demands: that land be made available to acquire through state agrarian credits, that INCRA and the ITC designate unproductive farms in Paraná for expropriations, that a commission from MASTRO be included in the process of surveying these areas, and that MASTRO organize alongside the authorities a commission to verify INCRA's surveys and projects in northern Brazil. The document ended with an affirmation that "MASTRO emerges to raise the voices of those without land. The present farmers once again confirm the demands of the movement: Land in Paraná. Land only for those who work it and need it to live."[73]

Like other agrarian reform movements of the late dictatorship period, MASTRO invoked the military's own laws as a basis for its political and legal legitimacy. Specifically, MASTRO sought to invert and redeploy the meanings of the 1964 Land Statute. The military regime had passed the statute almost immediately after it seized power. Written as a prerequisite for participating in the programs and financing opportunities of the Alliance for Progress, the statute was intended to regulate land reform and pacify the rural labor movements that had radicalized at the end of João Goulart's presidency. José de Souza Martins argues that this agrarian reform served the military's aim of expanding capitalist agro-industries in the countryside and de-escalating political struggles for land.[74] Although the military government tried to dictate the terms of agrarian reform, rural Brazilians consistently invoked certain aspects of the Land Statute to defend their own vision of agrarian change. In particular, MASTRO focused on two main clauses of the statute. Article 18 authorized land expropriation for the "social good" and also required the rational management of properties. Article 28 allowed for the transfer of property owned by individuals who "employ predatory activities and refuse to implement standards for the conservation of natural resources" and in areas "with high concentrations of tenant farmers, sharecroppers and squatters."[75] Although rarely followed in practice, these laws provided rural groups with the policy language to formulate a legal basis for direct action.[76]

The efforts of MASTRO within Paraná occurred in the context of a national economic crisis. Framed by an oil shock in 1979 and interest rate hikes by the US Federal Reserve in the early 1980s, the crisis of 1979–1983 became "the worst recession in [Brazil's] modern history."[77] During this period inflation rose from 77 percent to 179 percent, and the government's foreign debt nearly doubled, from US$50 billion to US$98 billion.[78] Subsequently, president João Baptista Figueiredo adopted International Monetary Fund prescriptions and implemented sweeping austerity measures that disproportionally placed the burden of adjustment policies on the lower classes.[79] Rising inflation led to a 246 percent increase in the price of staple foods between 1982 and 1983, a serious problem made worse when the federal government passed legislation in July 1983 that limited the wages of Brazilian workers. Having begun negotiations with the International Monetary Fund to curb inflation and bring down the national debt, the government enacted Decree Law No. 2045 that cut all salaries by 20 percent in relation to the newly introduced Consumer Price Index.[80]

In response, workers launched a wave of strikes in the middle of 1983 that culminated with a national day of protest on July 21. São Paulo "was like a holiday," and over two million people participated across the country—including a turnout of nearly 95 percent of all workers in the most concentrated industrial regions. Approximately one million workers in Rio Grande do Sul went on strike, and the city of Rio de Janeiro witnessed its largest demonstration since 1968's March of the 100,000.[81] The protesters denounced the dictatorship's financial policies and demanded the return of political freedoms, above all the return of direct presidential elections as championed by the Diretas Já campaign. At the same time that millions of people in cities were defending their hopes for a democratic future with few immediate repercussions, thousands of rural Brazilians continued to mobilize under increasingly repressive circumstances.

By July, the Padroeira occupation stretched into its third month among rising tensions. On July 1 a group of jagunços most likely paid by the Minolli family set fire to the houses of fifteen families.[82] And in early September farmers exchanged gunshots with the farm's hired security forces, though no injuries resulted. A rumor then circulated that state troopers would soon march on the farm to physically remove the occupiers.[83] The police never marched on the occupation, although they did arrest—and allegedly torture—two landless farmers.[84] This escalation of violence reverberated in other rural protests throughout the region.

The two concurrent land occupations with a MASTRO presence took place on the Anoni and Três Pinheiros farms, in the municipalities of Marmaleiro and Matelândia, respectively. Similar to the Padroeira farm, INCRA had previously cleared Anoni for expropriation, yet the property sat idly in private hands.[85] On July 17, 1983, forty families occupied the Anoni farm, and violence ensued within days. At seven in the morning on July 21, a jagunço named João Scarton arrived with a contingent of armed men and surprised five people outside of their tents. The landless farmers fled amid a scattering of gunfire, and a fifty-three-year-old father of nine named João Maria de Paula was killed.[86] The murder received national media attention, with a headline from O Estado de São Paulo declaring "A Death in the Fight for Land Already Expropriated."[87] In spite of the violence, the families maintained their occupation. As Luis Pozzolo recalls, "everyone was afraid, but if we had been too afraid nothing would have happened because we had no other options. It's [better to] die fighting."[88] Another participant, Afonso Camer, explained that the occupations persevered out of simple necessity: "We resisted because we had to. Hunger speaks louder than [fear], and it spoke for many people."[89]

Two weeks after the death at Anoni, fifty families staged another land occupation on the Três Pinheiros farm in Matelândia. Less than a month into the occupation, state troopers swarmed onto the farm and physically expelled all of the families. One article observed that police tried to seize a Brazilian flag that the occupation had "guard[ed] religiously."[90] This image of peasant farmers and police fighting for control of the Brazilian flag is emblematic of the deeper challenges facing poor rural communities during this period. Nearly two decades into Brazil's dictatorship, the expansion of grassroots actions suggested the military's loosening grip on power. But despite the reemergence of opposition forces, many Brazilians still lived in an authoritarian climate. Regions like the western Paraná countryside symbolized the unfulfilled promise of a new democratic era. For Brazilians like those in MASTRO, neither the abertura nor the official end of military rule in 1985 brought about any immediate change to the daily realities of rural poverty. So when state troopers tore down the Brazilian flag and forced the Três Pinheiros occupiers to set up a new camp along the side of the highway—in a heavy downpour of rain, no less—it represented more than just the end of their land occupation. It symbolized their recurring exclusion from mainstream society.

Whereas MASTRO had played a supportive role in the initial three land protests, the culmination of these recent events pushed the organization to lead its own occupations. On September 19 almost forty families occupied the

Cavernoso farm (also known as Lagoa Santa) in the municipality of Guarapuava. According to MASTRO, the farm's previous owner had used the two hundred hectares to grow drugs, but the police had since thrown him in jail, leaving the land vacant. One of the occupiers told the *Folha de Londrina*, "We are going to stay here, strong, and take control of the farm. I've never had a piece of land, and now I'll fight for a place to plant."[91] As pressure mounted, the Cavernoso occupation was visited by Paraná's governor José Richa, an earlier ally of the MJT movement at Itaipu who had been elected to office the previous year. The occupying families presented Richa a list of demands that reflected a new stage of mobilization. Determined to create entirely new communities, MASTRO now called on the government to provide materials for the construction of houses, schools, and medical facilities.[92] The occupation persisted for over a year before the government consented to a deal that eventually allowed 208 people to live permanently on the land.[93]

Some six months after MASTRO's occupation at Cavernoso, the group staged two follow-up actions. While Cavernoso stood almost two hundred kilometers from the group's center of operations in São Miguel do Iguaçu, the second occupation returned to MASTRO's symbolic birthplace: in May 1984 sixty families occupied land that belonged to the Itaipu Binational Corporation. These seventy alqueires formed part of the dam's security line rimming the reservoir, an area that INCRA planned to incorporate into an ecological reserve.[94] In contrast to the previous land occupations, which took place almost exclusively on private agricultural lands, landless farmers now targeted an area belonging jointly to the state government and the Itaipu dam. One of the participants said that by taking their fight directly to INCRA and Itaipu, MASTRO had "stepped on the right wound."[95] The occupation lasted only eight days before police dispersed the families, but its momentum resurfaced less than two months later when MASTRO mobilized for its largest action yet.

On June 17, 1984, members of MASTRO seized control of 1,280 hectares of land on the Mineira farm in the municipality of São Miguel do Iguaçu. This occupation became MASTRO's most challenging and longest-lasting direct-action protest; in the end, it was also the most successful. For two and a half years, MASTRO maintained its occupation of the Mineira property, and to raise public awareness and political pressure, it also staged an urban protest camp for four months outside of INCRA's headquarters in the state capital of Curitiba.[96] The growing profile of the Mineira occupation received a boost from the visit of Luiz Inácio "Lula" da Silva, the president of the Workers' Party (PT) and the most prominent Brazilian activist of the time. Addressing the occupying families, Lula declared that "every worker in this country needs to know the courageous fight of the landless farmers of western Paraná, because the day that all workers have the courage that you are showing here, the strength of will that you display, on that day there will be no more oppressors and exploiters."[97] The perseverance of the Mineira occupiers eventually secured the expropriation of nearly seven hundred hectares of land, redistributed among forty-one families.[98] When INCRA officially handed over the land in February 1987, it was renamed the Assentamento Sávio-Dois Vizinhos in honor of one of MASTRO's lead organizers, Miguel Isloar Sávio.

Prior to the victory, however, the occupation endured numerous challenges. Within the first month, fifty armed troopers entered the area and pushed out over a hundred families. According to one report, the police swept through the encampment and destroyed tents, furniture, and clothing.[99] The police also arrested and detained twelve members of MASTRO.[100] These events served as some of the largest police actions of the period against landless occupations in Paraná.

An interesting news angle came from a *Folha de Londrina* article regarding a dozen women who defiantly remained on the land after the police raid, demanding the release of their husbands.[101] The resolve of these women appears to have helped secure the eventual freedom of the arrested men. Their depiction in the media, however, hints at an underlying tension. Women were vital members of MASTRO, just as they were in the earlier fight at Itaipu and in other rural struggles. Yet they remained almost completely absent in news coverage of the movement. The few mentions of female farmers often contained little information beyond how many women and children were living in a given land occupation. Although news articles included images of suffering mothers holding or even breastfeeding their babies, the media rarely quoted women.

This silencing of women also existed within MASTRO. In interviews, female members still speak with pride in having participated in the land occupations, but they also explain how the men prohibited them from taking any leadership role whatsoever. Teolide Turcatel remembers the machismo that predominated in MASTRO, saying, "We wanted equality, we fought for equality, and the men got angry at us, the leadership didn't want us to get more involved."[102] Along with being excluded from the movement's decision-making progress, she recalls that when the police threatened to invade MASTRO's camps, the leadership sent women with their children to the front lines to lessen the chance of a violent attack. Another woman, Iraci Maino, offers a similar perspective: "In the camps, a woman was for cooking, for cleaning, for working, for taking care of things, but not for taking part in anything."[103] When asked about the role of MASTRO's female participants, male interviewees spoke enthusiastically about the courage of women during the occupation. But none offered any indication they saw women as having played anything more than a supporting role.

This book has presented numerous examples of the contradictions that exist within social movements. In the fight against Itaipu, the MJT neglected indigenous groups almost entirely and never prioritized the demands of landless farmers. The limitations placed on women like Turcatel and Maino show that MASTRO, despite originating as a movement marginalized by Brazilian society and by a previous rural struggle, nonetheless produced its own hierarchies and forms of exclusion. In spite of these internal tensions, landless occupations continued to spread throughout western Paraná and across the nation. The growing momentum culminated in a meeting in early 1984 that stood as a watershed moment in the history of Brazilian social movements.

Cascavel and the Formation of the Landless Workers Movement

From January 20 to 22, 1984, approximately a hundred people from twelve states gathered in the western Paraná city of Cascavel to discuss the situation of landless farmers in Brazil. Over these three days, the Landless Workers Movement (MST) officially formed.[104] This represented the largest attempt in Brazilian history to establish a nationwide organization devoted to agrarian reform. The MST has since become one of the most prominent social movements in Latin America. Its creation in 1984, one year before the official end of military rule, marked the emergence of landless workers as a nationally organized and politically potent force (figure 7.2).

This chapter has not aimed to draw a blind link between the struggle for land at Itaipu and the formation of the MST. As seen throughout this book, rural struggles had developed across generations and across regions. In the early 1980s, conditioned by the changing political climate of abertura, MASTRO was one of many organizations that helped propel the landless campaign to unprecedented levels. As such, I do not contend that the MST would never have formed without the MJT fight against the Itaipu dam. Rather, by understanding how MASTRO served as an important—but not singular—genealogy between the two movements, we can open new insights into the history of rural mobilizations in Brazil.

FIGURE 7.2 Cover image of conference proceedings, National Landless Meeting, Cascavel, January 20 to 22, 1984. Courtesy of Davi Schreiner.

The MST has inspired a robust body of scholarship. As Cliff Welch observes, this literature tends to depict the movement as a reaction to the elite concentration of land and the mechanization of agriculture.[105] Without diverting attention from the core issue of access to land and rural unemployment, the case of MASTRO demands that scholars expand their explanations for how the MST came into being. Along with denouncing the abuses of agricultural estates and an unresponsive government bureaucracy, the landless struggles in western Paraná suggest that the MST also emerged from inequalities *among* rural communities. The connections between Itaipu and the MST illuminate the continuities and the fissures between different forms of rural mobilization. Almost all anglophone scholars have written about the MST's founding conference without making a single reference to MASTRO's participation. Many Brazilians, in contrast, acknowledge MASTRO as an important piece in the 1984 creation of the MST.[106] Moreover, the MST's own website lists MASTRO alongside the Encruzilhada Natalino conflict as the two most influential antecedents of the MST.[107] An overview of MASTRO's role in the 1984 Cascavel meeting thus offers a starting point for understanding how the localized conflicts in western Paraná helped open a new era of landless struggle throughout Brazil.

It is no coincidence that the MST's national founding took place in western Paraná, less than 150 kilometers from the Itaipu dam. After hosting the Medianeira regional conference in July 1982, MASTRO established a leading presence among national landless movements. Along with serving as a logistically feasible meeting point for groups arriving from different regions, western Paraná had also become one of the country's most active zones of landless mobilization. Of Brazil's twelve largest land occupations in 1983, four took place in the state of Paraná.[108] The minutes of the Cascavel meeting provide further evidence of the respect and importance accorded to MASTRO. After introductions during the morning of the first day, the afternoon focused on a "presentation of the experiences of struggle." The very first group to recount its history was MASTRO.[109] On the summit's third and final day, attendees identified MASTRO's Cavernoso and Anoni occupations as some of the most notable victories across the country.[110] Finally, an SNI surveillance report noted that a representative from MASTRO, Dalézio Schmidt, served on the meeting's leadership committee.[111]

Acknowledging MASTRO's role at the 1984 Cascavel meeting provides more than just an update to anglophone historiography. It underscores how members of MASTRO went from being almost an afterthought in the fight at Itaipu to being key contributors in the creation of Brazil's largest social movement. For Brazilians who fought in movements like MASTRO and the MST, the idea of land as a collective right extended beyond the material goal of agrarian reform. At a moment rhetorically filled with the abertura's promise of a new era, the belief that land was a fundamental right held the potential to make poor rural Brazilians visible in the national imaginary, and to elevate their status as legitimate sociopolitical actors.

Despite the progress made at Cascavel—and perhaps because of it—rural families continued to face severe repression. The ongoing violence suggests that Brazilian elites remained determined to keep the countryside isolated from the broader return of democratic freedoms. Four months after the Cascavel meeting, hired gunmen killed a fifty-two-year-old father of ten named Raimundo Nonanto de Oliveira on the Padroeira land occupation—the site of MASTRO's first mobilization.[112] The murder of landless farmers became increasingly common during this period; the MST claimed that 116 rural Brazilians were killed in 1983 alone.[113] The death of Nonanto de Oliveira, however, offered particular cause for alarm because it happened three months *after* the state government brokered a deal between the farm's owners and the occupying families.[114] Although the ITC had theoretically secured the sale of almost two hundred hectares of land to be distributed among 116 families, the government had not yet begun processing the contracts. Nor did the state protect the lives of farmers as they waited for their new land titles.

On April 10, 1984, a month before the Padroeira murder, one million demonstrators took to the streets of São Paulo in the single largest protest in Brazilian history.[115] Part of the national Diretas Já campaign that fought (unsuccessfully, in the end) for direct presidential elections, the events in São Paulo marked the apex of mainstream opposition forces under the abertura. The torrent of urban opposition in the early to mid-1980s stands in contrast to the authoritarian realities that persisted in places like the western Paraná countryside. In both cases, Brazilians rallied around a particular vision of democratic rights. When urban citizens mobilized for electoral and political rights, they did so with relatively little pushback. But when landless Brazilians fought under a banner of agrarian rights, they confronted undulating waves of repression. Workers like those in MASTRO often saw themselves as participants in Brazil's democratization, yet this enduring violence suggested that the fruits of abertura did not belong to them. Whether shaped by military leaders, elite politicians, or even grassroots protests in the streets, the dominant framework of abertura looked to reverse the structures of dictatorship: civilian rule should be restored, political freedoms should flourish anew, and direct elections should again determine the country's future. Yet for landless workers, democracy promised more than just the absence of dictatorship, more than just the return to a supposedly better era before 1964. For impoverished and marginalized Brazilians—whether in the countryside or in cities—the official return of democratic rule did not mean they now lived in a democracy. For this reason, their struggles continued long after 1985.

Landless mobilizations in western Paraná during the early 1980s offer a complicated balance sheet. On the one hand, the region became a center of an emerging national movement, with MASTRO sparking a veritable alphabet soup of grassroots organizations throughout the state: MASTEL (Landless Farmers Movement of the Paraná Coast), MASTRECO (Landless Farmers Movement of Center-West Paraná), MASTEN (Landless Farmers Movement of Northern Paraná), and MASTES (Landless Farmers Movement of Southwest Paraná). Although rural discontent had simmered for decades, the climate of abertura allowed these movements to forge new platforms for challenging their marginalized standing in Brazilian society. With MASTRO as the first and largest of these groups, Paraná became one of Brazil's most active centers of landless mobilization and was chosen to host the 1984 founding of the MST. Moreover, many of the occupations of the early 1980s eventually achieved their goals of having land expropriated and redistributed into federally legislated assentamentos. Although it took fifteen years, the Anoni occupation eventually became the Assentamento José Eduardo Raduan, with 3,946 hectares of land redistributed among 436 families.[116] And as mentioned earlier, in 1987 MASTRO's Mineira occupation became the Assentamento Sávio-Dois Vizinhos.[117]

On the other hand, these achievements form part of a larger history of landless struggle that also includes a series of deaths, assaults, and forced displacements. Landless movements like MASTRO and later the MST sought to transform the existing structure of land tenure, a goal considered radical and thus unacceptable by elites throughout the country. The audacity of this challenge helps explain the resulting violence, both in the early 1980s and in the decades since. Connected to a history of rural repression that long predated the start of the dictatorship, the abuse suffered by MASTRO and other agrarian reform movements did not subside after the return to civilian rule in 1985. If anything, the growing profile and momentum of the MST actually escalated violence in the countryside. Whereas an estimated 1,500 land-reform activists and peasants were killed during the official period of dictatorship from 1964 to 1985, nearly 2,000 were killed between 1985 and 2016.[118] From this perspective, the fight for land has only become more authoritarian since the transition to democracy.

The point here is not to voyeuristically highlight instances of violence but rather to place them within the context of how rural repression existed before, during, and after the official parameters of military rule. Nor is it a suggestion that other regions in Brazil, both rural and urban alike, did not continue to face their own forms of physical and social repression in the waning years of dictatorship. Instead, the persistence of rural violence suggests that although abuses like those in the Paraná borderlands were amplified by the climate of authoritarian rule, they belonged to a broader history of authoritarianism. This perspective complicates the traditional periodization of dictatorships. More important, it also demands that scholars of modern Brazil, especially those studying the military era, attempt to look past the static boundaries of a given political system or time period in order to trace the deeper constructions of social exclusion and repression. Of the many realities of abertura, perhaps the starkest of all is the understanding that the incomplete process of democratization resulted not from the transition out of military rule but from the inequalities long embedded in the fabric of Brazilian society.

After the Flood

Over the course of two weeks in October 1982, almost thirty billion cubic meters of water spread out behind the Itaipu dam, submerging 1,350 square kilometers of land that had supported roughly sixty thousand people living along the Brazil-Paraguay border. The Itaipu flood was the culmination of two decades' worth of engineering and technical planning, and the purported solution to over a century's worth of geopolitical tensions between the neighboring countries. After such a long and conflict-ridden path to creating the reservoir basin, the 1982 flood set in motion a relatively straightforward process of producing the dam's much-heralded hydroelectric energy. The first power-generating unit became operational in May 1984, with seventeen more units installed over the following seven years. When two more stations were added in 2007, Itaipu's capacity stood at 14,000 megawatt-hours, making it the largest producer of hydroelectric power in the world. Between 1984 and 2016, Itaipu generated more than 2.4 billion megawatt-hours, providing almost 20 percent of the energy consumed in Brazil and a staggering 75 percent of the energy used in Paraguay.

None of this hydroelectricity would have been possible without the flood, and in many ways the history of Itaipu can be understood in terms of "before" and "after" the events of October 1982. Before the flood, Brazilian governments had struggled to fulfill their goals for development and industrialization; after the flood, the Itaipu dam steadily energized a new era of modernized growth. Before the flood, Brazil had jostled with its neighbors in the Southern Cone for political and economic dominance; after the flood, it emerged as the region's most powerful nation. Before the flood, it was uncertain which of the dictatorship's policies would persist into Brazil's potential democratic future; after the flood, the legacy of military rule was enshrined in the Itaipu reservoir that stretched across the now-inundated borderland. As a permanent fixture representing the dictatorship's geopolitical worldview, the waters of Itaipu offered physical proof of how the realities of authoritarian rule could survive long after the military was removed from power.

The flood also served as a turning point for many of the displaced communities. When asked about Itaipu, interviewees often framed their memories around notions of before and after. As one farmer, Adil Fochezatto, recalled, the dam "was terrible for you, and you know why? Because before we were a community . . . [but] then everything started to change, one person left for here, another moved over there, there was no way to maintain a community. Everything changed."[1] And in thinking about her life before Itaipu, Dona Suita fought back tears while sharing, "All of my family lived in the same place, we had a beautiful property, near a river with a waterfall, really pretty, marvelous. Even today we feel like we died of sadness. But what can you do?"[2]

Yet despite the rupture so clearly felt in the above quotations, the importance of what took place at Itaipu cannot fully be captured in the crisp timeline implied by before and after. The flood, like the experience of dictatorship more broadly, held different meanings for different groups, and any discussion of either before or after must account for the plurality of timelines that existed, whether in the western Paraná borderlands or any other region of Brazil. This book has argued that a rural perspective helps complicate the dominant periodization of Brazilian history, showing how the assumed boundaries between military and civilian rule begin to fall apart when seen from the countryside. To fully understand the grassroots rural histories at Itaipu—both in contrast to urban and elite spaces, and also on their own terms—we must explore the multiple and overlapping chronologies that blur the temporal lines of the Itaipu flood. By extension, this approach also challenges the dichotomy of dictatorship and democracy in Brazil.

Frameworks of Time, Place, and Struggle

To better understand the complicated relationship between ideas of before and after, we can revisit the three theoretical contributions of this book: the dialectic of land and legitimacy, the double reality of abertura, and the overarching theme of the book, the visibility of rural Brazil.

First, the dialectic of land and legitimacy shows how relationships to land can tether social standing to notions of place and time. In the Paraná borderlands, three categories of rural Brazilians lived in close proximity to one another. Despite inhabiting the same landscape and mobilizing against a common enemy in Itaipu, the experience of each group diverged according to its distinct connection to land. The title-holding farmers saw land as individual property; landless workers (peasants, sharecroppers, and day laborers, among others) saw land as a basis of their collective rights; and for the Avá-Guarani indigenous community, land existed as a way of life. These perceptions of land impacted the sociopolitical legitimacy of each group and the extent to which they were included in Brazil's reemerging climate of democracy.

It is no coincidence that each of the interviews on the previous page lamenting the rupture caused by Itaipu came from farmers whose families held the legal deed to their flooded lands. Without diminishing the traumas they experienced in the aftermath of Itaipu, their testimonies show how the ability to remember a relatively idyllic life before the flood was a privilege reserved mainly for the title-holding small farmers. To be sure, these rural communities were an impoverished sector of Brazil's population, both before and after Itaipu. But their ownership of small plots of land—and their status as Euro-descendant farmers—brought them a certain level of respect in the eyes of mainstream society. This sense of legitimacy increased in the politicized context of abertura and democratization, when the Justice and Land Movement (MJT) staged two protest camps that drew national attention and successfully forced Itaipu to pay higher land prices. The ability to purchase new properties helped these farmers navigate the hardships of displacement and maintain their status as legitimate, if still marginalized, citizens of Brazil.

The same could not be said for the region's landless peasants and indigenous groups, whose more radical notions of land tenure kept them on the margins of both the Justice and Land Movement and the mainstream abertura. As such, their participation in the most visible fight at Itaipu did not guarantee any immediate victories. In the aftermath of the standoff at Itaipu and the 1982 flood, the ongoing defense of their particular relationships to land emboldened these groups to carve a space in Brazil's reemerging democratic landscape. The peasants created a new movement called MASTRO (Landless Farmers Movement of Western Paraná) that used direct land occupations to make the question of landlessness and agrarian reform one of the most important issues in postdictatorship Brazil. And after being relocated to a new indigenous reserve, the Avá-Guarani used strategies and tools learned at Itaipu (solidarity networks, media coverage, appeals to federal laws) to advance their long-standing efforts to assert their political rights as Brazilians and their cultural rights as Indians. So while the title-holding farmers bought new lands and settled into a distinguishably new chapter of their lives after the flood, the region's landless and indigenous communities persisted in their pre-Itaipu and predictatorship struggle for land and legitimacy.

The concept of a double reality of abertura provides a second framework for reimagining notions of before and after. The core premise of the official abertura was that an elite-controlled and gradual process of reform could return Brazil to the type of democratic system prevailing before the 1964 coup. But because the benefits of that pre-1964 democracy had not been shared equally, the fight for a new society in the late 1970s and early 1980s included a chorus of competing voices and aspirations. The double reality of abertura posits that all Brazilians experienced democratization at two levels: the official abertura they understood to be dominant elsewhere and the version they experienced as their own reality and their own hope for the future. Mainstream opposition forces mobilized for institutional reform and direct presidential elections, yet even before the military seized power, rural communities had rarely benefited from these political freedoms. And because areas like the Paraná countryside had suffered repression and inequality regardless of whether Brazil was under military or democratic rule, local families saw few of their own concerns reflected in the official policies of abertura. While Brazilian elites and urban social movements inched along a gradual albeit inconsistent path of democratization, the displaced farmers, peasants, and indigenous communities confronted the reality that for Brazilians like them, the return of democracy would not automatically bring a less repressive life.

The gulf between the official and the lived versions of abertura explains why marginalized groups like those in the Paraná borderlands fought for a democracy that offered more than just the reversal of dictatorship. Rather than returning to a time before military rule, groups in the Itaipu flood zone strove to chart an entirely new foundation from which to grow Brazilian democracy. For rural communities living in Itaipu's shadow, these alternative visions included the abertura's stated goals of political rights and electoral freedoms, but they were premised above all on demands that had not yet been seen as pillars of a democratic society: access to land, respect for rural livelihoods, and the inclusion of the Brazilian countryside as a legitimate space in the national imaginary. So although the struggle at Itaipu emerged during the period of abertura, both its origins and its ripple effects extended beyond the immediacy of Brazil's political reopening. Life before the dictatorship diverged across lines of class, ethnicity, gender, regional background, and relationships to land, and as a result the transition out of military rule was experienced on overlapping timelines.

Despite the continuities before and after the dictatorship, the context of abertura did, in fact, cultivate a series of significant changes. As seen throughout this book, the process of confronting the Itaipu dam, such an important appendage of the dictatorship, fostered new levels of political engagement that allowed communities in western Paraná to adapt their existing notions of justice to new contexts. Protesting farmers referred to Itaipu as a big political classroom and a laboratory of consciousness; landless peasants remembered their participation—in spite of its limitations—as the spark that started their later independent mobilization; and members of the Avá-Guarani credited the conflict at Itaipu with teaching them how to tap into grassroots networks and the media to bring attention to their cause. Even if displaced communities could never fully access the rights promised by the abertura, the growth of political consciousness and social movement organizing in the early 1980s suggests that local groups were able to appropriate the meanings of democratization and refashion them toward their own parallel set of goals. So whereas the structural inequalities in the Paraná countryside did not fundamentally change before or after Itaipu and the abertura, what did change was the perceptions of what was politically possible and the tools available for attempting to bring those changes to fruition.

The struggles that formed in the shadow of the Itaipu dam represented a turning point in the history of rural mobilization and representation. Against a backdrop of abertura and the national movement for democracy, the conflicts at Itaipu offered a platform on which a wide range of rural Brazilians could articulate and attempt to make visible their visions of land and justice. Because these ideas were predicated on histories of inequality and social mobilization that long predated the official start of military rule, they positioned rural communities to develop strategies of collective action that extended beyond the impending return of democratic rule.

An Unbroken River

This book has used the Itaipu flood as an analogy for Brazil's military dictatorship. As the most repressive and most visible event in the construction of the Itaipu dam, the 1982 flood serves as a cogent symbol not only of the authoritarianism that loomed over Brazil between the 1960s and 1980s but also of the popular struggles that mobilized in response. For this book's guiding framework—the idea of rural visibility—the image of the flood offers a fitting conclusion for a history of the social and physical landscapes that dot the Brazilian countryside.

Although the flood permanently transformed the Paraná River, it did not erase it entirely. In the aftermath of the flood, the waters of the Paraná no longer flowed unobstructed as they did before, but they still remained in motion, only now as part of the dam's reservoir basin. Even the reservoir stayed in flux: to produce energy, water would be released through Itaipu's turbines before emptying out further downstream. The flood determined the shape and contours of the Paraná River at that particular spot, but the Itaipu dam sits on only a small section of the seventh-longest river on the planet. Running its course over nearly three thousand kilometers before emptying into the Plate basin and the Atlantic Ocean, the Paraná River continues to exist and move forward in spite of the Itaipu dam and its reservoir basin.

For communities in western Paraná, this broader view also helps contextualize the experience of living through Brazil's dictatorship. Despite the traumas suffered between 1964 and 1985, the realities of rural life under military rule were shaped, but never defined, by the actions and ideologies of the dictatorship. Like the Paraná River, life in the countryside was not determined solely by one bend in time or one cascading series of events. This reality was as true for instances of repression as it was for moments of opposition. Events like the Itaipu flood—and the violence of military rule more broadly—represented particularly concentrated efforts to literally and imaginatively remove certain groups from the national polity and its territories. Yet the history of marginalization in the countryside also emerged from everyday forms of violence on display throughout this book, including the dispossession of land, attacks on ethnic identities, and the systemic belief that rural livelihoods and rural demands were illegitimate. And although the farmers, peasants, and Indians directly mobilized against a branch of an authoritarian regime, the standoffs at Itaipu were not defined by the immediacy of military rule. Rather, the contingencies of dictatorship and the political climate of abertura magnified a deeper history of efforts to make the countryside visible.

When we see Itaipu in its larger context, the question is no longer what took place before or after. Because there is no common chronology to unify the meanings attached to paradigmatic events like the flood or the dictatorship, we must shift our attention instead to the scales of time and the degrees of visibility that help determine a given history. The tensions within and between the various groups displaced by Itaipu show that to fully understand the stories on display in this book, we must study rural communities in relation to both mainstream society and also their own neighbors. This approach guides us to questions of how rural Brazilians are seen, when, and by whom, allowing experiences like those at Itaipu to open new pathways into exploring the people and the landscapes that are too often left at the margins of history.

Both the flood and the military regime that produced it left communities devastated in ways that continue to provoke trauma and sadness to this day. Yet they also brought attention to a region that had long been ignored and created opportunities for marginalized communities to develop new strategies and networks toward the goal of overcoming entrenched inequalities. The violence of dictatorship and the mass displacement at Itaipu destroyed livelihoods and forever changed the region. But like the Paraná River after the flood, displaced Brazilians stayed in motion, taking the lessons and hardships learned at Itaipu and carving out new lives along new shores. Some of these families stayed close by in western Paraná, building homes just beyond the reservoir basin. Some flowed west across the border into Paraguay or north into the Amazon, and others spread throughout southern and central Brazil. Seen together, these rural Brazilians formed tributaries of displaced communities that, although separated by geography and social standing, were connected by the memories of having overlapped at a particular moment in a tucked-away borderland to confront, even if just briefly, a common threat.

NOTES

Introduction

Epigraph: As quoted in Bento Ribeiro, *Memórias do concreto*, 40.

1 This book focuses almost exclusively on Itaipu as it relates to Brazil, although an equally important and at times overlapping history took place in Paraguay. The Itaipu flood covered 570 square kilometers of Paraguayan lands (compared to 780 square kilometers in Brazil) and displaced over twenty thousand local Paraguayans, compared to over forty thousand Brazilians. For more on the Paraguayan story of Itaipu, see Gómez Florentín, "The Making of the Itaipú Hydroelectric Dam."

2 Hudson, *Brazil*, 195.

3 During military rule, elections for senators and federal deputies were held in 1966, 1970, 1974, and 1978. In 1982 Brazilians directly elected state governors, a victory of the opposition's campaign within the abertura. For more, see Fleischer, "The Constituent Assembly and the Transformation Strategy."

4 The official estimate was 40,000 displaced people, yet because Itaipu's statistics counted only those with legal title, it is impossible to calculate how many landless families were impacted. As will be shown in chapter 2, Guiomar Inez Germani places the number between 42,000 and 43,000. But even Germani's estimates (extrapolated from census data in 1970 and 1975) do not include the squatters, day laborers, and itinerant rural workers who might have left the region without being counted (Germani, *Expropriados*, 54). Moreover, Itaipu uses the unit of "families" (meaning individual expropriation cases) rather than the total number of people on a given plot of land. Itaipu calculated 8,500 families: 1,600 urban and 6,900 rural. Itaipu's only enumeration of the landless (as shown in chapter 6) involved the 4,082 people sent to three colonization projects. Two close observers at the time offer their estimates for how many landless Brazilians were impacted by Itaipu. Miguel Isloar Sávio, a leader of the landless movement, said that of the 6,900 displaced rural families, between 30 and 40 percent were landless (Miguel Isloar Sávio, interview with Davi Schreiner, São Miguel do Iguaçu, Brazil, October 15, 1996, transcript courtesy of Davi Schreiner). The journalist Juvêncio Mazzarollo places the number at 20 percent (Mazzarollo, *A taipa da injustiça*, 49). Using a conservative middle figure of 25 percent and based on

Germani's calculation that the 6,900 rural families represented 38,455 people in total, one can estimate a baseline of 9,500 landless people. Subtracting the 4,082 individuals sent to resettlement projects, it is fair to suggest that between 5,000 and 6,000 displaced people were not accounted for in Itaipu's statistics. As such, rather than the official estimate of 40,000, or even Germani's approximation of 42,000, the number might more accurately be in the range of 46,000 to 48,000.

5 For a more detailed study of Itaipu's construction, see White, "Itaipu," 62–107. Although the present book strategically gives more attention to the social, political, and rural histories of Itaipu, there is ample terrain for a future project explicitly on the engineering and environmental histories of the dam. Such a study would contribute to a budding literature on water management, technocrats, and the environment across Latin America; recent works in this vein include Wolfe, *Watering the Revolution*; and Buckley, *Technocrats and the Politics of Drought and Development*.

6 The history of the landless movement in western Paraná, and its absence in much of the historiography, is the subject of chapter 7. For an overview of the MST, see Wolford, *This Land Is Ours Now*.

7 Devine Guzmán, *Native and National in Brazil*.

8 For more on opposition movements to hydroelectric dams worldwide, see Khagram, *Dams and Development*.

9 The MJT fight at Itaipu predated—and directly influenced—what soon became a larger movement against the construction of megadams in Brazil, a group known first as the Regional Commission of People Affected by Dams and later renamed the Movement of People Affected by Dams.

10 To be sure, rural-based visions for democracy long predated the period of Itaipu. As far back as 1875, for example, the black abolitionist and engineer André Rebouças argued in his seminal book *A Democracia rural brasileira* that the dismantling of land monopolies, in conjunction with creating a rural workforce of emancipated former slaves, could unleash the country's full democratic potential. For Rebouças, breaking up the concentration of land, especially in a postabolition context, would cultivate a form of Brazilian democracy nourished by both individualism (*a iniciativa individual*, meaning the self-driven autonomy of independent farmers) and a "spirit of collectivism" (*espirito de associação*) among the farmers. Rebouças called this collectivism of autonomous rural Brazilians *yankismo*, for his admiration of the North American settler-farmer model. Compared to the more utopian vision of Rebouças, the history of Itaipu will show how different rural groups tended to form their political and social attachments to democracy not as a combination of individualism and collectivism but rather as a proclivity toward one or the other.

11 Two classic works on the period are Moreira Alves, *State and Opposition in Military Brazil*; and Skidmore, *The Politics of Military Rule in Brazil*. For political parties as opposition, see Keck, *The Workers' Party and Democratization in Brazil*; and Kinzo, *Legal Opposition Politics under Authoritarian Rule in Brazil*. For opposition and the church, see Serbin, *Secret Dialogues*. For the Diretas Já (Direct

Elections Now) campaign, see Tosi Rodrigues, *Diretas Já*. Examples of newer attempts to rethink the abertura include Dunn, *Contracultura*; Pinheiro, *Cale-se*; Green, *We Cannot Remain Silent*; Langland, *Speaking of Flowers*; McCann, *Hard Times in the Marvelous City*; Atencio, *Memory's Turn*; and Snider, "'An Incomplete Autonomy.'"

12 Existing literature has treated rural social movements and indigenous histories as almost entirely distinct fields. In her capstone study of twentieth-century rural struggles, for example, Leonilde Medeiros makes no mention of indigenous Brazilians. Medeiros, *História dos movimentos sociais no campo*. Although scholarship on rural mobilization has dramatically increased in the past two decades—largely a response to the rise of the MST—there has been little effort to view the struggles of indigenous people as part of the wider history of collective action in the Brazilian countryside. Only one study offers more than a casual reference to the role of indigenous communities in the radicalization of rural Brazil: Wright and Wolford, *To Inherit the Earth*. The history of Paraná is also largely absent in the vast literature on agrarian movements. Its most thorough treatment is a two-sentence mention of the protests at Itaipu in Branford and Rocha, *Cutting the Wire*, 150.

13 Nixon, *Slow Violence*. Nixon's framework of unimagined communities is a challenge to Anderson, *Imagined Communities*.

14 Nixon, *Slow Violence*, 151.

15 Scott, *Seeing like a State*, 4.

16 Rogers, *The Deepest Wounds*, 6.

17 Melià, "A experiência religiosa Guarani," 336.

18 For an overview of the early decades of rural unions, see Welch, *The Seed Was Planted*.

1. Borders, Geopolitics, and Itaipu

1 Galeano, *Crónicas latinoamericanas*, 139.

2 For an overview of the war, see Whigham, *The Paraguayan War*.

3 The region is spelled Guaíra in Portuguese and Guairá in Spanish; I will employ the former.

4 Arquivo Nacional, Brasília (henceforth AN-BSB), Itamaraty report, July 5, 1967, N8.0.PSN, EST.286, 736.

5 Brazil's geopolitical overtaking of Argentina began in the 1930s and accelerated in the 1940s when the government of Getúlio Vargas aligned the country with the United States in World War II. For more on the changing relationships during this time among Brazil, Argentina, and the United States, see Hilton, "The United States, Brazil, and the Cold War"; and Hilton, "The Argentine Factor in Twentieth-Century Brazilian Foreign Policy Strategy."

6 For a history of Brazil's early twentieth-century actions in the Amazon, with a focus on Euclides da Cunha as one of the main agents on the ground, see Hecht, *The Scramble for the Amazon*.

7   For more on the Alliance for Progress, see Taffet, *Foreign Aid as Foreign Policy*. For covert US actions, see Rabe, *The Killing Zone*.

8   The 1973 Treaty of Itaipu will be discussed later in this chapter.

9   Archivo Histórico de la Cancillería de Paraguay (hereafter AHCP), "Tratado de límites entre la República del Paraguay y el Império del Brasil," 1872. The holdings of the AHCP are not organized by category. Cited evidence therefore contains only the identifying numbers of the original documents themselves.

10 The Brazilian government cited international legal theory to argue that there was no need to outline those final twenty kilometers since they were already legally implied in the treaty of 1872's designation of the peak of the Mbaracajú hills and the tallest waterfall as "natural" frontier markers. Brazil cited the 1945 work of Stephen B. Jones, who argued that "unless the boundary is *clearly marked in nature* or is *uninhabited* or inaccessible country, it is desirable that monuments be intervisible." Jones, *Boundary-Making*, 215.

11 Key meetings of the Joint Border Commission included the Second Conference of July 29, 1933; the Eleventh Conference of August 21, 1939; the Thirteenth Conference of May 5, 1941; the Fifteenth Conference of May 29, 1945; the Twenty-First Conference of December 21, 1955; and the Twenty-Fifth Conference of November 20, 1961.

12 Soares de Lima, *The Political Economy of Brazilian Foreign Policy*, 352–57.

13 To counter Argentina's downstream claims, Brazil cited the 1895 Harmon Doctrine—named for Judson Harmon, the former US attorney general. Soares de Lima, *The Political Economy of Brazilian Foreign Policy*, 347.

14 Arguments for the importance of the policies of the Mitre government in Argentina come from McLynn, "The Causes of the War of Triple Alliance." Those who cite British commercial interests as the main cause include Pomer, *La Guerra del Paraguay*; Hobsbawm, *The Age of Capital*; and Peñalba, "Draft Dodgers, War Resisters and Turbulent Gauchos."

15 McLynn, "The Causes of the War of Triple Alliance," 43. More recently, Thomas Whigham has argued that the war's cause emerged "within a narrow realm of politics. Specifically, the war can be traced to political ambitions and how those ambitions expressed themselves in the construction of new nations." Whigham, *The Paraguayan War*, xiv.

16 AN-BSB, secret letter from João Baptista Figueiredo to President Emílio Médici, December 1, 1969, Exposição de Motivos No. 056/69, in N8.0.PSN, EST.285.

17 AHCP, DPI (Departamento de Política Internacional) no. 712, December 14, 1965; and "Suscinta informacion sobre el diferendo paraguayo-brasileño relativo al salto del guaira," March 15, 1966.

18 Macedo de Mendonça, "A geopolítica e a política externa do Brasil," 152.

19 Modeled on foreign projects like the Tennessee Valley Authority, CIBPU was a form of regional integration unprecedented in South America. It existed from 1951 to 1972 and helped oversee the construction of various river-based public

works projects in the states of São Paulo, Mato Grosso, Minas Gerais, Goiás, Paraná, Rio Grande do Sul, and Santa Catarina. Gardin, CIBPU.

20 Khagram, *Dams and Development*, 142.

21 Lima, *Políticas de governo e desenvolvimento*, 80.

22 Duarte Pereira, *Itaipu*, 53.

23 Marcondes Ferraz had previously overseen the construction of the Paulo Afonso dam on the São Francisco River in the northeastern state of Bahia, and in 1962 served on the board of the São Paulo–based electricity company Light. After the military coup of 1964, he was nominated by President Humberto Castelo Branco to serve as president of Eletrobras, a position he held through the entire tenure of Castelo Branco's administration (1964–1967). Centro de Pesquisa e Documentação de História Contemporânea do Brasil–Fundação Getúlio Vargas (hereafter CPDOC-FGV), Verbete biográfico, Otávio Marcondes Ferraz. It should also be noted that the Ministry of Mines and Energy had only recently been created as an official government body in July 1960.

24 CPDOC-FGV, "Relatório preliminar sobre o aproveitamento do Salto de Sete Quedas (Guairá) Rio Paraná," December 1962. Source: OMF 61.11.23, Folder VII.

25 AN-BSB, Foreign Ministry of Brazil letter No. 94, March 12, 1962, written to the Paraguayan embassy in Rio de Janeiro, in N8.0.PSN, EST.286.

26 Although the Brazilian government was aware of the results of the Joint Border Commission's efforts, it took no decisive action in response. Arquivo Histórico de Itamaraty, Brasília (hereafter AHI), Confidential Note No. 245, 930(42)(43), July 17, 1962.

27 AN-BSB, aaa/dam/sdf/daj/24/254.(43), September 12, 1962, in n8.0.psn, est.286.

28 AN-BSB, Foreign Ministry of Brazil letter No. 115, June 14, 1963, written to the Paraguayan embassy in Rio de Janeiro.

29 AHI, Note No. 358/254.(43), September 11, 1963.

30 Juan Antonio Pozzo Moreno, "Un reconocimiento pendiente," *ABC Color*, October 21, 2012, http://www.abc.com.py/edicion-impresa/suplementos/economico/un-reconocimiento-pendiente-467321.html.

31 Goulart is quoted in "Stroessner faz acôrdo com Goulart: Sete Quedas," *Jornal do Brasil*, January 29, 1964, 1; Stroessner's quotation is from AHI, Telegram No. 53, DAM/254.(43), February 27, 1964.

32 "Encontro de Presidentes: Paraguai Apóia Construção de Sete Quedas," *Última Hora*, January 21, 1964, 6.

33 "Encontro de Presidentes."

34 "Stroessner faz acôrdo com Goulart: Sete Quedas," *Jornal do Brasil*, January 21, 1964, 1.

35 "7 Quedas: Não há compromisso com USSR," *O Jornal*, January 5, 1964, 1; and "Goulart responderá à nota soviética, que não faz ofertas," *Jornal do Brasil*, January 5, 1964, 3.

36 Parker, *Brazil and the Quiet Intervention, 1964*.

37 Foreign Relations of the United States (hereafter FRUS), State Department paper, "Guidelines of U.S. Policy and Operations, Brazil," February 7, 1963, 1961–1963 vol. 12: 487–90.

38 Smith, *Brazil and the United States*, 154–56.

39 Weis, *Cold Warriors and Coups d'État*, 153.

40 FRUS, telegram from the Department of State to the embassy in Brazil, March 30, 1964, 1964–1968, vol. 31, doc. 194.

41 AHCP, Brazilian Embassy Note 322, November 8, 1965.

42 This was known as the Ata das Cataratas in Portuguese and the Acta de Iguazú in Spanish.

43 Given the importance of Brasil Grande in the ideological formation of modern Brazil, it has generated surprisingly little scholarship, though an important analysis on how it fit into the policies of the dictatorship is available in Fico, *Reinventando o otimismo*, esp. 73–88.

44 Ynsfrán, *Un giro geopolítico*, 70.

45 AHI, Operation Sagarana, Secret Report CTF/1, 254(43), paragraph 29, June 22, 1967.

46 "Hasteamento da bandeira paraguaia em Coronel Renato provocou a sua ocupação pelos militares brasileiros," *Jornal do Brasil*, January 6, 1966, 7. This article was the second in a five-part series on the border conflict. This report and testimony were then passed along to General Alvaro Tavares do Carmo, commander of the Fifth Military Region. AN-BSB, Ministry of War Report No. 994/S-102-CIE, April 24, 1969, in BR.DFAN.BSB.Z4.SNA.CFR.0007.

47 Tosta was especially alarmed by Paraguay's well-developed border presence, noting the existence of a school, numerous churches, a hotel, a police station, and even an airstrip. This stood in stark contrast to Brazil's side, which Tosta described as "completely abandoned." AHI, Operation Sagarana, Secret Report CTF/1, 254(43), paragraph 30, June 22, 1967.

48 The name *Sagarana* came from the title of a novel by the Brazilian writer and diplomat João Guimarães Rosa, a fictional account of Brazil's nineteenth-century empire. Tosta was a great admirer and close collaborator of Rosa; in 1962 Tosta received his job with Itamaraty thanks to a nomination from Rosa, who at the time was the head of the Foreign Ministry's Border Demarcation Service. Macedo de Mendonça, "A geopolítica e a política externa do Brasil," 157.

49 AHI, Operation Sagarana, Secret Report CTF/1, 254(43), paragraphs 31–32, 38, June 22, 1967.

50 Arquivo Nacional, Rio de Janeiro (hereafter AN-RJ), Ministry of War Report No. 994/S-102-CIE, April 24, 1969, in BR.DFAN.BSB.Z4.SNA.CFR.0007.

51 AN-RJ, Ministry of War Report No. 994/S-102-CIE, April 24, 1969, 4.

52 AHCP, "Antecedentes históricos del litigio Paraguay-Brasil," May 10, 1966.

53 AHCP, verbal note from Castelo Branco to Stroessner, September 1, 1965.

54 References to the small size of the detachment come from AN-BSB, Minutes of the National Security Council (hereafter CSN), March 16, 1966, in N8.0.PSN, EST.286;

the symbolism of the troops was noted by Foreign Minister Juracy Magalhães, CPDOC-FGV.JM pi 66.04.05/1, April 5, 1966.

55 AN-BSB, secret letter from João Baptista Figueiredo to President Emílio Médici, December 1, 1969, Exposição de Motivos No. 056/69, in N8.O.PSN, EST.285.

56 AN-BSB, Minutes of the CSN, March 16, 1966, in N8.O.PSN, EST.286.

57 AHCP, verbal note from Castelo Branco to Stroessner, September 1, 1965.

58 AHI, Telegram No. 408, Brazilian embassy in Asunción, November 28, 1965, DAM/DF/932.(42)(43).

59 Ynsfrán, *Un giro geopolítico*, 73. In the following months, six letters were exchanged between the foreign ministries on the following dates: September 25, October 22, October 29, November 8, November 9, and December 14. Source: AHI.

60 AHCP, DPI no. 604, October 22, 1965.

61 Carlos Saldívar, interview with author, Asunción, Paraguay, January 14, 2015.

62 Conrado Pappalardo, interview with author, Asunción, Paraguay, January 5, 2015.

63 AHCP, press release from the Ministry of Foreign Relations, October 26, 1965.

64 According to different versions of the story, the Paraguayans were detained between four and six hours.

65 AHCP, Brazilian Embassy Note 322, November 8, 1965.

66 "Hasteamento da bandeira paraguaia em Coronel Renato provocou a sua ocupação pelos militares brasileiros," *Jornal do Brasil*, January 6, 1966, 7.

67 Folch, "Surveillance and State Violence in Stroessner's Paraguay," 47.

68 This news comes from "Brasil propõe ao Paraguai arbitragem internacional," *Folha de São Paulo*, November 16, 1965, 11; and "Brasil quer arbitragem em 7 Quedas," *Jornal do Brasil*, November 18, 1965, 17.

69 FRUS, Memo of Conversation, State Department, 1964–1968, vol. 31, South and Central America; Mexico, doc. 465.

70 Nixon is quoted in Hanratty and Meditz, *Paraguay*, 46.

71 "Diplomacia," *Última Hora*, November 25, 1965, 6. Couto e Silva had been dispatched to Asunción at the personal request of President Castelo Branco, largely because he and Stroessner knew each other well from their time together in the Brazilian Army Mission in Paraguay.

72 Moreira Alves, *State and Opposition in Military Brazil*, 8.

73 Couto e Silva, *Geopolítica do Brasil*.

74 Descriptions of the November 27 demonstration come from Centro de Documentación y Archivo para la Defensa de los Derechos Humanos (henceforth referred to as CDyA), 1F 0974–981, November 27, 1965; CDyA 9F 1829–1831, January 24, 1966; "Hasteamento da bandeira paraguaia em Coronel Renato provocou a sua ocupação pelos militares brasileiros," *Jornal do Brasil*, January 6, 1966, 7; Ricardo Caballero Aquino, interview with author, Asunción, Paraguay, January 7, 2015; and AHI, Note 949, Brazilian embassy in Asunción, December 2, 1965.

75 Examples of news articles discussing the unifying perception of opposition to Brazil include "El partido R[evolucionario] Febrerista se pronuncia en diferendo

fronterizo con Brasil," *El Pueblo*, January 6, 1966; and "Centro paraguayo de ingenieros al condenar actitud inamistosa de Brasil se solidariza con el gobierno," *Patria*, January 14, 1966.

76 Stroessner, speech to Paraguay's House of Representatives, April 1, 1966, reproduced in Giménez, *Sobre el salto del Guaíra al oido de América*, 6–13.

77 Ricardo Caballero Aquino, interview by author, Asunción, Paraguay, January 7, 2015.

78 AHI, Secret Note 839. 930(42)(43), Brazilian embassy in Asunción, November 5, 1965.

79 "Paraguai vai indenizar o Brasil," *O Globo*, December 2, 1965, 8.

80 Gibson Barboza, *Na diplomacia, o traço todo da vida*, 85–87.

81 AHCP, DPI notes 17–42, 1966. The most widely distributed of these exchanges occurred in January 1966, when Paraguay sent out copies of a lengthy letter (DPI no. 712) it had written to Brazil on December 14, 1965, sharing it with twenty different embassies throughout the world.

82 AHCP, DPI no. 75, February 9, 1966. This drafting error occurred on pages 2 and 3.

83 Forty-eight hours after meeting with Tosta, the Brazilian Institute for Agrarian Reform's director of land resources, General Jaul Pires de Castro, signed a decree to expropriate lands in the border zone of Amambaí. AHI, Operation Sagarana, Secret Report CTF/1, 254(43), paragraphs 38–44, June 22, 1967.

84 AN-BSB, Minutes of the CSN, March 16, 1966, in N8.0.PSN, EST.286.

85 AN-BSB, ssn/188/502.52, March 11, 1966, in br.dfan.bsb.z4.sna.cfr.0006.

86 AN-BSB, Minutes of the CSN, March 16, 1966, in N8.0.PSN, EST.286, 2.

87 Minutes of the CSN, March 16, 1966, 24–26.

88 Department of State Airgram No. A-167, October 13, 1963, https://repository.library.brown.edu/studio/item/bdr:355471/.

89 Archibaldo Lanús, *De Chapultepec al Beagle*, 294.

90 AHCP, Ministerio de Relaciones Exteriores No. 18/73, August 18, 1973.

91 AHCP, DPI no. 192, April 14, 1966. For more on the economic role of the United States in the geopolitical landscape between Brazil, Paraguay, and Argentina, see Mora and Cooney, *Paraguay and the United States*; and Langley, *America and the Americas*.

92 Stroessner, speech to Paraguay's House of Representatives, April 1, 1966, reproduced in Giménez, *Sobre el salto del Guaíra al oido de América*, 6–13.

93 "Guaira al oído de America," *Patria*, April 1966.

94 "Los Saltos del Guairá son y serán Siempre Paraguayos!," *El Pueblo*, March 5, 1966.

95 Clippings of these international articles are included, respectively, in the following Itamaraty notes in the AHI: no. 132 from March 9, 1966; no. 485 from April 3, 1966; no. 401 from April 24, 1966; no. 237 from April 19, 1966; no. 134 from March 12, 1966; no. 107 from April 3, 1966; and no. 244 from March 19, 1966.

96 "Juracy entrega ao julgamento da história a acusação paraguaia," *O Globo*, April 27, 1966, 17.

97 AHI, Letter from Fernando Simas Magalhães to Foreign Minister Magalhães, in 930.1(42)(43) "Incidente na fronteira Brasil/Paraguai," Volume XII. Document written sometime between May 20 and May 31, 1966.

98 Sapena Pastor made this proposal directly to Brazil's ambassador, Souza Gomes, at a meeting in Asunción. Souza Gomes then took the message back to Rio de Janeiro, at which point Foreign Minister Magalhães became Brazil's primary negotiator.

99 Most of the descriptions of the Act of Iguaçu negotiations come from a confidential report to President Castelo Branco written afterward by Magalhães. CPDOC-FGV, AAA/DAM/DF/G/SG/75/930.1(42)(43), in JM 66.01.27/1(A) CMRE, July 28, 1966. Aspects of this account were confirmed and counterbalanced by a report from Paraguay's Special Border Commission, September 16, 1966, AHCP.

100 "Diário Oficial da União," August 8, 1966, 9061–62, the full document can be found at http://www.jusbrasil.com.br/diarios/2934808/pg-43-secao-1-diario -oficial-da-uniao-dou-de-08-08-1966/pdfView.

101 A full roster of the delegations can be found in "Relatório do Senhor Ministro de Estado" in JM 66.01.27/1(A) CMRE, July 28, 1966.

102 The General Staff of the Armed Forces made this argument on June 16 as part of the larger process of drafting Brazil's proposal for the eventual negotiations with Paraguay. CPDOC-FGV, AAA/DAM/DF/G/SG/75/930.1(42)(43), in JM 66.01.27/1(A) CMRE, July 28, 1966, appendix 7.

103 CPDOC-FGV, AAA/DAM/DF/G/SG/75/930.1(42)(43), JM 66.01.27/1(A) CMRE, July 28, 1966, appendix 21.

104 CPDOC-FGV, AAA/DAM/DF/G/SG/75/930.1(42)(43), JM 66.01.27/1(A) CMRE, July 28, 1966, appendix 16.

105 Paraguay's postnegotiation report celebrated Brazil reversing its position that the waterfalls and their potential energy belonged within Brazilian territory. AHCP, Special Border Commission Report, September 16, 1966.

106 CPDOC-FGV, AAA/DAM/DF/G/SG/75/930.1(42)(43), in JM 66.01.27/1(A) CMRE, July 28, 1966, appendix 22.

107 Both closing remarks reproduced in CPDOC-FGV, JM 66.01.27/1(A) CMRE, July 28, 1966.

108 "Culminaron con Positivo y Elocuente Resultado Tratativas de Cancilleres de Paraguay y Brasil," La Tribuna, June 23, 1966, 5; and "Retirada da Fôrça de Guaíra em Troca da Aceitação da Fronteira," O Globo, June 23, 1966, 11.

109 "Brasil Abandonou o Guaíra," O Globo, June 28, 1966.

110 This information comes from a report marked "secret/urgent" written on June 6, 1967. AN-RJ, N8.0.PSN, EST.286, 728–37.

111 AHI, Operation Sagarana, Secret Report CTF/1, 254(43), paragraph 98, June 22, 1967.

112 AN-BSB, Special Border Commission Report No. 00206, August 29, 1968, in N8.0.PSN, EST.286.

113 AHI, Operation Sagarana, Secret Report CTF/1, 254(43), paragraphs 104–10, June 22, 1967.

114 Nickson, "Brazilian Colonization of the Eastern Border Region of Paraguay," 121.

115 Magalhães, speech at the Conference of the Chancellors of the Plate Basin, February 27, 1967, reproduced in Magalhães, *Minha experiência diplomática*, 90–92.

116 Reports of Paraguay's increased border presence come from AHI, Operation Sagarana, Secret Report CTF/1, 254(43), paragraph 100, June 22, 1967; and AN-BSB, Ministry of War Report No. 259/69/S-102-CIE, May 12, 1969, in DFANBSB Z4 SNA CFR 0007.

117 AN-BSB, minutes of a meeting held in the Asunción office of Ambassador Mario Gibson Barboza, July 1967, in N8.0.PSN, EST.286, 772–73.

118 AN-BSB, CSN report, August 29, 1968, in N8.0.PSN, EST.286.

119 AHI, G/AAA/3/240.(43), letter from Ambassador Mario Gibson Barboza to João Baptista Figueiredo, secretary-general of the CSN, January 24, 1970.

120 AN-BSB, CSN report G/AAA/3/240.(43), January 24, 1970, in N8.0.PSN, EST.285.

121 This agreement emerged from two previous summits held in Buenos Aires, in February 1967, and Santa Cruz de la Sierra, Bolivia, in May 1968. The full text of the 1969 treaty can be found in "Treaty on the River Plate Basin," *International Legal Materials* 8, no. 5 (1969): 905–9.

122 Information on the Cooperation Accord and all subsequent details of the survey work come from AN-BSB, Ministry of Mines and Energy Report, MME no. 602.232/73, April 9, 1973.

123 AHI, "Anteprojeto de Tratado," September 1972. The earliest outline of the treaty circulated four months beforehand, but only after the Itaipu proposal in January did the deliberations begin in earnest.

124 "Tratado de Itaipu, Decreto Legislativo No. 23, de 1973."

125 Schilling and Canese, *Itaipu*, 29–31.

126 Kleinpenning, *Man and Land in Paraguay*, 180.

127 Duarte Pereira, *Itaipu*, 227–32.

128 Quoted in Nickson, "Itaipú Hydro-Electric Paraguayan Perspective," 7. There is a substantial body of literature on developmentalism and the muscular ideologies and political economies of military rule in Latin America. Two of the pioneering texts in the intellectual history of Latin American development are Evans, *Dependent Development*; and O'Donnell, *Bureaucratic Authoritarianism*. On the question of hydroelectric dam projects, specifically in the Paraná borderlands, see also Ferradás, *Power in the Southern Cone Borderlands*; Lins Ribeiro, *Transnational Capitalism and Hydropolitics in Argentina*; and Folch, "Surveillance and State Violence in Stroessner's Paraguay." Other recent works on development and dictatorship include Blackmore, *Spectacular Modernity*; and Field, *From Development to Dictatorship*.

129 CDyA, "Itaipu: La gran entrega," Bulletin of the National Committee of the Christian Democrat Party, August 1973, 224F.2171.

130 AHCP, Ministry of Foreign Relations DPI no. 264, September 12, 1973.

131 The conflict among Brazil, Argentina, and Paraguay over these competing binational dams persisted throughout the decade. Although the 1979 Tripartite Agreement officially quelled the regional dispute, it came only after primary

construction on Itaipu had already been completed. This agreement established rules and engineering parameters for how both the Itaipu and Corpus dams could simultaneously function on the same river. For more details on the Itaipu-Corpus conflict and the Tripartite Agreement, see Caubet, *As grandes manobras de Itaipu.*

132 As referenced in AHI, Telegram No. 1141, DAM-1/AIG from the Brazilian embassy in Buenos Aires, May 4, 1973. Criticisms also came from within Brazil, although they tended to focus on the engineering components of the treaty and argued that other alternatives could still be developed. Critics included the engineer Marcondes Ferraz and the former governor of São Paulo, Lucas Nogueira Garcez. "Marcondes Ferraz: Itaipu vai criar zona de atritos," *Diario Popular*, May 18, 1973; and "Itaipu não é a univa alternativa," *Folha de São Paulo*, June 8, 1973.

133 "A Argentina cria na ONU um problema para Itaipu," *Jornal da Tarde*, November 23, 1973, 2; and "Na ONU, a Argentina ganha do Brasil," *Jornal da Tarde*, December 13, 1974.

134 "'Itaipu es el simbolo de nuestra soberana cocacion fraternal', dijo ayer Stroessner," *ABC Color*, April 16, 1973, 7–9.

135 "Itaipu representa la superestructura del porvenir," *Patria*, June 8, 1973.

136 Amaral de Souza, speech, April 26, 1973, *Diário do Congresso Nacional*, Section 1, 1015–16.

2. The Project of the Century

1 This chapter offers several examples of Itaipu's leaders claiming to treat farmers in a "fair, Christian, and just" manner.

2 Green, *We Cannot Remain Silent*, 321.

3 Seidman, *Manufacturing Militance.*

4 Langland, *Speaking of Flowers*, 217. For more on Geisel and distensão, see Moreira Alves, *State and Opposition in Military Brazil*, 133–53.

5 The national security zones were established by Project Law No. 13, passed by Congress on April 17, 1968.

6 CPDOC-FGV, "José Costa Cavalcanti." Biographical folder, no date.

7 Itaipu's director controlled AESI and could dispatch it wherever "necessary to satisfy the political, structural, or development needs of the country." AN-BSB, CSN, Box 25 A2, February 18, 1975.

8 Stepan, *Rethinking Military Politics.*

9 In addition, AESI participated in Operation Condor, a secret system created in the 1970s by various South American military states in order to share information and persecute, torture, and kill political dissidents in each other's countries. In her study of Itaipu and Latin American dictatorships, Jussaramar da Silva concludes that "it is impossible to view the activities of AESI without connecting them to the actions of Operation Condor . . . and above all, without seeing the heavy hand of the State in the control of workers, local communities, and

opposition groups in the region." Jussaramar da Silva, "A ação das assessorias especiais," 244. For more on Operation Condor, see McSherry, *Operation Condor and Covert War in Latin America*.

10 Sanders, *The Itaipu Hydroelectrical Project*, 4.

11 Construction statistics come from White, "Itaipu," 1; and Monteiro, *Itaipu, a Luz*, 94.

12 Bento Ribeiro, *Memórias do concreto*, 27. The frost of 1975 proved especially destructive for coffee growers, ruining as much as half of the coffee produced across southern Brazil. "Frost in Brazil Said to Ruin Half of Coffee Crop and Peril Herds," *New York Times*, July 24, 1975, 10.

13 Comissão Pastoral da Terra (CPT), *O Mausoléu do faraó*, 2.

14 Agricultural statistics come from Mazzarollo, *A taipa da injustiça*, 32.

15 The flood impacted an additional 570 square kilometers of land on the Paraguayan side of the border.

16 Information in this paragraph was compiled and corroborated through many conversations with different interviewees. Among the most helpful sources were Werner Fuchs and Celso Anghinoni.

17 Brant de Carvalho, "Das terras dos índios a índios sem terra," 173–77.

18 Constitution of Brazil, 1967, Article 157, section VI, paragraph 1. The 1973 Treaty of Itaipu also helped govern the expropriation process. Article XVII of the treaty designated Itaipu Binacional as the sole entity responsible and gave Itaipu's board of directors the final say as to which lands could be expropriated. Institute for Latin American Integration, *Obras hidroeléctricas binacionales en América Latina*, 329.

19 The theme of land-for-land will be discussed in greater detail in chapters 3 and 6.

20 Mazzarollo, *A taipa da injustiça*, 49. The eight impacted municipalities were Guaíra, Terra Roxa, Marechal Cândido Rondon, Santa Helena, Matelândia, Medianeira, São Miguel do Iguaçu, and Foz do Iguaçu.

21 Centro de Documentação Itaipu Binacional (hereafter CDIB), Area Prioritária—Relatório final da Comissão Mixta Brasil/Paraguai, September 1974, 8000F.605–760, 146. Unless otherwise noted, all documents from the CDIB are categorized by their microfilm number.

22 CDIB, I/AJ/004/74, Memo from the Legal Directory, October 17, 1974, 360F.349–351.

23 CDIB, RDE-157/76, Resolution of the Executive Directory, November 24, 1976.

24 "Colonos querem maior indenização por suas terras junto a Itaipu," *O Globo*, January 5, 1974. An *alqueire* is a unit of land roughly equivalent to 2.5 hectares (25,000 square meters). The cruzeiro (Cr$) was Brazil's currency from 1942 to 1986.

25 CDIB, I/AJ/007/74, Memo from Legal Directory to General Director, November 22, 1974, 360F.0356. All exchange rates in this book, accounting for monthly inflation, are calculated from "Exchange Rate, 1954–Present," last revised May 2004. http://www.gwu.edu/~ibi/database/Exchange_Rate_1954-present.pdf.

26 CDIB, Area Prioritária—Relatório final da Comissão Mixta Brasil/Paraguai, September 1974, 8000F.605–760, 95.

27 "Itaipu e desapropriados," *Nosso Tempo*, September 30, 1981, 11.

28 For a discussion of propaganda and official publicity campaigns during the dictatorship, see Schneider, *Brazilian Propaganda*.

29 Reproduced in Germani, *Expropriados terra e agua*, 197.

30 Reproduced in Germani, *Expropriados terra e agua*, 218.

31 Edgard Raviche, interview with author, Toledo, Paraná, Brazil, November 4, 2014.

32 Elio Rusch, interview with author, Marechal Cândido Rondon, Paraná, Brazil, November 21, 2014.

33 "Colonos querem maior indenização por suas terras junto a Itaipu," *O Globo*, January 5, 1975.

34 CDIB, Evandro Stelle Teixeira, speech to the City Council of Foz do Iguaçu, March 26, 1975, 355F.1702–1705.

35 Miguel Isloar Sávio, interview with Davi Schreiner, São Miguel do Iguaçu, Brazil, October 15, 1996, transcript courtesy of Davi Schreiner.

36 Werner Fuchs, interview with author, Curitiba, Paraná, Brazil, July 13, 2013.

37 Bento Ribeiro, *Memórias do concreto*, 23.

38 Quoted in Mazzarollo, *A taipa da injustiça*, 53.

39 The progressive social currents that eventually led to the doctrine of liberation theology initially emerged during the Second Vatican Council (Vatican II) from 1962 to 1965 and arrived in Latin America at the 1968 general assembly of the Council of Latin American Bishops in Medellín, Colombia. For more on liberation theology, see Serbin, *Secret Dialogues*, 36–38, 115–16.

40 Mainwaring, "Grassroots Catholic Groups and Politics in Brazil," 2.

41 Edgard Raviche, interview with author, Toledo, Paraná, Brazil, November 4, 2014.

42 Welch, *The Seed Was Planted*, 359.

43 Silvênio Kolling, interview with author, Garuva, Santa Catarina, Brazil, February 28, 2015.

44 Aluízio Palmar, interview with author, Foz do Iguaçu, Paraná, Brazil, August 8, 2013.

45 Gernote Kirinus, interview with author, Marechal Cândido Rondon, Paraná, Brazil, September 17, 2014. Kirinus's observations on Fazza parallel the analysis in Germani, *Expropriados terra e agua*, 141.

46 CDIB, Circular No. 681/76, Town Hall of Marechal Cândido Rondon, March 6, 1976, 1316F.91.

47 CDIB, Circular No. 136/79, Town Hall of Marechal Cândido Rondon, September 9, 1979, 248F.873–874.

48 CDIB, Circular No. 051/79, Town Hall of Paraíso do Norte, June 5, 1979, 1316F.92.

49 CDIB, letter from State Deputy José Lázaro Dumont to José Cavalcanti, May 31, 1977, 356F.1574–1576.

50 Mezzomo, *Memórias dos movimentos sociais no oeste do Paraná*, 107.

51 Mazzarollo, *A taipa da injustiça*, 58.

52 Mezzomo, *Memórias dos movimentos sociais no oeste do Paraná*, 33.

53 Elio Rusch, interview with author, Marechal Cândido Rondon, Paraná, Brazil, November 21, 2014.

54 Albano Melz, interview with author, São Clemente, Paraná, Brazil, November 17, 2014.

55 Quoted in Mazzarollo, *A taipa da injustiça*, 58.

56 Details on this meeting come from CDIB, "Relatório da visita das representantes das igreja Católica e protestante, da região do reservatório," 729F.1041–1042. May 22, 1978.

57 "Um pesadelo para os lavradores: Itaipu," *Folha da Tarde*, July 17, 1978; and "Pastoral da Terra acusa Itaipu," *Folha de São Paulo*, August 18, 1978.

58 Centro de Documentação e Pesquisa Histórica, Universidade Estadual de Londrina (hereafter CDPH), "Programa da assembléia dos lavradores da área de Itaipu," October 16, 1978, doc. no. 1513.

59 Silvênio Kolling, interview with author, Garuva, Santa Catarina, Brazil, February 28, 2015.

60 Archive of CPT, Goiânia, Minutes of Santa Helena meeting, October 16, 1978, PRO547. General Geisel was scheduled to visit nearby Foz do Iguaçu four days later on October 20.

61 Archive of Federação dos Trabalhadores na Agricultura do Estado Paraná, Curitiba (hereafter FETAEP), Santa Helena Letter, October 16, 1978.

62 Mazzarollo, *A taipa da injustiça*, 64.

63 Moreira Alves, "Interclass Alliances in the Opposition to the Military in Brazil," 295.

64 For more on the amnesty movement, see Gonçalves, *O Preço do passado*.

65 Moreira Alves, *State and Opposition in Military Brazil*, 197–208.

66 Quoted in Matiello, "Narrativas tecnológicas," 71.

67 Matiello, "Narrativas tecnológicas," 195.

68 Carlos Grillmann, interview with author, Foz do Iguaçu, Paraná, Brazil, October 2, 2014.

69 Núcleo de Pesquisa e Documentação sobre o Oeste do Paraná, Universidade Estadual do Oeste do Paraná, Marechal Cândido Rondon (hereafter CEPEDAL), "Depoimento do Pastor G. G. Kirinus," Curitiba, April 19, 1978, "Kirinus" collection No. 4.

70 Deputy Paulo Marques, speech, June 10, 1978, *Diário do Congresso Nacional*, Section 1, 4740.

71 CDIB, Memo I/AJ.SCA/0377/78, December 5, 1978, 1681F.1104–1107.

72 Mazzarollo, *A taipa da injustiça*, 69.

73 Archive of FETAEP, Curitiba, Presidential Decree No. 83.225, March 1, 1979.

74 AN-RJ, Confidential AESI Report No. 0514/79-E/AESI.G/, May 7, 1979, paragraph 7, in AC.ACE.1798/79.

75 Mazzarollo, *A taipa da injustiça*, 70–73.

76 As cited in Veranisa Schmitt, "Os atingidos por Itaipu," 36.

77 Quoted in Matiello, "Narrativas tecnológicas," 100.

78 CDIB, "Terras no Paraná e indenização justa," document produced at the Santa Helena meeting, April 7, 1979, 1398F.1471–1480.

79 Constitution of Brazil, 1967, Article 153.

80 Archive of FETAEP, Curitiba, E/DG/0221/79, April 11, 1979.

81 This report was issued by the Institute of Land and Cartography in April 1981 at the height of the Foz do Iguaçu land encampment. The details of the report will be presented in chapter 3.

82 AN-RJ, Confidential AESI Report No. 0514/79-E/AESI.G/, May 7, 1979, paragraphs 9 and 12, in AC.ACE.1798/79.

83 "Cara a Cara," *Hoje*, May 31, 1979, 14–15.

84 "Cara a Cara," 15.

85 "Cara a Cara," 15.

86 The exchange rate between the Brazilian cruzeiro and the US dollar in 1979 fluctuated between 20:1 and 40:1. When the farmers at different points in 1979 demanded a price increase of around Cr$25,000 per alqueire, this represented a sum of US$831 if one takes an average exchange rate of 30:1. The average rural holding slated to be flooded by Itaipu was six alqueires; farmers thus sought an average indemnification equivalent to US$4,986. Over the next two years, the cruzeiro suffered from rampant inflation, and the farmers increased their price demands to keep pace with the resulting overspeculation in the land market. Even at the height of the farmers' movement in May 1981, when they demanded an increase of almost Cr$500,000, with inflation (at that time the exchange rate was 84:1) this still only amounted to the equivalent of roughly US$2,400 per alqueire.

87 CDIB, "Notas da reunião com a INCRA," December 5, 1978, Rio de Janeiro, 728F.1273–1285.

88 A 2010 report on Itaipu quoted Aníbal Orué Pozzo, the communications director of Itaipu in Paraguay, as saying that although the official estimate of worker deaths had tended to be in the range of 130 to 150, it was likely that the actual number was closer to the total of 1,000 that many critics of the dam have alleged. "37 anos do tratado de Itaipu," Paraná Online, April 26, 2010. http://www.parana-online.com.br/colunistas/sopa-brasiguaia/76320/37+ANOS+DO+TRATADO+DE+ITAIPU.

89 "Itaipu é campo de concentração," *Nosso Tempo*, March 4, 1981, 8–12; and "Dener," interview with author, Assentamento Antonio Tavares, São Miguel do Iguaçu, Paraná, Brazil, November 3, 2014.

90 "As críticas de Sérgio Spada são injustas," *Hoje*, June 28, 1979, 8.

91 CDIB, AJ/003/79, "Instrução ao setor de desapropriação," Memo from the Legal Office, June 1, 1979, 2110F.0016.

92 Although Itaipu first established its guidelines for expropriations in the reservoir area in July 1977, its bylaws shifted throughout the next several years. Only in April 1979 did the legal office officially receive the mandate to process expropriations. Yet "a series of irregularities and errors" continued until a Central Expropriation Archive was created in March 1980. All sources from CDIB: Memo 1/

AJ.SCA/0377/78, December 5, 1978, 1681F.1104–1107; and Memo I/AJ.SEC/0003A/80, "Situação no arquivo central de desapropriação," February 12, 1980, 2110F.431–433.

93 CDIB, I/AJ.SEC/006/80, "Montagem e tombamento de processos encerrados," Memo from the Legal Office, March 18, 1980, 2100F.438–441.

94 Untitled article, *Folha de Londrina*, July 5, 1979, 28.

95 CDIB, Confidential Memo, "Cálculo do índice para o 2 reajuste da tabela de preços do reservatório," June 27, 1979, 1684F.1588–1593.

96 AN-RJ, Confidential AESI Report No. E/AESI.G/IB/BR/0549/79, November 20, 1979.

97 Regional archive of INCRA, Cascavel, Paraná, Report PJR/NO.312/79, September 24, 1979.

98 Moreira Alves, *State and Opposition in Military Brazil*, 173.

99 For example, the Party Reform Bill prohibited the use of terms in official party names that appealed to class or race, a stipulation targeting the nascent Workers' Party (PT, Partido dos Trabalhadores). The PT would not receive official recognition by the state until October 1980, when it fulfilled the requirement of obtaining 20 percent of municipal representatives in at least thirteen states. For more on the Party Reform Bill, see Moreira Alves, *State and Opposition in Military Brazil*, 212–15.

100 Green, *We Cannot Remain Silent*, 349.

101 Kucinski, *O Fim da ditadura militar*, 139.

102 Gaspari, *A ditadura encurralada*, 221.

103 Mainwaring and Share, "Transitions through Transaction."

104 All descriptions of this document come from "Você e as hidroelétricas," Office of the CPT-Paraná, Marechal Cândido Rondon, 1979, courtesy of Werner Fuchs.

105 "Você e as hidroelétricas," 18–19.

106 "Questão de Itaipu, Tércio quer diálogo," *O Paraná*, May 6, 1979, 1.

107 CDIB, Confidential Memo, I/AC/0017/78, January 31, 1979, 1399f.1393–1394.

108 CDIB, Of.INCRA/P/No./74/80, March 6, 1980, 2136F.972–977.

109 "Comemoração dos 25 anos do Movimento Justiça e Terra," video recording from Santa Helena, 2007, courtesy of Tarcísio Vanderlinde.

110 Quoted in Mezzomo, *Memórias dos movimentos sociais no oeste do Paraná*, 15.

111 "Colonos do Oeste ameaçam ir a Brasília se a Itaipu se recusar a indenizá-los," *Correio de Notícias*, May 8, 1980, 11.

112 "Itaipu: A ameaça dos lavradores," *Folha de São Paulo*, June 25, 1980, 33.

113 CDIB, letter from CPT leadership to General Cavalcanti, June 23, 1980, 2135F.958–995.

3. The Double Reality of Abertura

1 Barth, in Füllgraf, *Os desapropriados*.

2 For example, the headline "Oz fuzis de Itaipu são o símbolo da abertura?," *Hoje*, March 28, 1981; and a speech by deputy Paulo Marques to Congress, declaring "bayonets and guns pointed at those responsible for a large part of this country's [agricultural] production and wealth, this is the symbol of abertura." March 19, 1981, *Diário do Congresso Nacional*, Section 1, 778.

3 McCann, *Hard Times in the Marvelous City.*

4 For its insight into the relationship between legality and legitimacy, the case of Itaipu offers a rural complement to Brodwyn Fischer's study of inequality and informality in Rio de Janeiro, *A Poverty of Rights.* And because Fischer ends her history in the early 1960s, the present book can extend her analysis of a poverty of rights not only to the countryside but also to the period of military rule.

5 Archive of the CPT, Londrina, Paraná (hereafter CPT-Londrina), Relatório Geral, Movimento Reivindicatório "Justiça e Terra," Santa Helena, July 31, 1980, 1.

6 Marcelo Barth, interview with Catiane Matiello, reproduced in Matiello, "Narrativas tecnológicas," 102.

7 Mazzarollo, *A taipa da injustiça,* 84–86.

8 Reproduced in Germani, *Expropriados terra e agua,* 216.

9 CPT-Londrina, "Ao Povo, ao governo, e à Itaipu," included in Relatório Geral, Movimento Reivindicatório "Justiça e Terra," Santa Helena, July 31, 1980, 8.

10 "Queremos paz, justiça e terra," *O Paraná,* July 15, 1980, 6.

11 Quoted in "Queremos paz, justiça e terra."

12 CPT-Londrina, Relatório Geral, Movimento Reivindicatório "Justiça e Terra," Santa Helena, July 31, 1980, 2.

13 Werner Fuchs, interview with author, Garuva, Santa Catarina, Brazil, February 28, 2015.

14 "Agricultores em pé-de-guerra," *O Paraná,* July 15, 1980, 1; "700 agricultores invadem os escritórios da Itaipu," *O Globo,* July 15, 1980, 6; and "Agricultores invadem escritório," *Jornal do Brasil,* July 15, 1980, 8.

15 Quoted in "Queremos paz, justiça e terra," *O Paraná,* July 15, 1980, 6.

16 "A 'rádio justiça e terra' divulga diariamente as notícias," *Poeira,* no. 12, July/August 1980, 8.

17 Silvênio Kolling, interview with author, Garuva, Santa Catarina, Brazil, February 28, 2015.

18 Germani, *Expropriados terra e agua,* 118.

19 "Itaipu: Inalterada a situação dos colonos," *Diário Popular,* July 20, 1980, 6.

20 Claudio Pizzato, interviewed in Füllgraf, *Os desapropriados.*

21 CDPH, Internal Memo from Paulo da Cunha, July 16, 1980, CPT doc. no. 1762, Tombo 1828. The five demands that da Cunha conceded in theory were to readjust land prices every 120 days, to pay within fifteen days of the contract's signing, to compensate farmers for their previous investments in electrical power and development, to survey the available lands in Paraná for possible resettlement, and to allow farmers to stay on their lands until May 1982.

22 Mazzarollo, *A taipa da injustiça,* 90.

23 Mazzarollo, *A taipa da injustiça,* 90.

24 "Expropriados pretendem iniciar greve de fome," *Folha de Londrina,* July 17, 1980; and "Agricultores ameaçam greve de fome em Itaipu," *Gazeta do Povo,* July 17, 1980, 40.

25 CDPH, "Exigências de 14 de julho de 1980," MJT, July 14, 1980.

26 Archive of FETAEP, Curitiba, "Manifesto de apoio e solidariedade dos sindicatos de trabalhadores rurais das micro-regiões 1, 2 e 3 do extremo oeste do Paraná," July 18, 1980.

27 "Itaipu: Paraguaios aderem ao movimento," *Diário do Paraná*, July 20, 1980, 7.

28 "Apoio e solidariedade," *Poeira*, no. 12, July/August 1980, 8. Although much of the support came from labor and political groups, the farmers received letters of solidarity from groups as diverse as the Lions Club of Santa Helena and the Housewives Association of Toledo. Germani, *Expropriados terra e agua*, 125.

29 Reproduced in Germani, *Expropriados terra e agua*, 125.

30 Both quotations from "Solidariedade dá força política a expropriados," *Gazeta do Povo*, July 25, 1980.

31 Scott Mainwaring shows that from 1980 to 1981, Brazil's gross domestic product dropped nearly 10 percent, inflation was over 90 percent, and the external debt rose 33 percent to a total of US$72 billion. Mainwaring, *Rethinking Party Systems in the Third Wave of Democratization*, 90.

32 Quotation from AN-RJ, AESI Report No. E/AESI.G/IB/BR/0034/80, August 11, 1980, in SNI ACE.967/81.01-02.

33 AN-RJ, SNI telex, CT/189 AC 1451/117/ACT/80, July 28, 1980, in SNI ACE.967/81.01-02. This report poses the unanswerable question of which member of the MJT was the military's informant.

34 Marcelo Barth, interview with Catiane Matiello, reproduced in Matiello, "Narrativas tecnológicas," 108.

35 Werner Fuchs, interview with author, Curitiba, Paraná, Brazil, July 13, 2013.

36 Albano Melz, interview with author, São Clemente, Paraná, Brazil, November 17, 2014.

37 Adil Fochezatto, interview with author, Santa Helena Velha, Paraná, Brazil, November 14, 2014.

38 Itamar da Silva, interview with author, Santa Helena, Paraná, Brazil, November 16, 2014.

39 At the time of the protest, Germani was a graduate student at the Federal University of Rio Grande do Sul and conducted research as a participant-observer that was published as a book in 2003.

40 Germani, presentation at the twenty-fifth anniversary of the Justice and Land Movement, Santa Helena, August 30, 2007, event organized by Werner Fuchs, Juvêncio Mazzarollo, Marcelo Barth, and Silvênio Kolling, video recording courtesy of Tarcísio Vanderlinde.

41 "Acima de tudo, amor à terra," *Folha de São Paulo*, March 29, 1981, 6.

42 Weinstein, *The Color of Modernity*, 6.

43 Weinstein, *The Color of Modernity*, 9.

44 For relevant analysis of gender roles within labor and agrarian reform movements in a similar Latin American context, see Tinsman, *Partners in Conflict*.

45 A particularly rich set of interviews concerning the role of women during the Santa Helena encampment is included in Matiello, "Narrativas tecnológicas."

46 "Agricultores invadem escritório," *Jornal do Brasil*, July 15, 1980, 9.

47 "Sindicatos apóiam expropriados de Itaipu," *Folha de São Paulo*, July 20, 1980, 9–10.

48 CDIB, letter from da Cunha to Cavalcanti, June 20, 1980, Register No. 0533/80, Office of the Director General, included in the appendix of the Sixteenth Meeting of Itaipu's Executive Council, July 24, 1980, 23865F.0025-0554.

49 CDIB, Minutes of the Meeting of the Director General, July 24, 1980, 23865F.0063, item no. 4.

50 As will be shown later in this chapter, on April 14, 1981, the Institute for Lands and Cartography released a report stating that Itaipu had paid roughly 30 percent less than the actual value of land in the region.

51 "Ato contra a Itaipu reúne 5 mil colonos," *Folha de São Paulo*, July 25, 1980. Whereas national media outlets like the *Folha de São Paulo* reported that roughly five thousand demonstrators participated in the Day of the Farmer events in Santa Helena, MJT leaders placed the number between eight thousand and ten thousand. CPT-Londrina, Relatório Geral, Movimento Reivindicatório "Justiça e Terra," Santa Helena, July 31, 1980, 5.

52 Mazzarollo, *A taipa da injustiça*, 95.

53 Mazzarollo, *A taipa da injustiça*, 93; and CPT-Londrina, Relatório Geral, Movimento Reivindicatório "Justiça e Terra," Santa Helena, July 31, 1980, 5–6.

54 "Itaipu: Amanhã marcha até Foz," *O Estado do Paraná*, July 27, 1980.

55 Mazzarollo, *A taipa da injustiça*, 96.

56 CPT-Londrina, Relatório Geral, Movimento Reivindicatório "Justiça e Terra," Santa Helena, July 31, 1980, 6, 16.

57 CPT-Londrina, Relatório Geral, Movimento Reivindicatório "Justiça e Terra," Santa Helena, July 31, 1980, 17–18.

58 CPT-Londrina, Relatório Geral, Movimento Reivindicatório "Justiça e Terra," Santa Helena, July 31, 1980, 6, 17–18.

59 "Posseiros também assegura direitos," *Poeira*, no. 12, July/August 1980, 11.

60 CPT-Londrina, Relatório Geral, Movimento Reivindicatório "Justiça e Terra," Santa Helena, July 31, 1980, 6.

61 The two headlines, respectively, are from "Temendo a 'marcha' Itaipu recua," *O Paraná*, July 29, 1980, 6; and "Os agricultores de Itaipu decidem aceitar proposta," *O Estado de São Paulo*, July 30, 1980, 12.

62 "Itaipu explica as suas razões," *O Estado do Paraná*, July 30, 1980, 1.

63 Quoted in "Itaipu anuncia reajuste nas desapropriações," *Folha de Londrina*, July 26, 1980.

64 CDIB, Minutes of the Meeting of the Director-General, July 24, 1980, 23865F.0063, item no. 8.1.

65 No title, *Poeira*, no. 12, July/August 1980, 11.

66 Wright and Wolford, *To Inherit the Earth*, 34. The Encruzilhada Natalino camp took place from December 1979 to June 1983.

67 Gernote Kirinus, interview with author, Marechal Cândido Rondon, Paraná, Brazil, September 17, 2014.

68 Silvênio Kolling, interview with author, Garuva, Santa Catarina, Brazil, February 28, 2015.

69 Nelton Friedrich, interview with author, Foz do Iguaçu, Paraná, Brazil, October 9, 2014.

70 AN-RJ, Minutes of Meeting on August 26, 1980, Office of Itaipu Binational, Foz do Iguaçu, Brazil, Memo 967/81, in SNI ACE.967/81.01-02.

71 "Classificação das terras irrita desapropriados," *Hoje*, August 3, 1980.

72 CDIB, letter from General Cavalcanti to the Commission of Farmers, October 10, 1980, Memo E/DG/0758/80, R2134.1716.

73 CDIB, Meeting between Itaipu Executive Directory and Commission of the Expropriated, October 1, 1980, 2135.0926–930.

74 A confidential AESI report noted Barth's suggestion of occupying lands. AN-RJ, Confidential AESI Report No. E/AESI.G/IB/BR/0052/80, October 13, 1980, in SNI ACE.967/81.01-02.

75 Mazzarollo, *A taipa da injustiça*, 98.

76 "O preço de paz: Justiça e terra," *Nosso Tempo*, March 18, 1981, 6–8.

77 Christopher Byrons, Jonathan Beaty, and Gisela Bolte, "Big Profits in Big Bribery," *Time*, March 16, 1981, 60–65.

78 Allegations of scandal had dogged Itaipu since the original 1973 treaty. Throughout the 1970s many reports claimed that Alfredo Stroessner had accepted over US$100 million from the Brazilian government for his approval of the "uneven" 1973 treaty. "Corrupción en Itaipú," ten-part series published in *ABC Color*, 1996. Even before the 1981 *Time* article, questions of corruption at Itaipu had been covered in the US media. In 1979 *Harper's* carried a story on similar claims about Brazil's 1973 bribes to Stroessner. Penny Lernoux, "Behind Closed Doors," *Harper's*, February 1979, 20–29.

79 "No Brasil, 'matéria de sedução,'" *O Estado de São Paulo*, March 17, 1981, 1.

80 For example, the bribery scandal was denounced in CDIB, "Speech from Iram Saraiva," Chamber of Deputies, March 23, 1981, information request No. 148, 1–4; and "Speech from Brabo de Carvalho," Chamber of Deputies, April 2, 1981, 2682.1440–1443.

81 "140 milhões de dólares para subornar os tecnocratas de Itaipu enquanto 8 mil famílias lutam por indenizações justas," *O Estado do Paraná*, April 26, 1981, 1.

82 CDIB, 4146.1287-1302, September 13, 1983. Copies of Cavalcanti's letters to the editor of *Time* are included in a dossier presented to the Chamber of Deputies Foreign Relations Committee on September 13, 1983.

83 Archive of FETAEP, Curitiba, Minutes of the Assembly of Farmers Expropriated by Itaipu Binational, March 16, 1981, Itacorá.

84 "O preço de paz: Justiça e terra," *Nosso Tempo*, March 18, 1981, 6–8.

85 Quoted in "O preço de paz: Justiça e terra."

86 "Colonos iniciam marcha para Foz," *O Estado do Paraná*, March 17, 1981.

87 Marcelo Barth, interview in Füllgraf, *Os desapropriados*.

88 In the late 1960s, Guimarães had been the state secretary of public security, where he put down a series of protests from farming and peasant communities. Before being named Itaipu's chief of security, he had also worked as the head of intelligence and security for Petrobras at the Araucária oil refinery in southeastern Paraná. Arquivo Público do Paraná (hereafter APP), "Questões de Terra 'Lopei,'" Folder No. 003491.

89 "Baionetas e fuzis contra os colonos," *Hoje*, March 27, 1981.

90 João Adelino de Souza, interview with author, Foz do Iguaçu, Paraná, Brazil, October 6, 2014. De Souza worked for *Nosso Tempo*.

91 "Itaipu aponto baionetas contra agricultores," *Nosso Tempo*, March 18, 1981, 20.

92 "Itaipu resiste com armas," *Nosso Tempo*, March 18, 1981, 1; and "Os fuzis de Itaipu são o símbolo da abertura?," *Hoje*, March 28, 1981, 1.

93 CDIB, "Documento de reivindicações aprovado na Assembléia de Agricultores em Itacorá," March 16, 1981, included as annex of "Ata da 180a Reunião," Itaipu Executive Committee, 2823.591–592.

94 "Costa Cavalcanti chega a Foz, mas colonos recusam proposta de Itaipu," *Folha de Londrina*, March 19, 1981, 7.

95 Lauro Rocini, interview with author, Itaipulândia, Paraná, Brazil, December 26, 2014.

96 Aluízio Palmar, interview with author, Foz do Iguaçu, Paraná, Brazil, August 8, 2013.

97 Werner Fuchs, email exchange with author, January 16, 2018.

98 Headline quotations come respectively from "Desapropriados formam uma mini-cidade," *O Mensageiro*, April 1981, 13–14; and "Uma sociedade evoluida em torno de um acampamento de colonos," *Folha de Londrina*, March 29, 1981, 32.

99 "O acampamento do século," *O Estado do Paraná*, March 29, 1981, 14.

100 "Itaipu aumenta as indenizações, mas os desapropriados rejeitam," *O Estado de São Paulo*, March 21, 1981, 12.

101 "Cavalcanti não aceita reunião e renega Movimento Justiça e Terra," *Folha de Londrina*, March 21, 1981.

102 CDPH, "Resposta ao Comunicado da Itaipu Binacional," March 21, 1981.

103 "Brizola vai a Abi-Ackel pedir justiça a colonos," *O Paraná*, March 22, 1981, 1.

104 "Itaipu aumenta as indenizações, mas os desapropriados rejeitam," *O Estado de São Paulo*, March 21, 1981, 12.

105 Paulo Marques, congressional speech, March 19, 1981, *Diário do Congresso Nacional*, Section 1, 778–779.

106 CDIB, Jorge Arbage, speech to Chamber of Deputies, March 31, 1981, 2682.1427–1429.

107 "Ney fará gestões," *O Estado do Paraná*, March 27, 1981, 11.

108 AN-RJ, "Declaração," Pedro Fedalto and Olívio Fazza, April 1, 1981, in SNI ACE.841/81.

109 "Luta pela democracia e solidariedade política," *Diário do Paraná*, August 16, 1979. Further details on the 1979 meeting are compiled from various reports included in APP, "Encontro Latino Americano de Oposições," Folder No. 01431.

110 CEPEDAL, "Carta das oposições, Brasil/Paraguai," June 1, 1980, "Kirinus" collection.

111 CDIB, "Carta de Foz do Iguaçu," PTB, February 22, 1980, 2134.238–241. Further details on the PTB meeting come from CDIB, "Reunião do Leonel Brizola," 2134.235–237, no date.

112 For a historiographic discussion of abertura, see note 11 of the introduction. And for an overview of scholarship on the abertura as an elite process, see chapter 2, section "The Start of Abertura and a New Era of Opposition in Brazil."

113 APP, "O PMDB e a luta dos agricultores de Itaipu," October 8, 1980, Departamento de Ordem Política e Social, Folder no. 62999.

114 AESI Report No. E/AESI.G/IB/BR/056/81, November 30, 1981, 4, item 6, courtesy of Aluízio Palmar.

115 CDIB, Minutes of Itaipu Binational's Executive Committee, May 28, 1981, 2823.1245.

116 Itamar da Silva, interview with author, Santa Helena, Paraná, Brazil, November 16, 2014.

117 Aluízio Palmar, interview with author, Foz do Iguaçu, Paraná, Brazil, August 8, 2013; and Edgard Raviche, interview with author, Toledo, Paraná, Brazil, November 4, 2014.

118 "Expropriados de Itaipu dão mostras de desespero," Folha de São Paulo, March 25, 1981, 9.

119 "Esperança a expropriados de Itaipu," Folha de São Paulo, March 30, 1981.

120 Lauro Rocini, interview with author, Itaipulândia, Paraná, Brazil, December 26, 2014.

121 Marcelo Barth, interview with Catianne Matiello, reproduced in Matiello, "Narrativas tecnológicas," 107.

122 Gernote Kirinus, interview with author, Marechal Cândido Rondon, Paraná, Brazil, September 17, 2014.

123 AN-RJ, ITC Report, April 1981, in SNI ACE.841/81.

124 Quoted in "Itaipu não receberá agricultores," Nosso Tempo, April 15, 1981, 18.

125 AN-RJ, "Roteiro para reuniões por barraca," included in Confidential AESI Report No. E/AESI.G/IB/BR/021/81, 3, April 10, 1981, in SNI ACE.892/81. The results of this intracamp survey were made public and covered in many news outlets, for example, "Agricultores de Itaipu divulgam novas táticas," Diário do Paraná, April 9, 1981, 4; and "Expropriados querem falar com Stroessner," Folha de Londrina, April 9, 1981, 7.

126 AN-RJ, "Roteiro para reuniões por barraca," included in Confidential AESI Report No. E/AESI.G/IB/BR/021/81, 15, April 10, 1981, in SNI ACE.892/81.

127 "Em fim, Itaipu negociará com agricultores," Nosso Tempo, May 6, 1981, 5.

128 Mazzarollo, A taipa da injustiça, 114.

129 "Itaipu eleva preço de terras em 30% e colonos aceitam," Jornal do Brasil, April 29, 1981.

130 "Quando a violência se justifica," Nosso Tempo, May 6, 1981, 2.

131 "Em fim, Itaipu negociará com agricultores," Nosso Tempo, May 6, 1981, 5.

132 Mazzarollo, A taipa da injustiça, 114.

133 Germani, *Expropriados terra e agua*, 167.

134 "Agricultores aceitam proposta da Itaipu," *Gazeta do Povo*, May 10, 1981, 39.

135 "O document final," *Nosso Tempo*, May 13, 1981, 6.

136 "Dobrando o Leviathan," *O Estado do Paraná*, May 12, 1981; and "Em Itaipu, a união faz a força," *Gazeta do Povo*, May 11, 1981.

137 Archive of FETAEP, Curitiba, "Mensagem aos agricultores expropriados pela hideoelétrica Itaipu," May 8, 1981.

138 "O documento final," *Nosso Tempo*, May 13, 1981, 6–7.

139 "Pouca justiça e pouca terra," *Nosso Tempo*, May 20, 1981, 18.

140 "Itaipu: INCRA inicia remoção dos colonos," *O Estado do São Paulo*, May 17, 1981, 25.

141 AN-RJ, SNI Report No. 0229/117/ACT/81, July 21, 1981.

142 "Expropriados de Itaipu fazem passeata de protesto," *Folha de Londrina*, August 25, 1981, 1.

143 Archive of FETAEP, Curitiba, survey of farmers awaiting expropriation, June 28, 1982. The survey included ninety-five respondents.

144 CDIB, letter to Colonel Haroldo Ferreira Dias, state secretary of public safety, from Adelino Schmengler, Silvino Odilo Kerber, and Odalio Francisco dos Santos, June 22, 1982, 3359.1270–1271.

145 "Desapropriação em Itaipu é concluída," *Gazeta do Povo*, August 17, 1982, 14. Details on those still awaiting payment come from "Colonos ainda esperam indenização de Itaipu," *O Estado do Paraná*, October 2, 1982, 9.

146 Warren Hoge, "Brazil Creates a Lake, with Care for Man and Beast," *New York Times*, October 15, 1982.

147 CDIB, Memo from Bruno Castro da Graça, to the supervisor of human resources, Memo I/AESI/ASF/058/82, August 9, 1982, 9193.1385–1387.

148 AN-RJ, "Denúncia contra a Itaipu Binacional," SNI Report No. 08663/30/AC/82, December 10, 1982.

149 "No último dia de visita a Sete Quedas, 40 mil pessoas formam fila de 1 km," *O Globo*, September 20, 1982, 5.

150 CDPH, "Adeus Sete Quedas," poster, 1982.

151 Carlos Drummond de Andrade, "Adeus Sete Quedas," 1982, originally published in *Jornal do Brasil*, Section B, September 9, 1982.

152 "Os últimos a deixar a região devastada," *O Globo*, October 10, 1982, 12.

153 Quoted in "Os últimos e tristes dias em Itaipu," *O Estado de São Paulo*, October 1, 1982, 1–5.

154 "Usina atrai imprensa do mundo desenvolvido," *O Estado de São Paulo*, November 6, 1982, 14.

155 Both speeches reproduced in CDIB, "Relatório Anual, 1982," Itaipu Binational, 126–32.

156 During military rule, elections for senators and federal deputies had been held in 1966, 1970, 1974, and 1978. For a thorough account of the 1982 elections, see Fleischer, *Da distensão à abertura*.

157 Legally recognized parties needed to have formed directorates in 20 percent of municipalities.

158 Nohlen, *Elections in the Americas*, 175.

159 Stepan, *Rethinking Military Politics*, 63.

160 "A democracia vitoriosa," *Folha de São Paulo*, November 16, 1982, 2.

161 Biblioteca do Senado Federal, Brasília, José Richa, "Fuzis, a melhor maneira de calar os colonos do Paraná?," Senate speech, March 26, 1981.

162 "Resultados finais nas prefeituras," *Diário do Paraná*, November 21, 1982, 3.

163 As part of the military's negotiated transition out of power, Tancredo Neves was indirectly elected president in 1985. However, Neves died soon after his inauguration and was replaced by vice president José Sarney. Fernando Collor de Mello in 1989 became Brazil's first president elected directly by the general population.

4. Sem Tekoha não há Tekó

1 The Avá-Guarani are also known as the Avá-Chiripá, the Xiripá, or the Guarani Ñandeva.

2 Melià, "A experiência religiosa Guarani," 336.

3 Onorio Benites, interview with author, Aldeia Indígena Tekoha Itamarã, Paraná, Brazil, November 6, 2014.

4 While working for the National Foundation of Indigenous Affairs (FUNAI) in the early 2000s, Brant de Carvalho began a multiyear study of the community that later became a doctoral dissertation. Brant de Carvalho, "Das terras dos índios a índios sem terra."

5 Williams, "Land Rights and the Manipulation of Identity," 151.

6 Rodríguez-Piñero, *Indigenous Peoples, Postcolonialism, and International Law.* Other notable works include Ahrén, *Indigenous Peoples' Status in the International Legal System*; and D. Maybury-Lewis, *The Politics of Ethnicity.* For Brazil in particular, see Ramos, *Indigenism*; and Devine Guzmán, *Native and National in Brazil.*

7 Ramos, *Indigenism*, 95.

8 Ramos, *Indigenism*, 17–19.

9 Moog Rodrigues, "Indigenous Rights in Democratic Brazil," 492.

10 Williams, "Land Rights and the Manipulation of Identity," 138.

11 Garfield, *Indigenous Struggle at the Heart of Brazil*, 145.

12 Garfield, *Indigenous Struggle at the Heart of Brazil*, 198; and Ramos, *Indigenism*, 249.

13 Silva, "Folhas ao vento," 17.

14 Silva, "Folhas ao vento," 79.

15 Mallon, *Courage Tastes of Blood*, 236.

16 Herzog, "Guarani and Jesuits," 50–51.

17 Silva, "Walking on the Bad Land," 188.

18 Rivarola, "The Total War in Indigenous Territories."

19 For the Contestado War, see Vinhas de Queiroz, *Messianismo e conflito social a Guerra Sertaneja do Contestado*; and Diacon, *Millenarian Vision, Capitalist Reality.*

20 Carrão, *Impressões de viagem à Fóz do Iguassú e Rio Paraná*, 49–50. For contemporary accounts of the Prestes Column's passage through western Paraná, see Cabanas, *A Columna da morte sob o commando do Tenente Cabanas*; and Assis, *Nas barrancas do Alto-Paraná.*

21 Indigenous Missionary Council (CIMI), "Itaipu & FUNAI x os Indios," February 1981, reproduced in *Poeira*, no. 15, April 1981, 24–27. The Mbya-Guarani belonged to the same larger Tupi-Guarani linguistic family as the Avá-Guarani. In addition to slight variations in linguistic expression and social rituals, the Mbya are differentiated from other Guarani subgroups by the fact that, along with living in the Paraná borderlands, the Mbya have also lived in regions closer to the Atlantic coast. Ladeira, "Os índios Guarani/Mbya e o complex lagunar estuarino de Iguape—Paranaguá."

22 Garfield, *Indigenous Struggle at the Heart of Brazil*, 145–46.

23 Freitas, "The Guarani and the Iguaçu National Park," 20.

24 "Desapropriação de terras no Sul provoca clima de tensão," *Jornal do Brasil*, January 5, 1976, 7. Other examples of Avá-Guarani memories of the fire include Indigenous Missionary Council (CIMI), "Itaipu & FUNAI x os Indios," 25.

25 "Desapropriação de terras no Sul provoca clima de tensão," *Jornal do Brasil*, January 5, 1976, 7.

26 Quoted in Brant de Carvalho, "Das terras dos índios a índios sem terra," 366.

27 "Desapropriação de terras no Sul provoca clima de tensão," *Jornal do Brasil*, January 5, 1976, 7.

28 Examples from, respectively, Ramos, *Indigenism*, 252; Tibes Ribeiro, "O horizonte é a terra," 178; and Werner Fuchs, interview with author, Curitiba, Paraná, Brazil, July 13, 2013.

29 Fernando Martins, interview with Sarah Iurkiy Gomes Tibes Ribeiro, July 13, 2000, reproduced in Tibes Ribeiro, "O horizonte é a terra," 178.

30 French's analysis concerns the Xocó tribe in the northern state of Alagoas. French, *Legalizing Identities*, esp. 43–76.

31 CEPEDAL, Resolution No. 162, March 23, 1977, "Sarah" collection 13/20/2.

32 Subgrupo de trabalho XV, "Relatório final FUNAI-INCRA," no date, 3. Courtesy of of Maria Lucia Brant de Carvalho.

33 Subgrupo de trabalho XV, "Relatório final FUNAI-INCRA," 5.

34 Subgrupo de trabalho XV, "Relatório final FUNAI-INCRA," 6.

35 CEPEDAL, letter from FUNAI to Itaipu, Report No. 046/GAB/P, June 22, 1977, 2–3, "Sarah" collection, 13/20.

36 CEPEDAL, letter from Itaipu to FUNAI, E/DG/0450/78, September 4, 1978, 4, "Sarah," collection, 13/20, 1.

37 Célio Horst, "Relatório de Viagem," FUNAI Item No. 023/81, June 6, 1981, reproduced in Brant de Carvalho, "Das terras dos índios a índios sem terra," appendix 7.

38 No title, *Luta Indígena*, March 1982, 4.

39 Those who decided to cross back into Paraguayan territory might not have necessarily fared much better. Nearly 250 Avá-Chiripá lived on the western banks of
the Paraná River, and with the help of the Indigenous Association of Paraguay,
a campaign emerged to demand a fair relocation process. Above all, the Avá-
Chiripá demanded the acquisition of new lands of similar size and quality, seeking fifteen thousand hectares spread across four distinct community settlements.
CEPEDAL, "Situación de comunidades indígenas Avá-Chiripá cuya ocupación de
tierras se va afectada por los trabajos de la Itaipú Binacional," report prepared for
the National Missionary Committee of the Paraguayan Episcopal Conference,
1981, "Sarah" collection, 9/20, 1.

40 Connected to the progressive wing of the Catholic Church, CIMI was created in
1972 and became one of the largest groups under the dictatorship to support indigenous rights. For more on indigenous groups and the Church during military
rule, see Garfield, *Indigenous Struggle at the Heart of Brazil*, 178–80.

41 These portions of the Indian Statute (Law No. 6002/73), respectively, come from
Article 20; Article 20, paragraph 3; and Article 20, paragraph 4.

42 "Indios também estão reclamando de Itaipu," *Jornal do Brasil*, March 21, 1981.

43 Within the documents related to the MJT, the only extensive reference to the
parallel struggle of the Avá-Guarani is a 1981 article, "Itaipu & Funai x os índios,"
Poeira, no. 15, April 1981, 24–27.

44 Carlos Grillmann, interview with author, Foz do Iguaçu, Paraná, Brazil, October 2, 2014.

45 Adriano Tupã Rokenji, interview with author, Aldeia Indígena Tekoha Itamarã,
Paraná, Brazil, November 6, 2014.

46 "Indios vão exigir area de Itaipu," *O Estado de São Paulo*, March 24, 1981.

47 "Funai debate indenização de terras indígenas em Itaipu," *O Globo*, March 24,
1981, 5.

48 Letter from Wilmar D'Angelis (CIMI) to Harry Luis Telles (FUNAI regional del-
egate), March 24, 1981, courtesy of Werner Fuchs.

49 Horst, "Relatório de Viagem," FUNAI Item No. 023/81, June 6, 1981, reproduced in
Brant de Carvalho, "Das terras dos índios a índios sem terra," appendix 7. Although
Horst counted only nine families on the day of his visit, he later determined that a
tenth family—of indigenous origin—lived in other parts of the region.

50 Ramos, *Indigenism*, 19.

51 "Indios Guarani do Paraná não são índios para FUNAI," *O Estado de São Paulo*,
April 8, 1981; and "Prometida solução aos Guarani de Ocoí," *O Estado de São
Paulo*, December 22, 1981.

52 "'Antropólogo da FUNAI' foi ver índios mas só conversou com grileiro," *O Estado
de São Paulo*, November 22, 1981. All three of the above-cited news sources come

from Centro Ecumênico de Documentação e Informação (CEDI), *Povos indíge-nas no Brasil, 1981,* Newsletter no. 10, April 1982, 60–61, 87.

53 Maria Lucia Brant de Carvalho, "Laudo anthropológico" Part II, report on the Avá-Guarani submitted to Newton Machado Bueno, regional administrator for Bauru, FUNAI, November 30, 2005, 69, courtesy of Maria Lucia Brant de Carvalho.

54 The criteria were devised in January 1981 by two retired air force colonels, João Carlos Nobre da Veiga, FUNAI's president, and Ivan Zanoni Hausen, the director of FUNAI's Community Planning Department. Ramos, *Indigenism,* 249.

55 "'Critério fascista' da Funai ameaça os índios," *Folha de São Paulo,* October 4, 1981, 1.

56 "'Critério fascista' da Funai ameaça os índios," 10. Upon assuming FUNAI's presidency in 1979, Colonel Nobre da Veiga purged the agency of anthropologists and replaced them with military personnel. Schmink and Wood, *Contested Frontiers in Amazonia,* 75.

57 "Entidades acusam FUNAI de ocultar estudos oficias," *Folha de São Paulo,* September 29 1981, 7.

58 "Racismo: FUNAI estabelece 'critérios de indianidade,'" *Luta Indígena,* no. 15, November 1981, 4–7.

59 "Parecer da antropóloga Rosane Cossich Furtado," Assunto: área indígena Ocoí (Paraná), November 20, 1986, reproduced in Brant de Carvalho, "Das terras dos índios a índios sem terra," appendix 10.

60 CEPEDAL, Edgard de Assis Carvalho, "Avá-Guarani do Ocoí-Jacutinga," report prepared for the ABA, 1981, 4, "Sarah" collection, 9/20, 2.

61 Carvalho, "Avá-Guarani do Ocoí-Jacutinga," 2.

62 CDIB, letter from Octávio Ferreira Lime to José Cavalcanti, September 10, 1981, Report No. 357/PRES. 2683.1196–1197.

63 Goldman, *Imperial Nature,* 165–167.

64 "Carta a FUNAI," written to Dr. Paulo Moreira Leal, December 2, 1981, reproduced in *Luta Indígena,* March 1982, 9.

65 "Carta a FUNAI," written to Dr. Paulo Moreira Leal, December 2, 1981, reproduced in *Luta Indígena,* March 1982, 8.

66 Meeting notes, December 23, 1981, written by Harry Luis Telles, Report No. 16/81/4DR, reproduced in Brant de Carvalho, "Das terras dos índios a índios sem terra," appendix 9M.

67 "Indios e posseiros, o que ainda resta nos vastos domínios das águas de Itaipu," *Folha de Londrina,* December 19, 1981, 1–5; "Indios da região de Itaipu reivindicam lugar para morar," *Folha de Londrina,* December 22, 1981, 8; and "Que farão Funai e Itaipu com os indios?," *Nosso Tempo,* December 23, 1981, 18–19.

68 "Indio sem terra pode parar lago de Itaipu," *O Estado de São Paulo,* January 15, 1982, 10; and "Guaranis querem área de Itaipu," *Jornal do Brasil,* January 15, 1982, 4.

69 "Itaipu nega imposições aos guaranis," *O Estado de São Paulo,* January 16, 1982, 9.

70 "Itaipu oferece área para índios do Ocoí," *O Estado do Paraná*, January 14, 1982, 9.

71 "Carta a FUNAI," written to Dr. Paulo Moreira Leal, December 2, 1981, reproduced in *Luta Indígena*, March 1982, 10.

72 "Indios não aceitam ser confinados por Itaipu," *Folha de Londrina*, February 7, 1982, 9.

73 "Itaipu oferece área para índios do Ocoí," *O Estado do Paraná*, January 14, 1982, 9.

74 *Luta Indígena*, March 1982, 13.

75 CEPEDAL, letter from community leaders to Colonel Paulo Leal and General José Cavalcanti, Barra do Ocoí, February 5, 1982, "Sarah" collection, 2/20, 1.

76 "Indios não aceitam ser confinados por Itaipu," *Folha de Londrina*, February 7, 1982, 9.

77 "Os Avá-Guarani resistem a Itaipu," *Folha de São Paulo*, February 14, 1982, 2–3.

78 "Saiba como vivem os índios Avá-Guarani," *Nosso Tempo*, June 15, 1982, 1–4.

79 AN-RJ, Report No. e/aesi.g/ib/br/005/0503/82, March 10, 1982, 3.

80 AN-RJ, Report No. e/aesi.g/ib/br/005/0503/82, March 10, 1982, 6.

81 *Luta Indígena*, March 1982, 13.

82 CEPEDAL, letter from Avá-Guarani to Colonel Paulo Leal, March 22, 1982, "Sarah," collection, 2/20, 3.

83 "Os ava-guaranis rejeitam a nova oferta de Itaipu," *Folha de São Paulo*, April 4, 1982, 8.

84 News outlets incorrectly reported that this third offer was accepted: "Indios aceitam última proposta de Itaipu," *O Estado do Paraná*, April 29, 1982, 9; and "Os guarani aceitam as terras de Itaipu," *Folha de Londrina*, May 7, 1982, 7.

85 "Guaranis apelam a Itaipu," *O Estado de São Paulo*, May 8, 1982, 12.

86 "Avá-guaranis irão receber nova terra," *Folha de São Paulo*, May 7, 1982, 6.

87 CEPEDAL, Agenda of Meeting to Deal with the Resettlement of the Ava-Guarani Indigenous Group, Itaipu office, Curitiba, Paraná, Brazil, May 7, 1982, "Sarah" collection, 2/20, 6.

88 "Mais guaranis beneficiados," *Folha de São Paulo*, May 8, 1982, 6.

89 CEPEDAL, Minutes of Meeting in Jacutinga-Ocoi, May 12, 1982, "Sarah" collection, 2/20, 7. The community later called this site Santa Rosa do Ocoí.

90 "Itaipu decide indenizar os índios Avá-guarani," *O Estado do Paraná*, May 14, 1982, 9.

91 "Indios da região tranforsmam-se em bóias-frias," *Hoje*, May 22, 1982, 6.

92 Teodoro Tupã Alves, interview with author, Aldeia Indígena Tekoha Itamarã, Paraná, Brazil, November 6, 2014.

93 "FUNAI não cumpre acordo e deixa índios com fome," *O Paraná*, February 5, 1983, 1.

94 For more on the Avá-Guarani in the 1980s and 1990s, see Brant de Carvalho, "Das terras dos índios a índios sem terra," 408–78; and Deprá, "O lago de Itaipu e a luta dos Avá-Guarani pela terra," 71–128.

95 Adriano Tupã Rokenji, interview with author, Aldeia Indígena Tekoha Itamarã, Paraná, Brazil, November 6, 2014.

96 Comissão Nacional da Verdade, *Relatório*.

5. The Last Political Prisoner

1 News articles include an April 12, 1979, piece in *Hoje* titled "Itaipu: O preço desumano do progresso." In 1980 he published a book on the Santa Helena land encampment and the early iteration of the farmers' movement called *A taipa da injustiça: Itaipu x agricultores exproriados.*

2 CDIB, Confidential Memo, Itaipu Binational, Report No. E/AESI.G/1B/BR/0061/80, November 19, 1980.

3 "Tortura," *Nosso Tempo*, March 12, 1980, 4.

4 "Políticos condenam prefeitos biônicos," *Nosso Tempo*, December 17, 1980, 7–9.

5 "Cunha Vianna ficará até 82," *Nosso Tempo*, December 24, 1980, 10–11.

6 As noted in chapter 2, in 1968 the military regime designated the region around Foz do Iguaçu as a "national security zone" and canceled all direct elections for mayor.

7 "Prefeito dá uma de juiz e cai do cavalo," *Nosso Tempo*, February 25, 1981, 13.

8 "Prefeito tem vergonha de ser coronel?," *Nosso Tempo*, March 4, 1981, 12.

9 Descriptions of this encounter come from "Depoimentos," *Nosso Tempo*, April 15, 1981, 5–7.

10 "Enquadrados na Lei de Segurança Nacional," *Nosso Tempo*, September 30, 1981, 8.

11 Amnesty International, document AMR 19/04/82, April 4, 1982, courtesy of the Mazzarollo family.

12 The text of Article 14 of the LSN comes from "Juvêncio condenado," *Nosso Tempo*, October 7, 1982, 2.

13 "Delegado comprova que processo é injusto," *Nosso Tempo*, April 15, 1981, 2. The original editorial stated, "Está louco ou é comendo conscientemente pedras por manteiga" ([He] is crazy or is consciously eating rocks as butter).

14 "Ques abertura é esta?," *Nosso Tempo*, April 15, 1981, 7.

15 "Juiz-Auditor recusa denúncia contra *Nosso Tempo*," *Nosso Tempo*, September 22, 1982, 2.

16 "Enquadrados na Lei de Segurança Nacional," *Nosso Tempo*, September 30, 1981, 8.

17 "Não se tira leite de vaca morta," *Nosso Tempo*, July 29, 1981, 12.

18 "Enquadrados na Lei de Segurança Nacional," *Nosso Tempo*, September 30, 1981, 8.

19 Chinem, *Jornalismo de guerrilha*, 18.

20 Dassin, "The Brazilian Press and the Politics of Abertura," 396. For more on oppositional media, see Molica and Luiz, *10 reportagens que abalaram a ditadura*.

21 "Condenado pela Espúria Lei de Segurança Nacional," *Nosso Tempo*, July 30, 1982, 8.

22 "Condenado pela Espúria Lei de Segurança Nacional," 8.

23 "Juvêncio condenado," *Nosso Tempo*, October 7, 1982, 2.

24 Macedo sent Juvêncio a copy of his speech, from April 3, 1981, and a personal note that "the threats suffered by your newspaper are limited to the arrogance of a colonel and the bitterness of a judge." Courtesy of the Mazzarollo family.

25 AN-RJ, Report No. 224/81/03/DSI/MJ, July 14, 1981, in SNI ACE.18410/81.

26 "Quando a violência se justifica," *Nosso Tempo*, May 6, 1981, 2; and "Pouca justiça e pouca terra," *Nosso Tempo*, May 20, 1981, 18.

27 AN-RJ, Report No. 0290/19/AC/81, August 12, 1981, in SNI ACE.18410/81; and Report No. AESI.G/IB/BR/010/81, July 13, 1981, courtesy of Aluízio Palmar.

28 CDIB, I/AJ.ADV/0153/81, R3530.1075–1083, October 6, 1981.

29 E/AESI.G/IB/BR/056/81, November 30, 1981, courtesy of Aluízio Palmar.

30 "Mazzarollo condenado na LSN," *O Estado do Paraná*, June 23, 1982.

31 LSN, Law No. 6.620. Published officially in *Diário Oficial da União*, Section 1, December 20, 1978, 20465.

32 "Juvêncio condenado," *Nosso Tempo*, October 7, 1982, 2.

33 Werner Fuchs, interview with author, Curitiba, Paraná, Brazil, July 13, 2013.

34 "Juvêncio condenado," *Nosso Tempo*, October 7, 1982, 2.

35 Confidential Federal Police report 0300/83-SI/DPF.1/FI/PR, October 21, 1983, courtesy of Aluízio Palmar.

36 *Poeira*, no. 25. November/December 1982, courtesy of Werner Fuchs.

37 "Teotônio visita Juvêncio na prisão," *Nosso Tempo*, March 10, 1983, 2.

38 Statement by the National Labor Front, October 22, 1982, courtesy of the Mazzarollo family.

39 Document from the PT, October 1983, courtesy of the Mazzarollo family.

40 "Teotônio visita Juvêncio na prisão," *Nosso Tempo*, March 10, 1983, 2.

41 Letter from Juvêncio Mazzarollo to Aluízio Palmar, courtesy of the Mazzarollo family.

42 Vilma Macedo, interview with author, Foz do Iguaçu, Paraná, Brazil, September 27, 2014.

43 "Juvêncio em greve de fome," *Nosso Tempo*, November 4, 1983, 23.

44 "Juvêncio encerra greve de fome," *Nosso Tempo*, November 11, 1983, 1.

45 Juvêncio's personal files contain copies of over 1,500 letters from fifteen countries: the United States, Canada, France, Spain, Italy, the United Kingdom, Sweden, Switzerland, Austria, Germany, Belgium, Greece, Tasmania, New Zealand, and Australia. Courtesy of the Mazzarollo family.

46 Open letter from David Chiel, associate director of the Committee to Protect Journalists, November 28, 1983, courtesy of the Mazzarollo family.

47 Statement written by Juvêncio Mazzarollo, November 9, 1983, courtesy of the Mazzarollo family.

48 Letter from prison written by Juvêncio Mazzarollo, March 28, 1984, courtesy of the Mazzarollo family.

49 Details on solidarity actions come from "Todos querem Juvêncio em liberdade," *Nosso Tempo*, April 7, 1984, 20; and "Vencemos," *Nosso Tempo*, April 13, 1984, 15.

50 "Vencemos," *Nosso Tempo*, April 13, 1984, 15.

51 "Supremos liberto o último preso político do País," *O Estado de São Paulo*, April 7, 1984.

52 "Vencemos," *Nosso Tempo*, April 13, 1984, 15.

6. "Men without a Country"

1 Although it is difficult to establish the exact number of Brazilians living in Paraguay, most estimations fall between 400,000 and 500,000. A commonly cited number, 459,147, comes from a 2002 report by the Brazilian Foreign Ministry. Albuquerque, *A dinâmica das fronteiras*, 59.

2 For the 1964 law's resettlement policies, see Wolford, *This Land Is Ours Now*, 45. Earlier state policies also attempted to transform the Brazilian "hinterlands." Seth Garfield provides an insightful example of how the Amazon region became an ideological and material pillar of Getúlio Vargas's Estado Novo (New State) regime (1937–1945). Garfield, *In Search of the Amazon*.

3 Moreira Alves, *State and Opposition in Military Brazil*, 25.

4 Quoted in Wagner, *Brasiguaios*, 11.

5 Nixon, *Slow Violence and the Environmentalism of the Poor*, 151.

6 Quoted in Albuquerque, *A dinâmica das fronteiras*, 67.

7 Gerd Kohlhepp offers the one-sixth cost estimation, while J. M. G. Kleinpenning quotes the price as one-tenth of that in Brazil. Kohlhepp, "Incorporação do espaço fronteiriço," 209; and Kleinpenning, *Man and Land in Paraguay*, 178.

8 Kohlhepp, "Incorporação do espaço fronteiriço," 210.

9 *Jornal do Brasil*, July 7, 1977, quoted in Menezes, *La herencia de Stroessner*, 173. Menezes only provides the newspaper title and date, but no title or page number for the source of his quotation.

10 Kohlhepp, "Incorporação do espaço fronteiriço," 208.

11 "A migração brasileira no Paraguai," *Cadernos de Justiça e Paz*, no. 2, June 1981, 13.

12 Fogel and Riquelme, *Enclave sojero*, 124.

13 Quoted in "Por um sonho, a travessia de uma fronteira," *Veja*, March 3, 1971, 34.

14 Kleinpenning, *Man and Land in Paraguay*, 179. The Institute for Rural Well-Being was created in 1963 to incorporate Paraguay's peasant population into the nation's economic development. Despite the declarations of a fair system of land management, the Paraguayan state distributed rural deeds in a manner that consolidated existing hierarchies. Elites throughout Paraguay received most titles distributed by the institute, yet in the border regions specifically, a disproportionate number of government lands were given to Brazilians. Menegotto, *Migrações e fronteiras*, 41.

15 Feliú, *Los Brasiguayos*, 47.

16 Fogel and Riquelme, *Enclave sojero*, 126.

17 Wagner Rocha D'Angelis and Juvêncio Mazzarollo, "A migração brasileira no Paraguai," *Cadernos de Justiça e Paz*, no. 2, June 1981, 15.

18 "Encontro analisa a vida dos 'brasiguaios,'" *Folha de São Paulo*, September 2, 1982, 17.

19 "As terras sem títulos, problemas pelos colonos," *Folha de São Paulo*, November 23, 1981, 8.

20 "Colonos brasileiros no inferno Guarani," *Revista Panorama*, June 18, 1980, 16–17.

21 AN-BSB, Report No. 0100/S-102-AI-CIE, Defense Ministry, January 24, 1975, in N8.0.PSN, EST.285.

22 The organizers included Paraguay's Domingo Laino—Stroessner's main critic—and several Brazilian politicians from the PMDB opposition party. CEPEDAL, "Carta das oposições-Brasil/Paraguay," Asunción, Paraguay, June 1, 1980, Collection "Kirinus," unmarked folder.

23 Between 1972 and 1977, the area under cultivation in Paraguay rose at an annual rate of 16 percent, and 25 percent of this area produced soybeans. Menezes, *La herencia de Stroessner*, 14. By the early 2000s, Paraguay had become the world's sixth-largest producer of soybeans, with the crop occupying over 50 percent of all cultivated lands in the country. Albuquerque, *A dinâmica das fronteiras*, 83.

24 Riquelme, "Notas para el estudio de las causas y efectos de las migraciones brasileñas," 136.

25 Albuquerque, *A dinâmica das fronteiras*, 107.

26 *Última Hora*, June 20, 1977, 13, quoted in Laino, *Paraguay*, 80.

27 "Explorados no Paraguai," *Folha de Londrina*, August 7, 1985.

28 Ozorio de Almeida, *The Colonization of the Amazon*, 1–29.

29 Garfield observes that Travassos's ideologies combined "Rudolf Kjellen's theory of the porousness of territorial boundaries with Halford Mackinder's creed that control of the continental 'heartland' held the key to military superiority." Garfield, *In Search of the Amazon*, 31.

30 Ozorio de Almeida, *The Colonization of the Amazon*, 4.

31 Alston, Libecap, and Mueller, *Titles, Conflict, and Land Use*, 41.

32 The Araguaia War will be discussed more in chapter 7.

33 Various scholars have analyzed the limitations of the PIN and the process through which the military government largely abandoned the goal of developing state-run colonization projects, shifting instead toward the end of the 1970s to private initiatives of large-scale cattle ranching. See Schmink and Wood, *Contested Frontiers in Amazonia*, 76; Alston, Libecap, and Mueller, *Titles, Conflict, and Land Use*, 42–43; and Ludewigs et al., "Agrarian Structure and Land-Cover Change," 1350.

34 Ministry of Agriculture, INCRA, Projeto Integrado de Colonização Altamira—1, INCRA, Brasília, 1972, quoted in Fearnside, "Brazil's Settlement Schemes," 47.

35 Ozorio de Almeida, *The Colonization of the Amazon*, 28.

36 CDIB, "Desaproriações, área do reservatório (margen esquerda)," 1983, 4148.187–195.

37 Archive of FETAEP, Curitiba, E/DG/0221/79, April 11, 1979.

38 CDIB, letter from Laurenço Vieira da Silva, president of INCRA, to General José Cavalcanti, president of Itaipu, August 14, 1978, Circular INCRA P/no. 296, 728.1259–1261. Other exchanges between INCRA and Itaipu over these issues included the following documents housed in the CDIB: Meeting between Itaipu

Legal Department and INCRA, May 24, 1978, 729.1043–1053; and letter from Gen. Cavalcanti to INCRA president Vieira da Silva, May 30, 1978, 728.1262–1263.

39 CDIB, letter from Construtora Andrade Gutierrez S.A. to General Cavalcanti, March 16, 1979, 8241.974–978; and letter from Indeco S.A. to General Cavalcanti, December 9, 1979, 1398.1822.

40 CDIB, letter from Colonizadora Sinop S.A. to General Cavalcanti, August 4, 1978, 728.323–325.

41 CDIB, letter from General Cavalcanti to President of INCRA, E/DG/0461/78, September 13, 1978, 694.785–786.

42 CDIB, "Notas da reunião com o INCRA," December 5, 1978, Rio de Janeiro, 728.1273–1285.

43 CDIB, "Notas da reunião com o INCRA e empress colonizadoras," December 15, 1978, Rio de Janeiro, 728F.1299–1317.

44 CDIB, "Subsídios sobre despapropriações," Itaipu internal memo, 1979, 1316.135–136.

45 "Desapropriações: E começa o êxodo para o Norte," *Jornal da Tarde*, April 9, 1979, 12.

46 CDIB, letter from General José Cavalcanti to Irmut Helmet Krugel, president of the Association of Council Deputies of the Border Region, January 23, 1979, 1397.338–340.

47 "Agricultores x Itaipu," *Hoje*, April 12, 1979, 4.

48 CPT-Londrina, "Ao povo, o governo, e à Itaipu," July 14, 1980 (original capitalization).

49 Only a single item concerned lands in Paraná, relating to the possibility of reactivating the Agrarian Fund (*Bolsa Agrária*). CDIB, "Ata da reunião realizada em Itaipu," July 27, 1980, 2135.901–904.

50 CDIB, "Reunião entre a diretoria da Itaipu Binacional e a Comissão de Expropriados," Santa Helena, October 1, 1980, 2135.926–930.

51 The project's official name was Poti, but it was commonly referred to as Arapoti, the name of the nearby town.

52 Examples include CDIB, letter from General Cavalcanti to Minister of Agriculture Angelo Amauri Stabile, E/DG/0142/82, April 2, 1982, 3358.327–328; and CDIB, letter from the governor of Minas Gerais, Francelino Pereira dos Santos, to General Cavalcanti, GM No. 259, April 30, 1982, 3359.291.

53 CDIB, "Desaproriações, área do reservatório (margem esquerda)," 1983 report, 4148.187–195.

54 The Bahia project was initially established in 1975 to accommodate families displaced by the Sobradinho dam. The Acre colony began in 1977 and at the time was the second-largest agricultural project in all of Brazil. INCRA webpage, "Deputados homenageiam os 43 anos do Incra no Acre," August 23, 2013, http://www.incra.gov.br/web-deputados-homenageiam-os-43-anos-do-incra-no-acre.

55 "Comissão Pastoral da Terra critica Itaipu pelo envio de colonos da usina para o Acre," *Folha de Londrina*, July 25, 1981.

56 Schmink and Wood, *Contested Frontiers in Amazonia*, 69.

57 Quoted in "Encontro sobre colonização em São Paulo," January 16–19, *Poeira*, no. 32, February 1984, 16.

58 In Füllgraf, *Os desapropriados*.

59 "Colonos paranaenses com malária no Acre," *O Estado de São Paulo*, August 27, 1981.

60 Interviewed in Füllgraf, *Os desapropriados*.

61 "Agricultores de Itaipu no Acre," *Poeira*, no. 18, September 1981, 24.

62 Schmink and Wood, *Contested Frontiers in Amazonia*, 77.

63 Quoted in "Colonos do Sul estão abandonados no Acre," *Folha de Londrina*, November 25, 1983.

64 Interviewed in Füllgraf, *Os desapropriados*.

65 Of the 401 families relocated to Arapoti, 312 (77 percent) were *arrendatários*, 40 (10 percent) were small farmers, 36 (9 percent) were rural waged workers, and 13 (3 percent) lived on private lands. CDIB, "Desaproriações, área do reservatório (margen esquerda)," 1983 report, 4148.187–195. Statistics on the settlers' financial situation come from AN-RJ, "Situação do Projeto Poty, no município de Arapoti/PR," SNI Report No. 130/17/AC/83, February 18, 1983, in SNI ACE.3721/83.

66 Interviewed in Füllgraf, *Os desapropriados*.

67 "Fome em Arapoti," *Hoje*, September 17, 1982, 5.

68 "Arapoti vive cenário de uma herença cruel, diz deputado," *Diário Popular*, December 25, 1982; and "Colonos removidos do Oeste passam até fome em Arapoti," *Folha de Londrina*, January 4, 1983, 24–26.

69 AN-RJ, Paraná, State Coordination of Civil Defense—CEDEC/PR, "Relatótio sobre o problema dos agricultores reassentados pelo INCRA da área do lago de Itaipu para Arapoti," December 29, 1972, in SNI ACE.4068/83.

70 AN-RJ, Federal Public Service, "Relatótio sobre PROJETO POTY," INCRA-4(09) No. 018, January 12, 1983, 2, in SNI ACE.4068/83.

71 Federal Public Service, "Relatótio sobre PROJETO POTY," 5–6.

72 Federal Public Service, "Relatótio sobre PROJETO POTY," 5–7.

73 Federal Public Service, "Relatótio sobre PROJETO POTY," 8.

74 Although the national media began providing more in-depth coverage, newspapers in Paraná still produced a much higher volume. One INCRA report noted that in the month of November 1983 alone, sixty-five articles in newspaper within Paraná covered the resettlement projects, thirty-five of which it deemed positive, twenty-one negative, and nine neutral toward the projects. INCRA state office, Curitiba, "Resenha dos jornais do Paraná, avaliação mensal," November 1983.

75 "Ex-colonos de Itaipu agora passam fome em Arapoti," *Folha de São Paulo*, July 3, 1983, 11.

76 "Ex-colonos de Itaipu agora passam fome em Arapoti," *Folha de São Paulo*, July 3, 1983, 11.

77 AN-RJ, Confidential SNI Report No. 130/17/AC/83, August 8, 1983, in SNI ACE.3721/83.

78 Confidential SNI Report No. 130/17/AC/83, 2.

79 "Colono de Arapoti pode perder terra," *O Estado do Paraná*, August 12, 1983, 9.

80 "Projeto Poti desaponta famílias de agricultores," *O Estado do Paraná*, November 2, 1984.

81 AN-RJ, Confidential SNI Report No. 096/130/AC/85, November 4, 1985, in SNI ACE.53321/85.

82 Albuquerque, *A dinâmica das fronteiras*, 231.

83 Quoted in "A ilusão brasileira no Paraguai," *Folha de São Paulo*, November 22, 1981, 8.

84 Albuquerque, *A dinâmica das fronteiras*, 229.

7. Land for Those Who Work It

1 "Posseiro será indenizado," *O Estado de São Paulo*, December 15, 1974.

2 As explained in the note on terminology and orthography at the start of this book, the category of "landless" (*sem terra*) covers a wide range of rural Brazilians who did not have the legal deed to the lands they worked. Among others, this includes squatters (*posseiros*), tenant farmers (*arrendatários*), sharecroppers (*parceiros*), day laborers (*empregados*), and itinerant workers (*boias-frias*). In this chapter, as throughout the book, the landless are described at different points as peasants, peasant farmers, landless farmers, or landless workers.

3 In more contemporary landless struggles, the category of farm (*fazenda*) has been up for debate. Some consider the term appropriate only for a productive enterprise of small scale, akin to a family farm in the United States. The properties targeted for occupation by the MST, in contrast, are often called *estates* (*latifundias*) if they are deemed unproductive, or *plantations* if they are large in size. In this book the targets of MASTRO occupations are all referred to as *farms*, the designation used at the time.

4 Other land occupations in western Paraná included the following farms: Giacomet-Marodim in Chopinzinho (1983), Quinhnão 11 in Sertaneja (1983), Imaribo in Mangueirinha (1984), Rio das Cobras in Quedas do Sul (1984), Brilhante in Cascavel (1984), and Serra Igreja in Morretes (1984). Fabrini, "Os assentamentos de trabalhadores rurais," 109; and Schreiner, "Entre a exclusão e a utopia," 61.

5 *State troopers* refers to the Polícia Militar (Military Police), a body unaffiliated with the military. The Polícia Militar originated in the state militias prior to the dictatorship, and although it mimics a military hierarchy, the state government controls it.

6 "Pastel" Adriano, interview with author, Santa Terezinha, Paraná, Brazil, November 3, 2014.

7 Delfino Becker, interview with author, Querência do Norte, Paraná, Brazil, November 23, 2014.

8 For more on other rural mobilizations during Brazil's dictatorship, see Souza Martins, *A militarização da questão agrária no Brasil*; B. Maybury-Lewis, *The*

Politics of the Possible; Medeiros, *Reforma agrária no Brasil*; Pereira, *The End of Peasantry*; and Rogers, *The Deepest Wounds*. The Peasant's Truth Commission offers an especially useful resource for the study of rural mobilization and repression during Brazil's dictatorship. Comissão Camponesa da Verdade, *Relatório final*.

9 Favareto, "Agricultores, trabalhadores," 30.

10 Although mostly linked to the frontier states of Mato Grosso and Goiás, the March to the West also involved the settlement of western Paraná. Foweraker, *The Struggle for Land*, 29.

11 Alston, Libecap, and Mueller, *Titles, Conflict, and Land Use*, 5, 131–32.

12 Although the Brazilian Communist Party's Peasant Leagues had been repressed and disbanded by 1948, the party's *setor do campo* (its rural branch) and *setor especial* (its military training) remained active. For more on the Porecatú War, see Welch, *The Seed Was Planted*, 129–139; Joaquim da Silva, *Terra roxa de sangue*; and Priori, *O levante dos posseiros*. Responding, in part, to new laws under the Vargas regime that gave labor rights to farmworkers, the Peasant Leagues—a front organization established by the Brazilian Communist Party (PCB)—emerged in the mid-1940s with dozens of organizations in Paraná, São Paulo, Rio de Janeiro, Minas Gerais, and Pernambuco. Welch, "Camponeses," 129. For more on the Peasant Leagues, see Santos de Morais, "Peasant Leagues in Brazil," 453–501; and Souza Martins, *Os camponesas e a política no Brasil*, 21–102. Most scholarly work on the Peasant Leagues focuses on movements in the northeast; examples include Mallon, "Peasants and Rural Laborers in Pernambuco," and Pereira, *The End of Peasantry*, esp. 3–32, 63–65, 165.

13 Zanoni Gomes, *1957*.

14 Nildemar Silva, interview with author, Assentamento Antonio Tavares, São Miguel do Iguaçu, Paraná, Brazil, November 3, 2014.

15 Milton Serres Rodrigues, the mayor of Encruzilhada do Sul, founded MASTER. Serres Rodrigues had the support of Governor Brizola. Both men belonged to the Brazilian Workers' Party (PTB). Carvalho Rosa, "Sem-terra," 200–207.

16 Ondetti, *Land, Protest, and Politics*, 79, 13.

17 Welch points in particular to a speech on March 13, 1964—two weeks before the eventual military coup—given by President Goulart to almost 200,000 people that advocated for radical agrarian reform. General Humberto Castelo Branco, who would soon serve as the first military president, remembers hearing Goulart's speech and feeling motivated to get even more involved in planning the coup. Welch, *The Seed Was Planted*, 333.

18 For more on Araguaia, see Campos Filho, *Guerrilha do Araguaia*; and also Comissão Nacional da Verdade, *Relatório*, ch. 14.

19 APP, "Documentos sôbre 'gang' de grileiros e corruptos do sudoeste do Paraná," report sent to the Paraná secretary of public safety, 1969–1970; "'Jagunços' voltaram a atacar no sudoeste," *Tribuna do Paraná*, September 25, 1972, 5; "Paraná: O temor aos posseiros," *Folha de São Paulo*, October 29, 1972; and "Problemas de

terra," No. 219/73-CISESP/DI, August 1, 1973. All of the preceding files are found in APP, PT 159A.15A.

20 APP, Paraná Military Police, Report No. 026 PM/2/69, "Problemas de terras no sudoeste," May 7, 1969, in PT 159A.15A.

21 Statistics come from B. Maybury-Lewis, *The Politics of the Possible*, 12. Another useful study of rural mobilization under dictatorship and the subsequent return of civilian rule is Houtzager, *Os últimos cidadãos*.

22 Welch, "Camponeses," 138.

23 Land occupations were also staged in other Latin American countries during the second half of the 1970s, most notably the *tomas* (land seizures) in Chile and Peru.

24 "O que os colonos querem de Itaipu," *Hoje*, November 2, 1978, 4.

25 Carlos Grillmann, interview with author, Foz do Iguaçu, Paraná, Brazil, October 2, 2014.

26 CDIB, "Ata da reunião realizada em Itaipu em 27/07/80," July 27, 1980, 2135.901–904.

27 "Posseiros também assegura direitos," *Poeira*, no. 12, July/August 1980, 11.

28 Adil Fochezatto, interview with author, Santa Helena Velha, Paraná, Brazil, November 14, 2014.

29 Dona Suita, interview with author, Santa Helena, Paraná, Brazil, November 16, 2014.

30 Dona Suita, interview with author, Santa Helena, Paraná, Brazil, November 16, 2014.

31 Itamar da Silva, interview with author, Santa Helena, Paraná, Brazil, November 16, 2014.

32 Wife of Afio Genaro [name unknown], interview with author, Assentamento Antonio Tavares, São Miguel do Iguaçu, Brazil, November 3, 2014.

33 "Terra por terra," *Poeira*, no. 13, September 1980, 15–16.

34 "Movimento dos agricultores sem terra," *Nosso Tempo*, July 29, 1981, 12.

35 Quoted in Mazzarollo, *A taipa da injustiça*, 151.

36 Ribeiro de Moraes Junior, "MASTRO," 25–63.

37 Afonso Camer, interview with author, Medianeira, Paraná, Brazil, November 3, 2014. For a contemporary account of Canudos, see Cunha, *Rebellion in the Backlands*. A more recent scholarly interpretation is Levine, "'Mud-Hut Jerusalem.'"

38 João Pedro Stedile, an eventual leader of the MST, provides good insight into the role of the Syndicate of Rural Workers in the formation of landless movements in the early 1980s in Stedile and Mançano Fernandes, *Brava gente*, 15–56.

39 Werner Fuchs, email correspondence with author, January 3, 2017.

40 AN-RJ, "1A ATA," September 2, 1981, in SNI ACE.2632/82.

41 Examples of state surveillance include AN-RJ, Department of Federal Police, Request No. 130/81, in BR.AN.BSB.ED.03.4, 50/57, October 1981; AN-RJ, Paraná Military Police, Report No. 763/81-PN/2, in SNI ACE.2632/82, December 21, 1981; and APP, SNI Report on MASTRO, 0143/116/ACT/81, November 23, 1981.

42 Survey statistics come from Sindicato dos Trabalhadores Rurais-São Miguel do Iguaçu (hereafter STR-SMI), "Levantamento de agricultores sem terra," no date

given. Although this survey has no date attributed, a later document suggests that it was conducted between late 1981 and early 1982. STR-SMI, "MASTRO em 28/1/1982," January 28, 1982.

43 Although almost all MASTRO members were landless, a few participants owned very small tracts of land. In the above survey, eight people (1.2 percent) were categorized as small farmers. And a document from early in MASTRO's formation mentioned that one could still join provided they owned no more than six alqueires of land. AN-RJ, "1a ata," September 2, 1981, in SNI ACE.2632/82.

44 Baller, "Fronteira e fronteiriços," 245.

45 Souza Martins, *A militarização da questão agrária no Brasil*, 99.

46 APP, "Atividades de MASTRO na região oeste do estado do Paraná," Report No. 052-82-PM/2-PMPR, in "Questnões de terras do oeste do Paraná e sudoeste," No. 003496.

47 STR-SMI, open letter to the Senate Agricultural Commission, Brasília, February 27, 1982, Report No. 059/82.

48 AN-RJ, letter to Valter da Costa Reis, General Chief of the SNI, from José Guilherme Cavagnari, Regional Coordinator of INCRA Paraná, March 12, 1982, Report INCRA-4(02) No. 225, in SNI ACE.2632/82.

49 AN-RJ, SNI Report No. 0031/117/ACT/82, May 11, 1982, in SNI ACE.2632/82.

50 AN-RJ, SNI Report No. 0064/16/ACT/82, September 16, 1982, in SNI ACE.3302/82.

51 "O Grito dos Sem Terra," *Poeira*, no. 22, May/June 1982, 6–9.

52 Mançano Fernandes, "The Formation and Territorialization of the MST in Brazil," 119. Additional information on the July 9–11 Medianeira meeting comes from AN-RJ, SNI Report No. 256/119/APA/82, August 16, 1982, in SNI ACE.3486/82.

53 An SNI report observes that the Goiânia meeting was organized by Leadership Training Center of the Archdiocese of Goiânia, the Pastoral Land Commission (CPT), MASTRO, and the Movement of Rural Cristianity. AN-RJ, SNI Report No. 019/19/AGO/SNI/82, November 18, 1982, in SNI ACE.3526/82.

54 AN-RJ, SNI Report No. 259/15/AC/82, item 7, September 10, 1982, in SNI ACE.29096/82.

55 SNI Report No. 259/15/AC/82, item 8.

56 STR-SMI, letter to STR-SMI from Regional Coordinator of INCRA Paraná, Of.INCRA-4(09) No. 560, August 16, 1982.

57 STR-SMI, "Relato da 2a assembleia geral, MASTRO, Medianeira, Paraná," August 28, 1982.

58 "MASTRO realiza mini assembléias," *Poeira*, no. 25, November 1982, 17.

59 AN-RJ, José Guilherme L. Cavagnari, "Bases para uma política de assentamento de agricultores: Propostas para o estado do Paraná," September 1982, SNI Report No. 135/17/AC/82, 2, in SNI ACE.29309/82.

60 Cavagnari, "Bases para uma política de assentamento de agricultores," 3.

61 Cavagnari, "Bases para uma política de assentamento de agricultores," 8.

62 Instituto Paranaense de Desenvolvimento Econômico e Social, "Assentamentos rurais no Paraná," 1992, 24.

63 Celso Anghinoni, interview with author, Querência do Norte, Paraná, Brazil, November 23, 2014.

64 "Previsões para 1983," *Poeira*, no. 25, November 1982, 18.

65 Luis Pozzolo, interview with author, Guaraniaçu, Paraná, Brazil, November 12, 2014.

66 Nildemar Silva, interview with author, Assentamento Antonio Tavares, São Miguel do Iguaçu, Paraná, Brazil, November 3, 2014.

67 The Padroeira occupiers were seeking to have four thousand alqueires of the property deeded to them.

68 Information on MASTRO's role in the different land occupations in western Paraná in 1983 and 1984 comes mainly from AN-RJ, SNI Report No. 0125/17/ACT/83, October 3, 1983, in SNI ACE.4372/83. The final document from the MST's 1984 founding meeting also provides details on MASTRO's role in these occupations. "Ocupações de terra no ano de 83," National Landless Meeting, January 1984, Cascavel, 9, courtesy of Davi Schreiner.

69 "Invasão," *Nosso Tempo*, April 21, 1983, 10.

70 "Secretário promete paz a colonos de Matelândia," *Folha de Londrina*, May 21, 1983, 6.

71 "Invasão," *Nosso Tempo*, April 21, 1983, 12.

72 AN-RJ, Report on MASTRO's Third General Assembly, May 25, 1983, Medianeira, compiled by the Municipal Office of Medianeira, in SNI ACE.4372/83.

73 MASTRO, "Em marcha para a terra prometida," document crafted at the third general assembly of MASTRO, May 25, 1983, Medianeira, courtesy of Davi Schreiner.

74 Souza Martins, *A militarização da questão agrária no Brasil*, 32.

75 As reproduced in *Nosso Tempo*, May 5, 1983, 7.

76 For more on the legal components of rural mobilizations in Brazil, see Mézsáros, *Social Movements, Law and the Politics of Land Reform*.

77 Musacchio and Lazzarini, *Reinventing State Capitalism*, 91.

78 Mainwaring, *Rethinking Party Systems in the Third Wave of Democratization*, 90.

79 Baer, "Brazil's Rocky Economic Road to Democracy," 51.

80 Moreira Alves, *State and Opposition in Military Brazil*, 235–40.

81 Moreira Alves, *State and Opposition in Military Brazil*, 243–44.

82 "Jagunços já expulsam famílias em Matelândia," *Folha de Londrina*, July 2, 1983, 8.

83 "Aumenta a tensão na Fazenda Padroeira," *Nosso Tempo*, September 9, 1983, 2.

84 "Violência irrompe em vários pontos, na luta pela terra," *Folha de Londrina*, September 1, 1983.

85 The Anoni farm was officially expropriated by INCRA on March 31, 1980, via Decree No. 84.603. AN-RJ, SNI Report No. 0125/17/ACT/83, October 3, 1983, in SNI ACE.4372/83.

86 Details of the Anoni camp and violence are drawn from "Conflito de terra: Uma pessoa morre," *O Estado do Paraná*, July 29, 1983; and "João de Paula: Na Cruz do latifúndio," report compiled July 28, 1983, by the Syndicate of Rural Workers

of Capanema, Dois Vizinhos, Ampére, Nova Prata do Iguaçu, Francisco Beltrão, and Santa Izabel D'Oeste, courtesy of Davi Schreiner.

87 "Um morto em luta por terra já desapropriada," *O Estado de São Paulo*, July 29, 1983, 12.

88 Luis Pozzolo, interview with author, Guaraniaçu, Paraná, Brazil, November 12, 2014.

89 Afonso Camer, interview with author, Medianeira, Paraná, Brazil, November 3, 2014.

90 "Violência irrompe em vários pontos, na luta pela terra," *Folha de Londrina*, September 1, 1983, 7–8.

91 "Colonos do MASTRO ocupam uma fazenda em Guarapuava," *Folha de Londrina*, September 24, 1983.

92 "Cavernoso: Era uma fazenda sem gente," *Poeira*, no. 31, December 1983, 18–19.

93 "Cavernoso: Acordo garante plantio," *Jornal dos Trabalhadores Sem Terra*, no. 41, January 1985, 5.

94 "Ocupação da área do INCRA em São Miguel," *Poeira*, no. 33, March 1984, 31.

95 "Invadidas terras da Itaipu," *O Estado de São Paulo*, June 9, 1984, 8; and "Mais uma invasão de terra," *Folha de Londrina*, June 21, 1984, 21.

96 "Colonos invadem o Incra," *O Estado do Paraná*, July 24, 1984; and "Sob pressão, INCRA promete agir," *Jornal dos Trabalhadores Sem Terra*, no. 40, November 1984, 7.

97 "Com o coração ferido de desgosto por serem brasileiros," *Nosso Tempo*, September 27, 1984, 14.

98 Schreiner, "Entre a exclusão e a utopia," 456.

99 "Polícia usa violência contra os sem terra," *Jornal dos Trabalhadores Sem Terra*, no. 37, August 1984, 9.

100 "Posseiros expulsos," *Jornal do Estado*, July 1, 1984, 1.

101 "As mulheres resistem," *Folha de Londrina*, July 1, 1984, 12.

102 Teolide Turcatel, interview with author, Medianeira, Paraná, Brazil, November 2, 2014.

103 Iraci Maino, interview with author, Medianeira, Paraná, Brazil, November 2, 2014.

104 For a detailed account of the Cascavel meeting, see Branford and Rocha, *Cutting the Wire*, 21–25.

105 Welch, "Camponeses," 127–28.

106 Schreiner, "Entre a exclusão e a utopia"; Mazzarollo, *A taipa da injustiça*; Ribeiro de Moraes Junior, "MASTRO"; and Stedile and Mançano Fernandes, *Brava gente*.

107 Friends of the MST website, "History of the MST," February 12, 2003, http://www.mstbrazil.org/content/history-mst.

108 "Ocupações de terra no ano de 83," National Landless Meeting, January 1984, Cascavel, appendix 4, courtesy of Davi Schreiner.

109 Draft of Minutes, Encontro Nacional dos Trabalhadores Sem Terra, Cascavel, Paraná, January 20–22, 1984, 3, courtesy of Werner Fuchs.

110 Draft of Minutes, Encontro Nacional dos Trabalhadores Sem Terra, Cascavel, Paraná, 21.

111 AN-RJ, SNI Report No. 0016/19/ACT/84, February 7, 1984, 3, in SNI ACE.4741/84.

112 "Assassinado líder dos posseiros em Padroeira," *Jornal dos Trabalhadores Sem Terra*, no. 36, July 1984, 4.

113 "Trabalhadores rurais assassinados no ano de 83," National Landless Meeting, January 1984, Cascavel, appendix 3, courtesy of Davi Schreiner.

114 "Fazenda Padroeira: Acordo é decidido," *Tribuna do Paraná*, March 20, 1984.

115 Skidmore, *The Politics of Military Rule in Brazil*, 243.

116 Schreiner, "Entre a exclusão e a utopia," 456.

117 Members of MASTRO also resettled in two additional successful land occupations: the Assentamento Abapan in the municipality of Castro and the Assentamento Vitória da União in Manguerinha. Schreiner, "Entre a exclusão e a utopia," 456.

118 An estimated 1,556 deaths occurred in response to land struggles between January 1964 and December 1989. Comissão Camponesa da Verdade, *Relatório final*, 73. This number rises to 1,833 between 1985 and 2016. Comissão Pastoral da Terra, *Conflitos no Campo Brasil*.

Conclusion

1 Adil Fochezatto, interview with author, Santa Helena Velha, Paraná, Brazil, November 14, 2014.

2 Dona Suita, interview with author, Santa Helena, Paraná, Brazil, November 16, 2014.

BIBLIOGRAPHY

Archives

Archivo Histórico de la Cancillería de Paraguay (AHCP), Asunción, Paraguay

Arquivo Estadual de São Paulo

Arquivo Histórico de Itamaraty (AHI), Brasília

Arquivo Nacional, Brasília (AN-BSB)

Arquivo Nacional, Rio de Janeiro (AN-RJ)

Arquivo Público do Paraná (APP), Curitiba, Brazil

Biblioteca do Senado Federal, Brasília

Biblioteca Pública do Paraná, Curitiba, Brazil

Centro de Documentação Itaipu Binacional (CDIB), Foz do Iguaçu, Brazil

Centro de Documentação e Pesquisa Histórica (CDPH), Universidade Estadual de Londrina, Brazil

Centro de Documentación y Archivo para la Defensa de los Derechos Humanos (CDyA), Asunción, Paraguay

Centro de Pesquisa e Documentação de História Contemporânea do Brasil–Fundação Getúlio Vargas (CPDOC-FGV)

Comissão Pastoral da Terra (CPT), national office, Goiânia, Brazil

Comissão Pastoral da Terra (CPT), regional office in archdiocese of Londrina, Brazil (CPT-Londrina)

Federação dos Trabalhadores na Agricultura do Estado Paraná (FETAEP), central office, Curitiba, Brazil

Instituto Nacional de Colonização e Reforma Agrária (INCRA), regional office, Cascavel, Brazil

Instituto Nacional de Colonização e Reforma Agrária (INCRA), state office, Curitiba, Brazil

Núcleo de Pesquisa e Documentação sobre o Oeste do Paraná (CEPEDAL), Universidade Estadual do Oeste do Paraná, Marechal Cândido Rondon, Brazil

Sindicato dos Trabalhadores Rurais-São Miguel do Iguaçu (STR-SMI), central office, Brazil

Individuals with Personal Holdings

Almada, Martin
Fuchs, Werner
The Mazzarollo family
Palmar, Aluízio
Schreiner, Davi
Vanderlinde, Tarcísio

Digital Collections

Foreign Relations of the United States (FRUS), https://history.state.gov/
Nosso Tempo digital, www.nossotempodigital.com.br
Opening the Archives Project, http://library.brown.edu/openingthearchives/

Newspapers and Magazines

ABC Color (Paraguay)
Cadernos de Justiça e Paz
Correio de Notícias
Diário do Congresso Nacional
Diário do Paraná
Diário Popular
O Estado do Paraná
O Estado do São Paulo
Folha da Tarde
Folha de Londrina
Folha de São Paulo
Gazeta do Povo
O Globo
Harper's (USA)
Hoje
O Jornal
Jornal da Tarde
O Jornal do Brasil
Jornal do Estado
Jornal dos Trabalhadores Sem Terra
La Libertad (Paraguay)
Luta Indígena
Nosso Tempo
O Mensageiro
New York Times (USA)
O Paraná

Patria (Paraguay)
Poeira
El Pueblo (Paraguay)
Revista Panorama
Time (USA)
La Tribuna (Paraguay)
Tribuna do Paraná
Última Hora
Veja
Zero Hora

Interviews with Author

Adriano, "Pastel." Santa Terezinha, Paraná, Brazil. November 3, 2014.

Anghinoni, Celso. Querência do Norte, Paraná, Brazil. November 23, 2014.

Becker, Delfino. Querência do Norte, Paraná, Brazil. November 23, 2014.

Benites, Onorio. Aldeia Indígena Tekoha Itamarã, Paraná, Brazil. November 6, 2014.

Caballero Aquino, Ricardo. Asunción, Paraguay. January 7, 2015.

Camer, Afonso. Medianeira, Paraná, Brazil. November 3, 2014.

"Dener" [nickname]. Assentamento Antonio Tavares, São Miguel do Iguaçu, Paraná, Brazil. November 3, 2014.

Fochezatto, Adil. Santa Helena Velha, Paraná, Brazil. November 14, 2014.

Friedrich, Nelton. Foz do Iguaçu, Paraná, Brazil. October 9, 2014.

Fuchs, Werner. Curitiba, Paraná, Brazil. July 13, 2013.

Fuchs, Werner. Garuva, Santa Catarina, Brazil. February 28, 2015.

Grillmann, Carlos. Foz do Iguaçu, Paraná, Brazil. October 2, 2014.

Kirinus, Gernote. Marechal Cândido Rondon, Paraná, Brazil. September 17, 2014.

Kolling, Silvênio. Garuva, Santa Catarina, Brazil. February 28, 2015.

Macedo, Vilma. Foz do Iguaçu, Brazil. September 27, 2014.

Maino, Iraci. Medianeira, Paraná, Brazil. November 2, 2014.

Melz, Albano. São Clemente, Paraná, Brazil. November 17, 2014.

Palmar, Aluízio. Foz do Iguaçu, Paraná, Brazil. August 8, 2013.

Pappalardo, Conrado. Asunción, Paraguay. January 5, 2015.

Pozzolo, Luis. Guaraniaçu, Paraná, Brazil. November 12, 2014.

Raviche, Edgard. Toledo, Paraná, Brazil. November 4, 2014.

Rocini, Lauro. Itaipulândia, Paraná, Brazil. December 26, 2014.

Rusch, Elio. Marechal Cândido Rondon, Paraná, Brazil. November 21, 2014.

Saldívar, Carlos. Asunción, Paraguay. January 14, 2015.

Silva, Itamar da. Santa Helena, Paraná, Brazil. November 16, 2014.

Silva, Nildemar. Assentamento Antonio Tavares, São Miguel do Iguaçu, Paraná, Brazil. November 3, 2014.

Souza, João Adelino de. Foz do Iguaçu, Paraná, Brazil. October 6, 2014.

Suita, Dona. Santa Helena, Paraná, Brazil. November 16, 2014.

Tupã Alves, Teodoro. Aldeia Indígena Tekoha Itamarã, Paraná, Brazil. November 6, 2014.

Tupã Rokenji, Adriano. Aldeia Indígena Tekoha Itamarã, Paraná, Brazil. November 6, 2014.

Turcatel, Teolide. Medianeira, Paraná, Brazil. November 2, 2014.

Wife of Afio Genaro. Assentamento Antonio Tavares, São Miguel do Iguaçu, Paraná, Brazil. November 3, 2014.

Books, Articles, and Theses

Ahrén, Mattias. *Indigenous Peoples' Status in the International Legal System*. New York: Oxford University Press, 2016.

Albuquerque, José Lindomar. *A dinâmica das fronteiras: Os brasiguaios na fronteira entre o Brasil e o Paraguai*. São Paulo: Annablume, 2010.

Alston, Lee J., Gary D. Libecap, and Bernardo Mueller. *Titles, Conflict, and Land Use: The Development of Property Rights and Land Reform on the Brazilian Amazon Frontier*. Ann Arbor: University of Michigan Press, 1999.

Anderson, Benedict. *Imagined Communities: Reflections on the Origin and Spread of Nationalism*. London: Verso, 1983.

Archibaldo Lanús, Juan. *De Chapultepec al Beagle: Política exterior Argentina, 1945–1980*. Buenos Aires, Argentina: Emecé Editores, 1984.

Assis, Dilermando Cândido de. *Nas barrancas do Alto-Paraná: Fragmentos históricos da Revolução de 1924*. Rio de Janeiro: Ed. Irmãos Pongetti, 1926.

Atencio, Rebecca J. *Memory's Turn: Reckoning with Dictatorship in Brazil*. Madison: University of Wisconsin Press, 2014.

Baer, Werner. "Brazil's Rocky Economic Road to Democracy." In *The Political Economy of Brazil: Public Policies in an Era of Transition*, edited by Lawrence S. Graham and Robert Hines Wilson, 41–61. Austin: University of Texas Press, 1990.

Baller, Leandro. "Fronteira e fronteiriços: A construção das relações socias e culturais entre brasileiros e paraguaios (1954–2014)." PhD diss., Universidade Federal da Grande Dourados, 2014.

Bento Ribeiro, Maria de Fátima. *Memórias do concreto: Vozes na construção de Itaipu*. Cascavel, Brazil: Edunioeste, 2002.

Branford, Sue, and Jan Rocha. *Cutting the Wire: The Story of the Landless Movement in Brazil*. London: Latin America Bureau, 2002.

Brant de Carvalho, Maria Lucia. "Das terras dos índios a índios sem terra o estado e os Guarani do Oco'y: Violência, silêncio e luta." PhD diss., Universidade de São Paulo, 2013.

Buckley, Eve E. *Technocrats and the Politics of Drought and Development in Twentieth-Century Brazil*. Chapel Hill: University of North Carolina Press, 2017.

Cabanas, João. *A Columna da morte sob o commando do Tenente Cabanas*. Rio de Janeiro: Almeida e Torres, 1928.

Campos Filho, Romualdo Pessoa. *Guerrilha do Araguaia: A Esquerda em armas.* 2nd ed. São Paulo: Anita Garibaldi, 2012.

Carrão, Manuel. *Impressões de viagem à Fóz do Iguassú e Rio Paraná.* Curitiba, Brazil: Lith. progresso, R. S. Francisco, 1928.

Caubet, Christian Guy. *As grandes manobras de Itaipu: Energia, diplomacia e direito na Bacia do Prata.* São Paulo: Acadêmica, 1991.

Chinem, Rivaldo. *Jornalismo de guerrilha: A imprensa alternativa brasileira, da ditadura à internet.* São Paulo: Disal, 2004.

Comissão Camponesa da Verdade. *Relatório final: Violações de direitos no campo, 1946–1988.* Brasília: Comissão Camponesa da Verdade, 2014.

Comissão Nacional da Verdade. *Relatório.* Brasília: Comissão Nacional da Verdade (CNV), 2014.

Comissão Pastoral da Terra (CPT). *O Mausoléu do faraó: A usina de Itaipu contra os lavradores do Paraná.* Curitiba, Brazil: Comissão Pastoral da Terra Paraná, 1978.

Comissão Pastoral da Terra (CPT). *Conflitos no campo Brasil 2016.* São Paulo: Expressão Popular, 2017.

Couto e Silva, Golbery do. *Geopolítica do Brasil.* Rio de Janeiro: Livraria J. Olympio, 1967.

Cunha, Euclides da. *Rebellion in the Backlands.* 1902. Chicago: University of Chicago Press, 2014.

Dassin, Joan R. "The Brazilian Press and the Politics of Abertura." *Journal of Interamerican Studies and World Affairs* 26, no. 3 (August 1984): 385–414.

Deprá, Giseli. "O lago de Itaipu e a luta dos Avá-Guarani pela terra: Representações na imprensa do oeste do Paraná (1976–2000)." Master's thesis, Universidade Federal da Grande Dourados, 2006.

Devine Guzmán, Tracy. *Native and National in Brazil: Indigeneity after Independence.* Chapel Hill: University of North Carolina Press, 2013.

Diacon, Todd A. *Millenarian Vision, Capitalist Reality: Brazil's Contestado Rebellion, 1912–1916.* Durham, NC: Duke University Press, 1991.

Duarte Pereira, Osny. *Itaipu: Pros e contras.* Rio de Janeiro: Editora Paz e Terra, 1974.

Dunn, Christopher. *Contracultura: Alternative Arts and Social Transformation in Authoritarian Brazil.* Chapel Hill: University of North Carolina Press, 2016.

Evans, Peter B. *Dependent Development: The Alliance of Multinational, State, and Local Capital in Brazil.* Princeton, NJ: Princeton University Press, 1979.

Fabrini, João Edmilson. "Os assentamentos de trabalhadores rurais sem terra do centro-oeste/PR enquanto território de resistência camponesa." PhD diss., Universidade Estadual Paulista, 2002.

Favareto, Arilson. "Agricultores, trabalhadores: Os trinta anos de novo sindicalismo rural no Brasil." *Revista Brasileira de Ciências Sociais* 21, no. 62 (October 2006): 27–44.

Fearnside, Philip M. "Brazil's Settlement Schemes: Conflicting Objectives and Human Carrying Capacity." *Habitat International* 8, no. 1 (1984), 45–61.

Feliú, Fernanda. *Los Brasiguayos: Canindeyú Zona Alta*. Asunción, Paraguay: Imprenta LEO S.R.L., 2004.

Ferradás, Carmen. *Power in the Southern Cone Borderlands: An Anthropology of Development Practice*. Westport, CT: Bergin and Garvey, 1998.

Fico, Carlos. *Reinventando o otimismo: Ditadura, propaganda e imaginário social no Brasil*. Rio de Janeiro: Fundação Getulio Vargas, 1997.

Field, Thomas C. *From Development to Dictatorship: Bolivia and the Alliance for Progress in the Kennedy Era*. Ithaca, NY: Cornell University Press, 2014.

Fischer, Brodwyn. *A Poverty of Rights: Citizenship and Inequality in Twentieth-Century Rio de Janeiro*. Stanford, CA: Stanford University Press, 2008.

Fleischer, David. "The Constituent Assembly and the Transformation Strategy: Attempts to Shift Political Power in Brazil from the Presidency to Congress." In *The Political Economy of Brazil: Public Policies in an Era of Transition*, edited by Lawrence S. Graham and Robert H. Wilson, 210–58. Austin: University of Texas Press, 1990.

Fleischer, David. *Da distensão à abertura: As eleições de 1982*. Brasília: Editora UNB, 1998.

Fogel, Ramón, and Marcial Riquelme, eds. *Enclave sojero: Merma de soberanía y pobreza*. Asunción, Paraguay: Centro de Estudios Rurales Interdisciplinarios, 2005.

Folch, Christine. "Surveillance and State Violence in Stroessner's Paraguay: Itaipu Hydroelectric Dam, Archive of Terror." *American Anthropologist* 115, no. 1 (March 2013): 44–57.

Foweraker, Joe. *The Struggle for Land: A Political Economy of the Pioneer Frontier in Brazil from 1930 to the Present Day*. Cambridge: Cambridge University Press, 1981.

Freitas, Frederico. "The Guarani and the Iguaçu National Park: An Environmental History." *ReVista* 14, no. 3 (Spring 2015): 18–22.

French, Jan Hoffman. *Legalizing Identities: Becoming Black or Indian in Brazil's Northeast*. Chapel Hill: University of North Carolina Press, 2009.

Füllgraf, Frederico. *Os desapropriados*. Documentary film. Curitiba: Mutirão Produções Cine-Áudio-Visuais, 1983.

Galeano, Eduardo. *Crónicas latinoamericanas*. Montevideo, Uruguay: Editorial Girón, 1972.

Gardin, Cleonice. *CIBPU: A commissão interestadual da Bacia Paraná-Uruguai no planejamento regional brasileiro (1951–1972)*. Dourados, Brazil: Editora UFGD, 2009.

Garfield, Seth. *Indigenous Struggle at the Heart of Brazil: State Policy, Frontier Expansion, and the Xavante Indians, 1937–1988*. Durham, NC: Duke University Press, 2001.

Garfield, Seth. *In Search of the Amazon: Brazil, the United States and the Nature of a Region*. Durham, NC: Duke University Press, 2013.

Gaspari, Elio. *A ditadura encurralada*. São Paulo: Companhia das Letras, 2004.

Germani, Guiomar Inez. *Expropriados terra e agua: O conflito de Itaipu*. Salvador de Bahia, Brazil: EDUFBA/ULBRA, 2003.

Gibson Barboza, Mario. *Na diplomacia, o traço todo da vida.* Rio de Janeiro: Record, 1992.

Giménez, L. R. *Sobre el salto del Guaíra al oido de América.* Asunción: Anales del Paraguay, 1966.

Goldman, Michael. *Imperial Nature: The World Bank and the Struggles for Social Justice in the Age of Globalization.* New Haven, CT: Yale University Press, 2005.

Gómez Florentín, Carlos. "The Making of the Itaipú Hydroelectric Dam: The Unanticipated Consequences of Bringing Development to the Upper Paraná Region (1957–1992)." PhD diss., New York University, 2018.

Gonçalves, Danyelle Nilin. *O Preço do passado: Anistia e reparação de perseguidos políticos no Brasil.* São Paulo: Editora Expressão Popular, 2009.

Green, James. *We Cannot Remain Silent: Opposition to the Brazilian Military Dictatorship in the United States.* Durham, NC: Duke University Press, 2010.

Hanratty, Dennis, and Sandra Meditz. *Paraguay: A Country Study.* Washington, DC: Library of Congress, Federal Research Division, 1990.

Hecht, Susanna B. *The Scramble for the Amazon and the "Lost Paradise" of Euclides da Cunha.* Chicago: University of Chicago Press, 2013.

Herzog, Tamar. "Guarani and Jesuits: Bordering the Spanish and the Portuguese Empires." *ReVista* 14, no. 3 (Spring 2015): 50–52.

Hilton, Stanley E. "The Argentine Factor in Twentieth-Century Brazilian Foreign Policy Strategy." *Political Science Quarterly* 100, no. 1 (1985): 27–51.

Hilton, Stanley E. "The United States, Brazil, and the Cold War, 1945–1960: End of the Special Relationship." *Journal of American History* 68, no. 3 (December 1981): 599–624.

Hobsbawm, E. J. *The Age of Capital: 1848–1875.* New York: Scribner, 1975.

Houtzager, Peter P. *Os últimos cidadãos: Conflito e modernização no Brasil rural.* São Paulo: Editora Globo, 2004.

Hudson, Rex A., ed. *Brazil: A Country Study.* Washington, DC: GPO for the Library of Congress, 1997.

Institute for Latin American Integration. *Obras hidroeléctricas binacionales en América Latina.* Buenos Aires, Argentina: Banco Interamericano de Desarrollo, Instituto para la Integración de América Latina, 1985.

Instituto Paranaense de Desenvolvimento Econômico e Social (IPARDES). *Assentamentos rurais no Paraná.* Curitiba: Instituto Paranaense de Desenvolvimento Econômico e Social, 1992.

Jones, Stephen B. *Boundary-Making: A Handbook for Statesmen, Treaty Editors, and Boundary Commissioners.* Washington, DC: Carnegie Endowment for International Peace, Division of International Law, 1945.

Keck, Margaret E. *The Workers' Party and Democratization in Brazil.* New Haven, CT: Yale University Press, 1992.

Khagram, Sanjeev. *Dams and Development: Transnational Struggles for Water and Power.* Ithaca, NY: Cornell University Press, 2004.

Kinzo, Maria D'alva G. *Legal Opposition Politics under Authoritarian Rule in Brazil: The Case of the MDB, 1966–79.* New York: St. Martins, 1988.

Kleinpenning, J. M. G. *Man and Land in Paraguay.* Providence, RI: FORIS, 1987.

Kohlhepp, Gerd. "Incorporação do espaço fronteiriço do leste do Paraguai na esfera de influência brasileira." In *El espacio interior de América del Sur: Geografía, historia, política,* edited by Gerd Kohlhepp, Karl Kohut, and Barbara Potthast, 205-25. Frankfurt am Main: Vervuert, 1999.

Kucinski, Bernardo. *O Fim da ditadura militar: O colapso do "milagre econômico," a volta aos quartéis, a luta pela democracia.* São Paulo: Contexto, 2001.

Ladeira, Maria Ines. "Os índios Guarani/Mbya e o complex lagunar estuarino de Iguape—Paranaguá." Report for the Centro de Trabalho Indigenista (CTI), Brasília, 1994.

Laino, Domingo. *Paraguay: Fronteras y penetración brasileña.* Asunción, Paraguay: Ediciones Cerro Cora, 1977.

Langland, Victoria. *Speaking of Flowers: The Making and Remembering of 1968 in Military Brazil.* Durham, NC: Duke University Press, 2013.

Langley, Lester D. *America and the Americas: The United States in the Western Hemisphere.* Athens: University of Georgia Press, 1989.

Levine, Robert M. "'Mud-Hut Jerusalem': Canudos Revisited." *Hispanic American Historical Review* 68, no. 3 (August 1988): 525-572.

Lima, José Luiz. *Políticas de governo e desenvolvimento do setor de energia elétrica: Do Código de Águas à crise dos anos.* Rio de Janeiro: Centro da Memória da Electricidade no Brasil, 1995.

Lins Ribeiro, Gustavo. *Transnational Capitalism and Hydropolitics in Argentina: The Yacyreta High Dam.* Gainesville: University of Florida Press, 1994.

Ludewigs, Thomas, Eduardo Sonnewend Brondízio, and Scott Hetrick. "Agrarian Structure and Land-Cover Change along the Lifespan of Three Colonization Areas in the Brazilian Amazon." *World Development* 37, no. 8 (2009): 1348-59.

Macedo de Mendonça, Ariel. "A geopolítica e a política externa do Brazil: Interseção dos mundos militar e diplomático em um projeto de poder a Ata das Cataratas e o equilíbrio de forças no Cono Sul." Master's thesis, Universidade de Brasília, 2004.

Magalhães, Juracy. *Minha experiência diplomática.* Rio de Janeiro: Loje, 1971.

Mainwaring, Scott. "Grassroots Catholic Groups and Politics in Brazil, 1964-1985." Working Paper No. 98, Helen Kellogg Institute for International Studies, Notre Dame University, Notre Dame, IN, August 1987.

Mainwaring, Scott. *Rethinking Party Systems in the Third Wave of Democratization: The Case of Brazil.* Stanford, CA: Stanford University Press, 1999.

Mainwaring, Scott, and Donald Share. "Transitions through Transaction: Democratization in Brazil and Spain." In *Political Liberalization in Brazil: Dynamics, Dilemmas, and Future Prospects,* edited by Wayne Selcher, 175-215. Boulder, CO: Westview, 1986.

Mallon, Florencia E. *Courage Tastes of Blood: The Mapuche Community of Nicolás Ailío and the Chilean State, 1906-2001.* Durham, NC: Duke University Press, 2005.

Mallon, Florencia E. "Peasants and Rural Laborers in Pernambuco, 1955–1964." *Latin American Perspectives* 5, no. 4 (Fall 1978): 49–70.

Mançano Fernandes, Bernardo. "The Formation and Territorialization of the MST in Brazil." In *Challenging Social Inequality: The Landless Rural Workers Movement and Agrarian Reform in Brazil*, edited by Miguel Carter, 115–48. Durham, NC: Duke University Press, 2015.

Matiello, Catiane. "Narrativas tecnológicas, desenraizamento e cultura de resistência: História oral de vida de famílias desapropriadas pela construção da usina hidrelétrica de Itaipu." Master's thesis, Universidade Tecnológica Federal do Paraná, 2011.

Maybury-Lewis, Biorn. *The Politics of the Possible: The Brazilian Rural Workers' Trade Union Movement, 1964–1985*. Philadelphia: Temple University Press, 1994.

Maybury-Lewis, David, ed. *The Politics of Ethnicity: Indigenous Peoples in Latin American States*. Cambridge, MA: Harvard University David Rockefeller Center for Latin American Studies, 2002.

Mazzarollo, Juvêncio. *A taipa da injustiça: Esbanjamento econômico, drama social e holocausto ecológico em Itaipu*. 2nd ed. Curitiba, Brazil: Comissão Pastoral da Terra, 2003.

Mazzarollo, Juvêncio. *A taipa da injustiça: Itaipu x agricultores expropriados*. Curitiba, Brazil: Comissão Pastoral da Terra, 1980.

McCann, Bryan. *Hard Times in the Marvelous City: From Dictatorship to Democracy in the Favelas of Rio de Janeiro*. Durham, NC: Duke University Press, 2013.

McLynn, F. J. "The Causes of the War of Triple Alliance: An Interpretation." *Inter-American Economic Affairs* 33, no. 2 (Autumn 1979): 21–43.

McSherry, J. Patrice. *Operation Condor and Covert War in Latin America*. Lanham, MD: Rowman and Littlefield, 2005.

Medeiros, Leonilde Sérvolo de. *História dos movimentos sociais no campo*. Rio de Janeiro: Fase, 1989.

Medeiros, Leonilde Sérvolo de. *Reforma agrária no Brasil: História e atualidade da luta pela terra*. São Paulo: Editora Fundação Perseu Abramo, 1996.

Melià, Bartomeu. "A experiência religiosa Guarani." In *O rosto índio de Deus*, edited by Manuel M. Marzal, 293–357. Petrópolis, Brazil: Vozes, 1989.

Menegotto, Ricardo. *Migrações é fronteiras: Os imigrantes brasileiros no Paraguai e a redefinição da fronteira*. Santa Cruz do Sul, Brazil: Editora da Universidade de Santa Cruz do Sul, 2004.

Menezes, Alfredo da Mota. *La herencia de Stroessner: Brasil-Paraguay, 1955–1980*. Asunción, Paraguay: Carlos Schauman Editor, 1990.

Mézsáros, George. *Social Movements, Law and the Politics of Land Reform: Lessons from Brazil*. New York: Routledge, 2013.

Mezzomo, Frank Antonio. *Memórias dos movimentos sociais no oeste do Paraná*. Campo Mourão, Brazil: Editora da Faculdade Estadual de Ciências e Letras de Campo Mourão (FECILCAM), 2009.

Molica, Fernando, and Antero Luiz. *10 reportagens que abalaram a ditadura*. Rio de Janeiro: Editora Record, 2005.

Monteiro, Nilson. *Itaipu, a Luz*. Curitiba, Brazil: Itaipu Binacional, Assessoria de Comunicação Social, 1999.

Moog Rodrigues, Maria Guadalupe. "Indigenous Rights in Democratic Brazil." *Human Rights Quarterly* 24, no. 2 (2002): 487–512.

Mora, Frank O., and Jerry W. Cooney. *Paraguay and the United States*. Athens: University of Georgia Press, 2007.

Moreira Alves, Maria Helena. "Interclass Alliances in the Opposition to the Military in Brazil: Consequences for the Transition Period." In *Power and Protest: Latin American Social Movements*, edited by Susan Eckstein, 278–98. Berkeley: University of California Press, 1988.

Moreira Alves, Maria Helena. *State and Opposition in Military Brazil*. Austin: University of Texas Press, 1988.

Musacchio, Aldo, and Sergio G. Lazzarini. *Reinventing State Capitalism: Leviathan in Business, Brazil, and Beyond*. Cambridge, MA: Harvard University Press, 2014.

Nickson, R. Andrew. "Brazilian Colonization of the Eastern Border Region of Paraguay." *Journal of Latin American Studies* 13, no. 1 (1981): 111–31.

Nickson, R. Andrew. "Itaipú Hydro-Electric Paraguayan Perspective." *Bulletin of Latin American Research* 2, no. 1 (October 1982): 1–20.

Nixon, Rob. *Slow Violence and the Environmentalism of the Poor*. Cambridge, MA: Harvard University Press, 2011.

Nohlen, Dieter, ed. *Elections in the Americas: A Data Handbook*. Vol. 2, *South America*. New York: Oxford University Press, 2005.

O'Donnell, Guillermo A. *Bureaucratic Authoritarianism: Argentina, 1966–1973, in Comparative Perspective*. Berkeley: University of California Press, 1988.

Ondetti, Gabriel. *Land, Protest, and Politics: The Landless Movement and the Struggle for Agrarian Reform in Brazil*. University Park: Pennsylvania State University Press, 2008.

Ozorio de Almeida, Anna Luiza. *The Colonization of the Amazon*. Austin: University of Texas Press, 1992.

Parker, Phyllis R. *Brazil and the Quiet Intervention, 1964*. Austin: University of Texas Press, 1979.

Peñalba, José Alfredo Fornos. "Draft Dodgers, War Resisters and Turbulent Gauchos: The War of the Triple Alliance against Paraguay." *The Americas* 38, no. 4 (April 1982): 463–79.

Pereira, Anthony. *The End of Peasantry: The Rural Labor Movement in Northeast Brazil, 1961–1988*. Pittsburgh, PA: University of Pittsburgh Press, 1997.

Pinheiro, Manu. *Cale-se: A MPB e a ditadura military*. Rio de Janeiro: Livros Ilimitados, 2010.

Pomer, León. *La Guerra del Paraguay: Gran negocio*. Buenos Aires, Argentina: Ediciones Caldén, 1968.

Priori, Angelo. *O levante dos posseiros: A revolta camponesa de Porecatu e a ação do Partido Comunista Brasileiro no campo*. Maringá, Brazil: Editora da Universidade Estadual de Maringá, 2011.

Rabe, Stephen G. *The Killing Zone: The United States Wages Cold War in Latin America*. New York: Oxford University Press, 2012.

Ramos, Alcida Rita. *Indigenism: Ethnic Politics in Brazil*. Madison: University of Wisconsin Press, 1998.

Rebouças, André. *A Democracia rural brasileira*. Rio de Janeiro, 1875.

Ribeiro de Moraes Junior, Leozil. "MASTRO: A formacão do movimento dos agricultores sem terra do oeste do Paraná (1970–1990)." Master's thesis, Universidade Estadual do Oeste do Paraná, 2010.

Riquelme, Marcial. "Notas para el estudio de las causas y efectos de las migraciones brasileñas en el Paraguay." In *Enclave sojero: Merma de soberanía y pobreza*, edited by Ramón Fogel and Marcial Riquelme, 118–55. Asunción, Paraguay: Centro de Estudios Rurales Interdisciplinarios, 2005.

Rivarola, Milda. "The Total War in Indigenous Territories: The Impact of the Great War." *ReVista* 14, no. 3 (Spring 2015): 61–64.

Rodríguez-Piñero, Luis. *Indigenous Peoples, Postcolonialism, and International Law: The ILO Regime, 1919–1989*. New York: Oxford University Press, 2005.

Rogers, Thomas D. *The Deepest Wounds: A Labor and Environmental History of Sugar in Northeast Brazil*. Chapel Hill: University of North Carolina Press, 2010.

Rosa, Marcelo Carvalho. "Sem-terra: Os sentidos e as transformações de uma categoria de ação coletiva no Brasil." *Lua Nova*, no. 76 (2009): 197–227.

Sanders, Thomas G. *The Itaipu Hydroelectrical Project*. UFSI Reports 1982/no. 35. Hanover, NH: Universities Field Staff International, 1982.

Santos de Morais, Clodomir. "Peasant Leagues in Brazil." In *Agrarian Problems and Peasant Movements in Latin America*, edited by Rodolfo Stavenhagen, 453–501. New York: Doubleday, 1970.

Schilling, Paulo R., and Ricardo Canese. *Itaipu: Geopolítica e corrupção*. São Paulo: Centro Ecumênico de Documentação e Informação, 1991.

Schmink, Marianne, and Charles H. Wood. *Contested Frontiers in Amazonia*. New York: Columbia University Press, 1992.

Schneider, Nina. *Brazilian Propaganda: Legitimizing an Authoritarian Regime*. Gainesville: University of Florida Press, 2014.

Schreiner, Davi Felix. "Entre a exclusão e a utopia: Um estudo sobre os processos de organização da vida cotidiana nos assentamentos rurais (região sudoeste/oeste) do Paraná." PhD diss., University of São Paulo, 2002.

Scott, James C. *Seeing like a State: How Certain Schemes to Improve the Human Condition Have Failed*. New Haven, CT: Yale University Press, 1998.

Seidman, Gay. *Manufacturing Militance: Workers' Movements in Brazil and South Africa, 1970–1985*. Berkeley: University of California Press, 1994.

Serbin, Kenneth P. *Secret Dialogues: Church-State Relations, Torture, and Social Justice in Authoritarian Brazil*. Pittsburgh, PA: University of Pittsburgh Press, 2000.

Silva, Evaldo Mendes da. "Folhas ao vento: A micromobilidade de grupos Mbya e Nhandéva (Guarani) na Tríplice Fronteira." PhD diss., Universidade Federal do Rio de Janeiro, 2007.

Silva, Evaldo Mendes da. "Walking on the Bad Land: The Guarani Indians in the Triple Frontier." In *Big Water: The Making of the Borderlands between Brazil, Argentina, and Paraguay*, edited by Jacob Blanc and Frederico Freitas, 186–208. Tucson: University of Arizona Press, 2018.

Silva, Joaquim Carvalho da. *Terra roxa de sangue: A guerra de Porecatu.* Londrina, Brazil: Editora da Universidade Estadual de Londrina, 1996.

Silva, Jussaramar da. "A ação das assessorias especiais de segurança e informações da usina binacional de Itaipu no contexto das atividades de cooperação extrajudiciais no Cone Sul." *Cordis: Revoluções, cultura e política na América Latina*, no. 11 (July–December 2013): 219–51.

Skidmore, Thomas E. *The Politics of Military Rule in Brazil, 1964–1985.* New York: Oxford University Press, 1990.

Smith, Joseph. *Brazil and the United States: Convergence and Divergence.* Athens: University of Georgia Press, 2010.

Snider, Colin M. "'An Incomplete Autonomy': Higher Education and State-Society Relations in Brazil, 1950s–1980s." *Latin Americanist* 60, no. 1 (March 2016): 139–159.

Soares de Lima, Maria Regina. *The Political Economy of Brazilian Foreign Policy: Nuclear Energy, Trade and Itaipu.* Brasília: Fundação Alexandre de Gusmão, 2013.

Souza Martins, José de. *A militarização da questão agrária no Brasil: Terra e poder, o problema da terra na crise política.* Petrópolis, Brazil: Vozes, 1984.

Souza Martins, José de. *Os camponeses e a política no Brasil: As Lutas sociais no campo e seu lugar no processo político.* Petrópolis, Brazil: Vozes, 1981.

Stedile, João Pedro, and Bernardo Mançano Fernandes. *Brava gente: A trajetoria do MST e a luta pela terra no Brasil.* 3rd ed. São Paulo: Fundação Perseu Abramo, 2012.

Stepan, Alfred C. *Rethinking Military Politics: Brazil and the Southern Cone.* Princeton, NJ: Princeton University Press, 1988.

Szekut, Andressa, and Jorge Eremites de Oliveira. "'Aquí todos somos migrantes o hijos de migrantes, tanto los brasileños como los paraguayos': Memórias de migrantes brasileiros sobre a situação de colonização recente no Distrito de Santa Rita, Departamento de Alto Paraná, Paraguai." *Fronteiras: Revista de História* 19, no. 34 (July–December 2017): 319–52.

Taffet, Jeffrey F. *Foreign Aid as Foreign Policy: The Alliance for Progress in Latin America.* New York: Routledge, 2007.

Tibes Ribeiro, Sarah Iurkiv Gomes. "O horizonte é a terra: Manipulação da identidade e construção do ser entre os Guarani no Oeste do Paraná (1977–1997)." PhD diss., Pontifícia Universidade Católica do Rio Grande do Sul, Porto Alegre, Brazil, 2002.

Tinsman, Heidi. *Partners in Conflict: The Politics of Gender, Sexuality, and Labor in the Chilean Agrarian Reform, 1950–1973.* Durham, NC: Duke University Press, 2002.

Tosi Rodrigues, Alberto. *Diretas Já: O grito preso na garganta.* São Paulo: Editora Fundação Perseu Abramo, 2003.

Travassos, Mário. *Projeção continental do Brasil.* São Paulo: Companhia Editora Nacional, 1935.

Veranisa Schmitt, Judite. "Os atingidos por Itaipu: História e memória; Oeste do Paraná, décadas de 1970 a 2000." Master's thesis, Universidade Estadual do Oeste do Paraná, Marechal Cândido Rondon, 2008.

Vinhas de Queiroz, Mauricio. *Messianismo e conflito social a Guerra Sertaneja do Contestado, 1913–1916.* Rio de Janeiro: Civilizacao Brasileira, 1966.

Wagner, Carlos. *Brasiguaios: Homens sem pátria.* Petrópolis, Brazil: Vozes, 1990.

Weinstein, Barbara. *The Color of Modernity: São Paulo and the Making of Race and Nation in Brazil.* Durham, NC: Duke University Press, 2015.

Weis, W. Michael. *Cold Warriors and Coups d'État: Brazilian-American Relations, 1945–1964.* Albuquerque: University of New Mexico Press, 1993.

Welch, Cliff. "Camponeses: Brazil's Peasant Movement in Historical Perspective (1946–2004)." *Latin American Perspectives* 36, no. 4 (July 2009): 126–155.

Welch, Cliff. *The Seed Was Planted: The São Paulo Roots of Brazil's Rural Labor Movement, 1924–1964.* University Park: Pennsylvania State University Press, 1999.

Whigham, Thomas. *The Paraguayan War.* Vol. 1, *Causes and Early Conduct.* Lincoln: University of Nebraska Press, 2002.

White, John Howard. "Itaipu: Gender, Community, and Work in the Alto Paraná Borderlands, Brazil and Paraguay, 1954–1989." PhD diss., University of New Mexico, 2010.

Williams, Suzanne. "Land Rights and the Manipulation of Identity: Official Indian Policy in Brazil." *Journal of Latin American Studies* 15, no. 1 (1983): 137–161.

Wolfe, Mikael D. *Watering the Revolution: An Environmental and Technological History of Agrarian Reform in Mexico.* Durham, NC: Duke University Press, 2017.

Wolford, Wendy. *This Land Is Ours Now: Social Mobilization and the Meanings of Land in Brazil.* Durham, NC: Duke University Press, 2010.

Wright, Angus Lindsay, and Wendy Wolford. *To Inherit the Earth: The Landless Movement and the Struggle for a New Brazil.* Oakland, CA: Food First Books, 2003.

Ynsfrán, Edgar. *Un giro geopolítico: El milagro de una ciudad.* Asunción, Paraguay: Instituto de Estudios Geopolíticos e Internacionales, 1990.

Zanoni Gomes, Iria. *1957: A revolta dos posseiros.* Curitiba, Brazil: Criar Edições, 1986.

ABC Labor Strikes, 9, 71, 79, 91–93, 201
abertura, 2–8, 10–19, 55, 71, 77–79, 91;
  limitations of, *see* double reality of
  abertura; mainstream policies of, *see*
  Amnesty Bill, Direct Elections Now
  campaign, and Party Reform Bill
Act of Iguaçu, 30, 42–44, 47, 49, 50; and
  Brasiguaio immigration, 45, 176
Agrarian Leagues, 180
Agrarian Statute, 45
Alliance for National Renovation, 77,
  79, 107
Alliance for Progress, 22, 29, 217
Alvorada do Iguaçu, 62
Amazon, 22, 55, 69, 91, 173, 234, 237n6,
  265n2; and frontier expansion 179–82,
  185–87; resettlement projects in, 19,
  170, 174, 188, 190, 212, 217
Amnesty Bill, 2, 77
Anghinoni, Celso, 209, 214
Anoni occupation, 198–99, 219, 223, 226.
  See also Landless Farmers Movement
  of Western Paraná
Araguaia War, 182, 204
Arapoti resettlement project, 101–11, 171,
  184, 187, 189, 191–96
Assentamento Sávio-Dois Vizinhos,
  221, 226
Avá-Guarani Indians, xi, xviii, 3–5, 8–19,
  12–13, 17–18, 60, 125; and allegations
  of FUNAI abuse, 133–34; and collective landownership, 128, 135, 145, 149;
  depictions in the media, 146; living in
  the Triple Frontier zone, 130–31, 143;
  as measured by the government,

see indicators of Indianness; and
  political consciousness, 127–29, 139,
  147, 152, 230, 232; relationship to land,
  13, 126, 128, 135; relocation, 132–33,
  149–50; size of community, 130,
  140–41, 143, 146, 149

bandeirantes, 10, 38
Bank of Brazil, 50, 73
Barra do Ocoí, xviii, 125–27, 130,
  146, 149, 152. *See also* Avá-Guarani
  Indians
Barth, Marcelo, 69, 82, 86, 92, 101, 103,
  112, 208
boias-frias, xi, 177
Bom Jesus da Lapa resettlement project,
  111
Braga, Ney, 107, 110, 112, 123, 212
brasiguaios, 19, 61, 170–71, 175, 178–79;
  and the Act of Iguaçu 45, 176; as ag-
  ricultural shock troops, 172; popula-
  tion size, 172, 177; return migration
  to Brazil, 181, 195–196; and soybean
  agriculture, 177, 180
Brasil Grande, 31, 37, 40–41, 47, 52
Brazilian Anthropological Association,
  140, 142–43, 146
Brazilian Democratic Movement
  (MDB), 77–78
Brazilian Democratic Movement Party
  (PMDB), 107, 109–10, 117, 123, 162,
  192, 212
Brazilian Institute for Agrarian Reform,
  39–40, 242n83
Brazilian Lawyers Association, 91

Brazilian Workers' Party (PTB), 106, 109, 270n15
Brito, Oliveira, 28
Brizola, Leonel, 9, 29; and 1982 elections, 123; and support for farmers, 106, 109, 204

Campos, Roberto de Oliveira, 40
Canudos War, 209
Cardoso, Fernando Henrique, 108
Carvalho, Edgard de Assis, 143
Cascavel, 15, 117, 198–99; 1984 meeting, 222–25
Castelo Branco, Humberto, 34, 40, 56, 239n23, 270n17
Catholic Church, 65–67, 112, 131, 152, 208
Cavagnari, José Guilherme, 213
Cavalcanti, José Costa, 55, 80, 97, 106–07, 110, 112; and the Avá-Guarani Indians, 136; and colonizadoras, 185–86; political background, 56–57; private deliberations, 79, 96, 99, 162; and public relations campaign, 74–75, 102
Cavernoso occupation, 198–99, 220, 223. See also Landless Farmers Movement of Western Paraná
Christian Democrat Party, 51
Cold War, 1, 15, 22, 24, 29; and Brazil's domestic policies, see Doctrine of National Security; and Brazil's territorial expansion, see fronteiras vivas; and US foreign aid, see Alliance for Progress
Committee for Amnesty, 91
colonizadoras, 171, 185–86; coordination with Itaipu Binational, 173–74
Constitution of 1967, 5–6, 61, 133
Contestado War, 132
Costa e Silva, Artur da, 32, 56
Couto e Silva, Golbery do, 37, 78, 181
Cruz, Sérgio, 175
Cuban Revolution, 22, 172
Cunha Vianna, Clóvis, 104, 156–57, 159, 168
Cunha, Vasco Leitão da, 32

da Cunha, Paulo, 67, 72, 75–76, 87, 89, 96, 97, 113–15, 162, 185

da Silva, Luiz Inácia "Lula," 9, 71, 108, 220–21
Dantas, Francisco San Tiago, 27
Democratic Social Party (PDS), 107
dialectic of land and legitimacy, 11–13, 84, 200, 207, 229–30
Diretas Já (Direct Elections Now), 14, 201, 218, 225
disease: hepatitis, 190; malaria, 72, 190–91; measles, 190; smallpox, 132
distensão, 55–57, 71
Doctrine of National Security, 22, 37, 52, 181; and developmentalism, 172, 188; and frontier expansion, see Fronteiras vivas
Dominican Republic: US invasion of, 22, 37
double reality of abertura, 18, 83, 92, 207, 229, 231; in the Paraná borderlands, 108, 155

ecclesial Base Communities, 66
economic crisis of 1979–1983, 91, 122, 218
elections of 1982, 2, 85, 122–23, 211, 213–14, 235n3, 257n156
Eletrobras, 48, 239n23
Encruzilhada Natalino, 99–100, 205, 223
Estado Novo, 202–03
Evangelical Church of the Lutheran Confession, 65

Fernandes, Nicolás, 128, 135, 141–42
Figueiredo, João Baptista, 34, 77–78, 122, 161–62, 168, 218
First National Landless Meeting, 212
Folha da Tarde, 69
Folha de Londrina, 146, 220–21
Folha de São Paulo, 69, 93, 110–11, 123, 142, 146, 148, 179, 193
Foz do Iguaçu encampment, 2–3, 9, 12, 18, 80–82, 102, 137–138, 159, 162, 168, 183, 188, 194, 198, 205, 209, 214, 230; armed standoff at start of, 103; concessions won, 115–16; demands of, 104, 115–16; hierarchies within, 4, 106, 110–14, 117–18; impact of ICT report, 110–12, 114; life in the camp, 104; media cover-

age of, 104, 106, 114, 116; negotiations with Itaipu Binational, 106, 113–15; political consciousness at 83–84, 110. *See also* double reality of abertura; potential escalation of tactics, 113–14, 118–19; solidarity received, 106–8, 123

Friedrich, Nelton, 76, 88, 91–92

fronteiras vivas, 37, 47, 172

Fuchs, Werner, 64, 71, 80, 86–87, 92–93, 97, 106, 117, 188, 209

Füllgraf, Frederico, 82, 188, 190

Galeano, Eduardo, 20

Geisel, Ernesto, 64, 70, 72, 77–78, 205; and policy of distensão, 56

Germer, Claus, 215

Gordon, Lincoln, 29, 41

Goulart, João, 14–15, 21, 26, 56, 204, 217; meeting with Alfredo Stroessner, 28–29

Grande River, 27

Guaíra waterfalls, xvii; conflict of demarcation, 20, 23, 24–27; flooding of, 121–22

Horst, Célio, 140–44, 149

Hosken de Novais, José, 212

Iguaçu National Park, 133

Indian Statute, 5, 129, 149; and relationship to land rights, 135, 141–43; as a tool for political empowerment, 128, 135, 137

indicators of Indianness, 13, 140, 152; as federal policy, 141–42

Indigenous Missionary Council, 106, 137–39, 142, 144, 148–50

Indigenous Protection Service, 132–33

Institute for Rural Well-Being, 177

Institute for Lands and Cartography, 98, 107, 110–11, 215, 217, 225; 1981 report, 112–14, 212–213

Institutional Act No. 5, 56, 71, 77

Interstate Commission of the Paraná-Uruguay Basin (CIBPU), 26

Itacorá, 102–4

Inter-American Development Bank, 176

Interconsult-SPA, 48

International Engineering Co., 48

International Labor Organization, 128

International Monetary Fund, 218

International Telephone and Telegraph, 29

Itaipu Binational Corporation: archives of, 16–17, 185; creation of, 49–51; and military surveillance, 16, 57–58; public relations campaign, 63–64

Itaipu dam: construction of, 53–59; cost of building, 6, 55, 75, 173; energy capacity of, 228; fatalities during construction, 75; financial details of, 50; impact on surrounding regions, 59, 61–62; indigenous origin of name, 150

Itamaraty, 17, 31, 39, 42

Joint Border Commission, 27–28

Joint Technical Commission, 47–49

Jornal do Brasil, 36, 73, 88, 95, 114, 138

Justice and Land Movement (MJT), 3–12, 82–123; demands of, *see* Santa Helena encampment and Foz do Iguaçu encampment; demographics of, 93–95; formation of, 82; limitations of landless participants in, 98–99, 110–12, 205–8; overlap with Avá-Guarani, 129, 137–38; and religious leaders, 10, 66–67, 80, 86, 93, 112; resettlement of members, 119; role of women, 94–95

Justice and Peace Commission, 113, 148–49

Kennedy, John F., 29

Kirinus, Gernote, 72, 92, 100, 108, 112, 192

Kopytowsky, João, 156–57, 159, 168

Kubitschek, Juscelino, 26, 181

Labre, João Guilherme da Costa, 156, 159, 162

land prices, 111; and farmers' demands, 65, 69–70, 73, 86, 96; increases in, 72, 76, 97, 116; and overspeculation, 101

land reform, 4–5, 12, 15–16, 111, 187; as demanded by landless farmers, 73, 198, 201, 207–8, 217, 230; frontier settlement as government policy of, 182; and Goulart presidency, 29, 204; and rural trade unions, 202; strategy of land-for-land, 61, 85, 110–12, 187, 206

Land Statute, 5, 217–218
Landless Workers Movement (MST), 5, 15, 198–99; 1984 Cascavel meeting, 222–225
Landless Workers Farmers Movement of Western Paraná (MASTRO), 19, 230; Anoni occupation, 198–99, 219; and Cascavel meeting, 198, 222–25; Cavernoso occupation, 198–99, 219–20; demands of, 200, 208–9, 214, 217, 220. *See also* dialectic of land and legitimacy; demographics of, 210; formation of, 198, 208; growth of, 198, 201, 210–12; influence in Paraná, 226; Itaipu reserve occupation198–99, 220; leadership, 209; as legacy of earlier landless movements, 201–4; Mineira occupation, 198–99, 220–21; Padroeira occupation, 198–99, 215–18; role of women, 221–22; and rural unions, 213–14; support for, 215, 220–21; Três Pinheiros occupation, 198–99, 219; violence against, 12, 200, 219, 221, 226–27

Movement of Landless Farmers (MASTER), 15, 202–4
Magalhães, Juracy, 34, 42–43, 47
March to the West, 202
Marcondes Ferraz, Otávio, 27
Marechal Cândido Rondon, 65, 67–68, 97
Mato Grosso, 28, 31, 101, 171, 188, 212
Mato Grosso do Sul, 199
Mazzarollo, Juvêncio, 1, 15, 18; charges against, 160; on hunger strike, 165–66; reporting on the farmers movement, 74–75, 97, 114, 118, 156, 162; reporting on political corruption, 156–57, 159; as symbol of abertura, 164, 167; trial of, 161–63
Mbaracajú mountains, 24–25, 27–28
mechanization of agriculture, 15–16, 211, 223
Médici, Emílio, 49, 56, 182
Melo Franco, Afonso Arinos de, 28
Memórias Reveladas project, 17

Metallurgical Workers of São Bernardo, 91. *See also* ABC Labor Strikes
Meza Guerrero, Emilio, 32, 35–36
Minas Gerais, 62, 93, 171, 174, 183, 185, 188, 210
Mineira occupation, 198–99, 220–21, 226. *See also* Landless Farmers Movement of Western Paraná

National Confederation of Agricultural Workers, 202, 214
National Conference of Brazilian Bishops, 65, 166
National Electricity Administration, 48
National Foundation of Indigenous Affairs, 127, 128, 130; interactions with the Avá-Guarani Indians, 133–152; and the tutela system, 141, 151
National Indigenous Action Association, 148, 149
National Information Service, 71, 92, 110, 120, 162, 179, 194, 210–12, 223
National Institute for Colonization and Agrarian Reform (INCRA): and the Avá-Guarani Indians, 133–34, 148–49; and landless farmers, 212–13, 215, 217, 219, 220–21; policies of, 70, 72, 74, 77, 79, 101–04, 111, 185; and resettlement projects, 119, 171, 173–74, 185–96
National Integration Plan, 182–83
National Security Act, 154; and charges against Juvêncio Mazzarollo, 160–64
National Security Council, 31, 40, 47
National Truth Commission, 17, 153
National Union of Students, 91
Nixon, Richard, 37
Nixon, Rob, 10, 175–76
New York Times, 42, 120
Noah's Ark Project, 67–68
Nosso Tempo, 74, 114; and conflict with authorities, *see* Juvêncio Mazzarollo; and coverage of the Avá-Guarani Indians, 146; and coverage of farmers, 101–3, 105, 114, 116, 208, 216

O Estado de São Paulo, 73, 102, 119, 121, 138, 141, 161, 190, 197, 219

O Globo, 44–45, 73, 88, 138, 161
O Jornal do Brasil, 36, 73, 95, 114, 138
Ocoí Integrated Settlement Project, 133, 136
Operation Sagarana, 17, 24, 31–32, 34, 39, 40
Os desapropriados, 82, 170, 190

Padroeira occupation, 198–99, 215–19, 225. *See also* Landless Farmers Movement of Western Paraná
Palmar, Aluízio, 66, 104, 110, 160
Pappalardo, Conrado, 35
Paraná Federation of Agricultural Workers (FETAEP), 116, 119
Paraná River, xvii-xviii, 2, 17, 20–21, 44, 51–52, 59, 76; and the Avá-Guarani Indians, 128, 131–33, 136–37, 143, 150; demarcation of, 24, 27; and energy development, 14, 22, 25–30, 37, 41; and 1982 flood, 1, 60, 121, 176, 232–34; standoff at, 32, 34–35, 43, 49
Paranapanema River, 27
Paranhos, José, 22
Party Reform Bill, 77–78
Pastoral Land Commission (CPT), 65–67, 78–79, 117, 214
Patria, 42, 51
Pedro Peixoto resettlement project, 171, 184, 188
Peasant Leagues, 15, 203
Pinochet, Augusto, 131, 205
Pizzato, Claudio, 89, 116
Porecatú War, 199, 203
Porto Renato, 24, 32–36, 39–40, 42, 45–46
Pozzolo, Luis, 214, 219
Prestes Column, 132
El Pueblo, 42

Quadros, Jânio, 26

Revolutionary Febrerista Party, 38, 42
Richa, José, 123, 165, 213, 220
Rio das Cobras, 132–33, 137, 139–40, 143–45
Rural Assistance Fund, 66, 205
rural unions, 66, 202, 204; conflict with farmers, 66, 214; elsewhere in Latin America, 205; support for military welfare program, *see* Rural Assistance Fund
rural violence, 119–20; against Indians, 153; against peasants, 200, 203, 218–19, 225–27
Rusk, Dean, 29, 37

Saldívar, Carlos, 35–36
Santa Helena encampment, 2–3, 9, 18, 54, 68, 80–82, 159, 187, 205–06, 214; concessions won, 97–99; demands of, 86, 89, 96; hierarchies within, 4, 93–96, 98; life in the camp, 89; media coverage of, 88, 93–94; negotiations with Itaipu Binational, 86–87, 89, 96–97; political consciousness at, 83–86, 92, 100–1, 208. *See also* double reality of abertura; potential escalation of tactics, 97; solidarity received, 91
Santa Helena Letter, 70
San Tiago Dantas, Francisco, 27
São Miguel do Iguaçu, xviii, 68, 209–10, 220
São Paulo: city, 7, 71, 79, 89, 91, 109, 191, 218, 225; state, 2, 41, 59, 94, 132–33, 171, 183, 199, 202, 210
Santa Catarina, 12, 94, 167, 171, 185, 199, 210
Sapena Pastor, Raul, 27–28, 34–35, 39, 42–45, 50
Sávio, Miguel Isloar, 64, 209, 221
Schmidt, Dalézio, 223
Serra do Ramalho resettlement project, 171, 184, 187–88
Seventh International Conference of American States, 26
Silva, Nildemar, 203, 215
Sinop Company, 185
Sobradinho dam, 79, 185
Somero, Maria Angela, 217
Souza Gomes, Jaime, 34
Souza, João Adelino de, 74, 160
Souza, Amaral de, 51
Soviet Union, 29
soybean agriculture, 60, 177; mechanized cultivation of 180. *See also* brasiguaios

Special Committee of Security and Information (AESI), 57–58, 74, 76, 79, 92, 146; as part of Operation Condor, 245n9
Special Border Commission, 31
Squatters Rebellion, 14, 199, 203
Stroessner, Alfredo, 14, 21, 29, 34, 42, 49–50, 57, 113; agrarian policies of, 45, 47, 177, 180; connections to Brazil, 38–39; development goals of, 22–23, 27, 41; meeting with João Goulart, 28; nationalist approach to the border conflict, 28, 30–31, 37–38; praise for Itaipu dam, 51, 122
Syndicate of Rural Workers, xv, 209

Tekoha Iñetete, 150
Tekoha Itamarã, 126, 150–51
Thibau, Mauro, 40
Tietê River, 27, 41
Time magazine, 102, 162
Tosta, Octávio da Silva, 31–32, 39, 45
Train, Hans, 189
Trans-Amazonian Highway, 57, 182
Travassos, Mário, 181
Treaty of Itaipu, 18, 20–21, 53–54, 61; criticism of, 51; stipulations of, 22–23, 49–50; praise for, 50–51
Treaty of Loizaga-Cotegipe, 23–25, 30, 43–44
Treaty of the Plate Basin, 48

Três Pinheiros occupation, 198–99, 219. See also Landless Farmers Movement of Western Paraná

Ueki, Shigeaki, 70
United Nations, 37; Argentina denounces Brazil at, 25, 51; Paraguay denounces Brazil at, 45; and indigenous rights, 128
United States, 10, 16, 48, 51, 121; Cold War policies of, 22, 29; support for Brazil, 21–23, 37
Unified Workers Central, 166

Van de Ven, Adriano, 209
Veja, 73
Venturini, Danilo, 212
Vargas, Getúlio, 202, 265n2, 270n12
Villare, Pedro Godinot de, 35

War of the Triple Alliance, 20, 24–27, 30–31, 35, 47, 51; impact on Guarani, 132
women, 10, 113, 175; in MASTRO, 221–22; in Mineira occupation 221; in Santa Helena camp, 94–96
Washington Post, 42
Workers' Party (PT), 164, 220, 250n99. See also Luiz Inácia "Lula" da Silva
World Bank, 176; and hydroelectric projects, 143–44

Yacyretá dam, 41, 50